Law and Liturgy in the Latin Church,
5th–12th Centuries

Roger E. Reynolds

Law and Liturgy in the Latin Church, 5th–12th Centuries

VARIORUM
1994

This edition copyright © 1994 by Roger E. Reynolds.

Published by
Ashgate Publishing Limited
Wey Court East
Union Road
Farnham
Surrey, GU9 7PT
England

Ashgate Publishing Company
110 Cherry Street
Suite 3-1
Burlington
VT 05401-3818
USA

British Library CIP Data

Reynolds, Roger E.
Law and Liturgy in the Latin Church, 5th-12th Centuries.
(Variorum Collected Studies Series; CS 457)
I. Title II. Series
262. 9

US Library of Congress CIP Data

Reynolds, Roger E. (Roger Edward), 1936-
Law and Liturgy in the Latin Church, 5th-12th Centuries / Roger E.
Reynolds.
p. cm. -- (Collected Studies Series; CS457) Includes index.
ISBN 0-86078-405-3 (alk. paper)
1. Canon law--Sources. 2. Catholic Church--Liturgy--History--
Sources. 3. Liturgies (Canon law)--History--Sources.
I. Title. II. Series: Collected Studies; CS457.
LAW   94-4774
262. 9' 2--dc20   CIP

Transferred to Digital Printing in 2012

ISBN 978-0-8607-8405-0

COLLECTED STUDIES SERIES CS457

CONTENTS

> This volume contains xii + 318 pages

PUBLISHER'S NOTE

The articles in this volume, as in all others in the Collected Studies Series, have not been given a new, continuous pagination. In order to avoid confusion, and to facilitate their use where these same studies have been referred to elsewhere, the original pagination has been maintained wherever possible.

Each article has been given a Roman number in order of appearance, as listed in the Contents. This number is repeated in each page and is quoted in the index entries.

Corrections noted in the Addenda and Corrigenda have been marked by an asterisk in the margin corresponding to the relevant text to be ammended.

PREFACE

This volume can be seen simply as a collection of eighteen miscellaneous articles on law and liturgy by the author that have appeared in the past quarter century. But it should also be regarded as an invitation to liturgiologists to be aware of the riches of their own subject in medieval legal sources and to legal historians to appreciate and understand the wealth of liturgical material that is a principal ingredient in the law of the church. Liturgiologists often discuss such notions as the 'canon' of the Mass or *lex orandi lex credendi* with little appreciation of the legal implications of these terms. On their side, historians of canon law in their concentration on the more 'juridical' aspects of ecclesiastical legislation, such as procedural norms, appellate law, jurisdiction, episcopal primacy, and the like, have often neglected or misunderstood the liturgical legislation with all of its complexity and specialized language that issued from both conciliar and pontifical sources. It is forgotten that some of the greatest liturgical scholars in the Middle Ages were also legal experts and practitioners: bishop Ivo of Chartres, Lotario of Segni (Innocent III), and bishop William Durandus of Mende, to mention but three.

Since the late twelfth century and the well-known separation of legal and theological specialists, the former have often viewed liturgy primarily within the domain or as an object of theological study, especially sacramental theology, and the latter have regarded liturgy, especially in its rubrical manifestations, within the compass of legal study. Although in the later Middle Ages there was, to be sure, specialization in various disciplines, it was not nearly as great as is commonly thought today. The modern student is surprised, for example, to learn that the theologian-philosopher par excellence of the Middle Ages, St Thomas Aquinas, wrote not only one of the most sublimely beautiful liturgical offices, that for Corpus Christi, in which part of the *Decretum* of Gratian was used, but also an exposition on two decretals formulated at the fourth Council of the Lateran (1215) that had been incorporated into the *Decretales* of Gregory IX. Even as specialization of disciplines became the norm in the high and later Middle Ages, many learned individuals were fully capable of functioning in and relating disciplines that today are often considered as separate.

It was originally thought that the present collection of articles and notes should be divided into two sections, law and liturgy, with articles then arranged in approximate medieval chronological order in each section. The collection does contain, indeed, some articles that are rather narrowly limited to either liturgy or law. Among the former is the article on an eighth-century southeast German lectionary fragment that appeared in the Festschrift for Bernhard Bischoff, and among the latter is the article on the nineteenth-century fragmentary copy of the ninth-century Salzburg canonical *Collection in Two Books* found among the papers of the famous book thief, Guilelmo Libri. But in the vast majority of articles law and liturgy are usually tied closely together. One of the most striking examples is the article on the south Italian commentary on the Mass. Although the text deals with a liturgical subject, it originally was a canonical piece containing a pseudo-correspondence between Pope Damasus I with Jerome on a pseudo-canon of the council of Nicea. Its earliest appearance in the manuscripts, moreover, was in a canonical collection. Very quickly, however, what was a legal piece became primarily liturgical as layer upon layer of fanciful interpretations of elements of the Mass were added. Even with this heavy liturgical overlay, in the end the text was transmitted primarily in manuscripts of canon law. Thus, given the close association of law and liturgy in the vast majority of articles in this collection, it seems best to present them in approximate medieval chronological sequence.

In selecting articles one has written long ago, it is always tempting to pass over items from which in part or in whole one would now like to disassociate one's name. There are two such articles, both written early in the author's career as a graduate student, but both of which several scholars have suggested be reprinted notwithstanding: the first because it has often been cited and has been especially controversial; the other because it is often cited and most scholars still agree with it in substance. The first of these pieces, on the *virgines subintroductae* in Celtic Christianity, originally appeared as a student essay for the Utrecht patristic scholar, Gilles Quispel, who urged its publication and was still citing it approvingly less than ten years ago at the Oxford Patristic Conference. Since its appearance in the staid *Harvard Theological Review*, some friends, including the Hollis Professor of Divinity at Harvard, have said a more appropriate venue would have been *Playboy*. Others have correctly contested the use of the ninth canon of the First Synod of St Patrick as reflecting *syneisactism* (the spiritual marriage of a cleric and woman companion) because not included in the published text was the important qualifier 'the [cleric] from one place, the [virgin] from another.' Another scholar has argued that the poem *An Crinog* must refer to a cleric or boy living with his Psalter, not a *virgo subintroducta*. Yet another scholar has noted that the cold-water bathing facilities used by Ailred to control his lust were much more sophisticated than the article indicates. Beyond a host of other quibbles one may still have with the article, it seems clear that *syneisactism* was not confined to Celtic or even Insular Christians but was far more widespread to judge by the number of times the famous third canon of the First Council of Nicea was repeated or slightly modified in canonical collections (especially in systematic ones, where compilers were making conscious selections of canons) and by the number of times medieval synods re-enacted the substance of the canon. In short, one does not have to 'pick on' the pristine Irish church for maintaining *syneisactism* as a relic of early Christian practice; clerics throughout Europe seem to have relished its continuance far into the Middle Ages and beyond.

The second early controversial article included here, the one on the Turin *Collection in Seven Books*, was written while in the final throes of completing a doctoral dissertation and obtaining a teaching position. Perhaps articles produced under such pressures should never be published, but it was saved from the dustbin through the kindness and incomparable editorial skills of Stephan Kuttner. Over the years the problem in the article has been whether or not the collection can legitimately be numbered among Poitevin collections of the late eleventh century. While the article has been repeatedly cited whenever legal scholars mention the collection, it has been pointed out, especially forcefully by Linda Fowler-Magerl, that the collection contains canons that may point to an Italian origin. This is correct and should have been stressed even more in the article. But given the number of canons found primarily in Poitevin collections, including a peculiar version of the liturgical Ordinals of Christ and the *De distantia graduum*, it is still probable that, despite the Italian canons within it, the collection is at base a Poitevin one, even if compiled or copied in an Italian centre.

The perceptive reader of this collection of articles will surely notice that there are no items concentrating exclusively on the author's abiding interest in clerical orders and ordination rites. These will be gathered together and augmented in another volume. But it was on the good advice of Karl Morrison that articles largely outside these areas are collected in a volume like this. For his encouragement and his kindness in seeing this collection to publication, I am grateful to John Smedley of Variorum.

Acknowledgements of assistance in the preparation of various articles can be seen in the reprints herein. But acknowledgements of three kinds need to be added here. First, the periodical *Mediaeval Studies*, in which a number of the articles first appeared, has had the policy that assistance from any member of the Pontifical Institute of Mediaeval Studies not be acknowledged in articles in the journal because we work as a 'fellowship.' Such a policy may make sense in religious orders where acknowledgements can be interpreted as a symbol of pride both for the one thanked or for the one thanking (who may also be attempting to shift his mistakes to someone else). But this policy has always struck me as bordering on ingratitude, almost unchristian. Assistance should be acknowledged from whatever source, and it is a pleasure to thank here the fellows of the Institute, especially Virginia Brown and Walter Principe, for their help in improving many articles herein.

A second type of acknowledgement must go to the Social Sciences and Humanities Research Council of Canada, which for years has supported the manuscript research represented in many of the articles. Most recently the Council has generously funded a team programme at the Pontifical Institute entitled *Monumenta Liturgica Beneventana* to study and edit manuscripts and texts from the Beneventan-script zone of south Italy and Dalmatia. It is this funding that largely explains the number of articles on south-Italian canon law and liturgy.

The final acknowledgement must be to my wife, Ruth. She has read and improved many of the articles, and more important, she has often made travel for research in the many legal and liturgical manuscripts and texts studied and presented in this volume the constant delight it has been and continues to be.

ROGER E. REYNOLDS

Pontifical Institute of Mediaeval Studies, Toronto
1994

I

VIRGINES SUBINTRODUCTAE IN CELTIC CHRISTIANITY

SEVERAL years before his death the Irish novelist and playwright, George Moore, wrote his "one joyous book," *A Story Teller's Holiday*.[1] Combining "oddments of folklore" and the "rich Anglo-Irish idiom," Moore traced in Boccaccian fashion the ancient Christian practice of syneisactism[2] in early Celtic Christianity. In his work Moore was admittedly stimulated by the great Celticist, Kuno Meyer,[3] and by the then burgeoning translations of ancient Irish manuscripts describing syneisactism.[4]

Since Moore's novel, and perhaps in reaction to it, modern Irish historians have almost all passed over the subject of the *virgines subintroductae* in Celtic Christianity or have relegated it to the crude and heterodox past of ancient Irish history.[5] The early existence of the practice is admitted, but taking the lead of Hans Achelis,[6] most Irish historians prefer to say that by the sixth century in Ireland the *virgines subintroductae* had disappeared. Thus, at the risk of being accused of dredging up ancient unmentionables, this essay will consider the practice of syneisactism as it existed in early medieval Celtic Christianity, some of the explanations, both theological and environmental, for its existence, and the possible sources of the practice.

[1] GEORGE MOORE, *A Story Teller's Holiday*, 2 vols. (London, 1928).

[2] For economy of words, the term "syneisactism" will be used in this essay to denote the living together of a male ascetic and a *virgo subintroducta*. Other terms used to describe these women were *"agapetae"* (BONIZO of Sutri, *Liber De Vita Christiana*, ed. E. Perels [Berlin, 1930], 55, 205), *"conhospitae"* (infra, p. 556), *"mulieres extraneae"* (Conc. Nicea, c. 3), *"mulieres adoptivae"* (Conc. Bracar. II, c. 32, *PL* 84:579), *"sisters"* (infra, n. 52), and combinations of these terms.

[3] MOORE, *op. cit.*, viii.

[4] Irish scholars have been slow to publish ancient Celtic source material and slower yet in the publication of source material relating to syneisactism. As will be seen from the citations in this essay, the majority of texts dealing with the *virgines subintroductae* were published in the early decades of this century.

[5] A similar reaction met the publication of H. ACHELIS, *Virgines Subintroductae* (Leipzig, 1902). See M. BLACK, *The Scrolls and Christian Origins* (N.Y., 1961), 86.

[6] ACHELIS, *op. cit.*, 223.

Our dredging is justifiable for several reasons. First, recent studies in Jewish Christianity and Encratism tend to show the widespread and often orthodox [7] practice of syneisactism in the ancient Church.[8] Second, numerous studies have appeared in the past decades showing the "Jewish" characteristics of early Celtic Christianity.[9] Given these factors, the time would seem ripe to dredge up syneisactism, not to explore the subject exhaustively, but to show that the practice existed far into the Middle Ages particularly in Celtic and then in Anglo-Saxon milieus and that, far from being a Celtic skeleton-in-the-closet, Celtic syneisactism represented one of the most primitive aspects of Christianity to survive in medieval Western Europe.

Several factors are responsible for the caution of modern Irish scholars in treating the subject of the *virgines subintroductae* in Ireland. First the condemnation of syneisactism by numerous councils and synods [10] has made these scholars reticent to attribute

[7] It must be remembered that syneisactism was carried on for several centuries in orthodox communities and was condemned officially only at a fairly late date in the early Church. Nicea, c. 3, is the best known of the early conciliar condemnations.

[8] See, for example, J. DANIÉLOU, *The Theology of Jewish Christianity* (London, 1964), 375; G. QUISPEL, The Syrian Thomas and the Syrian Macarius, *Vigiliae Christianae* 18 (1964), 226–35; and G. QUISPEL, Gnosticism and the New Testament, in *The Bible in Modern Scholarship*, ed. J. P. Hyatt (Nashville, Tenn., 1965), 252–71.

[9] Although all of the studies on these characteristics are too numerous to list here, perhaps the most impressive are those dealing with the distinctively Mosaic character of early Celtic canon law. There are, for example, references to clean and unclean foods, cities of refuge, tithes, and the Year of Jubilee. K. BÖCKENHOFF, *Speisatzungen mosaischer Art in mittelalterlichen Kirchenrechtsquellen des Morgen und Abendlandes* (Münster, 1907); P. FOURNIER, De quelques infiltrations byzantines dans le droit canonique de l'époque carolingienne, in *Mélanges offerts à G. Schlumberger* (Paris, 1924), 67–78; and P. FOURNIER, Le Liber ex lege Moysi et les tendances bibliques de droit canonique, *Revue Celtique* 30 (1909), 221–34. In a recent monograph by R. KOTTJE, *Studien zum Einfluss des Alten Testaments auf Recht und Liturgie des frühen Mittelalters (VI. bis VIII. Jhrt.)* (Bonn, 1964), 17, 27ff., the Celtic use of Old Testament names is treated extensively, as well as important parallels between the Irish *peregrinatores* and their Old Testament forebears.

[10] ACHELIS, *op. cit.*, 34. The history of the medieval canonical condemnation of syneisactism remains to be written. Briefly, it can be said that after the condemnations of the ancient Church, there followed a line of condemnations in the Spanish and Gallic councils of the sixth and seventh centuries. Except for a few specific conciliar condemnations of syneisactism, most conciliar decrees in the period from A.D. 700–1000 were more generally directed against association with all but a select group of women. Nonetheless, the early condemnations of syneisactism were kept alive in the canonical collections, almost all of which contain the

the practice to the *a priori* pristine church of St. Patrick. Second, the canons attributed to St. Patrick [11] seem to condemn the practice.

> Henceforth let not a monk and a virgin live together in one dwelling, travel about in one wagon from villa to villa, or discourse continuously together.[12]

And third, the myriad texts referring to the great chastity of the Celtic saints and to their avoidance and distrust of women are used to show that syneisactism could hardly have existed beside an almost fanatic misogyny.

In response to this *a priori* and somewhat propagandist approach, it may be said that even the Irish saw their saintly forebears as living with *virgines subintroductae*. *"Mulierum administrationem et consortia non respuebant, quia super Petrum Christi fundati, ventum tentationis non timebant."* [13] Individual saints, such as St. Scothine, St. Mel, St. Kentigern, the Anglo-Saxon St. Aldhelm and Robert of Abrissel, all recognized as saints by the very Church which condemned syneisactism, lived *in consortio mulierum*. Moreover, the fact that St. Patrick condemned the practice probably bespeaks its existence,[14] and the

---

ancient canons. Most notable is the Iro-Italian Collection in V Books (Vat. Lat. 1339), in which these ancient prohibitions run to almost four full folio pages (fol. 72v–76v). In the eleventh century there is a resurgence of conciliar decrees against syneisactism — Rome (1059 and 1063), Liseaux (1064), and Rouen (1072). Thereafter, many of the prohibitions are directed against the practice in clearly heterodox communities. That the practice is condemned as late as the eleventh century in orthodox circles in the West makes questionable the special pleading for Ireland made by J. CARNEY, Old Ireland and her Poetry, in *Old Ireland*, ed. R. McNally (N.Y., 1965), 155.

[11] These canons were probably drawn up sometime in the fifth century, although there are admittedly clauses which indicate a later date. See *The Works* of St. PATRICK, ed. L. Bieler (London, 1953), 13; J. F. KENNEY, *Sources of the Early History of Ireland*, I. Ecclesiastical (N.Y., 1929), 169ff.

[12] Canon 9. L. BIELER, *The Irish Penitentials* (Dublin, 1963), 54.

[13] *Catalogus Sanctorum Hiberniae*, in A. W. HADDAN and W. STUBBS, *Councils and Ecclesiastical Documents relating to Great Britain and Ireland*, vol. II, pt. I (Oxford, 1873), 292.

[14] NORA CHADWICK in *The Age of the Saints in the Early Celtic Church* (London, 1961), 149, claims that many of the extreme provisions in the penitentials are due to the Irish love of casuistry, hypothetical legal analysis, and theoretical cases. This must be admitted, but the sheer popularity and repetition of those texts and the later synodical injunctions against syneisactism would seem to indicate an interest in the *virgines subintroductae* somewhat beyond that which NORA CHADWICK indicates.

great chastity of the Celtic saints certainly is not inconsistent with their living with women. Although Achelis overstates his case in saying that the early Celtic Church was characterized by the practice of syneisactism,[15] the number of stories of the saints, clergy, and lay ascetics living with the *virgines* clearly demonstrates that the practice cannot have been as foreign to Celtic Christianity as is often presented.

Before considering these numerous accounts of syneisactism in Ireland, we should outline briefly first the environmental factors which lend support to the claim that syneisactism was a common phenomenon in Celtic Christianity, and second the sources by which the practice might have come to Ireland. An important geographical factor, which many scholars often tend to forget, is that Ireland lay beyond the outmost limits of the Roman Empire. Latin was probably not spoken there until after St. Patrick's journey,[16] and the social institutions were non-Roman. Urban centers were practically nonexistent,[17] and wandering was a way of life for almost everyone from the shepherd to the traveling bard and scholar.[18] Life was extremely hard due to the changes in weather [19] and the interminable wars. Although women were subjugated to their fathers and husbands, they appear to have assumed some of what we commonly consider to be masculine duties. In several instances, for example, Irish women served in the wars and were treated as severely as warriors when captured.[20]

Given these environmental factors, it is not surprising to find

[15] ACHELIS, *op. cit.*, 124.

[16] C. MOHRMANN, *The Latin of St. Patrick* (Dublin, 1961), 45f.

[17] L. GOUGAUD, *Christianity in Celtic Lands* (London, 1932), 65. Perhaps the great monasteries approached most closely what could be called an Irish metropolis.

[18] For the wandering of Irish scholars, see H. WADDELL, *The Wandering Scholars* (N.Y., 1955), 25–68.

[19] J. LECLERCQ, *et al.*, *La spiritualité du moyen âge*, II (Paris, 1961), 56. A caveat should be introduced, however, against the all-too romantic notion of a wild and bitter climate in Ireland. Professor Joseph Stevens has kindly referred me to the study by E. HUNTINGTON, *Mainsprings of Civilization* (N.Y., 1959), 598f., in which it is shown that the climate of early medieval Ireland was much less severe than it is today, mild enough for the growing of grapes.

[20] *Vitae Sanctorum Hiberniae*, ed. C. Plummer, I (Oxford, 1910), cviii, n. 2. As late as approximately A.D. 686, a document was signed the ostensible object of which was to exempt women and children from military obligation. See N. CHADWICK, *op. cit.*, 136.

Celtic Christianity adapting itself to them and developing almost *sui generis* customs as judged by later Roman standards. Since there were no urban centers, there was no diocesan system as found on the Continent.[21] Christianity was carried by wanderers, some of whom were wild men or *gielts*.[22] And due to the harshness of life it is not surprising to find Christian men and women living together and helping each other. A converted woman, who was often persecuted and rejected by her family,[23] needed the support which would be given only by another Christian. This support was thrown either on the early wandering Christian male[24] or on the later established convents, which in some instances were connected closely with monasteries.[25] And it is clear that the early Celtic Christian males often needed the help of these women.[26] The clergy especially used female assistance in catechizing[27] and in the "performance of ministries which pertain to the confession of the sacred altar."[28] Although,

---

[21] Celtic wanderers on the Continent were later to be scolded for their disregard of diocesan boundaries. Infra, p. 556.

[22] In Ireland a saga is told of a sixth-century king, Suibne, who flees into the wilderness, lives on herbs, grows feathers, and even inhabits the treetops. At his death, his anmchara or soul-friend, St. Molling, buries him in consecrated ground. In a later text, the *Book of Aicill*, it is recorded that in the days of Suibne there were numerous other hermits who were gielt or wild. See N. CHADWICK, *op. cit.*, 107. JAMES CARNEY, *Studies in Irish Literature and History* (Dublin, 1955), 129ff., discusses the literary history of Suibne and shows how the tale of the totally unhistoric Suibne was conflated with the story of the historical St. Molling. See also J. CARNEY, Old Ireland and her Poetry, in R. McNALLY, *op. cit.*, 159f. Perhaps these gielts are similar to the Boskoi of the East. A.-J. FESTUGIÈRE, *Les Moines d'Orient*, I (Paris, 1961), 43. An interesting pictorial representation of these gielts can be seen in the painting, "La Tebaide," by Gherardo Starnino (1360–1409) in the Uffizi Gallery in Florence. Among the numerous hermits are two living in trees, one of whom has very long hair.

[23] St. PATRICK, *Confessions*, c. 42. "Not that their fathers agree with them (the virgins); no — they often even suffer persecution and undeserved reproaches from their parents . . . . How many have been reborn there so as to be of our kind, I do not know — not to mention widows and those who practice continence." *Works* of St. PATRICK, ed. L. Bieler, p. 34. On these *continentes* and virgins, see BIELER, *Life and Legend of St. Patrick* (Dublin, 1949), 74.

[24] If one follows the chronology of the *Catalogus SS. Hiberniae*, this would have occurred in the first age.

[25] On the institution of double monasteries, see M. BATESON, Origin and Early History of Double Monasteries, *Transactions of the Royal Historical Society* (London, 1899), 137–98. Also see J. RYAN, *Irish Monasticism* (London, 1931), 141ff.

[26] St. PATRICK, *Confessions*, c. 49.

[27] RYAN, *op. cit.*, 134.

[28] J. T. McNEILL and H. GAMER, *Medieval Handbooks of Penance* (N.Y., 1938), 205.

552

as we shall see, a great number of these women lived chastely, a far greater number, if we may believe the later sources,[29] were married to their companions.

In terms of social and geographical factors the Celtic milieus were congenial to the rise of syneisactism. But this practice was not indigenous. The stimulus came from as far away as Syria. In an increasing number of articles and monographs scholars have dealt extensively with the multiple similarities in the Christianity and monasticism of the Celtic *disart* and the Syrian and Egyptian desert and have found that generally Celtic Christianity followed Jewish, Syrian, and Egyptian patterns, rather than the Roman patterns which some Irish scholars present.[30] Hence it is almost expected that the institution of the *virgines subintroductae*, which arose in early Jewish Christianity in Syria and Palestine, could be found in Ireland. Like the problem of the lines of transmission of Christianity to Ireland, however, the precise channels of transmission of the institution of syneisactism are extremely obscure. Scholars who follow Bury's argument that St. Patrick first brought Roman Christianity to Ireland [31] and who thus see Roman Christianity as the norm of the pristine Irish Church would, if they were to deal with the issue, probably claim that syneisactism was brought to Ireland by heterodox or corrupt means. And if one uses the synodical definitions of heterodoxy, the practice probably did, to a certain extent, arrive in Ireland through these channels.

In response to those scholars who hold that the Irish Church had Patrician origins, a number of scholars have recently argued that Christianity came to Ireland sometime before Patrick from

---

[29] That the early Roman clergy was often married is seen from the clerical forebears of St. Patrick himself. A great many of the Irish penitentials speak of married clergy. See BIELER, *The Irish Penitentials, passim.*

[30] Although not an exhaustive list, the following are representative of this literature: P. SCHEFFER-BOICHORST, *Zur Geschichte der Syren im Abendlande: Gesammelte Schriften,* II, Eberings Hist. Studien 43 (Berlin, 1905), 187–224; M. R. JAMES, Syriac Apocrypha in Ireland, *JThS* 11 (1910), 290f.; M. SCHLAUCH, On Conall Core and the Relations of Old Ireland with the Orient, *Journ. of Celtic Stud.* 1 (1960), 152–66; P. FEIST, *Untersuchungen zur Bedeutung orientalischer Einflüsse für die Künst des frühen Mittelalters, Wiss. Zs. d. Martin-Luthers-Univ. Halle-Wittemberg,* II (1952/3), Reihe 1, 27–79; and P. PAULSEN, *Koptische und irische Kunst und ihre Ausstrahlungen auf altgermanische Kulturen* (Stuttgart, 1952–53).

[31] J. B. BURY, *The Life of St. Patrick and his Place in History* (London, 1905).

Spain and North Africa.[32] It is particularly in these areas that syneisactism was practiced or at least found congenial theological sanctions. In North Africa, for example, the Montanists [33] and Abelites [34] practiced syneisactism and advocated it as an imitation of the paradisaic state of virginity. As early as Pseudo-Cyprian's *De singularite clericorum* [35] we find a North African Christian condemning syneisactism.[36] In Spain the asceticism of North Africa was taken over by the Priscillianists, who wandered about making converts of many women, preaching continence and a form of dualism,[37] yet who gathered men and women together for devotions and were thus condemned for immorality.[38] It was in these Priscillianist circles that the *Epistula Titi* and the *Acts of John* and *Acts of Andrew*, with their encratitic theology and practices, were found.[39]

Although these heterodox channels from North Africa and Spain were most likely influential in bringing syneisactism to Ireland, it is not necessary to look exclusively to these heterodox channels. Following the lead of de Labriolle, many scholars have argued that syneisactism was found only in heretical circles.[40] De Labriolle's interpretations of the documents are often, however, highly questionable,[41] and he is completely oblivious to a great number of references in orthodox writers of the Church

[32] N. Chadwick, *op. cit.*, 54f. Also see the filiations on the map of western monasticism in J. Daniélou and H. Marrou, *The Christian Centuries: The First Six Hundred Years* (London, 1964), 277. On the relations between Visigothic Spain and Ireland, see the articles by J. N. Hillgarth, The East, Visigothic Spain, and the Irish, *Studia Patristica* 4 (Berlin, 1961), 441–56; and Visigothic Spain and Early Christian Ireland, in the *Proceedings of the Royal Irish Academy*, LXII (Dublin, 1962), 167–94; and the condensation of these articles in Old Ireland and Visigothic Spain, in *Old Ireland*, ed. R. McNally (N.Y., 1965), 200–27.

[33] J. Daniélou and H. Marrou, *op. cit.*, 121.

[34] F. Van der Meer, *Augustine the Bishop* (N.Y., 1961), 119.

[35] B. Altaner, *Patrology* (N.Y., 1961), 200, considers this a third-century work.

[36] Achelis, *op. cit.*, 35ff.

[37] Although H. Lietzmann, *The Era of the Church Fathers* (London, 1958), 74, calls this Manichaeism, the sources of this dualism may be found much earlier than Mani, even in Palestinian Judaism.

[38] Lietzmann, *op. cit.*, 75.

[39] M. R. James, *The Apocryphal New Testament* (Oxford, 1960), 265, 337, 349. On the *Epistula Titi* and its Pseudo-Cyprianic dependence, see J. Quasten, *Patrology*, I (Westminster [Md.], 1950), 156f.

[40] P. de Labriolle, Le "mariage spirituel" dans l'antiquité chrétienne, *Revue Historique* 136 (1921), 204–25.

[41] For his strange interpretation of Tertullian's *De Exhortatione*, c. 12, see de Labriolle, *art. cit.*, 210f.

554

of the ancient West who do not disapprove of the practice.[42] In the East the practice of syneisactism is commonly found among the orthodox fathers of the Nitrian desert, where men and women lived chastely together but did not wander.[43]

One cannot say precisely how syneisactism (and probably Christianity with it) reached Ireland, but it is probable that the ubiquitous Sarabaites of which John Cassian [44] and St. Jerome [45] speak carried it to Ireland. We have seen that as early as St. Patrick the practice was condemned,[46] and together with this condemnation St. Patrick enjoined: *"Clericus vagus non sit in plebe."* [47] Also we have cited the eighth-century *Catalogus Sanctorum Hiberniae* describing and approving of syneisactism for the first age of Irish saints.[48]

The saints of the second age are characterized by the *Catalogus: "abnegabunt mulierum administrationem, separantes eas a monasteriis."* [49] From this quotation it has been argued that syneisactism ended, as Achelis said, in the sixth century. But as will be seen in numerous sources, the practice lingered into the twelfth century, not only in Ireland and England, but wherever Celtic Christians traveled. Thus, we look to the texts and will treat them, not chronologically or geographically, but rather as they apply first to the practice of syneisactism and second to the theological underpinnings of syneisactism.

The basic definition of syneisactism is the chaste living together of a male and female ascetic, and it is precisely this picture which the earliest Celtic sources present. In the *Tripartite Life*

[42] Even GREGORY of Tours uses approvingly the encratitic *Acts of Andrew.* JAMES, *op. cit.*, 349.

[43] PALLADIUS, *The Lausiac History*, trs. R. T. Meyer in *Ancient Christian Writers*, 34 (London, 1965), c. 8.1, p. 42.

[44] Collatio 18.

[45] Although he does not call them Sarabaites, St. JEROME speaks of this type of wanderer in Epistle 22.34.

[46] Supra, p. 549.

[47] Canon 3. It is interesting to see in later canonical collections that prohibitions against wandering clerics and *virgines subintroductae* were often placed side by side. See, for example, the collection in Paris BN Lat. 3859 (ex IXs) cited in A. THEINER, *Disquisitiones criticae in praecipuas canonum et decretalium collectiones* (Rome, 1836), 145f. For an extensive list of medieval canons directed against the *clericus vagus*, see H. WADDELL, *op. cit.*, 269–99.

[48] Supra, p. 549.

[49] HADDAN and STUBBS, *op. cit.*, 292.

of Saint Patrick [50] Bishop Mel is pictured as living with a woman and being assisted by her in prayer.[51] In this instance the woman appears to have been his aunt, but from the detailed prohibitions in the Irish penitentials it seems that ascetic males often lived with other female relatives or with women completely unrelated.[52] Further, the age of the partners might be greatly disparate. If we may believe that the poem, *An Crinog,* is written, not to a lost psalter,[53] but to a syneisacte who has returned after a long absence, the ascetic poet seems to have been "a gentle boy of seven sweet years" [54] when his companion first began to live with him. *An Crinog* also presents evidence that a *virgo* could travel successively with more than one male.

> Since then you have slept with four men
> > after me
> without folly or falling away:
> I know, I hear it on all sides,
> You are pure, without sin from men.[55]

[50] *The Tripartite Life of Patrick,* ed. Wh. Stokes, I (London, 1887), 89.

[51] "At a certain time Patrick was told, through the error of the rabble, that bishop Mel had sinned with his kinswoman, for they used to be in one habitation a-praying to the Lord." *Tripartite Life,* 89.

[52] T. OLDEN, On the Consortia of the First Order of Irish Saints, *Proceedings of the Royal Irish Academy,* III (Dublin, 1894), 415-20, holds that the word "suir" came to mean the sister living *in consortio.* To denote a blood sister, the term "derbhshiur" was used. Professor D. A. Binchy has assured me that Olden's interpretation cannot be maintained. Nonetheless, the *virgines subintroductae* were often called "sisters." In the Irish canonical collection of St. Germain (Paris BN Lat. 12444) L. II, c. 31 (fol. 23v) the third canon of the Council of Nicea is paraphrased: "In totum denuntiavit sancta et magna synodus neque episcopo neque presbytero neque diacono . . . licere adoptivam sororem habere nisi forte sororem veram . . . ." Again on fol. 99r-v the *virgines* are called adopted sisters.

[53] JAMES CARNEY argues that the poem is written to a psalter which has recently been found by an old ascetic. He holds that the name Crinog really means "old-young" and that the poem is merely a "donnish joke." F. O'CONNOR, *Kings, Lords, and Commons* (London, 1961), 61. CARNEY's view is further expanded in his recent article, Old Ireland and her Poetry, in *Old Ireland,* ed. R. McNALLY, 154ff. He dates the poem ca. A.D. 1100, and implies that this date is so far removed from the Council of Nicea that it could hardly speak of syneisactism. CARNEY has, however, forgotten the eleventh-century condemnations of syneisactism in the West. Even if it is admitted, moreover, that the poem is written to a psalter, the form of the allegory indicates that the poet was well-aware of the practice of syneisactism. I have Professor Binchy's support in this regard, when he says that CARNEY's interpretation by no means precludes a reference in the poem to syneisactism. For KUNO MEYER's discussion of the poem, see his An Crinog: Ein altirisches Gedicht an eine Syneisakte, *Sitzungsberichte der königlich preussischer Akademie der Wissenschaften,* XVIII (Berlin, 1918), 361-74.

556

Bishop Mel probably lived in one place with his kinswoman, but the majority of persons involved in syneisactism seem to have wandered as did the early Syrian ascetics. Crinog and her companion had many "weary wanderings," [56] and in the early sixth-century account of Lovocat and Catihern the two Celtic [57] priests and their *virgines* wander about the immigrant population of Amorica preaching and celebrating Mass.[58] The priests are scolded by the bishops, Melanius and Eustochius, first for their wandering about established diocesan territories without episcopal permission [59] and second for their living with *conhospitae.*

The earliest Celtic sources also make it clear that the purpose of the spiritual union was one of assistance. The saints of the first age *"mulierum administrationem et consortia non respuebant"*; [60] Bishop Mel is helped by his kinswoman in prayer; and Lovocat and Catihern are assisted by their *virgines*, who "take the chalice and administer the blood of Christ to the people." [61] In this last instance the *virgines* play a role much like that of the ancient encratitic "priestesses." The Amorican bishops are quick to note this, but in condemning Lovocat and Catihern they trace the "heresy," probably through St. Augustine [62] and Epiphanius,[63] to the "Pepundians" or Pepuzians.[64]

[54] An English translation of *An Crinog* may be found in KUNO MEYER, *Selections from Ancient Irish Poetry* (N.Y., 1911), 37.

[55] KUNO MEYER, *Selections*, 37.

[56] *Ibid.*

[57] M. E. ERNAULT, in his response to L. DUCHESNE, Lovocat et Catihern, prêtres bretons du temps de St. Melaine, *Revue de Bretagne et de Vendée* 57 (1885), I, 5–21, has indicated that the names are Celtic in origin.

[58] "We have learned that you do not cease from carrying to the huts of your compatriots certain tables on which you celebrate Masses with the aid of women, which you call *conhospitae*. While you distribute the Eucharist, they presume to take the chalice and administer the blood of Christ to the people. The novelty of such a thing and the unheard-of superstition sadden us not a little, since this abominable sect, which never before has appeared in Gaul, seems in our time to be emerging. The Eastern fathers call it 'Pepundian' from the name of Pepundius, the author of the schism, who presumed to have women aiding him in the Sacrifice." DUCHESNE, *art. cit.*, 6.

[59] DUCHESNE, *art. cit.*, argues that the first abuse to which the bishops object is not the celebration of Mass with portable altars or the partaking of the Eucharist within one's house, but the wandering of the Celtic priests within established diocesan boundaries.

[60] Supra, p. 549.

[61] See n. 58, supra.

[62] AUGUSTINE, *De haeresibus*, c. 27, *PL* 42: 30–31.

[63] EPIPHANIUS, *Panarion*, c. 49.

[64] These two early sixth-century bishops probably used as their direct source

Although the primary motive of syneisactism was assistance to a Christian of the opposite sex, the issue of chastity naturally arose. Ideally the partners lived a chaste life, but like the earlier Pseudo-Clementine tradition,[65] the Irish sources early hint of scandalous behavior. Bishop Mel is accused "through the error of the rabble"[66] of sinning with his kinswoman.[67] And although Lovocat and Catihern are not accused of immorality, the bishops warn them that their action "produces a certain shudder since it is one which defames the clergy and shames and discredits the holy faith."[68]

In Pseudo-Clement there is a fear of women or perhaps extreme misogyny which leads to a condemnation of even the *pax*. In Ireland there is a like reaction to the freedom between men and women presented in the accounts of syneisactism. A great number of stories are told of the fanatical avoidance of the female sex by the Irish saints. St. Ciaran, who was tutoring a young princess, would look only at her feet.[69] St. Enda would converse with his sister, who had traveled a long distance to see him, only through a veil.[70] And St. Coemgen fled whenever he heard the sound of a cow or sheep since *"ubi ovis, ibi mulier, ubi mulier, ibi peccatum, ubi peccatum, ibi diabolus, et ubi diabolus ibi infernus."*[71]

Since this extreme caution with respect to women was probably the prevailing sentiment when most of the Celtic hagiographies were composed, it is perhaps startling to find mention made at all of the *virgines subintroductae* in Celtic Christianity. When the practice is cited, however, in the great majority of instances, the account is presented to show the chastity of the saint in the face of extreme temptation. Cuimmin's poem on the saints of Ireland portrays the sanctity of Saints Ciaran and Scothine in

the *Praedestinatus*, c. 27, a work composed in Gaul ca. A.D. 450, which copies St. Augustine, *De haeresibus*. See Duchesne, *art. cit.*

[65] Pseudo-Clement, *De virginitate*.
[66] Supra, n. 51.
[67] On investigation St. Patrick finds that the accusations are untrue.
[68] Duchesne, *art. cit.*, 6.
[69] *Vitae Sanctorum Hiberniae*, I, 205f.
[70] Gougaud, *Christianity in Celtic Lands*, 89.
[71] *Vitae Sanctorum Hiberniae*, I, cxxi.

this way.[72] And in the ninth- or tenth-century poem, *Éirigh, a ingen an righ*, there is a long list of the temptations undergone by the heroic saints of old while in the embraces of fair virgins.[73]

Perhaps the most famous Celtic account of syneisactism as primarily a temptation is found in the *Martyrology of Oengus the Culdee*. Besides his accounts of virginal nuns assisting clerics [74] and caring for them "in their bosoms" as for Jesukind,[75] Oengus extensively presents the details of the nightly temptations of St. Scothine. Although the report is relegated in Latin

---

[72] WH. STOKES, Cuimmin's Poem on the Saints of Ireland, *Zeitschrift für celtische Philologie* I (1897), 63.

(25) "Chaste Ciaran of Cloumacnois, loved humility which was not hasty or unsteadfast; He never said a word that was false: since he was born he looked not on a woman."

(53) "Scuithin of sweet stories loved — a blessing on everyone who hath done it — damsels beautiful, white bosomed, and among them he kept his virginity."

[73] SÉAN O'FAÓLÁIN, Éirigh, a ingen an righ, *Revue Celtique* 47 (1926), 197–200.

I have pondered on victorious Fionnbarr,
whose mind was lofty,
who denied the raging princess,
the daughter of Dangail d'Uib Ennaig.

I have thought on Ciaran of Cluan,
much have I heard of his piety,
who denied Aillind the Daughter of Bran,
and slept beneath . . .
(The Irish reads "fo cígibh." O'FAÓLÁIN
speculates that among other meanings this
may be read, "beneath a woman's breasts.")

I thought also of the great piety
of Scuitin of Sliabh Maircce Moir
who used to lie, God willed it in his love,
between the white paps of women.

And I thought then of Columcille
who for the love of the King of Truth
denied — for all her great fame —
(the pleasure of) Aidan's fair daughter.

I recalled Patrick and his austerities
the chief apostle of Erin
who rejected the blazing brightness
of the maiden daughter of the valiant Milchu.

[74] *The Martyrology of Oengus the Culdee*, ed. Wh. Stokes (London, 1905), 43.

[75] *Ibid.*, 45. The Christ-child is either fondled or nursed by nuns in *Félire hUi Gormáin, The Martyrology of Gorman*, ed. Wh. Stokes (London, 1895), 65, and in the story of St. Íte, cited by J. CARNEY, Poems of Blathmac, Son of Cu Brethan, in *Early Irish Poetry*, ed. J. Carney (Cork, 1965), 51.

to the footnotes of some histories,[76] it is here worth quoting because it contains some of the nuances in syneisactism found almost exclusively in Celtic milieus.

> Now two maidens with pointed breasts used to lie with him every night that the battle with the Devil might be the greater for him. And it was proposed to accuse him on that account. So Brenainn came to test him, and Scothin said, "Let the cleric lie in my bed tonight," saith he. So when he reached the hour of resting the girls came into the house wherein was Brenainn, with their lapfuls of glowing embers in their chasubles; and the fire burnt them not, and they spill (the embers) in front of Brenainn and go into the bed to him. "What is this?" asks Brenainn. "Thus it is that we do every night," say the girls. They lie down with Brenainn, and nowise could he sleep with longing. "That is imperfect, O cleric," say the girls: "he who is here every night feels nothing at all. Why goest thou not, O cleric, into the tub [of cold water] if it be easier for thee? 'Tis often that the cleric, even Scothin, visits it." "Well," says Brenainn, "it is wrong for us to make this test, for he is better than we are." Thereafter they make their union and their covenant, and they part *feliciter*.[77]

Although this account of St. Scothine has often been hidden in footnotes in the hope that it would appear to be a rare occurrence in Celtic Christianity, there are a number of similar accounts within the annals of Celtic and English history. William of Malmesbury in the twelfth century gives an almost identical picture of the temptation of St. Aldhelm; [78] Giraldus Cambrensis warns against following the example of St. Aldhelm, who lay *"inter duas puellas, unam ab uno latere, alteram ab altero, singulis noctibus"*; [79] and Robert of Abrissel, the famous twelfth-century recluse, is scolded by Bishop Marbode and Geoffrey of Vendôme for his nocturnal associations with certain of his women followers.[80]

[76] An early example of this appears in J. H. Todd, *St. Patrick, Apostle of Ireland* (Dublin, 1864), 91, n. 1.

[77] *Martyrology of Oengus*, 41.

[78] William of Malmesbury, *De gestis pontif. Angliae*, V, PL 179:1633f.

[79] Infra, p. 563.

[80] Bishop Marbode, *Epistola* vi, PL 171:1481. "Mulierum cohabitationem, in quo genere quondam peccasti, diceris plus amare, ut qui antiquae iniquitatis contagium, novae religionis exemplo circo eamdem materiam studeas expiare. 'Has

These Celtic accounts present essentially the same story found as early as the *Shepherd* of Hermas, in which an ascetic spends the night "as a brother and not a husband" with beautiful virgins.[81] But unlike the syneisactism in the ancient Church, several new elements have been added to the Celtic accounts. First, the virgins are often presented as proving their chastity before they enter under the roof of the male ascetic. Bishop Mel's kinswoman comes "having fire in her chasuble and her raiment was not injured," [82] and the maidens of St. Scothine come to Bishop Brenainn "with their lapfuls of glowing embers in their chasubles and the fire burnt them not." [83] This ability to carry fire in one's chasuble as a sign of one's sanctity and chastity probably reflects a Celtic interpretation of Proverbs 6:27–28. This passage was connected with the *virgines subintroductae* as early as Caesarius of Arles, but Caesarius uses the passage as a warning against the undue confidence of those deliberately subjecting themselves to the temptation of the *virgines*.[84] Later in Ireland and the adopted home of the Celts stories are told of a certain Bercert of County Cork [85] and Saints Tudual and Malo of Brittany, in which the same phenomenon is mentioned. Bercert had a "sister" who nightly brought home "seeds of fire," and one night on her way home, pride seized her and the fire burned through her apron, which, due to her sanctity, was incombustible. For this sin, Bercert rejected the sister. And in the life of St. Gwennole there is a eulogy of St. Tudual,[86] appearing in the life of St. Malo,[87] in

---

etenim solum communi accubitu per noctem, ut referunt, accubante simul et discipulorum grege, ut inter utrosque medius jacens, utrique sexui vigiliarum et somni leges praefigas.' Has peregrinationis tuae loquuntur esse pedissequas, et disputanti tibi jugiter assidere."

[81] *Similitude*, c. IX. 10f.

[82] *Tripartite Life*, 91.

[83] Supra, p. 559.

[84] This passage from Sermon XLI of CAESARIUS of Arles (ed. G. Morin, I [Turnhout, 1953], 179ff.), has gone unnoted by scholars dealing with syneisactism. Dom MORIN found this sermon in a number of mss attributed to Augustine. It is significant, perhaps, for the continued existence of the practice of syneisactism that this sermon is actually inserted into the eleventh-century canonical Collection of Tarragone, L. VI, c. 218 (Vat. Lat. 6093, fol. 127v–129v). It is, to my knowledge, the only canonical collection in which this sermon appears.

[85] T. OLDEN, *art. cit.*, dates this story ca. A.D. 839.

[86] A. DE LA BORDERIE, Les trois vies anciennes de St. Tudual, *Histoire de Bretagne*, I (Paris, 1887), 112.

[87] Unsigned Review of A. DE LA BORDERIE's work, in *Revue Celtique* 10 (1889), 254.

which the saint is presented as ascending sanctified to heaven
"cum vestibus ignem." [88]

Another nuance in the practice of syneisactism in Celtic milieus
was the frequent use of baths. Havelock Ellis has charged that
the prudishness of early Christianity destroyed the bath,[89] yet in
Celtic milieus the bath remained a favorite pastime long into
the Christian era and, in fact, was used in the maintenance of
chastity.[90] In the asceticism of the East there are at least two
examples of ascetics bathing in cold water,[91] but it was particularly in Celtic Christianity that these immersions were used.

There are in the Celtic hagiographies numerous accounts of
immersion. Some saints immerse themselves in tubs,[92] some in
wells,[93] some in icy streams,[94] some habitually,[95] some suddenly,[96]
some singly, and even some with "their wives." [97] The reasons
given for these baths are almost as numerous as the methods.
The usual reason given is that the bath puts down concupiscence
and provides immunity to lust. St. Kentigern, a Scot, immersed
himself

> because the law of sin, which wars within the members, was thus
> weakened and the fire of desire done away with and extinguished, so
> that no rottenness of wanton flesh might pollute or stain the lily of his
> honor in waking or even in sleeping.

And when he had bathed, he became absolutely immune *"quod
non magis ad speciosissimi puelle visum aut tactus quam ad du-
rissimi scilis stimularetur."* [98]

---

[88] A. DE LA BORDERIE, *art. cit.*, 113. "Jamque tamen ternos precesserat ordine
sanctus/ Eximios istos Tutgualus nomine clarus/ Cum meritis monachus multorum
exemplar habendus/ Cuius cumque sinu caperet cum vestibus ignem/ Non tetigit
flamma sed leni rore madescit/ Sed cum coelitibus vitam tum forte gerebat."

[89] H. B. WORKMAN, *The Evolution of the Monastic Ideal* (London, 1913), 64.

[90] For purposes not particularly ascetic, Findchua de Bri Gobann habitually
took baths in a vat of cold water. *Betha Fhinnchua Bri Gobhann*, in *Lives of the
Saints from the Book of Lismore*, ed. Wh. Stokes (Oxford, 1890), 237f. L. GOU-
GAUD, *Dévotions et pratiques ascétiques du moyen âge* (Paris, 1925), 158.

[91] PALLADIUS, *op. cit.*, 113; and N. CHADWICK, *op. cit.*, 104.

[92] St. Scothine.

[93] This was the practice of Evagrius in the Nitrian desert.

[94] Infra, n. 101.

[95] St. Scothine.

[96] GOUGAUD, *Dévotions*, 160.

[97] *Ibid.*

[98] *Vita Kentigerni*, ed. Forbes (Edinburgh, 1874), 185, cited in L. GOUGAUD,

Another reason for these baths was that, in bathing, one's sins could be washed away as in a second baptism. An unknown hermit of the ninth century sings for "a clear pool to wash away sins through the grace of the Holy Spirit." [99] And like St. Aelred of Rievaulx,[100] Cadroë, a tenth-century Scot in Metz, bathed in a roaring glacial stream reciting fifteen psalms, the longest of which was Psalm 118, the *Beati Immaculati*.[101]

In tracing further the reason for immersion one finds that the same rationalizations are often given for syneisactism. Hence we turn to a consideration of the ideological and theological reasons given for syneisactism. In considering these, however, it must be remembered that our sources are generally hagiographical and do not contain the articulated theology which one might find, for example, in St. Augustine. Rather, our sources, like those of the Egyptian and Syrian Fathers, present brief and poignant reasons often based on Jewish and biblical precedents.

Although, as we have seen, syneisactism was on occasion justified on grounds of support or of showing Christian charity to a fellow Christian in need, the preoccupation with chastity of the hagiographers led them to stress the theological justification for chastity rather than for syneisactism *per se*. On perhaps the lowest level of theological justification the severe testings and consequent triumphs of the men and women living together were seen as a type of earnest for future heavenly reward. St. Aldhelm goes to search out women to tempt him so that in the future he will receive the crown of perseverance.[102] And St. Columcille, when tempted by the beautiful daughter of Aedhan, admits that he would "be inclined to lie with her," but that "it is he who foregoes this inclination to sin for God's sake that is crowned in heaven." [103]

Not only the heavenly reward for chastity is sought in these

Mulierum Consortia: Étude sur le syneisaktisme chez les ascètes celtiques, *Eriu* 9 (1923), 148.

[99] K. MEYER, The Hermit's Song, *Eriu* 1 (1904), 39.

[100] L. GOUGAUD, *Dévotions*, 163, holds that in his rule for recluses, St. Aelred is actually speaking of himself.

[101] GOUGAUD, *Dévotions*, 160.

[102] Infra, p. 563.

[103] *Betha Coluimba Chille*, trs. A. Kelleher, *Zeitschrift für celtische Philologie* 11 (1917), 125.

testings, but the rewards for humility and poverty are also pursued. In the accounts of the ascetics of the East the tale is told of a certain Theophilus and Mary, the children of Antiochene nobles, who wandered through the streets of Amida as a mime and his female companion, ostensibly a prostitute. In this action these ascetics were attempting to achieve the greatest humility and to give up everything they possessed, even their reputations.[104] In the West the same justification for sleeping between two virgins appears in St. Aldhelm.

> Let us not presume to attempt such things, therefore, according to the example of St. Aldhelm of Malmesbury, who, it is said, lay between two maidens every night, one on one side and the other on the other side, so that he might be defamed by men, but his continence rewarded the more copiously in the future by God, who understood his conscience.[105]

In the accounts of Celtic syneisactism the relish with which the ascetics approach their temptation seems, as it does to George Moore, almost ludicrous, yet the ascetics conceived of this temptation not as an excuse for promiscuity but as a battle with Satan. Louis Bouyer has shown that St. Anthony's first concern in his flight from society was to go into those places where the Devil would most likely dwell, the tombs or wilderness, to be able to battle directly with him.[106] And as the Celtic *peregrinatores* went forth into the *disart*, they did not hesitate to attack aggressively the Devil in holy war as he appeared to them in the form of concupiscence.[107] This is the primary reason which influenced St. Scothine in his life with his virgins.[108]

Closely related to the "military" justification of chastity is that of martyrdom. In Egypt the wandering Anthony yearned for martyrdom and even went seeking it in Alexandria,[109] and

---

[104] WORKMAN, *op. cit.*, 71.

[105] GIRALDUS Cambrensis, *Gemma ecclesiastica*, II, 15, ed. T. S. Brewer, *Rolls Series*, p. 235, cited in L. GOUGAUD, Mulierum consortia, 149.

[106] L. BOUYER, *The Spirituality of the New Testament and the Fathers* (London, 1963), 312. Here BOUYER is following K. HEUSSI, *Der Ursprung des Mönchtums* (Tübingen, 1936), 111.

[107] St. PATRICK, *Confessions*, c. 44, speaks of the striving with the flesh. In the *Loricae* of the early Irish the military theme is quite clear.

[108] Supra, p. 559.

[109] St. ATHANASIUS, *The Life of St. Antony*, c. 46, trs. R. T. Meyer (London, 1950), 59.

I

the *Vita Antonii* contains numerous comparisons of the wandering ascetic's and martyr's life.[110] This language of the martyr [111] was carried over into Ireland, where among the three colors of martyrdom, red, white, and green,[112] chastity was called a white martyrdom since in it one abandoned all he had for God.[113] Even as late as the twelfth century, Geoffrey of Vendôme upbraids Robert of Abrissel for seeking in syneisactism an *"infructuosum genus martyrii,"* and admonishes him to avoid the consequent evils of a *"martyrium martyribus sanctis penitus ignotum."* [114]

To the extent that the Celtic ascetics considered their living with *virgines subintroductae* an earnest for heavenly reward, they acted on the basis of a futuristic eschatology. But the Celtic ascetics, like the ancient Encratites and Messalians, were also motivated in their syneisactism by a strong sense of realized eschatology. The Irish wanderers lived in their *disart* as a provisional paradise,[115] and together with harmony with the wild creatures, they found virginity and chastity to be the chief attributes of the paradisaic state.[116]

Nowhere does the theme of chastity as realized eschatology appear more clearly than in several accounts of Adam and Eve as the prototype of the Celtic ascetic and his *virgo* living in paradise. In the *Sultair na Rann* there is an account of paradise, obviously taken from the *Book of Adam and Eve*, which has taken on the coloring of Celtic syneisactism. Adam and Eve live chastely together in the Garden of Eden until the Devil in the form of a serpent decides to deceive Eve.[117]

The fall in the *Sultair na Rann* and in *Eve's Lament* [118] is pre-

[110] *Ibid.*, c. 5.
[111] Also see H. WADDELL, *The Desert Fathers* (Ann Arbor [Mich.], 1960), 18.
[112] LECLERCQ, *et al., op. cit.*, 57.
[113] GOUGAUD, *Dévotions*, 209.
[114] GEOFFREY of Vendôme, *Epistola* 47, PL 167:182. A similar reference to syneisactism as martyrdom is found in CAESARIUS of Arles, supra, n. 84.
[115] G. H. WILLIAMS, *Wilderness and Paradise in Christian Thought* (N.Y., 1962), 46.
[116] BOUYER, *op. cit.*, 304, discusses this theme for the pre-history of monasticism.
[117] ST. JOHN D. SEYMOUR, The Book of Adam and Eve in Ireland, in the *Proceedings of the Royal Irish Academy*, Sect. C, XXXVI (1922), 121–33. On the *Saltair na Rann*, see also D. GREENE, The Religious Epic, in *Early Irish Poetry*, ed. J. CARNEY (Cork, 1965), 78f.
[118] K. MEYER, Eve's Lament, *Eriu* 3 (1907), 148.

sented in Jewish fashion. Eve eats the apple; immediately her form changes; her raiment falls off; and she is ashamed. It is then she knows that

> So long as they endure in the light of day
> So long women will not cease from folly.[119]

Sin is here seen in relation to concupiscence. Moreover, the author of the *Sultair na Rann* presents Cain as a "true son of the Devil," a reference to the old Jewish tradition that at the time of the temptation Satan seduced Eve and hence became the father of Cain.[120]

The distinctively Celtic element which is added to this account of the prototype *virgo subintroducta* appears after the fall and expulsion from paradise. With their chastity and paradise gone, Adam sadly suggests to Eve that they do penance. Then, like St. Adamnán, St. Fursa, and innumerable Celtic saints,[121] Adam and Eve cleanse themselves of their sins by standing submerged to their necks in the river, she in the Tigris and he in the Jordan, and by singing psalms and lifting up their hands to God at the appointed canonical hours.

As this story of Adam and Eve is told, it cannot with certainty be claimed that it was written either by or about Irish saints practicing syneisactism. But the elements within the story — pristine paradise, virginity, the fall as involving concupiscence and children, and penitential or cleansing immersion — all point to an environment in which syneisactism was known and practiced.[122]

In one of his most recent books on Irish Christianity the dean of modern historians of ancient Ireland, Ludwig Bieler, cites two of the texts which have been cited in this essay and brushes them aside with the implication that syneisactism could hardly have

---

> 'Tis I that brought the apple down from
> above and which went across my gullet: so
> long as they endure in the light of day
> so long women will not cease from folly.

[119] K. Meyer, *Selections*, 34.
[120] Seymour, *op. cit.*, 129.
[121] *Ibid.*, 128.
[122] For the ancient Syriac parallels, see G. Quispel, The Syrian Thomas, 235.

been present in Celtic Christianity.[123] In this essay evidence has been adduced to show that such out-of-hand dismissals of syneisactism in Celtic Christianity are highly questionable. But more than simply amassing evidence of the practice of syneisactism and its Celtic nuances, we have shown that the Celtic milieu was congenial to this practice. Celtic Christians who practiced syneisactism did not always do so for the prurient reasons of which they have often been accused. Rather they practiced syneisactism in an environment which made it both practical and charitable. More important, however, they often acted out of genuine and orthodox theological motives. Syneisactism in Celtic Christianity, far from being a perversion of early Christian morality, was the continuation of a Christian practice which dates from the origins of Christianity and which was spread throughout the early Church, both in the East and in the West. The existence of *virgines subintroductae* in Celtic Christianity is, then, a further demonstration that Irish Christianity was not a "wholly new and extremely original current," [124] but that it was the last flowering in the West of the most primitive Christianity.

[123] L. BIELER, *Ireland, Harbinger of the Middle Ages* (Oxford, 1963), 25.

[124] BOUYER, *op. cit.*, 521, actually makes this statement concerning Irish monasticism, but in the early Middle Ages Irish monasticism and Irish Christianity were almost synonymous. It is somewhat difficult to see why BOUYER makes this statement in light of his comments on p. 517.

Basil and the Early Medieval Latin
Canonical Collections

Collections of canon law compiled during the early Middle Ages in the West are well known for their paucity of canons drawn from the fathers. Unlike the Greek collections — one thinks especially of the Nomocanon, which fairly bristles with such texts — the Western collections are made up largely of the decisions of councils and papal decrees. Some twenty years ago Charles Munier in a widely acclaimed Strasbourg thesis investigated the use of patristic texts in the major collections down to the time of Gratian and found that patristic texts formed only a small proportion of the total legal statements. Of these the overwhelming majority, as one might expect, was from the Western doctors, Augustine, Ambrose, Gregory, Jerome, and Isidore. Only occasionally were the Eastern fathers used, and in several cases Basil ran a poor second or third to figures like John Chrysostom and Gregory of Nazianzus.[1]

[1] Ch. Munier, *Les sources patristiques du droit de l'Église du VIIIᵉ au XIIIᵉ siècle* (Mulhouse 1957). The following table, based on Munier's lists, pp. 30-40, 126, gives an idea of the comparative numbers of patristic texts *in toto* with those of Gregory of Nazianzus, John Chrysostom, and Basil.

COLLECTION	TOTAL PATRISTIC	GREGORY	JOHN	BASIL
Hibernensis	479	11	—	3
Ps.-Isidore	180	—	—	—
Regino	43	—	—	9
Burchard	247	—	5	11
Anselm of Lucca	180	—	—	2
Deusdedit	210	1	1	—
Ivo, *Decretum*	755	1	10	2
Ivo, *Panormia*	298	—	3	1
Polycarpus	254	1	4	2
Gratian	1200	—	14	14

Reprinted from *Basil of Caesarea: Christian, Humanist, Ascetic. A Sixteen-Hundredth Anniversary Symposium*, ed. Paul J. Fedwick, pp. 513-532, by permission of the publisher. © 1981 by the Pontifical Institute of Mediaeval Studies, Toronto.

Given his monumental task of sifting through and identifying patristic texts scattered through thousands of canons in the collections, Professor Munier limited his research largely to the collections printed to his time, the *Collectio hibernensis*, Pseudo-Isidore, Regino, Burchard, Anselm of Lucca, Deusdedit, Ivo, and Gratian.[2] But if one goes to the manuscripts of early medieval Western collections, both major and minor, and some of the collections edited since Munier's thesis, an unexpected number of canons attributed to Basil can be found, enough to show that Basil's role in the formation of Western canon law was not quite as insignificant as a hasty look at the collections might seem to indicate. To anyone familiar with the hundreds of manuscripts of the scores of canonical collections written to the time of Gratian, it will come as no surprise that the present contribution is not based on a complete investigation of all the collections and their manuscripts. But it seems appropriate in a volume dedicated to making better known the influence of Basil on the culture of both East and West that a beginning be made in establishing the place of Basil in the canonical sources of Western Christendom.

Specialists in early medieval canon law collections generally introduce their studies by making a distinction in the types of collections they examine, and in an essay dealing with the appearance of Basil's texts in the scores of early medieval collections one may examine, it is useful to repeat this distinction. There are first the so-called chronologically or historically arranged collections, and second the systematically or topically arranged collections, within which is the subdivision of penitential collections.[3] In the historically arranged collections the decisions of councils and popes are ordered in the temporal sequence in which they were given. Hence, in the conciliar parts of these collections one starts with the Councils of Arles or Nicea, etc., and in the papal sections one begins with the "decisions" of Clement, Anacletus, Damasus, or whomever. On the face of it, it would seem that to look in a chronological collection for the texts of Basil (or any other Eastern father

---

[2] For the *Polycarpus* Munier used Paris BN lat. 3881. For his typed thesis, which contains extensive tables not reproduced in the printed version, Munier also used the *Collection in 3 Parts*, and the *Sententiae Magistri A*. See Ch. Munier, "À propos des textes patristiques du Décret de Gratien," in *Proceedings of the Third International Congress of Medieval Canon Law, Strasbourg, 3-6 September 1968*, ed. S. Kuttner (Vatican 1971) p. 43, n. 2.

[3] On the distinction between historical and systematic collections see H. Mordek, *Kirchenrecht und Reform im Frankenreich: Die Collectio Vetus Gallica, die älteste systematische Kanonessammlung des fränkischen Gallien: Studien und Edition* (Berlin/ New York 1975) pp. 2-4.

for that matter) would be futile. This type of patristic canon simply did not fit within the chronological arrangement of papal and conciliar texts. But as will be seen, texts of Basil did occasionally find their way into the chronological collections as supplements to provide doctrinal support for the decisions of councils and popes.

The second major type of early medieval canonical collection is the systematic collection in which a compiler has arranged the canons he has found in historically arranged collections according to topic. In these collections compilers felt little compulsion to use only papal and conciliar texts, and, moreover, little compulsion to copy a "pure" text of any canon. It is in this systematically arranged type of collection where one would expect to find patristic texts supplementing those from popes and councils and where one looks for and indeed finds a great many texts genuinely and not-so-genuinely Basil's.

Before the ninth century most Western canonical collections were historically arranged, but a survey of these collections shows that Basil citations were inserted not so much in the decisions of the councils and popes themselves, but in the florilegia of patristic citations that the canonistic compilers added to lend support to doctrinal statements. One of the first examples of this is in the so-called *Collectio Palatina* that Schwartz found represented in at least nine manuscripts, two of which have well-known ancient collections, the *Collectio Vaticana* and the *Collectio Hadriana*.[4] In the *Collectio Palatina* a text from *De Sp. S.* 8 is used once in the *Gesta Ephesena*[5] and is repeated in the *Florilegium of Cyril of Alexandria*.[6] The same text is cited in the *Florilegium of Eutyches* found in the *Collectio Novariensis* of Novara BC 30.[7]

In another florilegium, with a title *Incipiunt testimonia sanctorum patrum duas naturas in Christo confitentium*, a Basil text from *C. Eun.* 1 is connected with the decisions of the Council of Chalcedon. Again this text

---

[4] Schwartz, *ACO* 1.51, based his edition of the *Collectio Palatina* on Vatican BAV Pal. lat. 234 (s. 6/7), Oxford BL 102 (s. 6/7), Berlin DSB 1743 (s. 8²); the *Collectio Vaticana* found in Vatican BAV Vat. lat. 1342 (s. 8), Barb. lat. 679 (s. 8/9), Florence BLM Aedil. 82 (s. 9³/⁴); and the *Collectio Hadriana aucta* found in Vatican BAV Vat. lat. 5845 (s. 10¹), Munich Clm 14008 (s. 9²), Rome BV A.5 (s. 9³/⁴). On these collections and MSS see Mordek, *Kirchenrecht*, pp. 10, 43, 59.

[5] *ACO* 1.5.1 (p. 94): 21 [xv] Basilii sanctissimi episcopi Caesariae Cappadocie Primae. Neque tantum caelum et terra ... inpassibilitatem donaret. (= *De Sp. S.* 8, PG 32: 100.)

[6] *ACO* 1.5.1 (p. 141): Cyrillus Apologeticus contra Orientales (cf. CPG 522).

[7] *ACO* 2.2.1 (p. 75): Basilii episcopi Caesariensis primae Cappadociae. Neque enim tantum caelum et terra et magnitudo pelagi et cetera.

is incorporated into many ancient canonical collections and manuscripts, including Novara BC 30.[8]

Closely related in the Novara codex to the *Testimonia sanctorum patrum* with its Basil text is a florilegium of texts under the title *Incipit exempla sanctorum patrum*.[9] This florilegium is especially well known to Basil textual experts as containing extracts from Basil's *HFide* [15], **EGNys*. [38], *De Sp. S.* 18.45, and a canon attributed to a *Sermo de incarnatione domini* of Basil but in reality from Rufinus' translation of Origen's *Peri archon*.[10] What has not been fully appreciated by the Basil textual experts is that this Novara manuscript is actually one of the great early medieval compilations of canonical collections and contains not only the third recension of the *Collectio Dionysio-Hadriana*, but also the ancient *Collectio Vaticana* and Spanish *Collection of Novara*.[11]

Another text attributed to Basil but again taken from Rufinus' translation of Origen's *Peri archon* is included in a letter of another participant in the events surrounding the Council of Chalcedon, Pope Leo I. In his *Ep.* 165, Leo used this Ps.-Basilian canon, and it came to be included in virtually all of the great chronological collections of canon law in the early Middle Ages, including the *Collectio Vaticana*, *Collectio Quesnelliana*, *Collectio Hadriana*, *Collectio Hispana*, and the *Pseudo-Isidorian Decretals*.[12]

Another pope, Gelasius I, in a Latin florilegium on the two natures of Christ entitled *Testimonia veterum de duabus naturis in Christo* cited three

---

[8] *ACO* 2.3.3 (p. 119): Sancti Basilii ex his quae contra Eunomium scripsit. Ego enim et hoc quod est ... sine dubitatione commendat. (= *C. Eun.* 1, PG 29: 552.) The Basil text in the *Gestorum Chalcedonensium versio a Rustico edita* was found by Schwartz in large numbers of MSS including Paris BN lat. 16832 (s. 9), Vatican BAV Reg. lat. 1045, Vat. lat. 1319 (s. 12), Vat. lat. 1322 (s. 6 ex.), Milan BA E 147 Sup. (s. 7), Montpellier BEM 58 (s. 9), Novara BC 30 (s. 9), Leyden BRU Voss. 122, Verona BC 58 and 59 (s. 6/7).

[9] Cf. A. Reifferscheid, *Bibliotheca Patrum Latinorum Italica*, 2: 251 f.

[10] For the texts of these extracts see *Exempla sanctorum patrum quod "unum quemlibet" < licet > "Ex beata trinitate" dicere*, CCSL 85: 126 f.

[11] For the date of this MS see Mordek, *Kirchenrecht*, p. 244; and E. Cau, "Osservazioni sul cod. lat. 1616 (sec. 8 ex.) della Biblioteca Nazionale di Vienna," in *Palaeographica diplomatica et archivistica* (Rome 1979) p. 90; and for the contents of the MS see G. Picasso, "I codici canonistici della biblioteca Capitolare di Novara nella recente storiografia," *Novarien* 5 (1973) 7-9, and literature therein. For the various collections in the MS see Mordek, *Kirchenrecht*, p. 242: pp. 10 f., nn. 40 f.; p. 43, n. 32, and literature cited therein.

[12] *ACO* 2.4 (p. 125) (cf. PL 54: 1185): XIIII Item sancti Basilii episcopi Cappadocis. Cum ergo quaedam in Christo ... inlusa imaginibus aestimentur. (= Rufinus' translation of Origen's *Peri archon* 2.6.2, ed. P. Koetschau, GCS [Leipzig 1913] p. 141.) For the collections in which this canon is contained see *ACO* 2.4 (p. 125), and the *Decretales Pseudo-Isidorianae*, ed. P. Hinschius (Leipzig 1863) p. 590.

texts of Basil also used by Theodoret of Cyrus in the *Eranistes*.[13] Two
were from the *HGrat*. [4] 5, and the other from *C. Eun*. 2.[14] Again, these
canons are found in a well-known early ninth-century canon law manuscript from Corbie, Berlin DSB Phill. 1776.[15]

Basil's *C. Eun.*, which was unknown in a Latin translation in the early
Middle Ages except in fragments in our canonical collections, is also
found embedded in the *Edictum Iustiniani Rectae fidei*. This time,
however, the extract is not from the genuinely Basil sections of *C. Eun.*
but from book 4.[16] Moreover, the Latin text of the *Edictum* with its Basil
text is not found in well-known early medieval canon law collections, but
in the fairly obscure ninth-century canon law manuscript, Montpellier
BEM 58 and Cambridge Pembroke Coll. 108 from Bury.[17]

It was perhaps from the *Edictum Iustiniani* that this same extract from
**C. Eun.* 4 entered the text of the acts of the Second Council of Seville
(619).[18] The extract, which is also found in the *Florilegium of Leontius of
Byzantium*,[19] was embedded into the florilegium associated with the
canons of the Council[20] and was given wide broadcast in the early Middle

---

[13] 2.146, 3.244; ed. G. H. Ettlinger, *Theodoret of Cyrus Eranistes* (Oxford 1975) pp.
166, 239.

[14] *Testimonia veterum de duabus naturis in Christo*, ed. Schwartz, *Publiz. Samm-
lungen*, pp. 99, 104: Gelasius de duabus naturis.

21. Basilii episcopi Caesareae ex libro Eunomium. Qui vel modice considerat ...
palam universis insinuans. (= *C. Eun*. 2, PG 29: 577.)

22. Eiusdem ex sermone gratiarum actionis. Quapropter deflens super amicum ...
tristitiam insensate feramus. (= *HGrat*. [4] 5, PG 31: 228; and for the Latin translation of
this homily see CPG 2848.)

51. Basilii episcopi Caesariae de gratiarum actione. Sicut ergo suscepit famem ...
humectationis onus egreditur. (= *HGrat*. [4] 5, PG 31: 228 f.)

[15] A. Siegmund, *Die Überlieferung der griechischen christlichen Literatur* (Munich
1949) p. 50 dates this MS as s. 8 ex.

[16] Edictum Iustiniani Rectae fidei, ed. Schwartz, *Drei dogmatische Schriften Iustinians*
(Milan 1973) pp. 142 f.: Sed et sanctus Basilius in quarto libro contra Eunomium
interpretans hoc quod est Dominus creavit me ... utriusque naturam existimantes. (= **C.
Eun*. 4, PG 29: 704.)

[17] On the Montpellier codex see Mordek, *Kirchenrecht*, p. 43, n. 32; and F. Maassen,
Geschichte der Quellen und der Literatur des canonischen Rechts (Graz 1870) p. 745. The
Cambridge MS, which Schwartz dates as s. 10, was one of the few pre-Conquest books at
Bury. It is primarily a collection of patristic texts, but has several canonistic texts.

[18] *Concilios Visigóticos e Hispano-Romanos*, ed. J. Vives (Barcelona/Madrid 1963)
p. 181: Sanctus quoque Basilius in quarto libro contra Eunomium ita scribit: Quid est:
'Dominus creavit ... in una persona ostenderet'.

[19] See R. Devreese, "Le florilège de Léonce de Byzance," *ReSR* 10 (1930) 566, n. 3;
560, nr. 22).

[20] On the florilegium of II Seville see J. Madoz, "El florilegio patrístico del II Concilio
de Sevilla (a. 619)," in *Miscellanea Isidoriana* (Rome 1936) esp. 205 f.

Ages by its inclusion in the chronological canonical collections that contained the acts of this Hispanic council.[21]

We now move from the early medieval chronological collections to the systematic collections, where Basil texts are much more plentiful. Of the few extant systematic collections antedating the ninth century that served as vehicles for texts attributed to Basil, three stand out. One of these collections is Irish, another Frankish, and the third "Franco-Irish." Also there are the penitentials, both Insular and Continental.

* The Irish systematic collection of canons is the *Collectio hibernensis*, the object of study of our Basilian father, Joseph Wey, for many years.[22] This collection, compiled in Irish circles in Europe ca. 700 is well known for its texts of the Eastern fathers, Gregory of Nazianzus, John Chrysostom, and others. According to Professor Munier's computations there are only three texts belonging to Basil.[23] And if one looks at the nineteenth-century edition of Wasserschleben, there are indeed only three snippets from Basil, all neatly labeled *Basilius dicit* or simply *Basilius*.[24] Of the brief snippets two are from Rufinus' translation of the *Asc. Ir*, and one is from the Pseudo-Basil *Admon.* used earlier by Defensor of Ligugé in his *Liber scintillarum*.[25] In the manuscripts underlying Wasserschleben's edition of the *Hibernensis* four, perhaps five, additional snippets can be found from Basil's *Asceticon*.[26] These additional texts appear in a long version (the

---

[21] Vives' edition of the canon is taken from the *Collectio hispana* in the Codex Vigilanus, El Escorial RBSLEE d.I.2. For the text as it appears in the *Pseudo-Isidorian Decretals*, see PL 130: 607.

[22] See J. J. Ryan, "Observations on the Pre-Gratian Canonical Collections: Some Recent Work and Present Problems," in *Congrès de droit canonique médiéval, Louvain et Bruxelles, 22-26 juillet 1958* (Louvain 1959) 91; and Mordek, *Kirchenrecht*, p. 259.

[23] Munier, *Les sources*, p. 30.

[24] *Die irische Kanonensammlung*, ed. H. Wasserschleben (Leipzig 1885) pp. 37, 65, 109:

12.14: Modus et qualitas temperabitur cibi ... diversitatis existit. (= *Asc. Ir, EApokr.* 9; *Codex Regularum monasticarum et canonicarum*, ed. L. Holste and M. Brockie [Augsburg 1759], 1: 75 f. The text of the *Asc. Ir* printed by Holste and used throughout this paper may also be found in PL 103: 487-554.)

21.11b: Cum Dominus aliquando dicit ... de hoc iudicare. (= *EApokr.* 77, Holste, 1: 87.)

31.16 f.: Nam et parentes ... non sepultura illis debetur. (= ***Admon.* 3, Holste, 1: 456. The text of the *Admonitio* printed by Holste and used throughout this paper may also be found in PL 103: 683-700.)

[25] *Defensoris Locogiacensis monachi Liber scintillarum* 56.14, CCSL 117: 182.

[26] In Wasserschleben's MS 6 (Rome BV T. XVIII) there are the following canons:

f. 65ᵛ, 10.7: Vocis mensuram definivit ... quod est mutabile. (= *Asc. Ir, EApokr.*

so-called Form B) of the *Hibernensis* with clear ties in southern Italy.[27]

These snippets from Basil's texts in the *Hibernensis* — all dealing with modes of Christian behavior and fasting — were widely scattered in the early Middle Ages wherever the *Hibernensis* went and became especially popular in southern Italy in the tenth century and beyond, as will be seen.

Turning from the earliest Insular systematic collection to the Continent, it had not been known until a few years ago that Basil's texts from the *Asc. 1r* played a prominent role in the earliest and most widely diffused collection of the Frankish Church, the *Collectio Vetus Gallica*. In its last recension dating to the second quarter of the eighth century this ancient Lyonese collection originally directed to clerics was supplemented at the monastery of Corbie with long and almost complete *Interrogationes* from Basil's *Asceticon*, all dealing with the monastic life.[28] In his splendid edition of this collection, Professor Mordek suggests that the monastic redactor at Corbie may have used the famous Leningrad codex of Basil's *Asc. 1r* for his text.[29] It could also be that the compiler used a manuscript

---

130, Holste, 1: 96. Cf. Wasserschleben, p. 27.)

f. 68v, 14.4: Ieiunii mensura non debet ... habuisse signantur. (= *EApokr.* 89, Holste, 1: 89 f.)

f. 89v, 28.30: Basilius interrogat Si is qui consentit ... Adam aequievit Eve. (= *EApokr.* 121, Holste, 1: 94.)

f. 136, 65.8: Omni [*sic*] sermo qui non ... otiosus est. (= *EApokr.* 40; Holste, 1: 83.)

Wasserschleben, p. 152, also notes that in Karlsruhe, BLB Aug. XVIII, p. 161, following 39.16, there are four capitula, the last of which is *De voce moderanda monachi (Basil.)*, which is like 10.7 of the Vallicelliana MS.

[27] On Rome BV T. XVIII see Mordek, *Kirchenrecht*, pp. 134 f., and on its ties with southern Italy, see below, pp. 526 f.

[28] Mordek, *Kirchenrecht*, pp. 540-543:

46.28: Eorum vero qui etate ... quis orabit pro eo? (= *EApokr.* 7, Holste, 1: 74).

46.29: Interrogatio 80: Si oportit ire ... culpabile est. (= *EApokr.* 80, Holste, 1: 88.)

46.30: Interrogatio 81: Si hoc alicui ... sed tua fiat. (= *EApokr.* 81, Holste, 1: 88.)

46.31: Quantum autem habeat periculi ... irae sicut ceteri. (= *EApokr.* 88, Holste, 1: 89.)

46.32: Interrogatio 26: Quale iudicium esse ... mittatur in gehennam. (= *EApokr.* 26, Holste, 1: 81.)

The chapters from Basil in the *Collectio Vetus Gallica* are found in Mordek's MSS P_1 (Paris BN lat. 1603; s. 8-9, northeastern France); C (Cologne DB 91; s. 8-9, perhaps Burgundian); B (Brussels BR 10127-44; s. 8-9, northeastern France or Belgium); S_2 (Stuttgart WLB HB VI.109; s. $9^1/_4$, perhaps southwestern Germany); W (only 46.28) Würzburg UB M. p. th. q. 31; s. 8-9, probably western Germany); and P_2 (Paris BN Lat. 10588; s. 9^1, southwestern France [Burgundy ?]).

[29] Mordek, *Kirchenrecht*, p. 89. On Leningrad F.v.I.2, see Lowe, *CLA* No. 1598 and *Suppl.*, p. 67.

somewhat like another famous early Basil codex, Laon BM 330, now known to have been written at Corbie.[30]

The third pre-ninth-century systematic collection containing Basil texts is the so-called *Collection of St.-Germain*. This collection includes both texts from the *Collectio hibernensis* and Frankish sources, and in the midst of the canons on penance the compiler has inserted canons from *Interrogationes* 15-28 of Basil's *Asc. 1r*.[31] The only "complete" manuscript of this collection, Paris BN lat. 12444, was written at Fleury in the late eighth or early ninth century,[32] and could the Basil texts there be compared with the now mutilated codex, Orleans BV 192, a southern French manuscript of the *Asc. 1r* that had come to Fleury by the late eighth century,[33] dependencies might be established.

Parts of the *Collection of St.-Germain* are found in at least eight other manuscripts,[34] and one of these, Munich BSB Clm 14508, a northern

---

[30] J. J. Contreni, *The Cathedral School of Laon from 850 to 930: Its Manuscripts and Masters* (Munich 1978) pp. 43 f.

[31] A. J. Nürnberger, "Über eine ungedruckte Kanonensammlung aus dem 8. Jahrhundert," in *25. Bericht der wissenschaftlichen Gesellschaft Philomathie in Neisse vom Oktober 1888 bis zum Oktober 1890* (Neisse 1890) 191 f.; and Paris BN lat. 12444, ff. 60-62^v:

20.13b: Qui penituerit pro aliquo ... similis cura exhibetur. (= *EApokr.* 22, Holste, 1: 80.)

20.14: Quomodo quis debet poenitere in unoquoque ... contristati sunt. (= *EApokr.* 18, Holste, 1: 79.)

Qui sunt fructus ... contraria sunt peccato (= *EApokr.* 19, Holste, 1: 80.)

Qui se verbo ... ad peccatum suum. (= *EApokr.* 20, Holste, 1: 80.)

20.15: Qui vult confitere ... a quibus baptizabantur. (= *EApokr.* 21, Holste, 1: 80.)

20.16: Erga eum qui pro peccato ... inquiete ambulante. (= *EApokr.* 28, Holste, 1: 81.)

Quale iuditium esse ... ad simile provocat malum. (= *EApokr.* 26, Holste, 1: 81.)

Poenitentiam ex corde ... quam perdideram (= *EApokr.* 27, Holste, 1: 81.)

20.20: Peccantem quomodo corripiemus ... dubio ad mensa [sic]. (= *EApokr.* 16, Holste, 1: 79.)

20.21: Si quis autem in parvis ... diligenter corripit. (= *EApokr.* 17, Holste, 1: 79.)

20.22: Quid sentire de se debet ... pro amicis suis. (= *EApokr.* 15, Holste, 1: 79.)

20.23: Quali effectu quis debet ... videtur et gravior. (= *EApokr.* 24-23, Holste, 1: 80.)

Also in 20.10 (f. 59), *De confessione*, a "Basil" text, also in the *Liber scintillarum* 8.39, CCSL 117: 38, is used: Basilius dicit Melior est ... superba gloriatio.

[32] See B. Bischoff, "Centri scrittorii e manoscritti mediatori di civiltà dal VI secolo all'età di Carlomagno," in *Libri e lettori nel medioevo: Guida storica e critica*, ed. G. Cavallo (Bari 1977) p. 250, n. 192; and R. Reynolds, *The Ordinals of Christ from their Origins to the Twelfth Century* (Berlin/New York 1978) p. 74.

[33] On this MS see Lowe *CLA* No. 805, where it is noted that the fragment has a strange "Nota" sign resembling one in Orléans BV 154, which was in Fleury by the late eighth century, and the Fleury Fulgentius fragment, Vatican BAV Reg. lat. 267.

[34] Albi BR 38bis, ff. 38^v-42, on which see R. E. Reynolds, "The *De officiis vii graduum*:

French manuscript of the third quarter of the ninth century,[35] draws heavily on Basil's texts.[36] The compiler of this Munich manuscript omitted several of Basil's texts in the *Collection of St.-Germain*, but he added one from the Pseudo-Basil *Admon.* not found in his model.[37]

Since at least the nineteenth century it has been widely recognized that one of the chief vehicles for the transmission of Basil's texts and ideas to the West were the penitential collections. Our knowledge of Western penitential literature is soon to be revolutionized by the circle of scholars working with Professor Kottje in Germany,[38] and hence it is perhaps premature to comment about the Basil texts found in the penitentials edited to date. But for our purposes a convenient distinction can be made between the penitentials that specifically cite Basil as the source of a particular canon and those that simply reflect his works. In both cases, however, the compilers of the penitentials seem to have known Basil's penitential discipline from Greek, perhaps Syriac, sources, especially the three *Canonical Epistles* to Amphilochius, epistles not translated into Latin until much after our period.[39]

Of the penitentials that cite Basil directly as an authority, several stand out. There are first the so-called Theodorian penitentials, including the *Canones Gregorii, Capitula Dacheriana, Canones Cottoniani*, and the

---

Its Origins and Early Medieval Development," *MS* 34 (1972) 137; St. Gall sb 40, p. 304; Florence br 256, f. 126; and Albi br 43 (15), f. 15ᵛ; on which see Reynolds, *Ordinals of Christ*, pp. 70, n. 6, 71, n. 9, and 91; Albi br 38, ff. 126ᵛ-127ᵛ; and El Escorial rbsi.ee Q.III.10, f. 127ᵛ, on which see Mordek, *Kirchenrecht*, pp. 145, n. 224, and 268-270; and Barcelona bu 228 (s. 10²), f. 134ᵛ. For the extract of the *Collectio sangermanensis* in the early medieval liturgical commentary *Ordo missae a sancto Petro institutus cum expositione sua*, see Reynolds, *Ordinals of Christ*, p. 40, n. 19.

[35] On this ms, which early went to St. Emmeram in Regensburg, see P. Landau, "Kanonistische Aktivität in Regensburg im frühen Mittelalter," in *Zwei Jahrtausend Regensburg: Vortragsreihe der Universität Regensburg zum Stadtjubiläum*, ed. D. Albrecht (Regensburg 1979) pp. 63 f.

[36] Ff. 78-80. In these folios are extracts from the *Collection of St.-Germain*, 20.13b, 15, 16, 20-23.

[37] F. 95. Bassilius [sic] dixit Qui caritate plenus ... ambulat iracundus (Holste, 1: 457).

[38] See R. Kottje, "Die frühmittelalterlichen kontinentalen Bußbücher: Bericht über ein Forschungsvorhaben an der Universität Augsburg," *BMCL* 7 (1977) 108-111. In the bulletin, "Information für die Interessenten an der Bußbücher-Forschung," dated 22 May 1979 several projects that may have a bearing on Basil texts in the penitentials have been announced, including a dissertation by Franz Kerff on the transmission and sources of the *Collectio Quadripartita*, a study by Dieter Simon on Byzantine penitentials, and the recently published book of R. Kottje, *Die Bußbücher Halitgars von Cambrai und des Hrabanus Maurus: Ihre Überlieferung und ihre Quellen* (Berlin/New York 1980) p. 241.

[39] Cf. cpg 2: 162.

widely diffused *Collection of the Discipulus Umbrensium.* This last penitential, compiled probably in England ca. 680-690, contains no less than five canons that cite Basil directly as a source[40] and twenty-six more that may have been inspired by Basil's *Canonical Epistles.*[41] One of the canons that cites Basil's name specifically as a source was also used in the eighth-century *'Confessional of Egbert,'*[42] and two anonymous canons from the *Collection of the Discipulus Umbrensium* on menstruous women were placed under Basil's name in the *Penitential of Martène,* found in a ninth-century Fleury manuscript now in Florence.[43]

Other penitentials that cite Basil directly are the *Excarpsus Cummeani,* the *Poenitentiale Remense,* and the *Canones Basilienses,* recently studied and edited by Dr. Asbach. All of these repeat at least two canons found already in the Theodorian penitentials.[44] Most surprising are three manu-

---

[40] P. W. Finsterwalder, *Die Canones Theodori Cantuariensis und ihre Überlieferungs-formen* (Weimar 1929) pp. 290, 301, 307, 322, 327:

1.2.7: Item hoc virile ... in consuetudine fuerit, ut Basilius dicit....

1.8.14: Basilius iudicavit puero ... I annum peniteat. (Cf. *Canones Gregorii* [G] 171; *Capitula Dacheriana* [D] 171; *Canones Cottoniani* [Co] 109.)

1.14.3: Trigamus et supra ... Basilius hoc iudicavit in canone autem IIII annos. (Cf. D 32; G 85; Co 178.)

2.7.3: Mulieres possunt sub nigro ... sacrificium ut Basilius iudicavit. (Cf. G 9; Co 181.)

2.12.6: Mulieri non licet virum ... Basilius hoc iudicavit. (Cf. G 67; D 164; Co 91.)

[41] Finsterwalder, *Die Canones,* p. 204, notes that the following canons may be based on Basil's works: 1.2, 3.4.17.19; 4, 6 (s. 2); 6, 1.2; (8, 6); 9, 1.10; 14, (2.3) 4.5.6.8; 2.2, 7.13; 7, 3.4; 12, 5.6.13.15.20.36.

[42] 37 (382-389), on which see J. T. McNeill and H. M. Gamer, *Medieval Handbooks of Penance: A Translation of the Principal Libri poenitentiales and Selections from Related Documents* (New York 1938) p. 248. Cf. Finsterwalder, *Die Canones,* p. 290.

[43] Florence BML Ashburnham 29 (Libri 82), on which see A. G. Martimort, *La documentation liturgique de dom Edmond Martène: Étude codicologique* (Vatican 1978) Nos. 121, 604. For the text see F. W. H. Wasserschleben, *Die Bußordnungen der abendländischen Kirche* (Halle 1851) p. 300; and W. von Hörmann, *Bußbücherstudien I: Das sogenannte poenitentiale Martenianum* (Weimar 1911-1914) pp. 448, 468. Hörmann, pp. 209 f., notes that several other canons, 50.5, 15, 16, in the penitential may derive from Basil's *Canonical Epistles.*

[44] See F. B. Asbach, *Das Poenitentiale Remense und der sogen. Excarpsus Cummeani: Überlieferung, Quellen und Entwicklung zweier kontinentaler Bußbücher aus der 1. Hälfte des 8. Jahrhunderts* (Regensburg 1975 [1979]) (notes) pp. 167, 174; (text) pp. 36 f., 75, 83:

Excarp. Cum. 3.20: Trigamus ut superius ... Basilius hoc iudicavit, in canone autem iiii annos. (Cf. Wasserschleben, *Die Bußordnungen,* p. 473.)

14.9: Mulieres possunt sub nigro ... sacrificium. Basilius hoc iudicavit. (Cf. Wasserschleben, p. 492.)

Poenit. Rem. 5.45: Trigamus et superius ... Basilius hoc iudicavit. In canonum autem iii annos. (Cf. Asbach, notes, p. 154, for parallel citations from Theodore.)

scripts containing the whole of or the preface to the Irish *Paenitentiale Cummeani*, Oxford BL 311, Munich BSB Clm 14466b, and Vatican BAV Vat. lat. 1349, ascribing the text to Basil.[45]

A rapid survey of the indices of Schmitz' study and edition of the Continental penitentials of the ninth century and beyond will show the large number of instances in which texts in Basil's *Canonical Epistles* appear to have influenced the Continental compilers.[46] Schmitz' citations are almost all to canons in the so-called *Penitentiale Vallicellanum I*, a penitential of the late eighth or early ninth century compiled in northern Italy,[47] but a close reading of other Continental penitentials will show the influences of Basil right through the early Middle Ages.

After the late eighth century the next large infusion of Basil texts into Western canonical collections was to come in the very late ninth century, but before dealing with this infusion an isolated ninth-century canonical manuscript should be mentioned as containing Basil's texts drawn from sources other than his *Asceticon* and *Canonical Epistles*. This codex, Paris BN lat. 1597A, a Rheims manuscript of the 880s, is our only source of materials relative to the Frankish Council of Paris of 825.[48] In one of the pieces, the *Libellus synodalis Parisiensis*, there are three texts attributed to Basil, one from the *De Sp. S.* 18.45,[49] another from the *HMart.* [19],[50] and the third from the Pseudo-Basil *EIuln.* [360].[51] The source of these Basil

---

5.54: Mulieri non licet virum ... Basilius iudicavit. (Cf. Asbach, notes, p. 154, for parallel citations from Theodore.)

15.41: Mulieres possunt sub nigro ... sacrificium. Basilius hoc iudicavit. (Cf. Asbach, notes, p. 161, for parallel citations from Theodore.)

Canones Basil. (34a) 34: Trigamus vel supra ... Bassilius [*sic*] iudicavit in canone autem iii annis.

(40) 40: Mulieri non licet virum ... Basilius iudicavit.

[45] In Oxford BI. 311, f. 33 (ascribed to a tenth-century Continental scribe by Asbach, p. 27) the title is "Incipit sancti Basilii penitentiale ad Comiani Longii" (on which cf. L. Bieler, ed., *The Irish Penitentials* [Dublin 1963] pp. 6 and 108). In Clm 14466b, f. 66ᵛ (dated by Bischoff and Asbach, p. 230, to s. 9¹/₄, Regensburg) the title is "Incipit dicta sancti Basilii episcopi de xiiii remissionibus peccatorum." And Vatican BAV Vat. lat. 1349, f. 193 (on which see below, n. 62, and Bieler, pp. 6 and 108) the title is "Incipit de remediis penitentiae. Expositus [*sic*] sancti Basilii inquisitio a Cumiani Longii."

[46] H. J. Schmitz, *Die Bußbücher und die Bußdisciplin der Kirche*, 1 (Mainz 1883) 252, 264, 265, 274, 285 f., 290 f., 295, 297.

[47] A new study of this penitential is being prepared by Günter Hägele.

[48] Ph. Lauer, *BN: Catalogue général des manuscrits latins*, 2 (Paris 1940) 82 f.

[49] MGH Conc. 2.510 f.

[50] Ibid., 511.

[51] Ibid., 511. On the spurious nature of this "Basilian" epistle see M. Bessières, "La tradition manuscrite de la correspondance de saint Basile," *JThS* 23 (1922) 345.

texts was almost certainly the *Actiones* of the Second Council of Nicea, where all can be found.[52]

By the very late ninth century there appeared in northern France a collection that would have enormous influence in the diffusion of Basil texts in the great classical medieval collections of canon law, the *Collectio Quadripartita*.[53] In at least two of its books, 3 and 4, there is over a score of texts from or attributed to Basil. The great majority is taken from Rufinus' translation of the *Asceticon*,[54] but others reflect the shadowy "Smaragdus" text[55] and even the Greek *EApokr. fus.*[56]

---

[52] G. D. Mansi, *Sacrorum Conciliorum nova et amplissima collectio* 12 (Florence 1758/1798) 1065; 13: 68, 70.

[53] For literature on the *Collectio Quadripartita* see R. Kottje, "Kirchenrechtliche Interessen im Bodenseeraum vom 9. bis 12. Jahrhundert," in *Kirchenrechtliche Texte im Bodenseegebiet*, ed. J. Autenrieth and R. Kottje (Sigmaringen 1975) p. 32; R. Kottje, "Eine Antwerpener Handschrift des Quadripartitus Lib. iv." *BMCL* 6 (1976) 65-67; Mordek, *Kirchenrecht*, pp. 172 f.; and R. Pokorny, "Zwei unerkannte Bischofskapitularien des 10. Jahrhunderts," *DA* 35 (1979) 491, n. 14. There are two late ninth-century mss of the whole or parts of the *Quadripartita*: Vatican bav Vat. lat. 1347 (on which see Mordek, p. 263, and V. Brown, *Hand-List of Beneventan mss* [= 2nd ed. of E. A. Lowe, *The Beneventan Script*] [Rome 1980] p. 145), and Stuttgart wlb HB VII.62 (on which see J. Autenrieth, "Die kanonistischen Handschriften der Dombibliothek Konstanz," in *Kirchenrechtliche Texte im Bodenseegebiet*, p. 13). I have been unable to examine a complete manuscript of the *Quadripartita* and hence have used the edition in pl. 112: 1337-98 for book 3 and Vatican bav Vat. lat. 1347 for book 4.

[54] pl. 112: 1342-82:
[3.1] Aut quis crederet tristitiam ... ad saeculum Deum contristamur. (Attributed to Basil and similar to *EApokr.* 50. Holste, 1: 84.)
[3.15] His enim iudiciis inanis gloria ... receperunt mercedem suam. (Cf. *EApokr.* 146, Holste, 1: 98.)
[3.17] ... Est etenim huius vitii medicina, prout sanctus Basilius episcopus ait, ut omnia propter Deum ... sectemur hominum laudes. (Cf. *EApokr.* 146, Holste, 1: 98.)
[3.23] Inter furorem autem ... iratus pro tempore concitatur. (Attributed to Basil and similar to *EApokr.* 159, Holste, 1: 100 f.)
[3.47] Audiant hi qui non carnis corruptione ... sententiam sancti Basilii Caesariensis episcopi. Mulierem inquit ignoro et virgo ... integritatem cordis.
[3.53] Duo sunt enim genera tristitiae ... legem tuam. (Attributed to Basil and similar to *EApokr.* 5, Holste, 1: 84.)
[3.61] Cognoscitur quidem hic nequissimus ... superiorem efficiat. (Attributed to Basil and similar to *EApokr.* 61, Holste, 1: 85.)
Vatican bav Vat. lat. 1347, ff. 79ᵛ, 152-169:
[4.2] Timorem quidem docet ... calicem domini percipit. (Attributed to Basil and similar to *EApokr.* 134, Holste, 1: 97.)
[4.19] Hoc sit in iudicio positum ... facit differentium poenae. (Attributed to Basil. *EApokr.* 194, Holste, 1: 106.)
[4.24] Poenitentem ex corde ... ovem meam quam perdideram. (Attributed to Basil. *EApokr.* 27, Holste, 1: 81.)

Not too long after the *Quadripartita* was compiled, no less than eight of its Basil canons were included in the *Libri duo de synodalibus causis* of Regino of Prüm (ca. 906).[57] Most of these canons were later to find their

---

[4.25] Affectum illum in se recipiat ... sicut Zacheus fecit. (Attributed to Basil. *EApokr.* 18. Holste. 1: 79.)

[4.26] Erga eum qui pro peccato ... tradidimus vobis. (Attributed to Basil. *EApokr.* 28. Holste. 1: 81.)

[4.32] Si quis semel notatus ... cura similis adhibetur. (Attributed to Basil. *EApokr.* 22. Holste. 1: 80.)

[4.42] Id [*sic*] omnimodis observari ... non est qui erigat eum. (Attributed to Basil. *EApokr.* 174. Holste. 1: 103.)

[4.109] Si quis preventus ... in irritum revocetur. (Attributed to Basil and similar to *EApokr. br.* 60. PG 31: 1121.)

[4.152] Apostolus dicit Omnia facite ... et opus eius abiciatur. (Attributed to Basil. *EApokr.* 71. Holste. 1: 87.)

[4.153] Si quis murmurans extiterit ... sacerdotis iudicio paeniteat. (Attributed to Basil and similar to *EApokr.* 93. Holste. 1: 90.)

[4.157] Si quis detrahit ... detraxit Moysi poeniteat. (Attributed to Basil and similar to *EApokr.* 43 f., Holste. 1: 83.)

[4.210] Si is qui praeest ... evangelizavimus vobis anathema sit. (Attributed to Basil. Snippet from *EApokr.* 13. Holste. 1: 78.)

[4.211] Si quis prohibet nos facere ... qui diligunt Deum. (Attributed to Basil. Snippet from *EApokr.* 13. Holste. 1: 78 f.)

[4.212] Is qui praeest si praeter voluntate ... aut sacrilegus habeatur. (Attributed to Basil and similar to *EApokr.* 15. Holste. 1: 79.)

[4.221] Firma autem tunc erit ... deputari ac perfecta. (Attributed to Basil. Snippet from *EApokr.* 7. Holste. 1: 74.)

[4.225] Oportet tamen infantes ... excludatur hominum pessimorum. (Attributed to Basil. Snippet from *EApokr.* 7. Holste. 1: 74.)

[4.240] Qui consentit peccantibus ... culpabilem iudicandum. (Attributed to Basil. but on the source see n. 55.)

[4.251] Qui alterius consentit peccato ... consentit contrahat poenam. (Attributed to Basil.)

The texts of these canons are in E. L. Richter. *Antiqua canonum collectio, qua in libris de synodalibus causis compilandis usus est Regino Prumiensis...* (Marburg 1844) pp. 3-43.

[55] 4.240. Cf. *Smaragdi abbatis Expositio in Regulam s. Benedicti*, ed. A. Spannagel (Siegburg 1974) p. 329 (3.68.1 = *Regula Pachomii, Praecepta atque Iudicia*, clxxvi [*Pachomiana latina: Règle et épitres de s. Pachome. Épitre de s. Théodore et "Liber" de s. Orsiesius: Texte latin de s. Jérome*, ed. A. Boon (Louvain 1932) p. 69] = *Concordia Regularum* 72.2, PL 103: 1360 f.).

[56] 4.78 (Vat. lat. 1347, f. 157, with no attribution): Si quis vult coniugatus ... voluntate castitatis consensum. The canon is taken from the *Regula Isidori* 4. as found in the *Codex Regularum* (Holste. 1: 189; PL 103: 559). But cf. PL 83: 872, where it is lacking. It may be based on the *EApokr. fus.* 12. PG 31: 948 f. In Regino and other collections this canon is often attributed to Basil.

[57] *Reginonis abbatis Prumiensis Libri duo de synodalibus causis et disciplinis ecclesiasticis*, ed. F. G. A. Wasserschleben (Leipzig 1840) pp. 91, 154 f., 256 f., 315:

way into Burchard, Ivo, and Gratian, but there are two other Basil canons, later added in the appendices to Regino, whose influence would have repercussions in theological debate even into the present century. These canons, dealing with the "secret tradition" of the church and studied a dozen years back by Dom Gribomont,[58] were drawn from Basil's *De Sp. S.* 27, 29.[59] We have already come upon fragments of the *De Sp. S.* in ninth-century manuscripts,[60] and hence cc. 27, 29 in Regino's appendix may well have come from a now lost early Latin translation of the tract, but it is also possible that a Greek source available in northern France in the early tenth century was used.

By the early eleventh century there were two flourishing traditions of Basil texts in our systematic canonical collections, one stemming from the *Collectio hibernensis* found especially in southern Italian manuscripts, and another in the *Quadripartita* and Regino's collection. The *Hibernensis* tradition as found in the Roman manuscript, BV T. XVIII, written in Beneventan territories,[61] quickly transmitted its Basil canons into the tenth-century Beneventan *Collection in Nine Books* of Vatican BAV Vat. lat.

1.166: Apostolus dicit Omnia facite ... opus eius abiiciatur. (= *EApokr.* 71, Holste, 1: 87.)

1.167: Si quis murmurans exstiterit ... sacerdotis iudicio peniteat. (Similar to *EApokr.* 93, Holste, 1: 90.)

1.168: Si quis detraxerit ... detraxit Moysi peniteat. (Similar to *EApokr.* 43 f., Holste, 1: 83.)

1.325: Penitentem ex corde ... ovem meam quam perdideram. (= *EApokr.* 27, Holste, 1: 81.)

1.326: Affectum illum in se ... et abominatus sum. (= *EApokr.* 18, Holste, 1: 79.)

1.328: Erga eum qui pro peccato ... quam tradidimus vobis. (= *EApokr.* 28, Holste, 1: 81.)

2.109: Si quis vult coniugatus ... castitatis consensum. (= *Quadripartitus* 4.78.)

2.259: Clericus vel monachus adolescentium ... deinceps iuvenibus coniungendus. (This canon, which Regino attributes to Basil, bears no attribution in the *Quadripartitus*, 4.81 [Vat. lat. 1347, f. 157ᵛ]. It derives from the *Regula Fructuosi* 16, Holste, 1: 205; PL 87: 1107.)

[58] See J. Gribomont, "Ésotérisme et tradition dans le Traité du Saint-Esprit de saint Basile," *Oecumenica* 2 (1967) 23.

[59] Wasserschleben, pp. 447 f.:

Append. 2.36: Ecclesiasticarum institutionum ... publicata scripto. (= *De Sp. S.* 27, PG 32: 188.)

Append. 2.37: Deficit me dies ... persuasibilius eruditis clarescat. (= *De Sp. S.* 29, PG 32: 200.)

[60] See above, pp. 515-523. The texts in Append. 2 are found in Wolfenbüttel HAB Aug. 83-21 (written in the late tenth century) and Stuttgart WLB HB VI.114 (written in the late tenth century), on which see Autenrieth, "Die kanonistischen Handschriften," p. 14.

[61] See Brown, *Hand-List of Beneventan MSS,* p. 131.

1349,[62] and then on to the eleventh-century southern Italian *Collection in Five Books*.[63] These latter collections also shared canons from penitentials perhaps inspired by Basil's *Canonical Epistles*.[64] They may have come from earlier Continental penitentials or Greek sources. That Greek sources were being used in some form in these collections is highly likely because the *Collection in Five Books* also contains an extract from the *Vita Basilii* of Amphilochius (the story of the Conversion of the Jew) in a recension quite unlike the only known Latin versions of the Amphilochian *Vita* listed by the Bollandists.[65]

During the course of the eleventh century the tradition in the *Collection in Five Books* with its Basil texts worked a significant influence on a number of minor southern Italian collections. Of these the *Collection of Vatican Vat. lat. 4977* was noted by Paul Fournier long ago[66] but he

---

[62] F. 126; 6.83: Cum Dominus aliquando ... de hoc iudicare. (= *Coll. hib.* 21.11b.)

   f. 135; 6.189: Nam et parentes ... sepultura ei debetur. (= *Coll. hib.* 31.16f.)

   f. 140ᵛ; 6.250: Omnis sermo ... otiosus est. (= *Coll. hib.* 65.8 in Vallicelliana T. xviii.)

   f. 171ᵛ; 7.198: Ieiunii mensura ... habuisse signantur. (= *Coll. hib.* 14.4 in Vallicelliana T. xviii.)

   On this ms see Brown, *Hand-List of Beneventan mss.*, p. 145; and Mordek, *Kirchenrecht*, p. 138, n. 185, who points out that although the ms itself was written in the eleventh century, the collection seems, according to Fournier, to have been compiled in the early tenth century. There is also in this ms, f. 193, the preface to Cummean's Penitential ascribed to Basil, on which see n. 45 above.

[63] 1.220.3: Cum Dominus aliquando ... de hoc iudicare. (= *Coll. hib.* 21.11b.)

   3.242.4: Omnis sermo ... otiosus est. (= *Coll. hib.* 68.5 in Vallicelliana T. xviii.)

   3.254.2: Scire debemus quia rationem ... opus Dei negligenter. (The text of these canons is found in *Collectio canonum in v libris [Lib. i-iii]*, cccm 6: 135, 433, 439.)

   4.69: Si quis sacerdos palam ... peregrinando finiat.   *

   4.99: Si his qui consentit ... Adam acquievit Evae. (= *Coll. hib.* 28.30 in Vallicelliana T. xviii.)

   4.176: Nam et parentes ... eis detur honor. (= *Coll. hib.* 31.16f.)

   4.271: Plurimi namque homines ... vestra de celo debere. (= **Admon.* 14, Holste, 1: 462.)

   4.348: Modus et qualitas temperabitur cibi ... aliqua diversa existit. (= *Coll. hib.* 12.14.)

   (The text of these canons in Lib. 4 may be found in Vatican bav Vat. làt. 1339, ff. 181, 186ᵛ, 200, 215, 227; on which ms see *Manuscripta* 21 [1977] 13, and Reynolds, *Ordinals of Christ*, p. 92.)

[64] In the *Collection in Nine Books*, Vat. lat. 1349, ff. 197-205ᵛ, there are a number of penitential periods of fifteen years, a favorite in the works of Basil, on which see P. Fournier, "Un groupe de recueils canoniques italiens des xᵉ et xiᵉ siècles," *MAIBL* 40 (1915) 153-155.

[65] 3.220.2: Quidam hebreus venit ... nostrum Ihesum Christum; cccm 6: 421. Cf. the editions listed in bhl 1: 153 f. (Nos. 1022-1027).

[66] On this collection see Reynolds, *Ordinals of Christ*, p. 92.

missed its four Basil canons.[67] Less well known are three other collections with Basil texts, the *Collection of Vatican Arch. San Pietro H 58*,[68] the *Collection of Rieti*,[69] and the Farfa *Liber multiloquiorum*.[70] Of special interest in this last collection is a Basil text from a Greek *Vita Basilii* like the one Combefis edited in which the ages of the world are described.[71]

Much more important for the transmission of Basil texts in Western canon law than these southern Italian collections were the transalpine collections and their derivatives. From Regino, Basil texts passed into Burchard's *Decretum*,[72] and from Burchard they were filtered down to

---

[67] F. 44ᵛ: Scire debemus quia rationem ... opus Dei neglegenter. (= *Coll. VL*, 3.254.2.)

f. 47ᵛ: Si quis sacerdos palam ... peregrinando finiat. (= *Coll. VL*, 4.69.)

f. 52ᵛ: Si hisque consentit ... Adam acquievit Ævae (= *Coll. VL*, 4.99.)

f. 69ᵛ: Qui consentit peccatibus et defendit ... iudicandum et excommunicandum. (On this canon, which bears the attribution *Ex dictis Basilii episcopi*, see above, n. 54, and below, n. 77.)

[68] F. 52ᵛ: Vocis mensuram diffinit ... quod est notabile. (= *Coll. hib.* 10.7 in Vallicelliana T. xviii.)

On f. 148ᵛ, there is a reference to Basil, "Basilius episcopus Cesariensis clarus Cappadocie babetur [sic] qui multa continentiae et ingenii bona uno superbiae malo perdidit." On this liturgico-canonical collection see R. E. Reynolds, "Excerpta from the Collectio Hibernensis in Three Vatican Manuscripts," *BMCL* 5 (1975) 4-9; P. Salmon, "Un 'Libellus officialis' du xiᵉ siècle," *RBen* 87 (1977) 257-288; idem, "Un témoin de la vie chrétienne dans une église de Rome au xiᵉ siècle: le *Liber officialis* de la basilique des Saints-Apôtres," *RSCI* 33 (1979) 65-73; Kottje, *Die Bußbücher Halitgars von Cambrai* esp. pp. 65-69; and for Professor Bischoff's dating of the manuscript see D. Sicard, *La liturgie de la mort dans l'église latine des origines à la réforme carolingienne* (Münster 1978) pp. xiv, 115, n. 33.

[69] Rieti ᴀᴄ 5, f. 36ᵛ: Nam et parentes nostros ... sepultura ei debetur. (= *Coll. VL*, 4.176.)

f. 42: Plurimi namque homines ... vestra de celo debere. (= *Coll. VL*, 4.271.)

f. 73: Si quis sacerdos palam ... peregrinando finiat. (= *Coll. VL*, 4.69.)

On this collection, for which I am preparing a short study, see F. A. Ferretti, *L'archivio e l'antica Biblioteca della Cattedrale di Rieti: La Lipsanoteca Episcopale* (Rieti 1939) p. 23 with pl.; and Brown, *Hand-List of Beneventan MSS.*, p. 120.

[70] Vatican ʙᴀᴠ Vat. lat. 4317, ff. 171ᵛ-172: xxxii. De etatibus mundi in vita sancti Basilii. Basilius. A primo plasto homine cui nomen ... ducenti nonaginta septem. Item Basilius. In prima vero die ... quadrupedia et reptilia.

f. 197ᵛ: Si quis sacerdos palam ... pergrinando finiat. (= *Coll. VL*, 4.69.)

On this ᴍs see R. E. Reynolds, "The 'Isidorian' *Epistula ad Leudefredum*: An Early Medieval Epitome of the Clerical Duties," *MS* 41 (1979) 306 f.

[71] Ff. 171ᵛ-172. Cf. *Acta Sanctorum* 23: 420ʙ.

[72] 3.127: Ecclesiasticarum institutionum ... publicata scripto. (Attributed to Basil in ᴘʟ 140: 698.)

8.9: Monacho non liceat votum ... frangendum erit. (= *Coll. Disc. Umb.* 2.6.9 [Finsterwalder, p. 321]. Cf. Munier, *Les sources*, p. 213. In ᴘʟ 140: 794 attributed to Basil.)

9.45: Si quis vult coniugatus ... voluntate castitatis consensum. (Attributed to Basil in ᴘʟ 140: 822.)

Bonizo of Sutri's late eleventh-century canon law collection, *De vita christiana*.[73]

At the very end of the eleventh century the canonical collections that nearly supplanted all other earlier ones belonged to Ivo of Chartres, his *Decretum, Panormia,* and *Tripartita.* Of these three, the *Panormia* with its one Basil text[74] was the most popular, but it is in the other two that Basil texts are most heavily represented. In the *Decretum* there are at least nine.[75] While Munier in his published thesis on patristic sources

---

10.52: Si quis murmurans ... sacerdotis iudicio peniteat. (Not attributed to Basil in PL 140: 852.)

10.54: Apostolus dicit: Omnia facite ... opus eius abiiciatur. (Not attributed to Basil in PL 140: 852.)

10.59: Si quis contristatus ... animo satisfactionem recipiat. (Not attributed to Basil in PL 140: 852.)

10.67: Si quis detraxerit ... detraxit Mosi peniteat. (Attributed to Basil in PL 140: 854.)

17.35: Clericus vel monachus adolescentium ... deinceps iuvenibus coniungendus. (Attributed to Basil in PL 140: 925.)

19.39: Penitentem ex corde ... ovem meam quam perdideram. (Attributed to Basil in PL 140: 987.)

19.64: Erga eum qui ... quam tradidi vobis. (Not attributed to Basil in PL 140: 998.)

19.79: Qui sub gradu peccat ... gradum venire difficile est. (= *Coll. hib.* 11.1b; falsely attributed to Basil in PL 140: 1001.)

[73] 4.130: Ecclesiasticarum institutionum ... publicata scripto. (= Burchard 3.127.)

6.16: Si quis vult coniugatus ... castitatus consensum. (= Burchard 9.45.)

8.46: Si quis vult coniugatus ... castitatis consensum (= Burchard 9.45.)

The texts of these canons may be found in Bonizo of Sutri, *Liber de vita christiana*, ed. E. Perels (Berlin 1930) pp. 173, 214 f., 265. For further examples of the use of the canon, Si quis coniugatus..., see Anselm of Lucca, *Collectio canonum* 10.20, ed. F. Thaner (Innsbruck 1906) p. 492; Cardinal Gregory's *Polycarpus* 6.4 (Paris BN lat. 3881, f. 127ᵛ); and the *Collectio Caesaraugustana* 10.65 (Vatican Barb. lat. 897, f. 196ᵛ). I am grateful to Professor J. T. Gilchrist for microfilm of this MS.

[74] 2.159: Ecclesiarum institutiones ... publicata scripto. (PL 161: 1119 f.)

[75] 4.69: Ecclesiasticarum institutionum ... publicata scripto. (Attributed to Basil in PL 161: 283.)

7.32: Monacho non licet votum ... frangendum erit. (Attributed to Basil in PL 161: 553.)

8.183: Si quis coniugatus ... castitatis consensum. (Attributed to Basil in PL 161: 622.)

13.53: Si quis murmurans ... iudicio peniteat. (Not attributed to Basil in PL 161: 814.)

13.55: Apostolus dicit Omnia facite ... opus eius abiiciatur. (Not attributed to Basil in PL 161: 814.)

13.60: Si quis contristatus ... animo satisfactionem recipiat. (Not attributed to Basil in PL 161: 814 f.)

13.67: Si quis detraxerit ... Moysi peniteat. (Attributed to Basil in PL. 161: 815.)

15.55: Penitentem ex corde ... ovem meam quam perdideram. (Attributed to Basil in PL 161: 871.)

15.78: Erga eum qui pro peccato ... quam tradidi vobis. (Not attributed to Basil in PL. 161: 880.)

530

specifically noted the Basil texts in the *Decretum*,[76] he did not deal with Ivo's third collection, the *Tripartita*. Yet here Basil is represented by almost a score of texts. Most are neatly grouped together in Part 2 and placed under a general rubric that attributes them to the Eighth Synod (although some are more specifically assigned to Basil or Isidore).[77] Given

---

[76] Munier, *Les sources patristiques*, p. 39.

[77] Cf. Alençon **BM** 135 (an incomplete **MS** of the *Tripartita*), ff. 86-87, 148ᵛ, 166ᵛ; and Paris, **BN** lat. 3858B, ff. 92ᵛ-93ᵛ, 146ᵛ, 162ᵛ:

2.14.8: Timorem quidem docet ... calicem Domini percipit. (= *Quadripartita* 4.2; here attributed to Basil.)

2.14.9: Hoc sit in iudicio ... differentiam paene. (= *Quadripartita* 4.19; not attributed to Basil by name.)

2.14.10: Ut pro qualitate ... tempus impendatur. (= *Quadripartita* 4.20; not attributed to Basil by name, but within a larger group of canons under Basil's name. The text resembles the *EApokr. br.* 106, **PG** 31: 1155 f., but it is actually drawn from the canons of Laodicea, c. 2. In the *Quadripartita* 4.20 of Vat. lat. 1347, f. 152, the canon is attributed to the Council of Laodicea.)

2.14.11: Paenitentem ex corde ... ovem meam quam perdideram. (= *Quadripartita* 4.24; not attributed to Basil by name.)

2.14.12: Affectum illum in se ... sicut Zacheus fecit (= *Quadripartita* 4.25; not attributed to Basil by name.)

2.14.13: Erga eum qui pro peccato ... tradidimus vobis. (= *Quadripartita* 4.26; not attributed to Basil by name in the Paris **MS**, but specifically assigned to Basil in the Alençon **MS**.)

2.14.14: Si quis semel notatus ... cura similis adhibetur. (= *Quadripartita* 4.32; not attributed to Basil by name.)

2.14.15: In omnibus observari ... non est qui erigat eum. (= *Quadripartita* 4.42; not attributed to Basil by name.)

2.14.16: Si quis preventus fuerit ... in irritum revocetur. (= *Quadripartita* 4.109; attributed to Isidore.)

2.14.17: Oportet infantes cum voluntate ... sacerdotis iudicio peniteat. (= *Quadripartita* 4.221, 225; not attributed to Basil or Isidore by name.)

2.14.18: Si is qui praeest fecerit ... evangelizavimus vobis anathema sit. (= *Quadripartita* 4.210; not attributed to Basil by name.)

2.14.19: Si quis prohibet nos facere ... qui diligunt Deum. (= *Quadripartita* 4.211; not attributed to Basil by name.)

2.14.19 [*sic*]: Is qui praeest si praeter voluntatem ... aut sacrilegus habeatur. (= *Quadripartita* 4.212; not attributed to Basil by name.)

2.14.21: Qui consentit peccantibus ... similmodo culpabilem iudicandum. (= *Quadripartita* 4.240; not attributed to Basil by name.)

2.14.22: Si quis vult coniugatus ... voluntate castitatis consensum. (= *Quadripartita* 4.78; not attributed to Basil by name.)

3.7.2: Ecclesiasticarum institutionum ... quam publicata scripto. (See above, nn. 58 f.; here attributed to Basil.)

3.12.9: Monacho non liceat votum ... frangendum erit (= Burchard, *Dec.* 8.9; Ivo, *Dec.* 7.32; *Polycarpus* 4.35.15 [Paris **BN** Lat. 3881, f. 99]; on which see U. Horst, *Die Kanonessammlung Polycarpus des Gregor von S. Grisogono. Quellen und Tendenzen* (Munich 1980) p. 158 here attributed to Basil.)

the peculiar readings, it seems clear that the primary source of the Basil texts in Ivo's *Tripartita* is L. 4 of the ninth-century *Quadripartita*.

Our survey of the diffusion of Basil's texts in early medieval Western canonical collections arrives finally at Gratian's *Decretum*. When Gratian uses a Basil text, it is rarely attributed to our Eastern doctor; more often it is Isidore or the Eighth Synod.[78] These attributions provide the clue to Gratian's major source. It was the *Tripartita* of Ivo. In only two cases of

---

[78] D. 11, c. 5: Ecclesiasticarum institutionum ... publicata scripto. (= Ivo, *Trip.* 3.7.2; here attributed to Basil.)

D. 47, c. 8: Sicut hi qui per insaniam mente ... prestare quod velis. (Extracts from Rufinus' translation of the *HDestr.* [6], PG 31: 1749-1752; cf. CPG 2850, and CPL 225a; here attributed to Ambrose.)

D. 81, c. 26: In omnibus observare ... qui erigat eum. (= Ivo, *Trip.* 2.14.15; here attributed to the Eighth Synod.)

D. 90, c. 4: Alienus sit a fratrum ... sacerdotis iudicio peniteat. (Drawn from Ivo, *Trip.* 2.14.17; here attributed to the Eighth Synod.)

D. 90, c. 10: Si quis contristatus ... animo satisfactionem recipiat. (Similar to *EApokr.* 72, Holste, 1: 87; attributed here to Pope Fabian; cf. Ivo, *Dec.* 13.60, above, n. 75.)

C. 11, q. 3, c. 100: Qui consentit peccantibus ... simili modo culpabilem iudicandum. (= Ivo, *Trip.* 2.14.21; here attributed to Isidore.)

C. 11, q. 3, c. 101: Si is qui preest ... aut sacrilegus habeatur. (= Ivo, *Trip.* 2.14.18-19 [sic]; here attributed to Isidore.)

C. 20, q. 1, c. 1: Firma autem tunc erit ... deputari ac perfecta. (Drawn from Ivo, *Trip.* 2.14.17; here attributed to the Ninth Synod.)

C. 20, q. 2, c. 4: Oportet infantes cum voluntate ... gratia excludatur hominum pessimorum. (Drawn from Ivo, *Trip.* 2.14.17; here attributed to the Ninth Synod.)

C. 20, q. 4, c. 2: Monacho non licet votum ... frangendum erit. (= Ivo, *Trip.* 3.12.9; here attributed to Basil.)

C. 22, q. 4, c. 19: Si quis preventus fuerit ... in irritum revocetur. (= Ivo, *Trip.* 2.14.16; here attributed to Isidore.)

C. 26, q. 7, c. 7: Pro qualitate delicti penitenciae tempus inpendatur. (= Ivo, *Trip.* 2.14.10; here attributed to the Eighth Synod.)

C. 26, q. 7, c. 8: Hoc sit positum in iudicio ... haberi differenciam penae (= Ivo, *Trip.* 2.14.9; here attributed to the Eighth Synod.)

C. 26, q. 7, c. 9: Penitentem ex corde ... ovem meam quam perdideram. (= Ivo, *Trip.* 2.14.11; here attributed to the Eighth Synod.)

C. 26, q. 7, c. 10: Affectum illum in se ... sicut et Zacheus fecit. (= Ivo, *Trip.* 2.14.12; here attributed to the Eighth Synod.)

C. 26, q. 7, c. 11: Erga eum qui peccata ... tradidimus vobis. (= Ivo, *Trip.* 2.14.13; here attributed to the Eighth Synod.)

C. 27, q. 2, c. 22: Si quis coniugatus ... castitatus consensum. (= Ivo, *Trip.* 2.14.22; here attributed to the Eighth Synod.)

De penit. D. 2, c. 1: Si quis semel notatus ... cura similis adhibetur. (= Ivo, *Trip.* 2.14.14; here attributed to the Eighth Synod.)

De consec. D. 2, c. 25: Timorem quidem docet ... calicem Domini percipit. (= Ivo, *Trip.* 2.14.8; here attributed to both the Eighth Synod and Basil.)

Gratian's nineteen or so Basil canons was the *Tripartita* not the source, and in one of these it was Ivo's *Decretum*.[79]

To conclude, several comments should be made about the Basil sources used by early medieval Western canonical compilers. The major source of Basil canons was the *Asc. I r* in its Latin translation by Rufinus.[80] Which of the different manuscripts and Western recensions the compilers used must await critical editions not only of the Rufinus translation but in most cases critical editions of the canonical collections themselves. Beyond the *Asc. I r*, the Western canonists used fragments from other Basilian writings for which there were Latin translations, among them being the *HMart.* [19], *HDestr.* [6], *HGrat.* [4], and the Pseudo-Basil *Admon*. Perhaps more interesting are the indications that Greek versions of several Basil texts were known and used by the canonists. The compilers of penitentials seem to have known the penitential discipline in the *Canonical Epistles*, and the compilers of the canonical collections had at hand at least parts of the *De Sp. S.*, *C. Eun.*, **C. Eun.*, and one or more versions of the Amphilochian *Vita* unknown in Latin translation. Thanks to the canonists we have some of our earliest evidence of the transmission of Basil's texts into the West. It is not inconceivable that further searches through early medieval canonistic manuscripts will turn up unexpected evidence of other Basil texts hitherto unknown in the early medieval Latin West.

---

[79] D. 90, c. 10 (= Ivo, *Dec.* 13.60).

[80] On the intended wide distribution of Rufinus' translation of Basil's *Asc. I r* see C. P. Hammond, "A Product of a Fifth-Century Scriptorium preserving Conventions used by Rufinus of Aquileia," *JThS* 29 (1978) 370 f.

III

AN EIGHTH-CENTURY UNCIAL LEAF FROM A MONDSEE *LIBER COMITIS* (HARVARD, HOUGHTON LIBRARY MS Typ 694)*

In the second volume of his *Die südostdeutschen Schreibschulen* Professor Bischoff described a number of liturgical manuscripts written in or near the ancient abbey of Mondsee in the diocese of Passau[1]. Among these are two magnificent uncial Gospel books and a lectionary fragment[2]. The Gospel books, the Ingolstadt Gospels and New York-Nürnberg Gospel fragment, are particularly noteworthy because they were deluxe books written in Mondsee itself in an uncial script of the late eighth century. The lectionary fragment, a less imposing product in Carolingian minuscule of the first or second quarter of the ninth century, is also noteworthy in that after its creation in some southeast German centre it wandered to Mondsee and eventually to the Österreichische Nationalbibliothek in Vienna. In this last depository it came under the scrutiny of Franz Unterkircher, who described it in an article entitled "Ein Lektionar-Fragment aus Mondsee (Cod. Vindob. Ser. N. 3202)" honouring the prefect of the Vatican Library, Eugène Cardinal Tisserant, on his eightieth birthday[3]. An offprint of this article was given to the present author by the current prefect of the Vatican Library, Leonard Boyle, almost simultaneously with news brought by Virginia Brown of the existence at Harvard University of another lectionary fragment in uncial script almost certainly from early Carolingian Mondsee. Hence, it is appropriate that the present article honouring Professor Bischoff on his eightieth birthday concerns this fragment that in its script is related to the Mondsee Gospels and in its extraordinary peregrinations is not unlike the Mondsee lectionary.

The fragment, Cambridge, Massachusetts, Harvard University, Houghton Library MS Typ 694, recently came into Houghton's possession from the collection of Philip Hofer, who himself had spent decades of his career in Houghton. This new accession now stands as the only item written entirely in uncial script in the Harvard collection[4]. According to notes on the outer and inner folders in which the fragment is kept – and even on the fragment itself – Hofer purchased the fragment in May of 1957 from the London firm of Maggs Brothers Ltd. In a type of 'Geheimschrift' Hofer reported that he had paid for the leaf £ CUE-R-O (£ 125-6-0) or about $MEC ($ 351)[5] including postage. According to these same notes the fragment had come to Maggs in 1956 from the collection of the Leiden dealer Erik von

---

* For their assistance in the preparation of this article I am grateful to the librarians of Houghton Library, where as an undergraduate and graduate student my interest in the study of early medieval liturgical manuscripts was first stimulated. Publication of this description and photographs of the leaf is by permission of the Houghton Library, Harvard University.

[1] Bernhard Bischoff, *Die südostdeutschen Schreibschulen und Bibliotheken in der Karolingerzeit*, Teil II: *Die vorwiegend österreichischen Diözesen* (Wiesbaden 1980), pp. 9–26.

[2] Ibid, pp. 18–20, describing Munich, Bayerische Staatsbibliothek Clm 27270 + Prag, Státní knihovna ČSR, VI.D.4, and New York, P. Morgan Library, M. 564 + Nürnberg, Stadtbibl., Fragm. Lat. 1; and pp. 25f. describing Vienna, ÖNB Ser. nov. 3202.

[3] Franz Unterkircher, "Ein Lektionar-Fragment aus Mondsee (Cod. Vindob. Ser. N. 3202)", in: *Mélanges Eugène Tisserant* V (Studi e Testi 235, Vatican City), pp. 413–26 + 3 pls.

[4] Information kindly supplied by Rodney G. Dennis, Curator of Manuscripts of Houghton Library.

[5] Like many collectors of manuscripts, Hofer had a code word whose letters correspond to numbers signifying the cost of manuscripts.

Scherling[6]. Various notes accompanying the fragment also state that the *Lectionarium* was written in Italy and that it could be dated to ca. A.D. 750 or ca. A.D. 800[7]. After Hofer's death in 1984 the question of the date and origin was reconsidered because a final note on one of the inner folders states that "On July 24–25, 1985 i [*sic:* probably one of the appraisers in the firm of Bernard M. Rosenthal[8]] checked *CLA* (Great Britain & Netherlands)" [presumably searching for references to the Maggs or von Scherling collections]. "This leaf is not listed." Had the search through E. A. Lowe's *Codices Latini Antiquiores* continued to volume eight, however, where Professor Bischoff's collaboration with Lowe is patently obvious, the connections of the Houghton leaf with the uncial script of early Carolingian Mondsee would have become abundantly clear.

The fragment, part of a *Liber comitis*[9], is written on a yellow parchment leaf of fairly good quality but with a few defects: in the upper left hand margin of the recto side there is staining, which on the verso side caused part of a large decorated 'F' on the succeeding folio of the codex to leave its traces on ours; the parchment has given way around several letters and partially in the interlace of the finial of the upper hasta of the 'F'; and there are numerous tiny worm holes. At some time the leaf was trimmed so that no prick marks are visible, and the whole of the upper margin and half of the first of the twenty-five lines of text has disappeared. As it now stands the measurements of the leaf are 286 mm × 209 mm, with a writing space of 254 mm × 172 mm in two columns of 254 mm × 67 mm each. Four sets of vertical double lines were scored on the recto flesh side of the leaf for margins (7 mm wide), and single horizontal lines were scored on the recto side for the text (11 mm apart), whose small uncial letters are 4 mm high.

The ink used for the text, which has in places rubbed off, is a brownish-black; and numbers and rubrics for the pericopes were and remain in part written in red. At some time, probably during the Carolingian era, the numbers above the second and third pericopes were modified from xxxiii to xxvii and from xxxiiii to xxviii by scraping off the appropriate strokes from the Roman numerals (not from the frame above them) and by adding others in a slightly darker red ink.

There are two decorated 'F's (132 mm × 47 mm and 79 mm × 38 mm), whose interlace, 'Profilblätter,' and lively colours of red, yellow, violet, green, and dark blue place the leaf within a southeast German context and more especially Mondsee itself[10]. Most important, however, is that there are extensive traces of gold on the stem of the large 'F' on the recto side of the leaf. Further traces of gold appear on the verso side of the leaf, where the faint reverse impression of a large decorated 'F', which would have been on the following leaf of the codex, can be seen. Clearly, then, the codex from which the Houghton leaf came was a deluxe manuscript, not unlike the Ingolstadt and New York–Nürnberg Gospels with their letters decorated in lively coloured interlace, 'Profilblätter,' and gold and silver[11].

From late medieval times through modernity a variety of additions has been made on the leaf: flourishes around the large 'F'; doodles and attempts at interlace in the margins in light brown ink; a parting "Vale Vale..." in light brown ink between the columns on the recto side; and more recently in pencil the citations of Romans xii.17 and xii.21 next to the first pericope, and the note regarding the purchase and proposed origins of the leaf.

---

[6] In the volumes held by Harvard University of von Scherling's *Rotulus,* vols. 1–7, I was unable to find this leaf described.

[7] The latter date is given on the back of a photograph of the leaf in the folders.

[8] The appraisal number of the leaf is BMR 43.

[9] For the definition of a *Liber comitis* see Klaus Gamber, *Codices Liturgici Latini Antiquiores* [hereafter CLLA] (Freiburg/ S [2]1968), p. 429.

[10] See Bischoff, Schreibschulen II, p. 20; and Katharina Bierbrauer, *Die Ornamentik frühkarolingischer Handschriften aus Bayern.* Bayer. Akad. d. Wiss., Philos.-hist. Kl., Abh., N.F., H. 54 (Munich 1979), p. 86, and Taf. 68.1 for a 'Profilblatt' in Clm 27270.

[11] Ibid.

One scribe seems to have been responsible for the text and rubrics; and the fact that the same original red of the numerals and rubrics is found in the margins and interlace of the decorated 'F's' suggests that the same scribe had a hand in the decoration of the leaf. That the scribe added the rubrics after writing the text is clear from the numbers added for the third pericope on the verso side. In the margin the scribe drew a frame, which is still visible, and then began to write beneath it a number, of which only x\..ii is visible under ultraviolet light. Lacking sufficient space to complete it, the scribe eradicated the number and placed it above the rubric. The vertical stem of the new frame cuts across the lower point of the colon, thereby showing that the rubric was added after the text.

The scribe wrote text and rubrics in a bold and regular uncial script very similar to that in the first sections of the Ingolstadt Gospels described by Professor Bischoff[12]. Especially noticeable is the hanging asymetrical leaf forming the bow of the 'A'. There are, however, some minor differences: light horizontal hair-lines at the extremities of some letters are used; the round letters are not as broad; and in the curved strokes of the round letters there is a slight thickening at the lower left and upper right.

Abbreviations are used for the *Nomina sacra* and for standard liturgical formulae such as F̄r̄s̄. At line ends a horizontal stroke signifies an 'm'; and in the rubrics *post* is abbreviated as 'p't'. Numbers in the rubrics are Roman. The text itself is written *per cola et commata,* and as punctuation marks triangular-pointed colons are used for major pauses, and for medial pauses a semicolon, an oblique over a medial point, or a medial oblique. The only corrections are those in the rubricated Roman numerals for the pericopes; in 'bu' in line 11 of the left column of the recto side; and the deletion of words under the rubics on the verso side.

The pericopes in the Houghton *Liber comitis* are for the third, fourth, and fifth Sundays after Epiphany drawn respectively from Romans xii.17–21, xiii.8–10, and Hebrews iii.1–6. They follow basically the Vulgate text[13] but with a few variants: in Romans xii.17–21 vindicta*m et* and bon*um*; in Romans xiii.8–10 qui*c*quam, proximum *suum,* fura*v*eris, the addition of *rem proximi tui* in Romans xiii.9, restaurabi*t*ur, and Dilig*i*s; and in Hebrews iii.1–6 domo *illius,* transposition of *habitus est,* Omnes, a missing 'est' after Deus, and testimoni*o* eorum. The rubrics themselves are significant in that the term *Theophania* is used rather than *Epiphania.* Dom Wilmart long ago noted that the term *Theophania* is the one used in the tradition of the Gelasian sacramentaries and hence a token of liturgical tradition antedating the coming of the Hadrian Sacramentary to Aachen[14]. Moreover, this same term is used in the *Comes* of Alcuin, his first great biblical work, predating even his Bible version[15].

Significant also in this leaf are the number of readings for Sundays after Epiphany and the exact texts chosen. Although a few early examples of lectionaries like ours had readings for the fifth and sixth Sundays after Epiphany, most did not. For the pericopes themselves the Houghton leaf follows the general pattern of eighth- and ninth-century lectionaries by using Romans xii.16–21 for the third Sunday after Epiphany and Romans xiii.8–10 for the fourth Sunday after Epiphany. But as is shown in the accompanying table surveying some sixteen pericope lists using the pericopes of the Houghton leaf, it is only the Houghton example that uses Hebrews iii.1–6 for the fifth Sunday after Epiphany. As can be seen in this table the use of Hebrews iii.1–6 varied considerably in early lectionaries, and the Houghton example is yet another testimony to the uncertain position of this pericope in liturgical use.

---

[12] Particularly striking is the regularity of the upper boundary of the letters where no scoring is visible. On double scoring for lines in the Ingolstadt Gospel see Bischoff, Schreibschulen II, p. 18.

[13] For variants of the Vetus Latina in Hb 3.1 ff. of the lectionary fragment of Vatican BAV lat. 5755 see CLLA, 1268, p. 485.

[14] André Wilmart, "Le Lectionnaire d'Alcuin", *Ephemerides liturgicae* 51 (1937), p. 172.

[15] CLLA, p. 439.

Table of lections

SOURCE	CapL	Wep	CoB	H	CoL	CoP	Mu7	C	CoTh	V	M	AmB	CoA	Mu14	P	BEN
Rm 12.16ff.	T^c	T^3	T^3	T^3	T^3	T^3		T^3	T^3			P^{12}	T^4			T^3
Rm 13.8	Q^2	T^4	T^4	T^4	T^4	T^4	T^4	T^4	T^4				T^5	T		T^4
Hb 3.1ff.		N^4			T^5			T^6		T^6	N^1		T^3		T^4	

ABBREVIATIONS OF FEASTS (Suprascript numbers or letter are Sundays or quotidians in a season.)

T = Theophania
P = Pentecost
Q = Quadragesima
N = Nativitas

ABBREVATIONS OF SOURCES

CapL Fulda LB Cod. Bonifatianus 1 (ca. 545, Capua), cf. CLLA 401
Wep Würzburg UB M.p.th.f.62 (sVIIIm, English monk), cf. CLLA 1001
CoB Besançon BM 184 (sVIIIex, Murbach?), cf. CLLA 1226
H Harvard Houghton Lib. MS Typ 694 (sVIIIex, Mondsee)
CoL Leningrad GPB Q.v.I Nr. 16 (sVIII/IX, Corbie), cf. CLLA 1005
CoP Paris BN lat. 9451 (s.VIII/IX, N. Italy), cf. CLLA 1210
Mu7 Munich BSB Clm 29303(7), fol.^{r} (sIX^1, Salzburg)
C Chartres BM 24 (sIX$^{1/2}$, Tours), cf. CLLA 1229
CoTh Beauvais MS 23 (lost) (sIX, Centula for Amiens), cf. CLLA 1050
V Vatican BAV lat. 5755 (sIX, N. Italy), cf. CLLA 1268
M Milan Bibl. Amb. C 228 inf. (sIX^m, Bobbio), cf. CLLA 1219
AmB Bergamo Bibl. S. Aless. in Colonna (sIX$^{2/2}$, N. Italy), cf. CLLA 505
CoA Paris BN lat. 9452 (sIX$^{3/4}$, St.-Amand), cf. CLLA 1040
Mu14 Munich BSB Clm 29303(14), fol. 3^r (sX): the fragment beginning with "... ulterabis non" with no rubric. The Epistle and Gospel, however, are immediately before those for the Purification.
P Vatican BAV Pal. lat. 510 (sXI, Germany), cf. CLLA 1029
BEN Vatican BAV Ottob. 576 (sXI/XII/XIII, SE. Italy) and lat. 6082 (sXII, Monte Cassino), cf. CLLA 450, 455

There is a final important feature in the pericopes of the Houghton leaf: the second and third originally bore the numbers xxxiii and xxxiiii, which were changed to xxvii and xxviii. Although the numbers assigned to the pericopes in early books of the *Comes* varied widely, readings for these Sundays after Epiphany generally were numbered in the late teens. In the Alcuinian *Comes,* for example, pericopes for these Sundays bear the numbers xvii–xviiii[16]. Hence, it is likely that the complete *Liber comitis* of the Houghton leaf contained an extraordinarily rich collection of pericopes, at least for the Christmas and Epiphany seasons. This would tend to corroborate the suggestion, indicated also by the uncial script itself and by the traces of gold in the decorated intials, that the *Liber comitis* of the Houghton leaf was a deluxe codex and fitting liturgical companion for the magnificent late eighth-century uncial Gospel books of Mondsee described by Professor Bischoff.

---

[16] Wilmart, art. cit., pp. 151f.

Cambridge, Mass., Harvard Univ., Houghton Libr. MS Typ 694, recto side

pisces recipror
mittit
Et siquod est aliud
commandatum inhoc
uerbo restaurabi
tur:
Diliges proximum
tuum sicut te ip
sum; dilectio pro
ximi malum non
operatur
plenitudo ergo
legis est dilec
tio XXIII
Dom uir theoph
Lege ii p ap adheb
rson
siderato
apostolu
et pontifi
cem con
fessionis nos
traei bar qui fi
delis est et qui

Sicut et moyses
Sin omni domo il
lius:
Amplioris enim
gloriae iste pre
moyse dignus
habitus est quan
to ampliore hono
norem habet do
mus qui fabri
uit illam:
Omnes namque
domus fabricatur
ab aliquo quiaute
omnia creauit ds:
Et moyses quidem
fidelis erat in to
ta domo eius:
Tam quam famulus
in testimonio eoru
que dicenda erant:
Xps uero tam qua
filius in domo sua
quae domus sumus

Cambridge, Mass., Harvard Univ., Houghton Libr. MS Typ 694, verso side

IV

Unity and Diversity in Carolingian Canon Law Collections:
The Case of the Collectio Hibernensis and Its Derivatives*

It is now conventional textbook wisdom that when the early Carolingian rulers, Pepin, Charlemagne, and Louis the Pious, went about trying to consolidate the Frankish realm, they attempted in matters religious and intellectual to impose a form of unity through the use of Roman texts. In the area of liturgical reform Charlemagne is said to have attempted to put down the "anarchy" of local Gallican uses of the eighth century by asking from Pope Hadrian a "pure" copy of the Roman *Gregorian Sacramentary*. This sacramentary was then placed in the scriptorium at Aachen and scribes from throughout the realm are said to have come to make copies from it. A similar procedure is said to have been used in monastic reform. A "pure" copy of the *Regula sancti Benedicti* was brought from Monte Cassino to Aachen and perhaps used there as a model for visiting scribes to copy. And finally, in matters of ecclesiastical law Charlemagne is said to have requested and received from Pope Hadrian a copy of the ancient *Collectio Dionysiana,* which was then copied and diffused throughout the Carolingian realm.

During the past two decades this neat textbook description of early Carolingian attempts to impose unity through "Romanity" has begun to fray at the edges. It has been shown that while there were indeed successful attempts at reform through the introduction of Roman books, there was immediate and very substantial modification of these texts and that local and regional traditions continued to flourish throughout the

* See Addenda and Corrigenda

late eighth and ninth centuries. For example, Raymund Kottje in a brilliant article in 1965 showed on the basis of extant manuscripts that in southern France and northern Italy of the late eighth and early ninth century the ancient canonical *Concordia Cresconii* and the newly compiled Lyonese *Collectio Dacheriana* were at least as popular as the *Collectio Dionysio-Hadriana*.[1] Hubert Mordek a few years later demonstrated that the popularity of the Gallican *Collectio Vetus Gallica* continued even as Charlemagne was "imposing" the *Collectio Dionysio-Hadriana* and that a manuscript of this competing Gallican collection was even made for Charlemagne's court library, presumably to supplement the Roman collection.[2] More recently Susan Keefe has shown that in the initiatory rite of baptism, old Gallican and Milanese traditions quickly infiltrated the newly imported Roman ceremonies.[3] And finally, in matters penitential Kottje has demonstrated that the celebrated "Roman" penitential book of Halitgar of Cambrai is filled with traditional Frankish texts.[4] In short, the Carolingian ideal of Roman unity was often deflected in matters canonical and liturgical by texts and practices traditional in the Frankish realm.

In the scholarship of the past twenty years another element in the Carolingian mixture of Roman and non-Roman traditions has received perhaps less recognition than it deserves—the Irish. The role of the Irish in Carolingian culture and religious life has, of course, long been recognized and studied intensively. And in one area of canon law—penitential discipline and its texts—scholars eagerly await the studies promised by Kottje's "Bussbücher-Forschung."[5] Nonetheless, there has been insufficient examination of the influence that the major Irish collection of canon law, the *Collectio Hibernensis*, had in the Carolingian period.

---

[1]Raymund Kottje, "Einheit und Vielfalt des kirchlichen Lebens in der Karolingerzeit," *Zeitschrift für Kirchengeschichte* 76 (1965), 336–341.

[2]Hubert Mordek, *Kirchenrecht und Reform im Frankenreich: Die Collectio Vetus Gallica, die älteste systematische Kanonessammlung des fränkischen Gallien: Studien und Edition,* Beiträge zur Geschichte und Quellenkunde des Mittelalters 1 (Berlin–New York, 1975), p. 282.

[3]Susan Ann Keefe, "Baptismal Instruction in the Carolingian Period: The MS Evidence" (Diss., Toronto, 1981).

[4]Raymund Kottje, *Die Bussbücher Halitgars von Cambrai und des Hrabanus Maurus: ihre Überlieferung und ihre Quellen,* Beiträge zur Geschichte und Quellenkunde des Mittelalters 8 (Berlin–New York, 1980), pp. 185–190.

[5]See Raymund Kottje, "Die frühmittelalterlichen kontinentalen Bussbücher: Bericht über ein Forschungsvorhaben an der Universität Augsburg [nunc Bonn]," *Bulletin of Medieval Canon Law,* n.s. 7 (1977), 108–111.

This has been due in part to the fact that the great nineteenth-century study by Paul Fournier, "De l'influence de la collection irlandaise sur la formation des collections canoniques,"[6] appeared to be definitive and in part because scholars have waited to base new studies on the edition of the *Collectio Hibernensis* promised by Professor Sheehy.[7] But even while awaiting the new edition, several advances make it possible to give further precision to Fournier's work and to go beyond it, especially for the Carolingian period. One of these advances has come in the identification of further ninth-century manuscripts by Mordek and in Professor Bischoff's dating and locating of these and many codices known to Fournier.[8] Moreover, a number of texts that appear in the *Collectio Hibernensis* and its derivatives have been edited or studied in more detail. Hence, without claiming to be exhaustive, it would seem appropriate in a volume on the Carolingian period in which Irish scholarship plays a prominent role to bring this new material together to emphasize that the Carolingian canonistic complex contained not only Roman and Frankish elements, but a strong Irish component in the *Collectio Hibernensis* and its derivatives.

That there continued to be an Irish canonistic component in an age when the Roman was dominant is surprising for several reasons. First, the types of canons and authorities in the *Collectio Hibernensis* were clearly unlike those in the Roman and Gallican collections and were, therefore, subject to suspicion. There were the expected conciliar and papal canons, but many books of the *Hibernensis* contained substantial amounts of biblical material and snippets from the Fathers. Often these were, as Fournier says, "plutôt destinés à poser des principes qu'à réglementer en termes rigoureux l'action des divers organes de la société ecclésiastique."[9] Such texts had occasionally accompanied non-Irish collections to add authority to papal and conciliar texts,[10] but never were as many genuine and suspect texts used or as liberally sprinkled through the collections. Second, while there was no denying that the Irish were among the foremost scholars and missionaries of the Carolingian age, elements of their ecclesiastical discipline were suspect—the

---

[6]Paul Fournier, "De l'influence de la collection irlandaise sur la formation des collections canoniques," *Nouvelle revue historique de droit français et étranger* 23 (1899), 27-78 [in this article the pagination is taken from the 'extrait' of Fournier's study].

[7]See Mordek, *Kirchenrecht*, p. 259.

[8]See especially Mordek, *Kirchenrecht*, pp. 255-259.

[9]Fournier, "De l'influence," p. 48.

[10]See Roger E. Reynolds, "Basil and the Early Medieval Latin Canonical Collections," in *Basil of Caesarea: Christian, Humanist, Ascetic: A Sixteen-Hundredth Anniversary Symposium*, ed. P. J. Fedwick (Toronto, 1981), p. 513.

wandering, unusual notions about the relationship of abbots and bishops, and the like. Hence, the canon law collection epitomizing this discipline would be suspect. Most important, however, Irish penitential discipline was vigorously attacked in the Carolingian period, and the books that contained this discipline, the penitentials, were condemned by several early ninth-century councils.[11] It might seem surprising that the attacks on the penitentials should also have touched the *Collectio Hibernensis*, until it is recalled that the *Hibernensis* itself had Irish penitential texts within it[12] and that the penitentials were often contained in the same manuscripts as the *Hibernensis*.[13] Hence, the attacks on the Insular, especially the Irish, penitentials also very probably cast a pall over the canonical *Collectio Hibernensis*.

It has been well documented that the Carolingian condemnation of the Insular penitentials was only partially successful and that as useful instruments of ecclesiastical discipline they continued to be copied and modified for centuries.[14] So it was in the ninth century with the *Collectio Hibernensis*. The canons themselves might have lacked the authority of those in the Roman collections the Carolingians promoted, but they dealt with a multitude of matters untouched by the Roman, and, just as important, they were systematically arranged.[15] To trace the continuation of the *Hibernensis* in the ninth century let us look at it in its own and its derivative forms under the following headings: (1) complete, partial, and fragmentary manuscript exemplars; (2) abridgments; (3) collections dependent on *Hibernensis* canons; (4) isolated extracts from the *Hibernensis*; (5) the *Collectio Sangermanensis* and its supplement; and (6) Carolingian *liturgica*.

1. Complete, Partial, and Fragmentary Manuscript Exemplars of the *Collectio Hibernensis*

Until the new edition of the *Hibernensis* by Professor Sheehy appears, we shall not know exactly what the contents of the various recensions of

---

[11]See Cyrille Vogel, Les *"libri paenitentiales,"* Typologie des sources du moyen âge occidental 27 (Turnhout, 1978), pp. 39f.

[12]See e.g., the critical apparatus in *The Irish Penitentials,* ed. Ludwig Bieler and D. A. Binchy, Scriptores latini Hiberniae 5 (Dublin, 1963), pp. 54–58.

[13]Bieler-Binchy, *The Irish Penitentials,* pp. 16–24.

[14]See Vogel, *"Libri paenitentiales,"* passim.

[15]See Allen J. Frantzen, "The Significance of the Frankish Penitentials," *Journal of Ecclesiastical History* 30 (1979), 411.

the collection were, but traditionally they have been divided into an A or shorter, and a B or longer version of the text. Both versions continued to be copied into the late tenth century and are represented relatively complete in three manuscripts of the first half of the ninth century. Form A is found in Orléans, Bibl. de la Ville 221 (193) (s. IXin., Brittany) and St. Gall SB 243 (s. IX[1], St. Gall); and Form B is found in Oxford, Bodl. Hatton 42 (s. IX[1-med.], Brittany).[16] Since these manuscripts date to a time precisely when both Roman and Frankish collections were dominating all others, one wonders why they were copied at all. But the places of origin provide us with the clue. The manuscripts were written in areas with significant Celtic traditions or populations, St. Gall and Brittany.

St. Gall, of course, had grown out of the Irish mission of St. Columbanus, and although in the late eighth and early ninth century a multitude of canonistic texts could be found there,[17] it was widely known as having been a Continental foyer for Insular texts. Brittany, too, had an established Celtic tradition, and it was in part due to the Celtic population there that the Carolingian rulers had difficulty exercising their authority. In his study of the diffusion of the manuscripts of the *Collectio Dionysio-Hadriana* Kottje pointed out that it was in southern and western France and in northern Italy with their indigenous collections that the *Collectio Dionysio-Hadriana* had its most modest diffusion in the first half of the ninth century.[18] And although Mordek's results have modified this view in part,[19] it still appears to be the case that the *Dionysio-Hadriana* made the least headway in areas with their own canonistic traditions and collections, such as the *Concordia Cresconii* and *Collectio Dacheriana*. Hence, it is not surprising to find that the *Hibernensis* was copied in the early ninth century in a region with its own Celtic canonistic tradition, Brittany. And indeed, Irish influence is seen in the Breton Orléans manuscript in the text that precedes the *Collectio Hibernensis*, the *Virtutes quas Dominus dominica die fecit*,[20] a tract that the late Professor McNally attributed to the Irish.[21] Moreover, it may be significant that a later

---

[16]Mordek, *Kirchenrecht*, pp. 256f.

[17]See Raymund Kottje, "Kirchenrechtliche Interessen im Bodenseeraum vom 9. bis 12. Jahrhundert," in Johanne Autenrieth and Raymund Kottje, *Kirchenrechtliche Texte im Bodenseegebiet*, Vorträge und Forschungen, Sonderbd. 18, Konstanzer Arbeitskreis für mittelalterliche Geschichte (Sigmaringen, 1975), pp. 32–36.

[18]Kottje, "Einheit und Vielfalt," p. 337.

[19]See Mordek, *Kirchenrecht*, pp. 243–249.

[20]P. 21.

[21]Robert E. McNally, "Dies Dominica: Two Hiberno-Latin Texts," *Mediaeval Studies* 22 (1960), 355–361; and Scriptores Hiberniae minores 1, Corpus christianorum, Ser. lat. 108B (Turnhout, 1973), pp. 181–186.

manuscript of the A Form of the *Hibernensis*, Paris BN Lat. 3182 (s. X^2), was written in Brittany. This later manuscript, however, contains also the *Collectio Vetus Gallica* and *Collectio Dionysio-Hadriana*,[22] suggesting a gradual penetration of Roman and Frankish collections into areas hitherto under Celtic domination.

In the origins of the partial and fragmentary forms of the *Hibernensis* written in the late eighth and early ninth century the influence of Irish centers of culture can again be seen. The fragment of Form B in Karlsruhe, Bad. LB Aug. XVIII, fols. 75r–90v (s. IXin.), was written on the island of Reichenau, renowned for the number of Irish texts copied there.[23] Futher, two of the three manuscripts copied with extracts containing the first half of the *Hibernensis* to L. 38, c. 18, originated in areas with heavy Irish influence: Cambrai, Bibl. mun. 679 (619) (between 763 and 790, northeast France, Peronne?) and Cologne, DB 210 (Darmst. 2178) (s. VIII^2, northeast France).[24] It is interesting, too, that Tours, Bibl. mun. 556, a manuscript of the *Hibernensis* with the same configuration of contents as that in the Cambrai and Cologne manuscripts, was written in the last quarter of the ninth century at Marmoutier near Tours, where, according to Kottje,[25] there was an obvious and significant lacuna in the production of manuscripts of the *Collectio Dionysio-Hadriana*.

Beyond these partial manuscripts of the *Hibernensis* there exist two fragments of codices that Mordek speculates may contain the collection with clear indicia of Irish origins. The fragment in Trier, SB 137/50, fols. 48r–61v, was written in the second half of the eighth century either in Ireland itself or on the Continent in an Irish center,[26] and Munich, Clm 29410/2, was written at the turn of the eighth century on the Continent in an Irish hand.[27]

2. Abridgments of the *Collectio Hibernensis*

Inasmuch as the *Hibernensis* could be found in the late eighth century in a variety of complete recensions and in versions containing only portions of the

[22]Mordek, *Kirchenrecht*, pp. 153, 244.

[23]See, e.g., Roger E. Reynolds, *The Ordinals of Christ from their Origins to the Twelfth Century*, Beiträge zur Geschichte und Quellenkunde des Mittelalters 7 (Berlin–New York, 1978), pp. 69–71.

[24]Mordek, *Kirchenrecht*, p. 257. Also see below, pp. 110, 127.

[25]Kottje, "Einheit und Vielfalt," p. 337.

[26]Mordek, *Kirchenrecht*, p. 257.

[27]Mordek, *Kirchenrecht*, p. 257; and cf. Bernhard Bischoff, *Die südostdeutschen Schreibschulen und Bibliotheken in der Karolingerzeit, 2: Die vorwiegend österreichischen Diözesen* (Wiesbaden, 1980), p. 291. In this fragment there is at least a part of the *Collectio Hibernensis*, L. 1, c. 18.

complete text, it is not surprising that collections were quickly compiled in which selected canons were extracted in full or partial versions. There exist seven manuscripts with such abridgments of the *Hibernensis*, five of which were written in the late eighth or early ninth century in areas or specific localities with long Insular traditions.

(a) The Abridgment of Cambridge, Corpus Christi College 279

The latest of the abridgments was written in the latter half of the ninth century in the vicinity of Tours, which, as was mentioned, conspicuously lacks extant manuscript witnesses to the *Collectio Dionysio-Hadriana*. The Celtic connection of this abridgment lies in the fact that it was a copy, according to Allen Frantzen,[28] of a Breton manuscript. Although the canons drawn from the *Hibernensis* number only eighty,[29] it is significant that many of them are drawn from the early chapters on the ecclesiastical hierarchy and that many collections dependent on the *Hibernensis* would also borrow these texts.[30]

(b) The Abridgment of Würzburg, UB M.p.th.q.31, fols. 1–41

A second manuscript with an abridgment of the *Hibernensis* was written in part by an Anglo-Saxon scribe at the turn of the eighth century, probably in Germany. It contains not only a peculiar section devoted almost exclusively to an abridgment of the *Hibernensis*, but also a second mixed collection, to be dealt with later, in which fragments that may be from, or inspired by, the *Hibernensis* appear.[31] In the first part of the manuscript is a vast florilegium of some 603 texts attributed to the fathers, Augustine, Jerome, Gregory, Ambrose, and Gregory Nazianzus, most of which come from the *Hibernensis*. The structure of the collection is unusual in that the books, beginning with L. 21 of the *Hibernensis*, are assigned *Hibernensis* titles after which there generally follow two or three rubrics again drawn from the *Hibernensis*, followed by the mélange of patristic texts. The sequence of books, however, does not follow the major recensions of the *Hibernensis* but often leaps from late to early books and back again. Most of the books from LL. 2–67 of the *Hibernensis* are represented in the Würzburg abridgment.

---

[28]Frantzen, "Frankish Penitentials," p. 419, n. 73.
[29]Fournier, "De l'influence," p. 5.
[30]See Reynolds, *Ordinals of Christ*, p. 62, n. 39; and below, p. 114.
[31]Fols. 52–59, on which see below, p. 110.

(c)   The *Collection in 250 Chapters*

Three manuscripts with what is known as the *Collection in 250 Chapters* based on the *Hibernensis* were written in southeast Germany. Two are now in Munich, Clm 4592 (s. IX2/4, prov. Benediktbeuren) and Clm 6434, fols. 41r–75r (s. VIIIex., Freising), and one is in Vienna, ÖNB 522 (s. IX2/3, Salzburg).[32] The canons in this collection are drawn from the *Hibernensis* beginning at L. 20. Although the three manuscripts are all now from southeastern German centers with long traditions of Irish texts, the version of the *Collectio Hibernensis* in them is like that found in northern French recensions of the widely diffused *Collectio Vetus Gallica*.[33] Of special interest is the Vienna manuscript, written in the second third of the ninth century in Salzburg and annotated by Magister Baldo.[34] Not only was this scholar interested in the Roman canonical collections there,[35] but he was also involved in the glossing and supplementing of the Insular canonistic texts written in this center which had as recently as the late eighth century had the Irishman Virgil for its abbot-bishop and John the Anglo-Saxon for bishop.[36] The Vienna manuscript, like its counterpart in Munich, Clm 4592, is also significant for the diffusion of the *Hibernensis* in that a second collection in them, the so-called *Collection in 400 Chapters,* has canons drawn from the *Hibernensis*.[37] Further, in the Vienna manuscript, fols. 1v–2v, there is a short Hiberno-Latin introduction to the Gospels.[38]

(d)   The *Sangermanensis* Abridgment

Related to the *Collection in 250 Chapters* is another abridgment of the *Hibernensis* in Paris, BN Lat. 12444, fols. 75v–96v and 105r–136v.[39] Again canons are drawn from the *Hibernensis* beginning with a form

---

[32]Roger E. Reynolds, "Canon Law Collections in Early Ninth-Century Salzburg," in *Proceedings of the Fifth International Congress of Medieval Canon Law, Salamanca, 21-25 September 1976,* ed. S. Kuttner and K. Pennington, Monumenta iuris canonici, Ser. C, Subsidia 6 (Vatican, 1980), p. 32; and Mordek, *Kirchenrecht*, p. 258.
[33]Mordek, *Kirchenrecht,* p. 52.
[34]Bischoff, *Schreibschulen,* 2:159f.
[35]Reynolds, "Canon Law Collections," p. 25.
[36]Reynolds, "Canon Law Collections," p. 19.
[37]See below.
[38]Bernhard Bischoff, "An Hiberno-Latin Introduction to the Gospels," *Thought: A Review of Culture and Idea* 54 [n. 214, Robert E. McNally Memorial Issue] (1979), 234.
[39]Fols. 97r–104v originally followed fol. 29v.

of the introduction and L. 19,[40] but due to the mutilated state of the manuscript, we can no longer tell how far they continued. Several aspects of this manuscript are interesting as they touch on its probable place of origin, Fleury, and the use and diffusion of the *Hibernensis* and Irish texts there. As has been noted, the region around Fleury seems to have produced few manuscript exemplars of the *Collectio Dionysio-Hadriana*, suggesting that other traditions were more popular.[41] That the Irish tradition was one of these is seen in our Paris manuscript, which contains not only the *Hibernensis* abridgment, but also the *Collectio Sangermanensis,* one of the most celebrated derivatives of the *Hibernensis.*[42] Moreover, we know that Irish liturgical and paracanonical texts had made their way from southeastern Germany, especially Salzburg, to Fleury because Orléans, Bibl. de la Ville 184, written in the early ninth century in the vicinity of Salzburg, with its "Alcuinian" prayers,[43] Bavarian litany, and copy of "Virgil's" *Liber de numeris,*[44] had been taken at least by the tenth century to Fleury.[45]

(e)   The Abridgment of London, BL Royal 5.E.XIII

At least two ninth-century manuscripts of the *Hibernensis* written on the Continent made their way to Worcester, Oxford, Bodl. Lib. Hatton 42 and Cambridge Corpus Christi College 279.[46] And in fact, Worcester seems to have been a center where Irish texts were used well into the twelfth century.[47] Hence, it is not surprising to find another ninth-century abridgment of the *Hibernensis* in a codex whose provenance is Worcester, London, BL Royal 5.E.XIII. The manuscript is a vast florilegium of texts, and on folios 52r–68v under a title "Incipiunt pauca fundamenta de sinodali libri" there is a text into which extracts from the *Hibernensis* have been woven. They are taken from L. 1 and following of the *Hibernensis* and are arranged in the sequence of the *Hibernensis.*

---

[40]Although sections drawn from or resembling L. 1, cc. 14–16 (on which cf. below, p. 109, n. 53) and L. 2, cc. 5–25, have been inserted into and after L. 37 on fols. 117r–v and 119r–121r.
[41]Kottje, "Einheit und Vielfalt," p. 337.
[42]See below, pp. 119–124.
[43]Cf. PL 101:1383–1416, and Aimé-Georges Martimort, *La Documentation liturgique de dom Edmond Martène: Étude codicologique,* Studi e Testi 279 (Vatican, 1978), p. 508, nr. 1131.
[44]Cf. Reynolds, *Ordinals of Christ,* p. 67, n. 58.
[45]Bischoff, *Schreibschulen,* 2:36.
[46]Mordek, *Kirchenrecht,* pp. 257f.
[47]Reynolds, *Ordinals of Christ,* p. 123, n. 30.

Included among the texts on the ecclesiastical hierarchy are an Ordinal of Christ and the *De officiis vii graduum*, two pieces that had an extraordinary diffusion thanks to the *Hibernensis*.[48]

3. Collections Dependent on *Hibernensis* Canons

Had the canons of the *Hibernensis* been contained only in the collection itself or in abridgments, their impact might have been much less in the Carolingian period than it actually was. Entire collections or abridgments could easily have been identified and suppressed, but insofar as many canons of the *Hibernensis* proved to be valuable supplements to other canon law collections, they lost their association with the suspect Irish collection and became useful parts of widely accepted canonical compilations. In this section some of these collections with their *Hibernensis* canons will be treated. It should be noted, however, that one of the most conspicuous of these is lacking here, the *Collectio Sangermanensis*, which because of its importance as a bridge between canonistic and liturgico-didactic collections will be treated later.

(a) The *Collectio Vetus Gallica*

One of the earliest Frankish collections to use sections from the *Hibernensis* was the first major systematic collection of the Gallican church, the *Collectio Vetus Gallica*. In its earliest recension no texts from the *Hibernensis* were used, but when the *Vetus Gallica* reached Corbie it seemed appropriate to add monastic canons from Insular sources including the *Hibernensis* and the so-called *Penitentiale Discipulus Umbrensium*. These canons were added, it seems, in several layers and derived from a text of the *Hibernensis* something like that in Vienna, ÖNB 522 and Munich, Clm 4592.[49] Within the body of the *Vetus Gallica* in many manuscripts, canons from the *Hibernensis*, LL. 39 and 42, were appropriately added to the books dealing with monasticism.[50] But many of these same canons were also inserted at less appropriate places in the ninth-century manuscripts Oxford, Bodl. Bodl. 572 (s. IX[1], northern France)[51] and Paris, BN Lat. 10588, fol. 73v (IX[1], southern France, Burgundy?).[52]

---

[48]Reynolds, *Ordinals of Christ,* p. 75.
[49]Mordek, *Kirchenrecht,* p. 52.
[50]Mordek, *Kirchenrecht,* pp. 535–538.
[51]Mordek, *Kirchenrecht,* p. 98, n. 3.
[52]Mordek, *Kirchenrecht,* p. 237.

Another layer from the *Hibernensis* was also added to conclude several southern French manuscripts of the *Vetus Gallica*, Berlin, DSB Phill. 1763 (s. IXin., France, rather southerly) and Albi, Bibl. Roch. 38bis (s. IXca. med., southern French). In these instances the *Hibernensis*, L. 1, c. 16a (the famous text attributed to the emperor Constantine granting judicial immunity to the clergy)[53] was attached to the Sylvestrian accusatorial canon that established the sequence of clerical accusations.[54] This same combination of texts from the *Hibernensis* and the Sylvestrian accusatorial canon was also used in a number of eighth- and ninth-century manuscripts as a preface to all the canons of the *Vetus Gallica*: Brussels, Bibl. Roy. 8654–72 (s. VIII/IX, prov. St. Bertin); Einsiedeln, SB 205 (s. IX2/4, Switzerland); St. Gall, SB 675 (s. IX[1], perhaps Bavaria); and Vienna, ÖNB 2171 (s. IX3/4, southwest Germany).[55] To place this "Constantinian" quotation as an introduction to the *Vetus Gallica* is something like the use of the same text (but deriving from the original, not the *Hibernensis*) in the Vatican manuscript of the Salzburg *Collection in Two Books*, Vatican, Reg. Lat. 407 (s. IX3/4, vicinity of St. Gall) as a prologue to L. 1.[56] Much later in the thirteenth century the *Hibernensis* text would also be used as an introduction to the *Collectio Dionysio-Hadriana* in Barcelona, Archivo de la Corona de Aragón, Ripoll 105.[57]

(b) The *Collection of Bonneval*

From the *Collectio Vetus Gallica* many texts passed to the first *Collection of Bonneval*, compiled sometime between 816 and the mid-ninth century and found in the unique codex, Paris, BN Lat. 3859 (s. IXm.–3/4, "Gallien"). Here again, canons from the *Hibernensis*, LL. 39 and 42, on the monastic life were borrowed from the *Vetus Gallica*.[58]

---

[53]To use the "Constantinian" text as an addendum to the collection is not far removed from the *Collection in 250 Chapters*, noted above, which concluded with a longer version of this text not found in the *Hibernensis* (Vienna, ÖNB 522, fol. 113v). It should be noted that a "longer" version of this canon, but truncated with "expectate iudicium rel." is in Paris, BN Lat. 12444, fol. 117r–v, on which see above n. 40.

[54]See Reynolds, *Ordinals of Christ*, p. 30.

[55]Mordek, *Kirchenrecht*, pp. 274f., 277, 291, 299.

[56]Fol. 5r. On this manuscript see R. E. Reynolds, "The Pseudo-Augustinian 'Sermo de conscientia' and the Related Canonical 'Dicta sancti Gregorii papae,'"*Revue bénédictine* 81 (1971), 313.

[57]Mordek, *Kirchenrecht*, p. 245.

[58]Mordek, *Kirchenrecht*, p. 535; and "Die Rechtssammlungen der Handschrift von Bonneval—ein Werk der karolingischen Reform," *Deutsches Archiv* 24 (1968), 373f., 384, 417f.

(c)   The *Collection of 450 Chapters* of Cologne, DB 210

It was noted in connection with fragments of the *Hibernensis* that one group of manuscripts breaks off with texts ending at L. 38, c. 18. Among this group was Cologne, DB 210 (Darmst. 2178). But this manuscript is not so much a "pure" example of a partial manuscript of the *Hibernensis* as a dependent collection. Not only has the traditional division of the *Hibernensis* texts into books and chapters been broken down, but many of the *Hibernensis* canons themselves have been reduced and many non-*Hibernensis* texts have been added. These additions include a host of canons from Greek, African, and Gallican councils, including Epaon, Clermont, and Orléans V, and several papal decrees.[59]

(d)   The Collection of Würzburg, UB M.p.th.q.31, fols. 52–59

It has already been seen that the collection in this Würzburg manuscript was preceded by an abridgment of the *Hibernensis* (fols. 1–41).[60] Between this abridgment and our collection on fols. 52–59 there was inserted a partial manuscript of the *Collectio Vetus Gallica* written at almost the same time in western Germany in a scriptorium under Irish influence. In the collection on fols. 52–59 there is a mélange of canons, papal documents, patristic fragments, and even works attributed to Boniface, one of which had wide circulation in southeastern Germany under the title *Dicta sancti Gregorii papae*.[61] According to Fournier, who followed Nürnberger's description of this collection, there are canons drawn from the *Hibernensis*, LL. 1, 11, 17, and 21, but in many instances they have readings differing from those Wasserschleben gives. Hence, until the new edition of the *Hibernensis* appears, it may be more prudent to say that these canons of the Würzburg collection were inspired by rather than drawn from the *Hibernensis*.

(e)   The *Collection in 400 Chapters*

The manuscripts Munich, Clm 4592 and Vienna, ÖNB 522, which as we have seen contained the abridgment of the *Collectio Hibernensis* called the *Collection in 250 Chapters*, also were the vehicle for another collection in

---

[59]See the description of this collection by Hermann Wasserschleben, *Die irische Kanonensammlung*, 2nd ed. (Leipzig, 1885), xxv.

[60]See above, p. 105.

[61]See Reynolds, "'Sermo de conscientia,'" pp. 310–317; and "Canon Law Collections," p. 23, n. 46.

400 chapters. This collection, compiled at the earliest in the late eighth or early ninth century, seems to have had a much wider diffusion in the Carolingian realms than did the Irish *Collection in 250 Chapters* and is found in manuscripts whose origins were far removed from southeastern Germany with its Irish connections: Paris, BN Lat. 2316 (s. IX2/4, southern France) and Metz, Bibl. mun. 236, fols. 143-206 (s. VIII/IX, perhaps Rhenan: destroyed during World War II).[62]

The material in the *Collection in 400 Chapters* is an unusual mix, almost as strange as the *Collectio Hibernensis* itself. There are first long passages from the Bible showing the parallels between Old and New Testament texts. In this material Fournier pointed out possible extracts from the *Hibernensis*,[63] but in many cases it is possible that they were taken from Scripture itself or other florilegia in which the Old and New Testament texts were juxtaposed. Then, there are large numbers of Insular and Frankish penitential texts such as the *Penitential of Theodore*, *Penitential of Martène*, and the like.[64] Together with this "suspect" material are found canons which were clearly drawn from the *Collectio Hibernensis*, such as those from L. 46, *De ratione matrimonii*,[65] which as will be seen had an extraordinary diffusion in manuscripts and canon law collections from the ninth century on.[66] Finally, there is material in the *Collection in 400 Chapters* that would have been perfectly acceptable in a Frankish milieu, extracts from the *Collectio Vetus Gallica*.[67] It is interesting, as Mordek has shown, that the *Collection in 400 Chapters* in the early ninth-century manuscript, Paris, BN Lat. 2316, contains a fragment of the *Vetus Gallica* in a form related to that in Würzburg, UB M.p.th.q.31, fols. 42-51, which was written in the late eighth or early ninth century in a scriptorium with Irish influence.[68] Moreover, in this same Paris manuscript there is a large extract from the *Collectio Dionysio-Hadriana*. This codex of the *Collection in 400 Chapters* is, therefore, striking evidence that the Carolingians did not hesitate to combine the officially sanctioned *Collectio Dionysio-Hadriana* with Frankish and suspect Insular texts.

---

[62]Mordek, *Kirchenrecht*, pp. 162, 262, and 283f.
[63]Fournier, "De l'influence," p. 15.
[64]See especially, Vienna, ÖNB 522, fols. 144r-149r.
[65]Vienna, ÖNB 522, fol. 148v.
[66]See below, pp. 115f.
[67]Mordek, *Kirchenrecht*, pp. 162-164.
[68]Mordek, *Kirchenrecht*, p. 301.

(f) The *Collection of Laon*

One of the most intriguing collections compiled before the middle of the ninth century is the collection which goes under the names of the *Collection of St. Petersbourg* or the *Collection of Laon*, but which might better be called the *Collection of Cambrai* because both of its extant manuscript witnesses were perhaps written there: Laon, Bibl. mun. 201 (ca. s. IXm., Cambrai?) and Leningrad, Publ. Bibl. Q.v.II.5 (s. IX4/4, Cambrai?).[69] This collection was written with Carolingian reform ideology in mind since its first canon is entitled, "De eo quod secundum ordinem Romanum facere debemus."[70] But it nonetheless has many of the same characteristics as the *Collectio Hibernensis* and its derivative, the *Collectio Sangermanensis,*[71] except one, systematization. The *Collection of Laon* contains extracts from the Fathers, conciliar and papal canons drawn from the *Collectio Dionysio-Hadriana*, penitential material, didactic pieces on the sacraments, and even liturgical formularies.[72] Also, like the *Collection in 400 Chapters* it contains canons drawn from the *Collectio Vetus Gallica.*[73] The canons from the *Hibernensis* derive primarily from L. 14 and following.[74] Since, as has often been pointed out,[75] there was a copy of the *Hibernensis* at Cambrai in the late eighth century, it might be expected that these canons of the *Collection of Laon* depend on it. But, alas, there are canons taken from books of the *Hibernensis* beyond those found in L. 38 of the Cambrai manuscript of the *Hibernensis*. Moreover, it has been by no means proven that the *Collection of Laon* was compiled at Cambrai.[76]

(g) The *Penitential of Martène*

In both the *Collection in 400 Chapters* and the *Collection of Laon* we have seen the combination of canons from the "acceptable" Frankish

[69]Mordek, *Kirchenrecht*, p. 164. nn. 312f.
[70]See Paul Fournier, "Notices sur trois collections canoniques inédites de l'époque carolingienne," *Revue des sciences religieuses* 6 (1926), 219.
[71]See below, pp. 119–124.
[72]See Michel Andrieu, *Les Ordines Romani du Haut Moyen Âge*, 1, *Les manuscrits* (Louvain, 1931), pp. 349f.
[73]Laon, Bibl. mun. 201, fol. 90r.
[74]Fournier, "Notices," p. 223.
[75]See, e.g., Fournier, "Notices," p. 229, and John J. Contreni, *The Cathedral School of Laon from 850 to 930, Its Manuscripts and Masters*, Münchener Beiträge zur Mediävistik und Renaissance-Forschung 29 (Munich, 1978), p. 82.
[76]See Mordek, *Kirchenrecht*, p. 165, n. 315.

Collectio Vetus Gallica, penitential material, and the *Hibernensis*. The same is true with the penitential named after its ancient editor, Dom Edmond Martène.[77] This Frankish penitential has been dated by its modern editor, Walther von Hörmann, to between 802 and 813,[78] but it may have been compiled later since the manuscript in which it is found, Florence, Bibl. Med.-Laur. Ashburnham 82 (32) [Cat. 29], was written in western France during approximately the third quarter of the ninth century.[79] The manuscript itself was in Fleury and then Orléans until the depredations of G. Libri,[80] when a portion of what is now Orléans, Bibl. de la Ville 116 (94) was removed, ultimately to be transferred to Florence. The codex as a whole is an extraordinary one, containing among other items prayers like those of the Salzburg, then Fleury manuscript, Orléans, Bibl. de la Ville 184,[81] the Mass commentary *Dominus vobiscum*[82] like the one attributed to Alcuin in the Salzburg manuscript Budapest, Ors. Széch. Kön. 316,[83] several Carolingian expositions on baptism and the Creed,[84] a unique Ordinal of Christ,[85] and extracts from the *Collectio Hibernensis* derivative, the *Collectio Sangermanensis*.[86]

In his study of the *Penitentiale Martenianum* Mordek has shown that substantial sections are based upon the *Collectio Vetus Gallica*,[87] but even more important he has shown that many of the canons that von Hörmann attributed to the *Vetus Gallica* were probably based on the *Collection in 400 Chapters* or a collection underlying both it and the *Penitentiale Martenianum*. But beyond this there are clear borrowings from the *Hibernensis*, LL. 15–18 and 45–47.[88] It is especially interesting to see that these latter canons are drawn from the celebrated book in the *Hibernensis* on matrimony

---

[77]See Vogel, *"Libri paenitentiales,"* p. 78.

[78]Walther von Hörmann, "Bussbücherstudien," *Zeitschrift der Savigny-Stiftung für Rechtsgeschichte, Kan. Abt.* 1 (1911), 195–250; 2 (1912), 111–181; 3 (1913), 413–492; 4 (1914), 358–483.

[79]Mordek, *Kirchenrecht*, p. 200, n. 525.

[80]On Libri's depredations, see Roger E. Reynolds, "An Unexpected Manuscript Fragment of the Ninth-Century Canonical Collection in Two Books," *Bulletin of Medieval Canon Law*, n.s. 8 (1978), 35–38.

[81]See above, p. 107.

[82]*Amalarii episcopi opera liturgica omnia,* ed. J. M. Hanssens, 1, Studi e Testi 138 (Vatican, 1948), pp. 284–338.

[83]See Reynolds, "Canon Law Collections," p. 31, n. 106.

[84]These are currently being studied by Dr. Keefe.

[85]See below, p. 130.

[86]See below, p. 122.

[87]Mordek, *Kirchenrecht*, pp. 199–201.

[88]Fournier, "De l'influence," p. 17.

and, as one might expect in a penitential, from the books in the *Hibernensis* entitled *De questionibus mulierum* and *De penitentia.*

4. Isolated Extracts from the *Collectio Hibernensis*

Despite the fact that such canonical collections as the *Dionysio-Hadriana* and the *Vetus Gallica* with their "authentic" papal and conciliar canons received the approval of the Carolingian rulers, the usefulness of the *Hibernensis* did not diminish because many of its texts — especially patristic and Scriptural ones — were lacking in these "official" collections. But just as important, several sections of the *Hibernensis* dealt with matters inadequately covered in the Roman and Frankish collections. Hence, these sections were often reproduced and used as isolated extracts in manuscripts or were added to canonical collections of Roman, Frankish, or Hibernian types and even to florilegial collections and biblical exegetical texts.

(a) Extracts on the Ecclesiastical Hierarchy

The early books of the *Hibernensis* contain a long line of definitions of the clerical grades based largely on Isidore's work and its derivatives, and these nicely supplemented the strictly legal material of the papal and conciliar canons. These texts were often used in such abridgments as those of Cambridge, Corpus Christi College 279,[89] but they were also abstracted from the *Hibernensis* and used in a variety of canonical, liturgical, and florilegial manuscripts. In the last section of this paper we will look at some of these extracts as they were modified and placed in Carolingian *liturgica*, but here several direct borrowings from the *Hibernensis* canons on sacred orders should be mentioned.

In L. 8 of the *Hibernensis* there are two valuable epitomes of the origins and duties of the clerics. The first, called an Ordinal of Christ, lists the grades which Christ is thought to have fulfilled in his life and is of a type called the Hiberno-Hispanic Hierarchical because the two lower grades of exorcist and lector are listed according to a sequence used in Isidore's work.[90] The second epitome in L. 8 is the little tract entitled *De distantia graduum*, which entered pontifical manuscripts of the tenth and eleventh centuries under the title *De officiis septem graduum.*[91] By

---

[89]See above, p. 105.

[90]Reynolds, *Ordinals of Christ*, pp. 34, 61-63.

[91]See Roger E. Reynolds, "The *De officiis vii graduum*: Its Origins and Early Medieval Development," *Mediaeval Studies* 34 (1972), 113-151.

the ninth century both of these texts on the ecclesiastical hierarchy in L. 8 had been used in the canonical *Collectio Sangermanensis*, Paris, BN Lat. 12444, and in the florilegial tract in London, BL Roy. 5.E.XIII.[92] Slightly later in the tenth century they would also appear in modified forms in the canonical manuscript, Vesoul, Bibl. mun. 73, with its snippets of the *Collectio Sangermanensis.*[93]

(b) Extracts on Matrimony from the *Collectio Hibernensis*, L. 46

In many of the abridgments and derivatives of the *Hibernensis* some of the most frequently reproduced texts were from L. 46 entitled *De ratione matrimonii.* Extracts from this book were reproduced in a variety of canon law collections and manuscripts well into the high Middle Ages, but of particular interest here is their wide diffusion in Carolingian manuscripts. Maassen, Fournier, and Mordek have all presented substantial lists of isolated texts with the whole or partial text of L. 46, and several more exemplars can be added to these with dates and places of origin. What is also of special interest is the connection of many of the earliest manuscripts of this text with southeastern Germany, particularly Salzburg with its long tradition of texts based on the *Hibernensis.* Among the early manuscripts from Salzburg or southeast Germany with texts from L. 46 are Vienna, ÖNB 424 (s. IX2/4, Salzburg),[94] the *Mondsee Pastorale*, Vienna, ÖNB 1370 (s. IX1/4, Mondsee) with its rich collection of Salzburg texts,[95] and Munich, Clm 6242 (s. IX1/3, Freising) and 6245, fol. 59v (s. IX/X, Freising).[96] Related to the early Salzburg manuscripts are slightly later codices that contain the addenda to the Salzburg *Collection in Two Books*, Vatican, Reg. Lat. 407,[97] and Pal. Lat. 973 (s. IX2/2, northeastern France).[98] More distantly related to these manuscripts is Vatican, Reg. Lat. 421,[99] with its extract from the *Hibernensis*, L. 46, and the tract popular in Salzburg and southeast Germany,

---

[92]Reynolds, *"De officiis vii graduum,"* pp. 131f.; and *Ordinals of Christ*, pp. 74f.
[93]Reynolds, *Ordinals of Christ*, pp. 74f., n. 21.
[94]Fol. 7r. Reynolds, "Canon Law Collections," p. 27, n. 70; and Bischoff, *Schreibschulen*, 2:145f.
[95]Fol. 90r. Reynolds, "Canon Law Collections," pp. 26f.
[96]Mordek, *Kirchenrecht*, p. 259.
[97]Fols. 74v–75r.
[98]Fol. 39r–v.
[99]Fol. 22v. Professor Bischoff has kindly written me that this section of the MS, once belonging to St. Gall, SB 899, is from St. Gall, s. 2–3/3 IX.

116

De observatione iiii temporum.[100] Slightly outside the orbit of southeast German and Salzburg influence is the Bodensee manuscript, Freiburg, UB 8 (s. IX^2) with its excerpt from L. 46 of the *Hibernensis.*[101] By the middle of the ninth century a section from L. 46 had found its way into manuscripts of the Pseudo-Isidorian forgeries: the Pseudo-Isidorian *Benedictus Levita,*[102] and the manuscript, Paris, BN Lat. 1557,[103] which Bernard Merlette suspects may originally have been part of the famous Laon Pseudo-Isidore manuscript, Paris, BN Lat. 9629, glossed by Hincmar of Laon.[104]

(c) Salzburg Fragments

Two late eighth- and early ninth-century products of Salzburg, both containing fragments of the *Collectio Hibernensis* not hitherto noted in canonistic studies, have recently been brought to light. One of these is in Wolfenbüttel, Herz.-Aug. Bibl. 579 (Helmst. 532) (s. IX2/4, Salzburg), which contains a vast miscellany of texts including canonistic fragments also found in the Salzburg *Collection in Two Books,*[105] an Ordinal of Christ,[106] and a group of patristic and canonistic texts. Worked into these have been snippets drawn from the *Collectio Hibernensis*, L. 27.[107]

The other item, in a manuscript now lost but whose contents in Froben's works have recently been described by Professor Bischoff, was clearly written in early Carolingian Salzburg. Besides its important witness to the Irish *Stowe Missal,*[108] the manuscript contained isolated extracts from the *Hibernensis* in two places. One is in a tract without title,[109] and the other is within a tract with the rubric, "Incipit epistola de

---

[100]For manuscripts of this text see Reynolds, "Canon Law Collections," p. 24, n. 53, to which add St. Gall, SB 899, p. 93 (partial text).

[101]Mordek, *Kirchenrecht*, p. 259; and Johanne Autenrieth, "Die kanonistischen Hand-schriften der Dombibliothek Konstanz," in Autenrieth and Kottje, *Kirchenrechtliche Texte im Bodenseegebiet*, p. 11.

[102]3.179; PL 97:820.

[103]Mordek, *Kirchenrecht*, p. 259.

[104]See Contreni, *Cathedral School of Laon*, p. 62, n. 81; and the forthcoming article by Professor Contreni in *Viator.*

[105]Reynolds, "Canon Law Collections," p. 27.

[106]Reynolds, *Ordinals of Christ*, p. 72, n. 13 (1).

[107]Fol. 133v.

[108]See Bernhard Bischoff, *Salzburger Formelbücher und Briefe aus Tassilonischer und Karolingischer Zeit*, Bayerische Akad. der Wissenschaften, Phil.-Hist. Kl., Sitzungsb. Jhg. 1973, Hft. 4 (Munich, 1973), pp. 51f.

[109]Bischoff, *Salzburger Formelbücher*, pp. 42–44.

apatibus vel de principibus."[110] Included in the snippets drawn from the *Hibernensis* are those from LL. 25 and 37, *De regno* and *De principatu*, whose influence would be felt far into the Middle Ages.[111]

(d) Fragments of the *Hibernensis* Associated with Sedulius Scottus

One of the most celebrated scholars of the ninth century, Sedulius Scottus, worked in the company of Irish scholars at Liège.[112] In light of his Irish origins it is not surprising to discover that his own works acted as a magnet for other Irish texts, including the *Collectio Hibernensis*. In the twelfth-century manuscript of his *Collectaneum*, Bernkastel-Kues, St. Nikolaus-Hosp., Bibl. der Cus.-Stift. 37 (C 14), there are excerpts from the *Hibernensis* not distantly removed from the *Proverbia grecorum*,[113] fragments of which also appear in the Karlsruhe manuscript of the *Hibernensis*,[114] Sedulius's *Liber de rectoribus*,[115] and in the eleventh-century Norman Anonymous, who also used the *Hibernensis*.[116] Moreover, in another twelfth-century manuscript, Bamberg, SB 127 (B V 24), fol. 106v, there are attached to Sedulius's *Collectaneum in omnes sancti Pauli epistolas* fragments from the *Hibernensis* L. 46.6,29,27.[117] In short, just as we have seen the *Hibernensis* attached to canonistic texts written in locations with long traditions of Irish scholarship, so with the Irishman Sedulius we find *Hibernensis* texts naturally clustering around his work.

(e) Miscellaneous Isolated Extracts from the *Hibernensis*

As a source of canonical authority the *Hibernensis* was, as we have seen, attractive to the compilers of legal collections because it provided them

---

[110]Bischoff, *Salzburger Formelbücher*, pp. 44–46.

[111]See below, n. 116.

[112]Contreni, *Cathedral School of Laon*, p. 83.

[113]S. Hellmann, *Sedulius Scottus*, Quellen und Untersuchungen zur lateinischen Philologie des Mittelalters 1 (Munich, 1906), pp. 96f.

[114]Hellmann, *Sedulius Scottus*, p. 132.

[115]According to Hellmann, *Sedulius Scottus*, pp. 11, 73, there are ninth-century manuscripts of this text.

[116]See Roger E. Reynolds, "The Unidentified Sources of the Norman Anonymous: C.C.C.C. MS. 415," *Transactions of the Cambridge Bibliographical Society* 5, 2 (1970), 123; and Roger E. Reynolds, "Liturgical Scholarship at the Time of the Investiture Controversy: Past Research and Future Opportunities," *Harvard Theological Review* 71 (1978), 121–123.

[117]I am grateful to Professor Bischoff for having pointed out this instance of the use of the *Hibernensis*.

118

with an abundance of patristic and scriptural texts not found in the standard collections of papal and conciliar canons. But more than that, these texts were arranged in the *Hibernensis* in a convenient systematic fashion. Hence, it is not surprising to find that the *Hibernensis* quickly became a sourcebook for scholars working in a variety of extracanonical disciplines. A careful search through the hundreds of florilegial tracts compiled in the Carolingian period[118] and the biblical exegetical texts written by Irish scholars or those working in their tradition[119] would undoubtedly turn up an abundance of such borrowings from the *Hibernensis*. But here it is necessary only to cite a few such isolated instances in several Carolingian florilegia and exegetical manuscripts to illustrate the point.

(i) Florilegia. Professor Bischoff has very kindly drawn my attention to an extraordinary example of a Carolingian florilegium into which texts from the *Hibernensis* have been liberally sprinkled. The manuscript in which it is found, Munich, Clm 6433, fols. 2r–24v, was written in Anglo-Saxon minuscule in the late eighth century at Freising.[120] Among the authors cited in addition to those of the books of the Bible are Gaseus or Commodian, Eusebius, Gregory, Sedulius, Cassian, Gregory Nazianzus, Augustine, Isidore, Jerome, Basil, Barnabas, Clement, Virgilius Maro, Pelagius, and Athanasius; and the subjects range from love and hate to the fear of God and watchfulness in prayer. The snippets from the *Hibernensis* include not only those from such popular books as L. 47, *De penitentia*, but also from other less likely books such as LL. 13, 14, and 38.

(ii) Biblical Commentaries. Professor Bischoff in his seminal article, "Wendepunkte in der Geschichte der lateinischen Exegese im Frühmittelalter,"[121] also has drawn attention to the influence of the *Hibernensis* in a variety of Hiberno-Latin biblical commentaries of the late eighth and early ninth century. In the Genesis section of the *Pauca problesmata*

---

[118]See H.-M. Rochais, "Contribution à l'histoire des florilèges ascétiques du haut moyen âge latin," *Revue bénédictine* 63 (1953), 246–291.

[119]See Robert E. McNally, *The Bible in the Early Middle Ages,* Woodstock Papers 4 (Westminster, Md., 1959), p. 71; and Martin McNamara, "A Plea for Hiberno-Latin Biblical Studies," *Irish Theological Quarterly* 39 (1972), 337–353.

[120]*Codices Latini antiquiores: A Paleographical Guide to Latin Manuscripts Prior to the Ninth Century,* ed. E. A. Lowe (Oxford, 1934–), ix, 1283.

[121]*Mittelalterliche Studien: Ausgewählte Aufsätze zur Schriftkunde und Literaturgeschichte,* 1 (Stuttgart, 1966), 205–273 trans. as "Turning-Points in the History of Latin Exegesis in the Early Irish Church: A.D. 650–800," in *Biblical Studies: The Medieval Irish Contribution,* ed. M. McNamara, *Proceedings of the Irish Biblical Association* 1 (Dublin, 1976), 74–160.

de enigmatibus ex tomis canonicis, for example, the etymology of the word *bestia* found in the works of the Irish Virgilius Maro[122] seems to have been drawn from the *Hibernensis*, L. 53.1.[123] This same etymology is also found in the Irish Pseudo-Hilarius, *Expositio in vii epistolas canonicas*,[124] recently edited by Professor McNally.[125] In his editions of other Hiberno-Latin exegetical works McNally also called attention to what he saw as the influence of the *Hibernensis*, especially L. 46, *De ratione matrimonii*.[126]

5. The *Collectio Sangermanensis* and Its Supplement

One of the most important collections deriving from the *Hibernensis* was not dealt with earlier in this paper[127] because of its special nature as a bridge between canonistic and liturgical texts in the Carolingian period. This derivative is one of several collections designated by canonists as the *Collectio Sangermanensis* because it was first found in a manuscript from the fonds St.-Germain in the Bibliothèque Nationale in Paris. But a significant number of fragments of this collection, many with additional texts, have more recently been found, and hence not only should there be a new edition and study of this derivative collection but perhaps a rechristening to accompany it.[128]

Among the distinctive traits of Hiberno-Latin literature in the eighth and ninth centuries are the use of Irishisms, puns,[129] and glosses explaining the who, when, and where of matters,[130] but none are as obvious

---

[122]Michael Herren, "The Pseudonymous Tradition in Hiberno-Latin: An Introduction," in *Latin Script and Letters: A.D. 400–900. Festschrift Presented to Ludwig Bieler on the Occasion of His 70th birthday*, ed. J.J. O'Meara and B. Naumann (Leiden, 1976), pp. 125f.

[123]Bischoff, "Wendepunkte," p. 233.

[124]Bischoff, "Wendepunkte," p. 267.

[125]Scriptores Hiberniae minores 1:70.

[126]Scriptores Hiberniae minores 1:23, 33, 59, 86, 119.

[127]See above, p. 108.

[128]The other *"Collectiones Sangermanenses"* are in Paris, BN Lat. 12012, 12098, and Wolfenbüttel, Herz.-Aug. Bibl. 212 Gud. [4517] (and the newly found manuscript, Gent, UB 235, studied by L. Waelken and D. Van den Auweele, "La collection de Thérouanne en IX livres à l'abbaye de Saint-Pierre-au-Mont-Blandin: le Codex Gandavensis 235," *Sacris Erudiri* 24 [1980], 115-153). On the problem of the use of the appellation *Collectio Sangermanensis*, see Roger E. Reynolds, "A Florilegium on the Ecclesiastical Grades in Clm 19414: Testimony to Ninth-Century Clerical Instruction," *Harvard Theological Review* 63 (1970), 248, n. 71; and Mordek, *Kirchenrecht*, p. 144, n. 216.

[129]Herren, "Pseudonymous Tradition," p. 122.

[130]Bischoff, "Wendepunkte," p. 218; and Reynolds, *Ordinals of Christ*, p. 93.

as the love of numerology,[131] etymologies, and a question-response or didactic structure. In the *Collectio Hibernensis* itself questions of all sorts abound, and many are the canons that contain numbered lists of explanations and etymologies. These distinctive traits in the Irish material made them perfect vehicles to effect the directives of the Carolingian capitularies and conciliar canons which stated that both clergy and laymen were to know and understand the basis of their religious practice. Hence, an Irish tract with, for example, its questions and answers as to how many verses there are in the Creed, who wrote each, and what they mean, responded exactly to the educational program of the Carolingian rulers.

Among the sacraments a priest in the Carolingian realm was specifically charged with understanding and being able to explain were sacred orders, baptism, and the Mass,[132] and, of course, the *Collectio Hibernensis* provided brief descriptions of all of these. Thus, at the very end of the eighth century these descriptions were combined with the legislative sources of the *Hibernensis* and cast in didactic form to become what is now called the *Collectio Sangermanensis*.

The longest form of the *Sangermanensis* is in the Paris manuscript, BN Lat. 12444 (olim Sangerm. 928, Corbie), dealt with earlier as an abridgment of the *Collectio Hibernensis*.[133] The manuscript was written not in Corbie, as has often been stated,[134] but probably at Fleury in the late eighth or early ninth century.[135] The first extensive section deals with the ecclesiastical and religious hierarchies, the second with the Church and baptism, the third with the Mass and the ecclesiastical calendar, the fourth with penance, and the last with matrimony. The greatest proportion of texts consists of modifications of the *Hibernensis*, but they are also supplemented with texts that were to have very wide broadcast in Carolingian liturgical tracts.

Beyond this long form of the *Sangermanensis* there are what appear to be[136] several partial manuscripts and manuscripts with isolated excerpta.

---

[131]See, e.g., Robert E. McNally, *Der irische Liber de numeris: Eine Quellenanalyse des pseudo-isidorischen Liber de numeris* (Diss., Munich, 1957), passim.

[132]On these directives see, e.g., H. Netzer, *L'Introduction de la Messe romaine en France sous les carolingiens* (Paris, 1910), pp. 40–48; and Keefe, "Baptismal Instruction," pp. 149–152.

[133]See above, pp. 106f.

[134]See, e.g., Rosamond McKitterick, *The Frankish Church and the Carolingian Reforms, 789–895* (London, 1977), p. 148.

[135]Reynolds, "Florilegium on the Ecclesiastical Grades," p. 248, n. 71.

[136]Mordek, *Kirchenrecht,* pp. 144f., correctly warns that until a full study of the *Sangermanensis* is made, one must reckon with the possibility that what appear to be partial

The longest of the extracts is in a manuscript written in northern France in the last quarter of the ninth century but early taken to St. Emmeram in Regensburg, Munich, Clm 14508, fols. 75r–ca.105v. In this codex there are several sections with canonical material including the *Sangermanensis*, the *Capitula* of Theodulf of Orléans, *Capitula a sacerdotibus preposita*, and the *Collection in 53 Titles*.[137] The canons in our section of the manuscript cover most of the topics found in Paris, BN Lat. 12444, ranging from LL. 1 through 21 according to Nürnberger's description,[138] but there are many omissions and additions of material not found in the Paris manuscript. Also, the sequence of books has been radically altered, and a supplement added containing the ordination rubrics from the *Statuta ecclesiae antiqua*.[139]

The second extensive extract from the *Sangermanensis* is in Cologne, DB 117, fols. 69r–89v (s. IXca. med., France).[140] In this manuscript topics ranging from sacred orders through penance are treated, but again in many instances texts found in the Parisian codex of the *Sangermanensis*, such as the Ordinal of Christ and the *De distantia graduum*, have been omitted.

The third extensive extract from the *Sangermanensis* is in a southern French manuscript from the mid-ninth century, Albi, Bibl. Roch. 38bis, fols. 38v–42r. This codex also contains the *Collectio Vetus Gallica*, again illustrating the close association of the Irish and Frankish collections in ninth-century manuscripts. The extract from the *Sangermanensis* is particularly interesting for two reasons. First, it deals almost exclusively with synods and the ecclesiastical hierarchy. Second, after the word "Explicit," on fol. 42r, there is a supplement in dialogue form dealing with the duties of the presbyter and beginning with the words, "INT. Dic mihi pro quid est presbiter benedictus?" and short discussions of baptism and the Mass. As will be seen, this supplement had an extraordinary diffusion in manuscripts from the ninth century on.

---

manuscripts or excerpta may indeed have provided the sources of the *Sangermanensis* as it appears in Paris, BN Lat. 12444.

[137]Peter Landau, "Kanonistische Aktivität in Regensburg im frühen Mittelalter," *Zwei Jahrtausende Regensburg: Vortragsreihe der Universität Regensburg zum Stadtjubiläum,* ed. D. Albrecht, Schriftenreihe der Universität Regensburg 1 (Regensburg, 1979), pp. 63f., 74; and Mordek, *Kirchenrecht,* p. 172, n. 356.

[138]August J. Nürnberger, "Über eine ungedruckte Kanonensammlung aus dem 8. Jahrhundert," *25. Bericht der wissenschaftlichen Gesellschaft Philomathie in Neisse vom Oktober 1888 bis zum Oktober 1890* (Neisse, 1890), 125–197.

[139]Fol. 104r–v.

[140]Mordek, *Kirchenrecht,* p. 145, n. 223.

There is a fourth extensive extract from the *Sangermanensis* in London, BL Harl. 3034, fols. 1r–10r, that has hitherto not been noted. Although this tenth-century manuscript dates from slightly beyond our period, it is of special interest because its extracts from LL. 12–16 are in the interrogatory form of M (*Magister*) and Δ (*Discipulus*) common to a variety of Irish and Carolingian didactic tracts.

Isolated fragments of the *Sangermanensis* frequently appear also in canonical manuscripts from the ninth century on. One of the manuscripts, Orléans, Bibl. de la Ville 116, has already been mentioned for its texts of the *Penitentiale Martenianum*.[141] But sprinkled into its miscellaneous prayers, liturgical expositions, and homilies is a series of interrogatories, among which are several from the *Sangermanensis*.[142] Another mid-ninth-century codex from Lorsch, Vatican, Pal. Lat. 485, contains many of the same didactic tracts and expositions as the Orléans manuscript, but it also has sections from the *Collectio Dionysio-Hadriana*,[143] penitential material,[144] and the *Capitula* of Theodulf of Orléans.[145] The isolated excerpta from the *Sangermanensis* are placed under the name of Isidore[146] and draw on material from L. 12.[147]

Two canonistic manuscripts written slightly after the ninth century but containing Carolingian canonical material also have isolated excerpts from the *Sangermanensis*. Albi, Bibl. Roch. 38, fols. 126v–127v, an early tenth-century codex from southern France, contains, like Albi 38bis, a great variety of canonistic material including the *Collectio Vetus Gallica*,[148] penitential material, *capitula*, and even parts of the Pseudo-Isidorian forgeries. But this later Albi manuscript includes only a few snippets from the *Sangermanensis*, drawn from the introduction and L. 1. The other canonistic manuscript, Vesoul, Bibl. mun. 73, again contains a mélange of material ranging from penitential canons and episcopal capitularies[149] to liturgical commentary. On fols. 81r–83v there is a short

---

[141]See above, p. 113.
[142]E.g., fol. 72r (cf. Nürnberger, p. 174) and fol. 84v (cf. Nürnberger, p. 161).
[143]Mordek, *Kirchenrecht*, p. 247.
[144]John T. McNeill and Helena Gamer, *Medieval Handbooks of Penance*, Records of Civilization: Sources and Studies 29 (New York, 1938), p. 449.
[145]PL 81:870.
[146]See PL 81:869.
[147]Fol. 44r (cf. Nürnberger, pp. 161–163).
[148]Mordek, *Kirchenrecht*, pp. 268f.
[149]Fournier, "Notices sur trois collections," pp. 79–92.

section in dialogue form that contains material drawn from the introduction and LL. 1-9 of the *Sangermanensis*.

In discussing the codex Albi 38bis it was noted that there was a supplement on the presbyter's duties, baptism, and the Mass cast in the same dialogue form found in the *Sangermanensis* extract itself. This supplement may or may not originally have been within the corpus of the *Collectio Sangermanensis*, and until there is a new edition and study of the collection and its contents, one cannot be certain. But these supplemental texts are of extraordinary interest for several reasons. First, at least some of them are closely related to Irish texts. For example, the first text has a close parallel in the *Liber de numeris* of the Irishman Virgil of Salzburg:[150]

[*Sangermanensis* Supplement]	[*Liber de numeris*]
INT. Dic mihi pro quid est presbiter benedictus?	
R. Ad adnuntiandum verbum divinum et ad tradendum baptismum vel paenitentiam lacrimarum, hostiis offerentem omnipotenti Deo pro salute vivorum et requiem defunctorum.[151]	Quattuor causis ordinantur sacerdotes id est, verbum Dei populis praedicare retinere baptismum in recta fide, penitentiam fideliter omnibus largire, hostias puras pro salute vivorum et reliquis [*sic*] defunctorum omnipotenti Deo semper offerre.[152]

Second, these texts were widely scattered in both didactic and canonistic manuscripts from the ninth century. And third, the texts were often arranged in different sequences or used in part only.

There are two manuscripts from the ninth century that contain the section of the supplemental text on the presbyter's duties. One, St. Gall, SB 40, p. 304, has the *Joca episcopi ad sacerdotes* consisting of a variety of material on sacred orders and baptism.[153] The other manuscript, Albi, Bibl. Roch. 43 (15) (s. IX4/4, probably southern France) contains the *Collectio Dacheriana* and an *Interrogatio sacerdotalis* beginning with the words, "Dic mihi pro quid es presbiter benedictus?"[154] Again, this section of the manuscript contains much of the same material found in the St. Gall *Joca*, but in a different sequence.

[150]McNally, *Liber de numeris*, p. 83.
[151]Albi, Bibl. Roch. 38bis, fol. 42r.
[152]Munich, Clm 14392, fol. 85r.
[153]s. IX2-3/3, Switzerland: Reynolds, *Ordinals of Christ*, p. 70, n. 6.
[154]Fol. 15v. On the manuscript see Mordek, *Kirchenrecht*, p. 261.

124

Several codices later than the ninth century also have the *Sangermanensis* supplement with the question on the presbyter's duties, and they all seem to point to a southern European tradition of the text. The earliest is in Barcelona, Bibl. Univ. 228, fols. 134v–39r (s. X^2, southern France or northern Italy),[155] a manuscript with material on sacred orders, baptism, and a variety of ninth-century penitentials including Halitgar's penitential and a penitential described as the *Penitentiale Vallicellianum I*.[156] Slightly later is the manuscript, Florence, Bibl. Ricc. 256 (K.III.27), fol. 126v. This codex again has treatises on the sacred orders, baptism, and the Creed in dialogue form, but preceding it are texts from the *Institutio canonicorum* of 816/17.[157] And finally, in the twelfth-century manuscript, El Escorial, RBSL Q.III.10, fol. 127v, there is the *Sangermanensis* supplemental text together with baptismal literature.[158]

At least two additional codices have material from the *Sangermanensis* supplement on baptism, unusual because the pedilavium of the Milanese, Gallican, and Irish rites is included. The elder of the two manuscripts is Laon, Bibl. mun. 288, fol. 37v (s. IX1/3, eastern France, Laon?).[159] The other one, Paris, BN Lat. 13092, fol. 136v (s. XII), is later, but the baptismal text is within a florilegium on the sacraments, parts of which may be very ancient indeed. The text of the Ordinal of Christ in the manuscript, for example, contains the unusual grade of gravedigger, found especially in ancient texts written in Spain, southern France, and northern Italy.[160] Hence, the baptismal text from the *Sangermanensis* supplement with its Milanese-Gallican pedilavium is not unexpected.

6. Carolingian *Liturgica*

The *Collectio Sangermanensis* with its canons on the sacraments and the didactic form in which they are stated clearly shows the connection between the Irish collection of canon law and Carolingian liturgical tracts. In this concluding section of this article we shall examine the way in which material in the *Sangermanensis* was modified and used in the abundant Carolingian liturgical *expositiones*. Although material from several sections of the *Sangermanensis* seems to have made its way into a

[155]Kottje, *Bussbücher Halitgars*, pp. 15f.
[156]Ibid.
[157]Reynolds, *Ordinals of Christ*, p. 91.
[158]Mordek *Kirchenrecht*, p. 145, n. 224.
[159]Keefe, "Baptismal Instruction," p. 59.
[160]Reynolds, *Ordinals of Christ*, pp. 50f.

variety of these expositions,[161] here we shall concentrate on two categories of expositions, those dealing with the Mass and sacred orders, to see how texts deriving from the *Sangermanensis* and *Hibernensis* were used.

(a) Mass Commentary

During the Carolingian period a plethora of commentaries on the Mass appeared in response to legislative directives,[162] and one of those most frequently found in manuscripts from the ninth to the thirteenth century carried with it a text from the *Sangermanensis*. The tract itself has been attributed by Hanssens to Amalarius of Metz and is entitled *Ordinis totius missae expositio prior*.[163] In Hanssens's descriptions of the thirty or so codices with the commentary[164] one is struck by two things. First, the manuscripts date from the eleventh century and beyond, probably because the majority contain the *Pontificale Romano-Germanicum* of the late tenth or early eleventh century.[165] Further, one notices that the commentary begins in two different ways. In one form[166] it starts abruptly by describing the introit of the Mass. In the other, however, there are two small prefaces, one entitled *Incipit ordo missae a sancto Petro institutus cum expositione sua*, with the incipit "Missa pro multis causis celebratur"; and the other *Cur cotidie iteratur ista oblatio . . .*, with the incipit "Pro multis causis . . . ."[167] As one reads these short prefaces, which have little to do with the subsequent Mass commentary,[168] he is impressed by what have been described as Irish characteristics — the didactic form, numerology, and simplified descriptions of the how and why of the Mass. Hence, the reader begins to suspect that these two short texts probably were written at least by the late eighth or early ninth century in a milieu with Irish influence. Moreover, one suspects that they perhaps circulated independently before being attached to the Mass commentary.

---

[161]See Keefe, "Baptismal Instruction," pp. 332–338.
[162]See Reynolds, "Liturgical Scholarship," p. 110.
[163]Hanssens, 3:297.
[164]Hanssens, 1:217–220.
[165]Cf. Cyrille Vogel and Reinhard Elze, *Le Pontifical romano-germanique du dixième siècle, Le texte,* 1, Studi e Testi 226 (Vatican, 1963), p. 329. To be added to the list of manuscripts with this tract are Fiecht, SB 113, fols. 32r–36r (s. XII, folios unnumbered but described to me by Dr. Peter Jeffery); Graz, UB 1002, fols. 51r–56r (s. XII); and Vic, Mus. Episcopal Frag. XII (s. XII, kindly brought to my attention by Dr. Jeffery).
[166]E.g., in Munich, Clm 14628, fol. 107v, on which see Hanssens, 3:296f.
[167]Hanssens, 3:297f.
[168]See Adolph Franz, *Die Messe im deutschen Mittelalter: Beiträge zur Geschichte der Liturgie und des religiösen Volkslebens* (Freiburg im. Br., 1902), pp. 408f.

There is now evidence to confirm these suspicions. First, we now know that the texts did circulate independently of the Mass commentary. In two ninth-century manuscripts, one whose provenance is Limoges, Paris, BN Lat. 1248, fols. 24v–25r (s. IXm., northern France)[169] and the other from Monte Cassino, 323, p. 56 (s. IX^2, mid-Italy),[170] the two texts stand alone not distantly removed from other Mass commentaries. Just as interesting is their appearance in the tenth-century English manuscript, London, BL Royal 8.C.III, fol. 61r–v,[171] where they are found not far from a version of a text on the seven heavens resembling Virgil of Salzburg's *Liber de numeris*.[172] But the suspicion that there is Irish influence behind the texts is further confirmed when it is discovered that the first text is in the *Collectio Sangermanensis*.[173] In the Paris codex of the *Sangermanensis* and in the Cologne extract, there is the title *Ordo missae a sancto Petro apostolo institutus est. Pro quod causis caelebratur missa?* followed by the incipit "Pro multis causis." But in the Munich manuscript of the *Sangermanensis* extract only the title survives. This suggests that both title and the first text were separable and might partially explain why at least one of Hanssens's codices lacks the title.[174]

The second text on the daily offering of the Mass may have been suggested by one part of the *Sangermanensis,* but much closer is a section from a didactic tract on liturgical and doctrinal matters found in the late ninth- and tenth-century manuscripts, Monza, Bibl. cap. e-14/127, fol. 74r; Montpellier, BEM 387, fol. 55r (s. IX2/3, France); and London, BL Royal 8.C.III, fol. 57r:

[Mass Exposition Preface]	[Didactic Liturgical Tract]
CUR COTIDIE ITERATUR ISTA	Interr. Q[u]ur cottidie offertur
OBLATIO. . . . Pro multis	corpus xpi et sanguis in ecclesia
causis: prima, eo quod peccamus	quando canimus missam? [Resp.]
cotidie; secunda, eo quod corpus	Idcirco cottidie offertur quia
Christi paenitentibus post	peccamus cottidie. septies enim

[169]On this manuscript see Andrieu, *Ordines Romani,* 1:265–269.

[170]On this manuscript see Maurus Inguanez, *Codicum Casinensium manuscriptorum catalogus,* 2.2 (Monte Cassino, 1934), pp. 161f.

[171]See T. A. M. Bishop, "Notes on Cambridge Manuscripts, Part IV: MSS. Connected with St. Augustine's Canterbury," *Transactions of the Cambridge Bibliographical Society* 2 (1954–1958), 335f. and pl. XIVa.

[172]Fol. 62v, and see McNally, *Liber de numeris,* p. 123 and Munich, Clm 14276, fol. 10r–v. In the London manuscript the incipit for the text is "De septem spatiis celorum Virgilius dixit . . . ."

[173]Reynolds, *O-dinals of Christ,* p. 40, n. 19.

[174]Cf. Nürnberger, p. 176. Also cf. the *Collectio Hibernensis* 2.9, Wasserschleben, pp. 14f.

peccata offerre iubeatur, ut	iustus in die cadit. ne obliuioni
salutem per corpus Christi	passio xpi traderetur. Ipse enim
inveniant, atque exeant post	dicit: quotienscumque feceritis
paenitentiam; tertia, ut magnum	in meam commemorationem facietis;
beneficium passionis Domini	uel significat diem iudicii in
oblivioni non tradatur; quarta,	ecclesia discernentem bonos et
ut similet diem iudicii in	malos.[176]
ecclesia, in quo iusti ab	
iniustis separabuntur.[175]	

(b)   Texts on the Ecclesiastical Hierarchy

Earlier it was noted that two texts on the ecclesiastical hierarchy from the *Hibernensis*, the Ordinal of Christ and *De distantia graduum*, were used in a variety of collections, including the *Sangermanensis*.[177] As an addendum to his article on the influence of the *Hibernensis* Fournier noted that another Ordinal of Christ that Carl Weyman had found in Munich, Clm 6330, seems to have been a modification of the one in the *Hibernensis*, L. 8, c. 1.[178] That particular Ordinal of Christ is, indeed, similar to that in the *Hibernensis* and *Sangermanensis*, but it has been shown since Fournier's article that it is of a distinct type and had an independent tradition of its own.[179] But the Ordinal of Christ in the *Hibernensis*, L. 8, c. 1, was, nonetheless, modified and used in a variety of Carolingian liturgical commentaries.

Even in the late eighth century the Ordinal of Christ in the *Hibernensis* was undergoing significant changes in the collection itself, where both a longer and shorter form can be found in the manuscripts.[180] But perhaps most surprising is the modification of the subdiaconal verse in the *Hibernensis* manuscript, Cologne, DB 210:[181]

[Cologne Ordinal]
De recapitulatione septem graduum. De gradibus in quibus
Christus adfuit.
Hostiarius fuit quando aperiebat ostia inferni.

---

[175]Hanssens, 3:297f.

[176]Heinrich Brewer, *Das sogenannte Athanasianische Glaubensbekenntnis ein Werk des heiligen Ambrosius. Nebst zwei Beilagen: I. Über Zeit und Verfasser der sog. Tractatus Origenis und verwandter Schriften; II: Symbolgeschichtliche Dokumente aus einer Handschrift von Monza,* Forschungen zur christlichen Literatur-und Dogmengeschichte 9, 2 (Paderborn, 1909), pp. 188f.

[177]See above, p. 115.

[178]Fournier, "De l'influence," p. 53.

[179]As the Hibernian Chronological type, on which see Reynolds, *Ordinals of Christ*, pp. 58, 72.

[180]Reynolds, *Ordinals of Christ*, p. 62, n. 39.

[181]Ibid.

Exorcista fuit quando eiecit septem demonia de Maria Magdalene.
Lectur [*sic*] fuit quando aperiebat librum Isaiae.
Subdiaconus fuit quando subditus fuit patri matrique.
Diaconus fuit quando lavabit pedes apostolorum.
Presbiter fuit quando accepit panem et benedixit.
Episcopus fuit quando elevavit oculos et benedixit apostolus
[*sic*] suos quando ascendit in celum.[182]

Here Christ is said to have been the subdeacon when he was obedient to his father and mother, an explanation not found in any other medieval Ordinal of Christ yet reported.[183]

Since the Ordinal of Christ in the *Hibernensis* itself was being altered in various manuscripts of the collection, it is not surprising that in Carolingian manuscripts containing *liturgica* the form found in the *Hibernensis* was also being changed. One of the more unusual examples of this is found in a ninth-century codex that may have been written at Laon,[184] but was more likely compiled at Metz,[185] Metz, Bibl. mun. 351:

[Metz Ordinal]
De vii gradibus in quibus Christus fuit ecclesiae traditis.
i. Hostiarius fuit quando percussit et apperuit ianua inferni.
ii. Exorcista quando eiecit vii demonia de Maria Magdalena.
iii. Lector quando apperuit librum Iesu Nave.
iiii. Subdiaconus quando fecit vinum de aqua in Chana Galileae.
v. Diaconus quando lavit pedes discipulorum suorum.
vi. Sacerdos quando accepit panem ac fregit.
vii. Episcopus quando levavit manus suas et benedixit panem et dedit discipulis ut adponerent turbis.[186]

In the grade of doorkeeper in this Ordinal it has been shown elsewhere that there are traces of the text in the B form of the *Hibernensis* found in Oxford, Bodl. Hatton 42.[187] But just as interesting is the modification of the dominical sanction for the bishop.

Much more unusual than any of the ninth-century Ordinals hitherto brought to light is one in the ninth-century Limoges manuscript, Paris,

---

[182]Fol. 29r-v.
[183]Cf. Reynolds, *Ordinals of Christ*, pp. 165-191.
[184]Cf. Contreni, *Cathedral School of Laon*, p. 62, n. 81.
[185]Cf. Roger E. Reynolds, "A Visual Epitome of the Eucharistic 'Ordo' from the Era of Charles the Bald: The Ivory Mass Cover of the *Drogo Sacramentary*," in *Charles the Bald: Court and Kingdom, Papers Based on a Colloquium Held in London in April 1979*, ed. Margaret Gibson and Janet Nelson, British Archeological Reports 120 (Oxford, 1981), p. 266.
[186]Reynolds, *Ordinals of Christ*, pp. 75f.
[187]Reynolds, *Ordinals of Christ*, p. 76.

BN Lat. 1248 (s. IXm., northern France), which also contained the short preface to the Mass commentary mentioned earlier.[188]

[Limoges Ordinal]

INT. Fuit Christus rex et sacerdos? R. Utrumque fuit rex, fuit quia semetipsum regit et nos regimur ab illo. Sacerdos fuit quia semetipsum obtulit Deo in holocaustum.

INT. Fuit Christus hostiarius? Fuit. INT. Ubi? R. Post pasionem [*sic*] suam quando aparuit portas inferni et dixit Tollite portas principes vestras.

INT. Fuit Christus exorcista? R. Fuit. INT. Ubi? R. Quando septem eieccit demon[es] de Maria Magdalene.

INT. Fuit Christus acolitus? R. Fuit. INT. Ubi? R. Quando fidelibus suis predicavit suum evvangelium et dixit Erat lux vere que inluminat omnem hominem venientem in hunc mundum.

INT. Fuit Christus subdiaconus? R. Fuit. INT. Ubi? Quando de aqua vinum fecit in Cana Galileae.

INT. Fuit Christus diaconus? R. Fuit. INT. Ubi? Quando lavit pedes discipulorum suorum et tersit linteo quo erat precintus [*sic*].

. . . .

INT. Fuit Christus presbiter? R. Fuit. INT. Ubi? In cena sua quando fecit pasca iudeorum de agno et postea quum cenatum est, accepit panem in sanctas ac venerabiles manus suas benedixit et fregit et communicavit discipulis suis de suo sancto sacrificio novo.[189]

The similarity between this version and that in the *Hibernensis* is seen in the arrangement of the grades of doorkeeper and exorcist, where the exorcist is placed next to the doorkeeper. But the normal *Hibernensis* arrangement of the remainder of the grades has been completely changed, and both augmented and reduced with the addition of the acolyte and priest-king and the omission of the lector. The appearance of the acolyte here may be the first instance of this in an Ordinal of Christ antedating the tenth century;[190] and Christ as priest-king is unique to the Ordinals of Christ thus far reported.[191] Further, the dominical sanctions for the grades of doorkeeper and presbyter have been substantially changed from the *Hibernensis* text. The phrase "post pasionem suam" is reminiscent of the "ante passionem" placed before the doorkeeper in the Hibernian Chronological Ordinals of Christ.[192] And in the unique dominical

---

[188]See above, p. 126.
[189]Fols. 67v–68v.
[190]Cf. Reynolds, *Ordinals of Christ*, pp. 93f.
[191]Cf. Reynolds, *Ordinals of Christ*, pp. 165–191.
[192]Cf. Reynolds, *Ordinals of Christ*, p. 58.

sanction for the presbyter, who has been tacked on to a long series of interrogatories after the deacon, there may be traces of southern French-Catalan or Insular influence in the reference to the "sanctas et venerabiles manus suas."[193]

Not quite as unusual as the Limoges Ordinal of Christ but still related to the one in the *Hibernensis* is one found in the Fleury liturgico-canonical manuscript already mentioned:[194]

> [Fleury Ordinal]
> De septem gradus. Hic sunt septem gradus in quibus Christus adfuit.
> Hostiarius quando in templo.
> Lector quando legit librum Isaiae prophete.
> Exorcista quando eiecit septem demonia de Maria Magdalenae.
> Subdiaconus quando fecit vinum de aqua in Chana Galilaeae.
> Diaconus quando lavit pedes discipulorum.
> Sacerdos quando obtulit corpus suum in crucae.
> Episcopus fuit quando accepit panem et benedixit dedit discipulis suis et elevatis manibus benedixit eos et post resurrectionem suam a montem Oliveti et ferebatur in caelum.[195]

It has elsewhere been pointed out that the dominical sanctions for the grades of lector through deacon in the Fleury Ordinal are simply those of the *Hibernensis* and that those for the grades of doorkeeper, *sacerdos*, and bishop are extremely unusual for ninth-century texts. But just as important is the modification of the arrangement of the lector and exorcist, which are placed in the Romano-Gallican sequence of orders that was being imposed in the ninth century on most texts describing the ecclesiastical hierarchy.[196]

This same Romano-Gallican sequence of the lector and exorcist in an Ordinal of Christ is found in the *Collectaneum* attributed to Bede:

> ["Bede's" Ordinal]
> Septem sunt gradus in quibus Christus adfuit.
> Ostiarius fuit quando destruxit ostia inferni et ligavit diabolum.
> Lector fuit quando aperuit librum Isaiae prophetae in quo invenit Spiritus Domini super me, evangelizare pauperibus misit me.
> Exorcista fuit quando eiecit septem demonia de Maria Magdalene.

---

[193]Cf. Reynolds, *Ordinals of Christ*, pp. 50, 85.
[194]See above, pp. 113, 122.
[195]Reynolds, *Ordinals of Christ*, p. 82.
[196]Reynolds, *Ordinals of Christ*, p. 77, n. 28.

Acolythus fuit etc. [*sic*]
Subdiaconus fuit quando lavit pedes discipulorum suorum.
Diaconus fuit quando fecit de aqua vinum.
Presbyter fuit quando fregit panem discipulis suis, dicens Accipite et comedite, hoc est corpus meum.[197]

If this text was indeed written in the early eighth century by Bede — and there are substantial doubts that it was[198] — the appearance of the Romano-Gallican sequence of grades is extremely unusual. But just as strange is the "addition" of the acolyte and the omission of the bishop, a phenomenon common enough in Insular and Continental Ordinals from the eleventh century on, but extremely rare in the eighth and ninth centuries. Also the reversal of the pedilavium and miracle at Cana for the subdeacon and deacon is very unusual.

The Romano-Gallican sequence of the Fleury and "Bede" Ordinals was eventually "canonized" in the

[Hiberno-Gallican Hierarchical Ordinal]
Ordo de septem gradibus in quibus Christus ascendit.
  i. Ostiarius fuit quando percutiebat portas inferni.
 ii. Lector fuit quando aperuit librum Æsiae prophetae.
iii. Exorcista fuit quando eiecit septem demonia ex Maria
   · Magdalenae.
iiii. Subdiaconus fuit quando fecit vinum de aqua in Chana
      Galileae.
  v. Diaconus fuit quando lavit pedes discipulorum suorum.
 vi. Sacerdos fuit quando accepit panem et benedixit.
vii. Episcopus fuit quando aelevavit manus suas et benedixit
     discipulos suos.[199]

The text, found in many manuscripts from the ninth through the twelfth century,[200] is clearly based on the *Collectio Hibernensis* L. 8, c. 1, but the sequence of the lector and exorcist has been reversed.

Incorporated into two of the most celebrated liturgical commentaries of the first half of the ninth century were verses from the Ordinal of Christ

---

[197]PL 94:555f.
[198]Cf. Eligius Dekkers and Aemilius Gaar, *Clavis patrum latinorum* 2 (= *Sacris Erudiri* 3, 1961) (Steenbrugge, 1961), 250f., nr. 1129.
[199]Reynolds, *Ordinals of Christ*, pp. 76f.
[200]To be added to the list of manuscripts in Reynolds, *Ordinals of Christ*, pp. 76f. n. 27, is Princeton University, Garrett 169, fols. 81v–82r (a manuscript from the eleventh or twelfth century from Admont, kindly brought to my attention by Professor Robert Somerville) containing both a Hiberno-Gallican Hierarchical Ordinal and the *De officiis vii graduum*, on which see below, p. 132. Also, Professor Kottje and Dr. Franz Kerff have generously brought to my attention another ninth-century manuscript which contains the two texts in the same recensions: Prag, Stání knihovna, Tepla Cod. 1, pp. 88–91, on which see Bischoff, *Schreibschulen*, 2:250.

taken from the Hiberno-Gallican version. In the *Disputatio puerorum* attributed to Alcuin verses from this form are pieced together with other material to make up a small text on the ecclesiastical hierarchy.[201] In the much more famous *Liber officialis* of Amalarius, Christ's lection and the pedilavium were used in a description of the ecclesiastical hierarchy in which the grades were arranged in the Romano-Gallican sequence.[202]

The other epitome of the ecclesiastical grades appearing in both the *Hibernensis* and *Sangermanensis* was the little text entitled *De distantia graduum*.[203] By the early ninth century this text was being modified in Carolingian *liturgica* in many of the same ways as the Ordinals of Christ. In a strange form found in the extract from the *Sangermanensis* in Albi, Bibl. Roch. 38bis, for example, the text of the *Hibernensis* form of the *De distantia graduum* has been modified in several sections:

> De distantia graduum. Episcopum decet iudicare et inter-
> pretari, consecrare et confirmare, ordinare et offerre.
> Sacerdotem oportet offerre, bene preesse et benedicere.
> Diaconum oportet evangelizare, ad altario [sic] ministrare,
> populo verbum Dei adnuntiare.
> Subdiaconum ministrare aquam altari diacono.
> Exorcistam oportet subicere demones et dicere his qui com-
> municant aquam ministeria effundere.
> Lectorem oportet legere ei qui praedicat et lectiones, bene
> dicere panes et fructus novos.
> Ostiarium oportet tangere cloccas et aperire ecclesiam et
> sacrarium et codicem quod praedicatur aut legitur.
> Acolitum oportet cereos accendere et ante evangelium deportare.[204]

Besides several minor alterations in the verses for the *sacerdos* and deacon, the most important change has been the addition of the acolyte, in some respects reminiscent of the addition of the acolyte in the Limoges and perhaps the "Bede" Ordinals of Christ.[205]

Just as the Hiberno-Hispanic Hierarchical version of the Ordinals of Christ in the *Collectio Hibernensis* was being altereᴅ by the reversal in sequence of the exorcist and lector, so the *De distantia graduum* was changed in the early ninth century to correspond more nearly to the sequence of grades found in Romano-Gallican ordination rites. Hence,

---

[201]Reynolds, *Ordinals of Christ*, p. 79.
[202]Reynolds, *Ordinals of Christ*, pp. 77f.
[203]See above, p. 115.
[204]Reynolds, *"De officiis vii graduum,"* p. 137.
[205]See above, pp. 129f.

there came into being a proto-pontifical form of the *De distantia graduum* in which the text was rechristened as the *De officiis septem graduum* and the verses arranged from lowest doorkeeper to highest bishop. But most important, the Romano-Gallican sequence of grades was followed.[206]

This same sequence was used, as has been seen, in the ordering of grades in the Alcuinian *Disputatio puerorum*, a liturgical exposition whose manuscript tradition is largely bound up with southeastern Germany.[207] Into this text there was inserted a highly modified fragment of the *De distantia graduum*, "Oportet enim illis [subdiaconibus] apostolum legere, honestare altare, et aquam praeparare in ministerio altaris."[208] This same fragment also appears in the so-called *Collection of Laon*, which, as was earlier seen, contained other extracts from the *Hibernensis*.[209]

Conclusion

"Naturam expellas furca, tamen usque recurret" is an old adage perhaps better suited to farming than to canon law texts, but in our study we have seen how it might also be applicable to the *Collectio Hibernensis* in the Carolingian period. Despite the promotion by the Carolingian rulers of Roman canonical texts and their apparent disapproval of the Irish, the *Hibernensis* continued to flourish and luxuriate in a variety of contexts both canonical and literary as well as geographical. We have seen, for example, how the collection was quickly modified and disguised in abridgments. Then, useful excerpta were incorporated or hidden within many other collections, including the ancient *Collectio Vetus Gallica*, which seems to have been the quasi-official Frankish systematic collection of the Carolingians, or such newly composed collections as the *Collection of Laon*. Extracts of *Hibernensis* texts dealing with subjects inadequately covered in the "officially" promulgated collections also cropped up in isolated contexts, especially chapters dealing with matrimony and the ecclesiastical hierarchy. As a source of biblical and patristic citations we have seen, moreover, how the *Hibernensis* was used within Carolingian florilegia and biblical commentaries. And finally, we saw how texts from the *Hibernensis* and its derivative, the *Collectio Sangermanensis*, were cast in interrogatory forms to further the Carolingian educational intention to instruct the clergy on sacramental topics ranging from the Mass to sacred orders.

---

[206]Reynolds, *"De officiis vii graduum,"* pp. 135f.
[207]See Reynolds, "Canon Law Collections," p. 29.
[208]Reynolds, *"De officiis vii graduum,"* p. 139.
[209]Ibid. See above, p. 112.

134

By examining the origins of the manuscripts of the *Collectio Hibernensis* and its derivatives according to geographical distribution, it has also been found that in the late eighth and ninth century the collection flourished especially in those localities and areas with long Celtic traditions or where the "officially" promulgated Roman texts seem to have been poorly represented in the manuscripts. Hence, St. Gall, Reichenau, Brittany and southeastern Germany with their long Celtic traditions and western and southern France with their relative paucity of manuscripts of the *Collectio Dionysio-Hadriana* all seem to have been areas where texts of the *Hibernensis* were copied and used. Even in northern France, where one might have expected the *Hibernensis* to have disappeared entirely, manuscripts of it under a variety of guises just enumerated were made. But perhaps the most surprising flowering of the *Hibernensis* took place in a geographical region over which the Carolingians claimed domination but which has not been noted here thus far because the only extant manuscripts date to the tenth century and beyond. Fournier in his "De l'influence de la collection irlandaise" and in his later article, "Un groupe de recueils canoniques italiens des Xe et XIe siècles,"[210] dealt with these texts, all from central and southern Italy, but did not dwell on the fact that they were probably based on Carolingian models of the *Hibernensis* that seem to have circulated widely in those areas. These texts that Fournier studied are in the collection of Rome, Bibl. Vallicelliana T. XVIII, famous for its recension of the B Form of the *Hibernensis*,[211] the *Collection in Nine Books* of the Beneventan codex, Vatican, Vat. Lat. 1349,[212] the *Collection in Five Books*,[213] and their nearly dozen derivatives.[214] Beyond these collections that Fournier treated as *Hibernensis* derivatives are several found more recently, such as the *Collection of Rieti*, written in Beneventan script,[215] and the *Multiloquiorum of Farfa*.[216] But most important are five additional Italian manuscripts with extracts from the *Hibernensis* itself. One of these,

---

[210]*Mémoires de l'Académie des Inscriptions et Belles-Lettres* 40 (1916), 95-212.

[211]For the date of this codex see E. A. Loew, *The Beneventan Script, a History of the South Italian Minuscule*, 2nd ed. Virginia Brown *II Hand List of Beneventan MSS.*, Sussidi eruditi 34 (Rome, 1980), p. 131.

[212]For the date of this manuscript see Loew-Brown, *Beneventan Script*, p. 145.

[213]A partial edition of this collection may be found in Mario Fornasari, *Collectio canonum in V libris: Libri I-III*, Corpus christianorum, Cont. med. 6 (Turnhout, 1970).

[214]See Fournier, "Un groupe," pp. 190-208.

[215]On this collection see Reynolds, "Basil," p. 526.

[216]On this collection see Roger E. Reynolds, "The 'Isidorian' *Epistula ad Leudefredum*: An Early Medieval Epitome of the Clerical Duties," *Mediaeval Studies* 41 (1979), 306.

Vatican, Vat. Ottob. 6, is a tenth-century manuscript from Nonantola with miscellaneous texts drawn from the *Hibernensis* from beginning to end.[217] The second, Vatican, Vat. Lat. 4162, has *Hibernensis* texts on the higher grades of the ecclesiastical hierarchy.[218] The third and fourth manuscripts, Florence BML VII sin. 1, and Calci 11 Archivio della Certosa, are Italian manuscripts of Burchard's *Decretum* to which extracts from the *Hibernensis* LL. 11–18 have been added.[219] The fifth codex, the early eleventh-century manuscript of the collection of Vatican, Archivio San Pietro H 58, with its extracts from the *Hibernensis*, LL. 1–10, cheek by jowl on "Sedulius in Carmen Alpha," is most surprising because it seems to have been written in Rome itself.[220] In the geographical area and in the city itself, then, where the Carolingians would have expected the Romanity of the ancient canonical collections to have obliterated traces of other collections, the leavening influence of the Irish collections of canons continued to be felt long after Charlemagne and his contemporaries.

[217]See Roger E. Reynolds, "Excerpta from the *Collectio Hibernensis* in Three Vatican Manuscripts," *Bulletin of Medieval Canon Law*, n.s. 5 (1975), 2f.

[218]Reynolds, "Excerpta," pp. 3f.

[219]Gérard Fransen, "Manuscrits des collections canoniques," *Bulletin of Medieval Canon Law*, n.s. 6 (1976), 67; and cf. Hubert Mordek, "Handschriftenforschungen in Italien," *QFIAB* 51 (1972), 637, 646.

[220]Reynolds, "Excerpta," pp. 4–9; and Kottje, *Bussbücher Halitgars*, pp. 65–69. For Professor Bischoff's dating of this manuscript, see Damien Sicard, *La Liturgie de la mort dans l'église latine des origines à la réforme carolingienne,* Liturgiewissenschaftliche Quellen und Forschungen 63 (Münster/W., 1978), pp. xiv, 115, n. 33.

V

Excerpta from the Collectio Hibernensis
in three Vatican manuscripts*

Since the fundamental studies of Paul Fournier, 'De l'influence de la collection irlandaise sur la formation des collections canoniques'[1] and 'Un groupe de recueils canoniques italiens des xe et xie siècles',[2] the role of the Irish *Collectio Hibernensis* in the formation of early medieval Italian canonical collections has been widely recognized. In those articles Fournier showed how the *Hibernensis* worked its influence on the important canonical manuscript, *Vallicelliana T. XVIII*, the Collection in nine books (= 9L) of Vat. lat. 1349, and the Collection in five books (= 5L),[3] together with a host of more minor collections. Undoubtedly Fournier could have listed many more[4] Italian manuscripts[5] showing the influences of the *Hibernensis*, had catalogues been more explicit in their descriptions of various manuscripts as canon law collections. But the *Hibernensis*, heavily laden as it is with extracts from the works of the Fathers, has been disguised in the catalogues, like many other canon law collections, under such descriptions as *Florilegium patrum* or *Sententiae patrum sanctorum*. The *excerpta* from the *Hibernensis* in central Italian manuscripts

---

* Support for research in this note has been provided by the American Council of Learned Societies, the American Philosophical Association, and the Canada Council.

[1] NRHD 23 (1899) 27-78.

[2] *Mém. Acad. Inscr.* 40 (1916) 95-212.

[3] For bibliography on these collections, see H. Mordek, 'Die historische Wirkung der Collectio Herovalliana', ZKG 81 (1970) 235f. n. 82; Reynolds, 'The *De officiis vii graduum*: Its origins and early medieval development', *Mediaeval Studies* 34 (1972) 130 n. 71. On the illuminations and liturgical material at the beginning and end of Vat. lat. 1339 of the 5 L, see C. Walter, 'Les dessins carolingiens dans un manuscrit de Verceil', *Cahiers archéologiques* 18 (1968) 107 n. 34; K. Gamber, *Codices liturgici latini antiquiores*, 1.2. (Freiburg/Sch. 1968) 573 nr. 1599. There is a color plate of the first illuminated folio of this MS in C. L. Ragghianti, *L'Arte in Italia* 2 (Rome 1968) 857f. Also see G. Barraclough, *The medieval Papacy* (London 1968) 109, illust. 46.

[4] In his 'De l'influence' Fournier listed Madrid BN MS lat. A 151 (nunc 373) separate from those collections under the influence of the Italian recension of the *Hibernensis*. In the text of the *De distantia graduum*. fol. 9r-v, a gloss, 'que vulgo campane dicuntur', often added in the Italian MSS to the verse for the doorkeeper, has been introduced incorrectly after the verse for the lector. See Reynolds, 'The *De officiis vii graduum*' 131.

[5] The *Hibernensis* in Livorno Bibl. com. Labronica MS 10 has been described by S. Williams, *Codices Pseudo-Isidoriani: A palaeographical-historical study* (MIC, Subsidia 3; New York 1971) 143f. There are also fragments from the *Hibernensis* in the well-known Bobbio MS of the *Collectio Cresconii*, Vat. lat. 5748 (s. ix/x) fol. 7r-v; on which see R. Kottje, 'Einheit und Vielfalt des kirchlichen Lebens in der Karolingerzeit', *Zeitschrift für Kirchengeschichte* 76 (1965) 339 n. 69.

which are the subject of this note have also been camouflaged by the works of the Fathers and liturgical material surrounding them.

VAT. OTTOB. LAT. 6

The earliest of the three manuscripts, Vat. Ottobon. lat. 6 (s. x/xɪ), is a small manuscript (ff. 75, 206 × 140) which Salmon in his catalogue of Vatican liturgical manuscripts calls an *Enchiridion sacerdotale Nonantulense*.[6] The larger portion of the manuscript is made up of a section of the *Liber scintillarum* of Defensor of Ligugé, which is a mosaic of works of the Fathers (fol. 31r-75v),[7] and the *De natura rerum* and *De temporibus* of the Venerable Bede (fol. 15r-27r).[8] The remainder of the manuscript consists almost entirely of liturgical material and what the Vatican inventory calls *Excerpta ss. patribus et conciliis*.[9] The liturgical material includes an *Ordo missae* (fol. 9v-11r);[10] an *excerptum* from Isidore's *De origine officiorum*, 1.15.1-3, on the Mass (fol. 11r-v);[11] an *Expositio missae*, which is an abbreviation of the tract of Remegius in Book 40 of the Pseudo-Alcuinian *Liber de divinis officiis* (fol. 11v-14v);[12] and the text of Isidore's *De*

---

[6] P. Salmon, *Les manuscrits liturgiques latins de la Bibliothèque Vaticane* 2 (Studi e Testi 253; Vatican City 1969) 292. Also see Salmon, *Les manuscrits* 5 (Studi e Testi 270; Vatican City 1972) 228. On the provenance of the MS see J. Ruysschaert, *Les manuscrits de l'abbaye de Nonantola: Table de concordance annotée et index des manuscrits* (Studi e Testi 182bis; Vatican City 1955) 62.

[7] See H.-M. Rochais, 'Defensoriana: Archéologie du Liber scintillarum', *Sacris erudiri* 9 (1957) 237. Also see Ruysschaert, *Manuscrits Nonantola* 27 n. 1, noting in connection with Nonantola two MSS in the Biblioteca Nazionale Centrale in Rome. Of these Sessorianus 87 (1396) (s. xɪ), fol. 157v-164v, contains a fragment of the *Liber scintillarum* not in Vat. Ottob. lat. 6, but the Vatican MS is physically smaller in size. Another eleventh-century MS of the *Liber scintillarum*, which the catalogue of the Biblioteca Nazionale lists as having come from Nonantola, is Sessorianus 112 (1484) fol. 1r-71r; on which see Rochais, 'Defensoriana' 236.

[8] See M. L. W. Laistner, *A Hand-list of Bede manuscripts* (Ithaca 1943) 92, 143, 146; and *Bedae Opera de temporibus*, ed. C. W. Jones (Cambridge, Mass. 1943) 162, 167.

[9] *Inventarii codicum . . . Ottobonianae* 1; see Ruysschaert, *Manuscrits Nonantola* 62: '. . . ms composite de textes patristiques et liturgiques'; H.-M. Rochais, 'Contribution à l'histoire des florilèges ascétiques du haut moyen âge', RB 63 (1953) 255.

[10] Salmon, *Manuscrits liturgiques* 2.292.

[11] PL 83.752f.

[12] PL 101.1246-71. Other Vatican MSS containing the *Expositio missae* are Vat. Reg. lat. 479, fol. 56r-59r; Vat. lat. 466, fol. 57r-77r; and Vat. Reg. lat. 234, fol. 1r-13r on which see the forthcoming article of Reynolds, 'Marginalia on tenth-century tracts on the ecclesiastical officers'. The conclusion of the *Expositio* in Vat. Ottob. lat. 6 is more like that in Vat. lat. 466 than Vat. Reg. lat. 479. Also, in the conclusion there are fragments from a tract on vestments something like that found in Vat. Reg. lat. 479, fol. 59v-60r, Vat. Reg. lat. 234, fol. 14r-v, Vat. lat. 466, fol. 77r-v or PL 101.1242f.

V

origine officiorum, 1.18, entitled *Sententia Isydori de corpore et sanguine Domini* (fol. 29r-30v).[13]

The *Excerpta ss. patribus et conciliis* in the first section of the manuscript (fol. 1r-9r) is the abbreviation of the *Collectio Hibernensis*. The *excerptum* begins with two long sections from the middle and final books of the *Hibernensis*, and after canons from the first books on the bishop, presbyter, deacon, and subdeacon have been repeated, extracts are taken from books running to Book 43 of the *Hibernensis*.[14]

Within the *excerptum* there are two noteworthy features. First, the compiler is in part dependent on the Italian recension of the *Hibernensis*. Secondly, there are additions from the works of the Fathers used to supplement the *Hibernensis*. In the texts on the clerics, especially, material from Isidore's *Origines*, 7.12,[15] bolsters the already heavily Isidorian canons of the *Hibernensis*. With this supplementary material the *excerptum* of Ottobon. 6 is like the Italian 9L and the 5L.

VAT. LAT. 4162

The second *excerptum* is found in a twelfth-century manuscript containing a miscellany of classical, patristic, and medieval texts, including the *Constitutum Constantini*.[16] The manuscript is made up of segments from a variety of manuscripts now bound together. The *excerptum* from the *Hibernensis* is

---

[13] PL 83.754-7.

[14] The following numbered capitula from Vat Ottob. lat. 6 are drawn from the *Hibernensis* as edited by H. Wasserschleben, *Die irische Kanonensammlung* (2nd ed. Leipzig 1885). An exact list of canons from the *Hibernensis* must await the completion of a new edition of the *Hibernensis*; on which see M. Sheehy, 'Influences of ancient Irish law on the *Collectio canonum Hibernensis*', *Proceedings Congr. Strasbourg* (MIC, Subsidia 4; Vatican City 1971) 31. W = footnotes in Wasserschleben; *Orig.* = Isidore's *Origines*; V = Vallicelliana T. XVIII. 27.10-17; 44.20a; 53.4; 52.3, 1, 5; 58.3, 5; 61.2a; 54.1, 2-4, 8a, c; 66.3b, c; 1.1, 3; *Orig.* 7.12.9; 1.6a[1], 21; W5(i); 1.10m, o, 21; 2.1a[1]; *Orig.* 7.12.20, 17; 2.2, 11e, 13a, b, 16, 22, 24, 26[1]; 3.1, 2, 5; 4.1, 4; 13.1, 7; 15.2, 8c; 16.2, 7a, b, 9f, g, 13e; 21.16, 10b, c, 12; 22.2, 3c-g; V fol. 82v; 27.8a, c-e; 67.4g; 27.8f; 67.4i; 27.19a-c; V fol. 89v; 28.12; 67.4k-q; 39.1, 2; 67.6; 29.2, 1, 4a, b[1]; 30.2a-c, 3a, b; 33.1a, c-f, 2a-d, 3a-d; 34.4; 37.1a, b, d, e, 25a, c, 11b, 13; V fol. 103v-104r; 37.14, 10a, b, e, f, 15, 39, 21[1]; V fol. 103v; 37.8, 17, 32a, c, 33b, 35[1]; 42.1, 2, 3, 4a, e-h, 10a-e; 43.7.

[15] PL 82.291f. G. Gullotta, *Gli antichi cataloghi e i codici della Abbazia di Nonantola* (Studi e Testi 182; Vatican City 1955) 435. Cf. M. Andrieu, *Les Ordines romani du haut moyen âge* 1 (Louvain 1931) 293, who reports that in an eleventh-century MS from Nonantola, Rome Bibl. Naz. Centr. Sessorianus 52 (2096), there is a recension of the *Origines* differing from that found in PL 82. In the section on orders (fol. 153v-155v), however, the differences between the MS and the Arevalo edition in Migne are minimal.

[16] See H. Fuhrmann, *Das Constitutum Constantini (Konstantinische Schenkung), Text* (MGH Fontes 10; Hannover 1968) 36, 54.

on three folios numbered 35-37, now inserted between fol. 33 and 34. Of the folios with the *excerptum*, fol. 35 (a partial folio: 143×128) should perhaps have been bound after fol. 36-37 (full folios: 204×139, 204×119). The texts from the *Collectio Hibernensis* are only those describing the higher clerical orders, but they are arranged in the unusual sequence of bishop, presbyter, and subdeacon with the diaconal texts added on the partial folio.[17] Why the deacon was originally omitted between the presbyter and subdeacon is difficult to say, but the same omission can be found in one section of the third Vatican manuscript containing a *Hibernensis excerptum*.

VAT. ARCHIVIO SAN PIETRO H 58

This central-Italian manuscript is much larger (ff. $II+152$, 285×200) than Ottob. 6 or Vat. lat. 4162 and has been dated as early as the ninth century[18] but is certainly younger.[19] It is best known as a liturgical manuscript, and Salmon includes it under no less than five categories of liturgical books: missals, rituals, martyrologies, passionals and lectionaries.[20] In fact, besides the liturgical formularies, there are liturgical commentaries dependent on the works of Rabanus Maurus,[21] Walafrid Strabo,[22] Amalarius,[23] and others.[24] But despite

---

[17] The following numbered capitula cf the *excerptum* correspond to Wasserschleben's edition: (fol. 36r) 1.3 (partial), 10g, 16a-c, 17d; 2.7-9 (fol. 37r) 2.10, 11a, b, d, e (variant text), f, g, 14 (variant text), 15, 16; 4.4 (fol. 35r) 3.2, 4a, b; 1.14.

[18] See A. Poncelet, *Catalogus codicum hagiographicorum latinorum bibliothecarum romanarum* (Brussels, 1909) 47f., and H. Barré, *Les homéliaires carolingiens de l'école d'Auxerre* (Studi e Testi 225; Vatican City 1962) 118.

[19] H. Quentin, *Les Martyrologes historiques du moyen âge* (Paris 1908) 39-42 dates the MS to the twelfth century. H. Delehaye, 'Martyrologium e codice basilicae Vaticanae nunc primum editum', *Analecta Bollandiana* 49 (1931) 51, says eleventh or even tenth century. Salmon, *Manuscrits liturgiques* 2.240; 3.149; 4.20, 232; and 5.348, says eleventh or twelfth century; the *Indice per autori e materie* 194f., dates it to the eleventh century. The *Inventarium* based on the work of C. Stornajolo 3.184, says eleventh or twelfth century. And the 'Censimento dei codici dei secoli x-xii', *Studi medievali* 11 (1970) 1133, says tenth century. G. Mercati, *Codici latini Pico Grimani . . . con una digressione per la storia dei codici di S. Pietro in Vaticano* (Studi e Testi 75; Vatican City 1938) 150, points out that the words *Lib S. Petri* on fol. 1r are in a fourteenth-century hand, so the codex is a very early one in the fondo Archivio S. Pietro. As to the origin of the MS, the 'Censimento' 1133, says central Italy. Quentin 41, notes that the Martyrology of Bede contains additions recalling Beneventan martyrologies.

[20] See the citations in Salmon's catalogues in the previous note.

[21] fol. 129v. Cf. *De institutione clericorum libri tres* 1.31, ed. A. Knoepfler (Veröffentlichungen aus dem Kirchenhistorischen Seminar München 5; Munich 1901) 59, citing Fulda MS Aa 2; Bamberg MS Liturg. 131, fol. 52v, and MS Liturg. 140, fol. 19r; and Clm 3909, fol. 9r-v, St. Gall MS 446, p. 76f., and Vat. lat. 1146, 1147, and 1148, described by Andrieu, *Les Ordines* 1.215, 298, 337. Also see Mantua Bibl. com. 331 (C. III. 11) (s. xi), fol. 15v and Oxford Holkham Misc. 17 (s. xi), fol. 18v.

the predominantly liturgical character of the manuscript, there are extensive sections from the *Collectio Hibernensis*, the Penitential of Halitgar, Regino's *Libri duo de synodalibus causis et disciplinis ecclesiasticis*, a collection something like the 5L, a collection resembling the Collection of Diessen of Clm 5541, the *Collectio Herovalliana*, and a penitential like the *Poenitentiale Vallicellianum primum*. The text has been written in different hands in one and two columns, and there is some confusion in the present binding of quires.[25]

An exact and extensive description of the individual canons and their sources is beyond the scope of this note and must wait further studies on and editions of early medieval canonical collections in central Italy.[26] But the following major groups of material can be found in the manuscript:

1. Material resembling the *Poenitentiale Vallicellianum primum* and the introductory letters to the Penitential of Halitgar (fol. 42r-45v).[27]
2. Material similar to the 5L, bk. 3 (fol. 45v-48v).[28]
3. Material based largely on the *Collectio Hibernensis* 1, and Isidore's *Origines* (fol. 135r-138r).[29]
4. The Penitential of Halitgar bks. 3-5 (fol. 138r-143r).[30]
5. Miscellaneous canons from the Greek councils, popes, and the *Collectio Herovalliana* (fol. 143r-149r).[31]

---

[22] fol. 131r. Cf. *De exordiis et incrementis quarundam in observationibus ecclesiasticis rerum* 29f. ed. A. Knoepfler (Veröffentl. Sem. München 1; Munich 1899) 95-8.

[23] fol. 131r. Cf. *Liber officialis* 1.37, 39; 3.44, ed. I. M. Hanssens, *Amalarii episcopi Opera liturgica omnia* 2: *Liber officialis* (Studi e Testi 139; Vatican City 1948) 178-81, 185f., 381-6.

[24] On fol. 128v-129r, there is a group of short texts on the divine offices.

---

[25] It is uncertain how the MS was originally constructed, but the last two quires (fol. 135-42, 143-50) belong immediately before the present quire beginning on fol. 49.

[26] Among these are editions of the *Hibernensis* (see above n. 14) and the last two books of the 5L, see M. Fornasari, *Collectio canonum in V libris: Libri I-III* (CCL, Cont. med. 6; Turnhout 1970) and studies on the penetration of Regino, Halitgar, and other collections into Italy.

[27] The *Ordo poenitentiae*, beginning on fol. 42r is, strictly speaking, liturgical, but it is contained in the *Poenitentiale Vallicellianum primum*. See H. J. Schmitz, *Die Bussbücher und die Bussdisciplin der Kirche* 1 (Düsseldorf 1883) 239. The introductory letters to the Penitential of Halitgar are found in Schmitz, *Die Bussbücher* 2.246f. and PL 105.651-4.

[28] Although this material is now found in the 5L, an earlier collection with the same material is not precluded as a source.

[29] Texts similar to those defining the word 'synod' and the principal synods are found in Vallicelliana T. XVIII, fol. 58v-59r. Sections defining the word 'synod' are found in Isidore's *Origines* 6.16 and 9.8; PL 82.234f.

[30] The texts are closer to those edited by Schmitz, *Die Bussbücher* 2.275-89, than those in PL 105.

[31] The canons from the Council of Neocaesarea are attributed to Ancyra. Only one of the canons from the *Herovalliana* (cc. 20, 27, 30; PL 99.1021, 1027f.) bears the characteristic word *hera*; on which see H. Mordek '*Aera*', DA 25 (1969) 216-22, and Mordek, 'Die historische Wirkung' 220-42.

6. Material from the *Collectio Hibernensis,* bks. 1-9 (fol. 149r-150v, 49r-53r).[32]
7. Isidorian material on clerics and a section from the *Collectio Hibernensis,* bk. 10 (fol. 53r-56v).[33]
8. *Carmen alpha* attributed to Sedulius, followed by material like that in the 5L, bk. 3 (fol. 57r-59r).[34]
9. Penitential material resembling the *Poenitentiale Vallicellianum primum;*[35] fragments from Regino's *Libri duo,* bk. 2; canons of the Council of Tribur in the order of Clm 5541,[36] and papal and conciliar canons (fol. 109v-121v).
10. Miscellaneous canons from Clement's *Epistula* 2; Gennadius' *Diffinitio ecclesiasticorum dogmatum;* and the *Collectio Hibernensis* bk. 10 (material missing in 7. above) (fol. 122r-128v).[37]

While these groupings represent the major categories of material used by the compilers, they fail to distinguish unusual variants in the canons themselves,[38] and they also do not reflect the rich admixture of patristic material in the groups of texts. Nowhere is this more clear than in the sections of the manuscript describing the ecclesiastical officers. This topic seems to have been one the compilers thought most important, and besides the texts from the *Hibernensis* and its derivatives, there are sections intruded from Isidore's *Origines* and *De origine officiorum.* In several instances, moreover, the Isidorian texts have been significantly modified.

In the first instance the compiler, after defining the word *ecclesia,* says: 'Et sunt septem primi ordines ecclesie Dei: episcopis, presbiteris (*sic*), diaconus, subdiaconus, exorcista, hostiarius, lector . . .',[39] and goes on to deal with the bishop. This catalogue of grades is similar to the short list given in Isidore's

---

[32] Many of these canons, which are not found in Wasserschleben's edition, are found in the *Hibernensis* of Vallicelliana T. XVIII, fol. 64r-66v, especially those following book 9 of the *Hibernensis.*

[33] On the Isidorian material see below.

[34] It must be emphasized that many of the canons only resemble the 5L, but are in a different form.

[35] On fol. 121v (a small inserted folio) the numbers assigned to the canons are almost the same as those in the *Poenitentiale Vallicellianum primum.* Further, in the margin the words 'era cañ cancrensi' (*sic*) are added; on which see Mordek, 'Die historische Wirkung' 232.

[36] See Emil Seckel, 'Zu den Acten der Triburer Synode 895', NA 18 (1893) 406. In the Vatican MS there are two numbers assigned to the *capitula,* the first of which corresponds to the text in Clm 5541.

[37] There is a mistake in the present foliation in this section of the MS. Following the canonical material on fol. 128v, there are the liturgical texts, on which see above, n. 24.

[38] E.g., the *Canones Gregorii* of Halitgar 4.22 (Schmitz, *Die Bussbücher* 2.284) have been replaced with the longer text found, among other places, in the *Collectio Dionysio-Hadriana* (PL 67.342ff.).

[39] fol. 135v-136r.

Origines 7.12.3, but the text there reads: '. . . quorum gradus et nomina hec sunt: ostiarius, psalmista, lector, exorcista, acolitus, subdiaconus, diaconus, presbiter et episcopus'.[40] In the text of the Vatican manuscript the compiler limits the grades of the Church to seven, lists the grades from highest to lowest, omits the psalmist and acolyte, and places the lector below the doorkeeper. All except the last of these variations on the Isidorian model are probably made so as to reflect the hierarchy of orders described in the *Hibernensis*. There the orders described are seven from the bishop down through the doorkeeper,[41] with the acolyte and psalmist added only after the texts of the Ordinal of Christ and the *De distantia graduum*,[42] both of which list only seven grades without the acolyte and psalmist. Why the compiler of the Vatican manuscript lists the lector as a grade below the doorkeeper is difficult to explain, but the same sequence can be found in such diverse medieval texts as a seventh-century Old Irish legal tract,[43] the *De distantia graduum* in Turin Bibl. Naz. Univ. D.IV.33 (Pasini 239) and Berlin SB Savigny lat. 3,[44] the Ordinal of Christ in the *Libellus de diversis ordinibus*,[45] the *Summa confessorum* of Thomas Chobham,[46] the *Summa de sacramentis* of Peter the Chanter,[47] and the Ordinal of Christ in Paris BN lat. 3265A.[48]

---

[40] PL 82.290.   [41] Wasserschleben, *Die irische Kanonensammlung* 3-25.

[42] *Collectio Hibernensis* 8.1, 2; Wasserschleben, *Die irische Kanonensammlung* 26; and Vat. Arch. S. Pietro H 58, fol. 51v. The Ordinal of Christ from the *Hibernensis* 8.1 may also be found in the Italian MS, Milan Ambrosiana M 79 Sup. (s. xi), fol. 21r-v (a text Mr. Paul Meyvaert kindly called to my attention). As *excerpta* from the *Hibernensis*, the Ordinal of Christ and the *De distantia graduum* are also in Verona Capit. MS LXIII (61), fol. 84v; on which see Reynolds, 'The *De officiis vii graduum*' 131. In the Italian 9L and the 5L, the *De distantia graduum* is drawn from the *Hibernensis*, but not the Ordinal of Christ, which, like the text in Vat. lat. 4977, fol. 37r and the liturgico-canonical *Liber multiloquiorum* in seven books of Farfa (1090-99), Vat. lat. 4317, fol. 103v-104r, depends on a different Irish tradition represented in Vallicelliana T. XVIII, fol. 149v, following the *Hibernensis*.

[43] *Uraicect Becc and certain other selected Brehon law tracts* (Ancient Laws of Ireland 5; Dublin 1901) 22-4, where the grades are listed once in the sequence of lector, doorkeeper, exorcist, subdeacon, deacon, presbyter, and bishop, and later in the sequence of doorkeeper, exorcist, lector, subdeacon, deacon, presbyter, and bishop, with the psalmist, acolyte, and cleric added as subgrades. I owe this reference to Professor D. A. Binchy.

[44] See Reynolds, 'The Turin Collection in seven books: A Poitevin canonical collection', *Traditio* 25 (1969) 512f.

[45] See Reynolds, 'The unidentified sources of the Norman Anonymous: *C.C.C.C. MS. 415*', *Transactions of the Cambridge Bibliographical Society* 5.2 (1970) 129, and the new edition and translation by G. Constable and B. Smith, *Libellus de diversis ordinibus et professionibus qui sunt in aecclesia* (Oxford 1972) 60.

[46] *Thomae de Chobham Summa confessorum*, ed. F. Broomfield (Analecta mediaevalia Namurcensia 25; Louvain-Paris 1968) 115f., 326.

[47] Pierre le Chantre, *Summa de sacramentis et animae consiliis* III 2a, ed. J.-A. Dugauquier (Analecta mediaevalia Namurcensia 16; Louvain-Lille 1963) 256.

[48] fol. xxxv-xxxir. On this MS see the articles by A. Teetaert, 'Quelques "Summae de

A second alteration in texts on the ecclesiastical grades appears in the description of the chorbishop. Rather than following Isidore's text in the *De origine officiorum*,[49] the text of the *Hibernensis* in Paris BN lat. 3182 (Bigot. 89),[50] or one like Ottob. 6, the compiler uses his own variant.

Vat. Ottob. 6	Vat. Arch. S. Pietro H 58
Corepiscopi, id est vicarii episcoporum, ab uno episcopo civitatis cui adiecet ordinatur.[51]	Coriepiscopii, id est vicarii episcopii, ab uno episcopo ordinentur. Ysidorus. Hii autem episcopo solo ordinentur civitatis cui adiecient.[52]

A third instance, where a change in an Isidorian text on orders has been made, is in the repetition of the list of grades from the *Origines* 7.12.3.[53] For no apparent reason the deacon is omitted in the Vatican text.[54]

At the conclusion of the section on the ecclesiastical grades in the Vatican manuscript there is a group of the standard etymological definitions from the *Origines* 7.12. But two extraordinary texts have been inserted listing the grades and their relationships. The first catalogues the grades in a way reflecting Isidore's *De origine officiorum* 2.5-15.[55]

> Omnes quidem gradus ecclesie generaliter autem clerici aut fideles aut Christiani nunccupantur. Quorum primus est gradus episcopus, cui secundo loco quasi ex eo pendens choriepiscoporum supponitur gradus; tribus presbiterorum; iiii. diaconorum, cui quinto loco vel ut pendens ex eo custos sacrorum supponitur; vi[tus] subdiaconus; vii. lector; viii. loco supponitus psalmista, quasi appendens ix. exorcista; x. loco hostiarius, cui quasi pendens xi. loco subponitus accolitus.[56]

Here the grades are listed in the sequence of the *De origine officiorum*, and the offices of chorepiscopate and *custos sacrorum* are given. Strangely, the compiler, below the doorkeeper, adds the acolyte, a grade not originally in the *De origine officiorum*.[57]

---

paenitentia" anonymes dans la Bibliothèque Nationale de Paris', *Miscellanea Giovanni Mercati* II (Studi e Testi 122; Vatican City, 1946) 333f., and 'La "Formula confessionum" du frère mineur Jean Rigaud (†1323)', *Miscellanea historica in honorem Alberti de Meyer* II (Louvain-Brussels 1946) 676.

[49] PL 83.786f.

[50] Wasserschleben, *Die irische Kanonensammlung* 5, and cf. R. Kottje, 'Isidor von Sevilla und der Chorepiskopat', DA 28 (1972) 536. On the date of the Paris MS, see B. Bischoff, 'Wendepunkte in der Geschichte der lateinischen Exegese im Frühmittelalter', *Mittelalterliche Studien: Ausgewählte Aufsätze . . .* I (Stuttgart 1966) 269; and R. E. McNally, *Scriptores Hiberniae minores* I (CCL 108B; Turnhout 1973) 177f.

[51] fol. 4r.   [52] fol. 136r.   [53] PL 82.290.

[54] fol. 53v.   [55] PL 83.780-94.   [56] fol. 54r.

[57] See Reynolds, 'The portrait of the ecclesiastical officers in the Raganaldus Sacramentary and its liturgico-canonical significance', *Speculum* 46 (1971) 440 n. 20. In a number of early manuscripts of the *De origine officiorum*, including Vat. Reg. lat. 191 (s. ix), fol. 29v, and Rouen Bibl. mun. 524 (I.49) (s. ix), fol. 48r, a small extra folio has been

The second text describing the relationship of the grades contains a mixture of Isidore's *Origines* and *De origine officiorum*, but in the grade of lector there is included a surprising array of offices.[58]

> ... sed hic exitus diversos in se abent ordines. Quorum primus episcoporum est ordo, quadripertitus ut diximus in patriarchis, in archiepiscopis, in metropolitanis, in episcopis, quorum maximi pontifices nunccupantur, minimi choriepiscopi dicitur, generaliter autem summi sacerdotes Dei vocantur. Secundus presbiterorum, qui et ipsi sacerdotes dicuntur, quia continuus et pene par est et episcopus. iii. levitarum in quibus sunt diaconi et archidiaconi et sacrorum custodes. iiii. ipodiaconorum quia et subdiacones nunccupantur. v. lectorum in quibus sunt filosophi, poete, magistri, doctores, sapientes, scribe, notarii, librarii, interpretes, discipuli, sapientes quibus contrarius insipientes. vi. psalmistarum in quibus sunt cantores, preceptores, succentores, concentores. vii. exorcistarum. viii. hostiariorum in quibus sunt acoliti.

These unusual recensions of texts on the ecclesiastical grades represent only a fraction of the texts which have been modified and supplemented by the compilers of the manuscript. Further study may well prove that Vat. Arch. S. Pietro H 58 is in its originality the equal of any of the Italian collections which Paul Fournier showed dependent on the *Collectio Hibernensis*.

---

added to the MS with a text from Isidore's *Origines* 7.12.29f. (PL 82.293). On these MSS, see C. Lawson, 'Notes on the "De ecclesiasticis officiis",' *Isidoriana: Estudios sobre San Isidoro de Sevilla en el XIV centenario de su nacimiento*, ed. M. C. Díaz y Díaz (León 1961) 300.

[58] fol. 55v-56r.

VI

Canon law collections in early ninth-century Salzburg *

This paper is both a postlude and prelude. It is a postlude to Dr. Mordek's monumental work on the canonical collections antedating Pseudo-Isidore.[1] It is a prelude—one might even say an *Ersatz*—to a better study which will undoubtedly be written after the appearance of Professor Bischoff's catalogues of ninth-century manuscripts, especially Salzburg manuscripts.[2] But in the afterglow of Dr. Mordek's work and in anticipation of Professor Bischoff's, this paper will attempt to do for early ninth-century Salzburg what Professors Autenrieth and Kottje have recently done for several centers of early medieval canon law activity encircling the Lake of Constance.[3] That is, in a general fashion this paper will describe the canon law production of one of the key Carolingian ecclesiastical centers as reflected in the extant codices originating there.

In his examination of Austrian manuscripts in the *Codices latini antiquiores*, E. A. Lowe emphasized that with the exception of Verona, St. Gall, and a few German cities, Salzburg, at least until the early nineteenth century, surpassed almost every other ancient center for the volume of late eighth- and early ninth-century codices preserved on the spot.[4] And a perusal of these manuscripts which Lowe described, as well as those studied by Holter, Forstner, Unterkircher, and others, shows Salzburg to

---

* In the preparation and presentation of this paper I am indebted to Carleton University for financial assistance and to the Hill Monastic Manuscript Library for microfilm facilities.

[1] H. Mordek, *Kirchenrecht und Reform im Frankenreich: Die Collectio Vetus Gallica, die älteste systematische Kanonessammlung des fränkischen Gallien: Studien und Edition* (Beiträge zur Geschichte und Quellenkunde des Mittelalters, ed. H. Fuhrmann 1; Berlin-New York 1975).

[2] See B. Bischoff, 'Le projet de catalogue paléographique des manuscrits latins du neuvième siècle', *Archives, Bibliothèques et Musées de Belgique* 30 (1959) 223-7; *Die südostdeutschen Schreibschulen und Bibliotheken in der Karolingerzeit, I Die bayrischen Diözesen* (2nd ed. Wiesbaden 1960) 180; and Lowe, *Codices Latini antiquiores* (CLA) X, p. xiv.

[3] J. Autenrieth and R. Kottje, *Kirchenrechtliche Texte im Bodenseegebiet* (Vorträge und Forschungen, Sonderb. 18; Sigmaringen 1975).

[4] CLA X, p. viii.

have been an unusually productive center in the copying and creation of canon law texts.[5] But just as impressive as the volume of canon law texts are their types and their relationship to contemporary collections elsewhere in Europe and to clerics and scholars whose keen interest in canon law is so obvious in the manuscripts.

That the supply of canon law manuscripts is as copious as it is for our period may be surprising since there is only one codex whatsoever of indisputably Salzburg origin from the time prior to the very late eighth century.[6] It is only with Arno's episcopacy that there is an outpouring of manuscripts sufficient to gauge the level of canonistic activity in Salzburg.

Before looking at the canon law collections from the time of Arno and his immediate successors, Adalram and Liuphram, a few of the prominent features of the careers of these first archbishops of Salzburg should be rehearsed to set the canon law manuscripts in their historical context.[7]

---

[5] W. Neumüller and K. Holter, *Der Codex Millenarius*, I: *Der Codex Millenarius als Denkmal einer bayrische-österreichischen Vulgata-Rezension*; II: *Der Codex Millenarius im Rahmen der Mondseer und Salzburger Buchmalerei* (Forschungen zur Geschichte Oberösterreichs 6; Linz 1959); K. Forstner, *Die karolingischen Handschriften und Fragmente in den Salzburger Bibliotheken (Ende des 8. Jh. bis Ende des 9. Jh.)* (Mitteilungen der Gesellschaft für Salzburger Landeskunde, 3. Ergänzungsband; Salzburg 1962); F. Unterkircher, *Inventar der illuminierten Handschriften, Inkunabeln und Frühdrucke der Österreichischen Nationalbibliothek*, I: *Die abendländischen Handschriften* (Museion, N.F. II, Bd. 2 Teil 1; Vienna 1957) 281; *Die datierten Handschriften der Österreichischen Nationalbibliothek bis zum Jahre 1400* (Katalog der datierten Handschriften in lateinischer Schrift in Österreich 1.1; Vienna-Cologne-Graz 1969); K. Foltz, *Geschichte der Salzburger Bibliotheken* (Vienna 1877); P. Lehmann, *Mitteilungen aus Handschriften VI*, '1. Handschriften deutscher Herkunft in Budapest' (Sb. Akad. Munich 1939, 4; Munich 1939) 3-17; A. Siegmund, *Die Überlieferung der griechischen christlichen Literatur in der lateinischen Kirche bis zum zwölften Jahrhundert* (Abh. der bayer. Benediktiner-Akad. 5; Munich-Pasing 1949) 305; *Mittelalterliche Bibliothekskataloge Österreichs*, IV: *Salzburg*, ed. Österreich. Akad. der Wissensch., bearb. G. Möser-Mersky und M. Mihaliuk (Graz-Vienna-Cologne 1966); and B. Lambert, *Bibliotheca Hieronymiana manuscripta: La tradition manuscrite des oeuvres de Saint Jérôme*, 4B (Instrumenta Patristica 4; Steenbrugge 1972) 211.

[6] On the *Liber confraternitatum* see CLA X, pp. viii-x, and pl. I(a); and *Verbrüderungsbuch von St. Peter in Salzburg (Archiv von St. Peter in Salzburg, Hs. A 1)*, comm. K. Forstner and intro. K. Hermann (Codices selecti 51; Graz 1974).

[7] The dark and confused period in the Salzburg area between Roman occupation and Virgilian times is now being illuminated in the studies by H. Baltl, 'Zur Datierungsfrage des hl. Rupert', ZRG Kan. Abt. 61 (1975) 1-16; 'Das frühe Christentum in Karantanien und der heilige Amandus', *Zeitschrift des historischen Vereins für Steiermark* 66 (1975) 41-63; and 'Zur karantanischen Geschichte des 6.-9. Jahrhunderts',

Arno, a Bavarian, was educated and ordained in Freising during the period in which the Irishman Virgil administered Salzburg.[8] After moving from Bavaria to northern France and spending a few years as a monk at St. Amand, Arno was made its abbot by Charlemagne and thereafter enjoyed in the court circle the friendship of figures such as Alcuin. In 785 Charlemagne appointed his friend Arno as bishop of Salzburg, thus forging the link so clearly seen in the canon law manuscripts between Salzburg and St. Amand. As bishop and then archbishop of Salzburg after it was raised to metropolitical dignity in 798, Arno pursued several goals: to missionarize lands recently recovered from the Avars, to rejuvenate the spiritual life of his own clergy, and later to extend his jurisdiction into lands formerly under the domination of Aquileia. For the conversion of the peoples to the East and for the instruction of his own clerics Arno took part in a series of synods.[9] Moreover, he wrote catechetical and pastoral tracts in which he ordered that schools were to be established with masters who would teach according to the Roman tradition.[10] Clerics, scholars, and manuscripts were imported into and exchanged with the great monasteries, such as Tours and St. Amand,

---

in *Festschrift Nikolaus Grass zum 60. Geburtstag dargebracht von Fachgenossen, Freunden und Schülern*, edd. L. Carlen and F. Steinegger 1 (Innsbruck-Munich 1974) 407-23.

[8] See B. Bischoff, *Salzburger Formelbücher und Briefe aus Tassilonischer und Karolingischer Zeit* (Sb. Akad. Munich 1973, 4; Munich 1973) 19f. On the career of Arno see G. Demmelbauer, *Arno, der erste Erzbischof von Salzburg* (diss. Vienna 1950).

[9] E.g., *Conventus episcoporum ad ripas Danubii* (796), MGH Conc. 2.172-6; and Alcuin Ep. 107, MGH Epp. 4.153-4; *Concilium Rispacense* (800), MGH Conc. 2.205-19; *Concilium Salisburgense* (807), MGH Conc. 2.234.

[10] See especially the *Instructio pastoralis*, c.4; 'Et hoc consideret episcopus, ut ipsi presbyteri non sint idiothae, sed sacras scripturas legant et intellegant, ut secundum traditionem Romane aecclesiae possint instruere et fidem catholicam debeant ipsi agere et populos sibi commissos docere, missas secundum consuetudinem caelebrare, sicut Romana traditio nobis tradidit. Baptismum publicum constitutis temporibus per II vices in anno faciat, in Pascha, in Pentecosten: et hoc secundum ordinem traditionis Romanae debet facere'; and c.8: 'Episcopus autem unusquisque in civitate sua scolam constituat et sapientem doctorem, qui secundum traditionem Romanorum possit instruere et lectionibus vacare et inde debitum discere,...', MGH Conc. 2.198f. For the segment of the *Instructio pastoralis* lacking in the edition of the MGH p. 200, see A. Werminghoff, 'Zu den bayrischen Synoden am Ausgang des achten Jahrhunderts', *Festschrift Heinrich Brunner zum siebzigsten Geburtstag dargebracht von Schülern und Verehrern* (Weimar 1910) 51f., n. 5, on the basis of Munich MS lat. (Clm) 28135.

connected with Arno through ties established early in his career.[11] For the use of his own clerics Arno saw to it that manuscripts were reproduced by the score, and according to the Salzburg Necrology he was personally responsible for the production of over 150.[12]

Arno's archiepiscopal successors Adalram (821-36) and Liuphram (836-59) continued the policies of their illustrious predecessor,[13] but more and more their ties with secular government were with the nearby court of Lewis the German.[14] In fact, Liuphram was a chaplain in the court of Lewis before becoming archbishop of Salzburg.[15] Throughout the careers of both Adalram and Liuphram the Salzburg scriptoria continued to produce a flood of manuscripts, some of which made their way to the court of Lewis the German, whose letters of gratitude are still extant.[16] Further, it was during the careers of Adalram and Liuphram that the *scholasticus* Baldo—the *clarus magister* celebrated in poems by both Lewis and Dungal—was active.[17]

Having briefly sketched some of the historical context, let us now turn to the manuscripts themselves of canon law collections, fragments, and para-canonical texts and consider them within four time frames roughly corresponding to the early Arnonian period, which extends back into

---

[11] See H. Widmann, *Geschichte Salzburgs* I (Gotha 1907) 110; and J. Wodka, *Kirche in Österreich: Wegweiser durch ihre Geschichte* (Vienna 1959) 41; and LThK 1.682.

[12] MGH Necrol. Germ. 2.98; Widmann, *Geschichte* I.110; Wodka, *Kirche in Österreich* 41; and CLA X, p. ix.

[13] See Widmann, *Geschichte* 1.129, for Adalram's missionary projects, and W. Wattenbach, *Deutschlands Geschichtsquellen im Mittelalter bis zur Mitte des dreizehnten Jahrhunderts* I (Stuttgart-Berlin 1904) 292, for Liuphram's concern to maintain and expand the library at Salzburg.

[14] See Widmann, *Geschichte* 1.113, 128, who stresses the loosening of ties between Arno and Charlemagne's successor, Louis the Pious.

[15] J. Fleckenstein, *Die Hofkapelle der deutschen Könige, I. Grundlegung, Die karolingische Hofkapelle* (MGH Schriften 16/1; Stuttgart 1959) 179f., 183f.

[16] MGH Poetae 2.643; Foltz, *Geschichte* 10-15; Widmann, *Geschichte* 1.197; J. Thompson, *The literacy of the laity in the Middle Ages* (repr. New York 1960) 31f.

[17] B. Bischoff, 'Paläographische Fragen deutscher Denkmäler der Karolingerzeit', *Frühmittelalterliche Studien* 5 (1972) 126. On Baldo see Foltz, *Geschichte* 15; W. Levison, 'Die älteste Lebensbeschreibung Ruperts von Salzburg', NA 28 (1902-3) 292-4; Wattenbach, *Deutschlands Geschichtsquellen* 1.292; Bénédictins du Bouveret, *Colophons de manuscrits occidentaux des origines au XVIe siècle, I: Colophons signés A-D* (Spicilegii Friburgensis Subsidia 2; Fribourg/S. 1965) 195, nos. 1571-3; and Bischoff, *Salzburger Formelbücher* 11. See addition below, n. 124.

the very late eighth century, the later Arnonian period of the first quarter of the ninth century, and the eras of Adalram and Liuphram.

Early Arnonian period

The largest number of our extant Salzburg manuscripts and manuscript fragments of canon law dates from the early Arnonian period. From the volume of manuscripts and fragments it appears that Arno very early determined to build up as rapidly as possible the canonical resources which were probably in short supply during the time of his predecessors, the Anglo-Saxon John and the Irishman Virgil. In the abundance of canon law manuscripts produced during this early Arnonian period, one would expect to find vestiges of the Insular presence in Salzburg, and indeed these do appear, but they are joined by newer influences from Freising and St. Amand, areas connected with Arno's early career.

Two penitential manuscripts have survived from the early Arnonian period. One of them, Vienna, Nationalbibliothek MS 2233,[18] contains two penitential collections, one purely Irish, the *Penitentiale Vinniani*, and the other continental, the *Excarpsus Cummeani*. For the *Penitentiale Vinniani* this Vienna manuscript holds pride of place as being the oldest exemplar of the earliest Irish penitential.[19] The importance of this same manuscript for the text of the *Excarpsus Cummeani* [20] will undoubtedly be clarified in Dr. Asbach's new edition,[21] but it can be emphasized here that the *Excarpsus* and a fragment of the *Excarpsus* are in codices of virtually the same age from Freising and St. Amand which are directly connected with Salzburg. The Freising manuscript, Munich, Staatsbibliothek lat. (Clm) 6243, which originated in Alemannia, contains the First Collection of Freising whose presence at Salzburg will be discussed in a

---

[18] On this MS see CLA X, p. xi, and no. 1509, and Suppl. p. 66; and Mordek, *Kirchenrecht* 198, n. 512. On the use of the penitentials in the *Concilium Baiuwaricum* (MGH Conc. 2.51-3), see J. Heer, *Ein karolingischer Missions-Katechismus* (Biblische und Patristische Forschungen 1; Freiburg/Br. 1911) 70f.

[19] Fols. 25v-58v. See *The Irish penitentials*, ed. L. Bieler with append. by D. Binchy (Scriptores latini Hiberniae 5; Dublin 1963) 17. The St. Gall MS of the *Penitentiale Vinniani*, MS 150, dates to s. 2/4 IX, on which see R. Kottje, 'Kirchenrechtliche Interessen im Bodenseeraum vom 9. bis 12. Jahrhundert', in Autenrieth-Kottje, *Kirchenrechtliche Texte* 32.

[20] Fols. 1r-25v. On the use of the *Excarpsus* in the Bavarian mission catechism, see Heer, *Missions-Katechismus* 45, 78.

[21] See Kottje, 'Kirchenrechtliche Interessen' 33, n. 42; and Mordek, *Kirchenrecht* 198, n. 512.

moment;[22] and the St. Amand manuscript, Paris, B.N. MS lat. 2296 was copied by two scribes, one of whom wrote the so-called *Arno Sacramentary* in Salzburg.[23]

The second early Arnonian penitential manuscript, Vienna 2195, bears further evidence to the Insular presence in Salzburg.[24] The penitential is that of the 'Discipulus Umbrensium',[25] and the manuscript fairly bristles with Insular abbreviation signs.[26] In this manuscript we meet for the first time the later marginalia and textual additions of the ninth-century master Baldo [27] as well as a brief series of para-canonical sentences on the daily reception of the Eucharist attributed to Cyprian, Ambrose, and Hilary which were to be sprinkled through later manuscripts written in Salzburg or under the influence of Salzburg collections.[28]

Certainly the best-known canonical collection from the early Arnonian period is the Collection of Diessen, Clm 5508.[29] It is unnecessary to dwell extensively on the contents of this manuscript,[30] but it is appropriate

---

[22] Fols. 217r-29r, on which see J. McNeill and H. Gamer, *Medieval Handbooks of Penance* (Columbia University Records of Civilization 29; New York 1938) 446. On this MS see CLA IX. no. 1255, and Suppl. p. 63; Kottje, 'Kirchenrechtliche Interessen' 40; and Mordek, *Kirchenrecht* 618-33, 672 (Index).

[23] Fols. 1r-2v. On this MS see CLA V no. 544, and Suppl. p. 53; C. Vogel, *Introduction aux sources de l'histoire du culte chrétien au moyen âge* (Spoleto 1975) 58, n. 185; *Sacramentarium Arnonis: Die Fragmente des Salzburger Exemplars*, edd. S. Rehle and K. Gamber (Textus patristici et liturgici 8; Regensburg 1970) 10, 23; and B. Moreton, *The Eighth-Century Gelasian Sacramentary: A Study in Tradition* (Oxford Theological Monographs; Oxford 1976) 196-8.

[24] On this MS see CLA X no. 1508; Holter, *Der Codex Millenarius* 163; *Mittelalterliche Bibliothekskataloge* 39; and Mordek, *Kirchenrecht* 235.

[25] Fols. 2v-24v.

[26] Esp. fols. 46v-57r, on which see P. Finsterwalder, *Die canones Theodori Cantuariensis und ihre Überlieferungsformen* (Untersuchungen zu den Bussbüchern des. 7., 8. und 9. Jahrhunderts 1; Weimar 1929) 94.

[27] On the additions of Baldo see CLA X no. 1508.

[28] Fol. 52r. These texts are also found in the later Salzburg MS Vienna 1322, fol. 64r-v; the Reginensis MS of the Coll IIL, Vatican MS Reg. lat. 407, fol. 60r; and the Palatinus containing fragments of the Coll IIL, Vatican MS Pal. lat. 973, fol. 42r. On the question of frequency of communion in Arno's time see P. Browe, *Die häufige Kommunion im Mittelalter* (Münster/W. 1938) 17; *De frequenti communione in ecclesia occidentali usque ad annum c.1000* (Textus et Documenta, Series Theologica 5; Rome 1932) 71, doc. 107. See addition below, n. 124.

[29] On this MS see CLA IX no. 1247, and Suppl. p. 63; and Mordek, *Kirchenrecht* 9, 66, n. 17.

[30] This MS was written perhaps shortly before 798; see Forstner, *Die karolingischen Handschriften* 19.

to stress several extraordinary features of the manuscript itself as they touch contemporary and later canon law texts and scholars in Salzburg. Unlike our early penitential manuscripts with their Insular vestiges, Clm 5508 is heavy with the influence of Freising and St. Amand. Common to both the manuscript of the Collection of Diessen and the Alemannic, then Freising manuscript mentioned a moment ago, Clm 6243, are canons from the First Collection of Freising,[31] the *Decretum Gelasianum*,[32] and the para-canonical *De vii ordinibus ecclesiae* attributed to St. Jerome.[33] Moreover, Professor Munier has illustrated the ties between the collection and St. Amand, or northern France, with his observation that in the text of the *Statuta ecclesiae antiqua* the variants of the Collection of Diessen and the Collection of the MS of St. Amand are remarkably similar.[34]

As it is related to canonistic activity slightly later in early ninth-century Salzburg, the manuscript of the Collection of Diessen is of special significance. First, there are unusual readings of the canons of the Council of Paris of 614 [35] and the Council of Agde,[36] and these were later to turn

---

[31] See Mordek, *Kirchenrecht* 9, n. 32.

[32] See E. von Dobschütz, *Das Decretum Gelasianum de libris recipiendis et non recipiendis in kritischem Text* (Texte und Untersuchungen zur Geschichte der altchristlichen Literatur 38.4; Leipzig 1912) 146, who notes that the text of the *Decretum Gelasianum* in Clm 5508 is clearly related to the text in Clm 6243 either directly or through an intermediate MS.

[33] Fol. 94ar, beginning with the words 'nostris iustificabimur' (*Pseudo-Hieronymi De septem ordinibus ecclesiae*, ed. A. Kalff [Würzburg 1935] 60, line 8). On the appearance of the *De vii ordinibus ecclesiae* in this MS see F. Maassen, *Geschichte der Quellen* 629; and J. Lechner, 'Der Schlusssegen des Priesters', *Festschrift für E. Eichmann* (Paderborn 1940) 670. On the appearance of the *De vii ordinibus ecclesiae* in Clm 6243, fol. 200r, see R. Reynolds, *The Ordinals of Christ from their origins to the twelfth century* (Beiträge zur Geschichte und Quellenkunde des Mittelalters, ed. H. Fuhrmann, 7; Berlin-New York 1978) 32, nn. 24, 26.

[34] *Les Statuta ecclesiae antiqua: Édition-Études critiques*, ed. C. Munier (Paris 1960) 61.

[35] Fol. 104r. Cc. 4 and 6 of this council are found in only one earlier collection, the Collection of Reims, Berlin, Deutsche Staatsbibliothek MS Phill. 1743. In Clm 5508 the number of c.4 is not as clear as it might be, and this obscurity is perhaps reflected in the Coll IIL, where there is neither council nor number assigned the canon. As for c.6, only Clm 5508 and the Coll IIL assign it this number, whereas in Berlin 1743, so Dr. Teitge has kindly written me, the canon bears the number 5. Sometime later c.6 of the Parisian council was used in the Collection of Paris BN Lat. 4278, c.131 (fol. 148r), on which see J. Rambaud-Buhot, 'Une collection canonique de la réforme carolingienne (ms lat. de la Bibliothèque nationale n° 4278, ff. 128-167)', RHD 34 (1956) 66.

[36] The canons of the Council of Agde (506), cc. 10ff., are under the rubric *Di-*

up in the Collection in Two Books [hereafter Coll IIL], a collection very probably originating in Salzburg, to be mentioned shortly. Further, under the name of Pope Gelasius there is a fragment of Arno's *Pastoral Instruction*,[37] which was later to be included in a Freising manuscript [38] and in the *Mondsee Pastorale*.[39] And finally, throughout the manuscript of the Collection of Diessen there are numerous marginalia by master Baldo next to many canons later incorporated into the Coll IIL.[40]

The last of the complete manuscripts with canon law collections from the early Arnonian period is Maassen's Collection of the Time of Sergius I.[41] Both textually and paleographically the codex, Vienna 418, is redolent of St. Amand influence.[42] One of the scribes wrote in a pure St. Amand style, and the same collection appears in another manuscript originating in St. Amand, Vatican MS Reg. lat. 1040.[43]

Among the canonical fragments from the early Arnonian period is one fragmentary manuscript and two patristic manuscripts supplemented with isolated canonical texts. It is not certain that the manuscript fragment, Clm 29085(b),[44] containing snippets from the Council of Verneuil (755), was originally part of a larger canon law codex, but the earliest complete codices with this conciliar text are canon law manuscripts, our Alemannic, then Freising manuscript, Clm 6243,[45] and a western German

---

lectissimo fratri Exsuperio Innocentius in Clm 5508, fol. 96v, and when c.20 was used in the Coll IIL the attribution of the synod was to Innocent not Agde. There is a marginal cross next to c.20 in Clm 5508, fol. 98r.

[37] Fol. 73v. Cf. MGH Conc. 2.198, lines 1-15.

[38] Clm 28135 (Freising), on which see Werminghoff, 'Zu den bayrischen Synoden', 52, n. 5; and Bischoff, *Schreibschulen* 93f.

[39] Vienna 1370, fol. 53v, on which see below, p. 26.

[40] Professor Bischoff kindly noted for me the numerous instances in which Baldo wrote the abbreviation 'dīm' next to the canons of the *Statuta ecclesiae antiqua* and crosses next to the canons of the Councils of Paris and Agde, fols. 98r, 104r.

[41] Maassen, *Geschichte* 760f. On this MS see CLA X no. 1478; and *Mittelalterliche Bibliothekskataloge* 50.

[42] Holter, *Der Codex Millenarius* 152.

[43] On this St. Amand MS (s. VIII/IX) which was corrected in Rome see CLA I no. 112, and Suppl. p. 45.

[44] On this MS fragment, which Lowe dated slightly later than Clm 5508, see CLA IX no. 1247; and Forstner, *Die karolingischen Handschriften* 19. The texts of cc. 1-6, 7, 9, 10, 12-14, 18-22 are now on small strips of parchment formerly bound into Clm 5675.

[45] Fol. 229v.

manuscript, Vatican MS Pal. lat. 577, which also has texts found in early ninth-century Salzburg manuscripts.[46] The two patristic manuscripts to which isolated canonical texts have been added are Clm 208 [47] and Salzburg, St. Peter Stiftsbibliothek MS a.IX.27,[48] both written in St. Amand style and both corrected by Baldo. The former manuscript, containing the works of Cyprian, is rounded off by the *Decretum Gelasianum*,[49] and the latter manuscript, with the Ps.-Clementine *Recognitiones*, is supplemented by two apocryphal letters of Clement to James,[50] one of which is also in the Collection of Diessen.[51]

To describe extensively the early Arnonian manuscripts with para-canonical texts—that is, patristic and early medieval texts which would be incorporated into canon law collections throughout the Middle Ages—would perhaps carry us too far beyond the confines of our topic. But two miscellaneous manuscripts should be singled out because they include one of the most frequently repeated para-canonical texts in medieval

---

[46] On this MS see CLA I no. 97, and Suppl. p. 44; Bischoff, 'Paläographische Fragen' 109; and Mordek, *Kirchenrecht* 242, 254. This MS, fol. 11-v, contains the tract with the incipit 'De eo quod laicis...', which appears in various forms in the Coll IIL (see below, p. 28), Vatican MS lat. 7222, and in the other MSS listed in my 'The Pseudo-Augustinian *Sermo de conscientia* and the related canonical *Dicta sancti Gregorii papae*', RB 81 (1971) 313. To be added to those MSS are Würzburg, Universitätsbibliothek MS M.p.th.q. 31, fols. 52r and 57v (on which MS see CLA IX no. 1439, and Suppl. p. 65; B. Bischoffan d J. Hofmann, *Libri sancti Kyliani: Die Würzburger Schreibschule und die Dombibliothek im VIII. und IX. Jahrhundert* [Quellen und Forschungen zur Geschichte des Bistums und Hochstifts Würzburg 6, ed. T. Kramer: Würzburg 1952] 108f.; and Mordek, *Kirchenrecht* 242, 254), Vatican MS Reg. lat. 1021, fol. 214r (a St. Amand MS, on which see below, p. 515), and Vat. lat. 4160, fols. 55r-56r, on which MS see *Diuersorum patrum sententie siue Collectio in LXXIV titulos digesta*, ed. J. Gilchrist (MIC, Ser. B, Corp. Coll. 1; Vatican City 1973) xlixf., and Mordek, *Kirchenrecht* 7, n. 18, and p. 258.

[47] On this MS see CLA IX no. 1237; X, p. xii; Holter, *Der Codex Millenarius* 153; and Lehmann, *Mitteilungen* 12. On the entries by Baldo see CLA IX no. 1237.

[48] On this MS see Forstner, *Die karolingischen Handschriften* 44f.

[49] Fols. 254v-57v, on which see v. Dobschütz, *Das Decretum Gelasianum* 145, who points out that the text of the MS is like that of Troyes, Bibl. de la Ville MS 581, a St. Amand MS, on which see CLA VI no. 839, and *Sacra mentarium Arnonis* 25.

[50] Pp. 217-30 (continued on p. 231 in hand of s. XII).

[51] Maassen, *Geschichte* 410f., who also notes that the text is in Vatican MS Pal. lat. 577.

[52] On this MS see CLA IX no. 1313, and Suppl. p. 64; and C. Lawson, 'Notes on the *De ecclesiasticis officiis*', *Isidoriana: Estudios sobre San Isidoro de Sevilla en el XIV centenario de su nacimiento*, ed. M. Díaz y Díaz (León 1961) 300.

canon law collections. The two manuscripts, Clm 16128 [52] and Vienna 808,[53] bear, among other para-canonical material, the *De ecclesiasticis officiis* of Isidore of Seville in a recension later to be used in the Coll IIL.[54]

Later Arnonian period

In the many early Arnonian manuscripts we have found that the practical collections of penitentials and texts instructing clerics on their status and obligations were plentiful. During the later Arnonian period, canonical manuscripts are almost as copious as they were in the early period, but the type of collection changes. First, more theoretically-oriented collections appear, and secondly, the desire of Arno to have his clerics trained according to the Roman tradition is seen in the copying and reworking of the *Collectio Dionysio-Hadriana* in Salzburg and the immediate vicinity.

From the later Arnonian period there are several codices with the *Dionysio-Hadriana* or reworked versions thereof. Of these manuscripts two were written in the near vicinity of Salzburg, Clm 29083(m) and Salzburg, Carolino-Augusteum Museum MS 2163. The Munich manuscript is, unfortunately, only a fragment of what was probably the *Dionysio-Hadriana*,[55] and the Salzburg manuscript contains only substantially

---

[53] On this MS see Holter, *Der Codex Millenarius* 165; Forstner, *Die karolingischen Handschriften* 20; and Unterkircher *Inventar* 210 (who dates the MS to 802-804). Also in this MS, fols. 98r-100v, is a well-known text on the quatember days, *De observatione iiii temporum*, which also appears frequently in Salzburg MSS, including Clm 18524b and 14766 (from which the text was edited by G. Morin, 'Notes liturgiques: Un opuscule de l'époque carolingienne sur la raison d'être de Quatre-Temps', RB 30 [1913] 231-4), and MSS related to Salzburg, including Vatican Reg. lat. 407, fols. 70r-71v, and Vat. Pal. lat. 973, fols. 123v-25r. On the quatember days in Bavaria see the *Concilium Baiuwaricum*, c.10 (MGH Conc. 2.53); Heer, *Missions-Katechismus* 72; and L. Fischer, *Die kirchlichen Quatember: Ihre Entstehung, Entwicklung und Bedeutung in liturgischer, rechtlicher und kulturhistorischer Hinsicht* (Veröffentlichungen aus dem Kirchenhistorischen Seminar München, ed. A. Knöpfler, 4.3; Munich 1914) 150.

[54] The recension of the *De ecclesiasticis officiis* in Vienna 808, so C. Lawson kindly tells me, is like that of Clm 14766 and 18524b (on which see below, p. 29). In Vienna 808, fol. 41r, the acolyte is not described among the ecclesiastical grades, on which see my 'Excerpta from the Collectio Hibernensis in three Vatican manuscripts', BMCL 5 (1975) 8.

[55] On this fragment with canons from the councils of Ancyra and Nicea (PL 56.152A-153B), see Mordek, *Kirchenrecht* 247. After the explicit for the canons of Nicea there are no episcopal subscriptions like those in Vatican MS lat. 7222.

reworked extracts from the *Dionysio-Hadriana*.[56] But there is one almost complete manuscript of the *Dionysio-Hadriana*, Vatican MS lat. 7222,[57] which in its text and marginalia is closely related to the contemporary St. Amand codex of the *Dionysio-Hadriana*, Vatican MS Reg. lat. 1021.[58] Both manuscripts derived from a common intermediary (intermediaries?) defective in many passages. An investigation of the subsequent correction of the intermediary and its dependent St. Amand and Salzburg manuscripts would make for a fascinating study of the circulation of texts between northern France and Bavaria, but here it is necessary to stress only that of the hundreds of corrections, marginalia, and added texts in the Salzburg codex, the great majority is in the hand of master Baldo.[59]

There is one collection of canon law in a manuscript from the later Arnonian period which Friedrich Maassen specifically designated as the Collection of Salzburg.[60] The manuscript, Vienna 489,[61] contains the *Acta* of the Council of Ephesus and was based on an Insular model as can be seen in the abbreviation symbols, one of which was expanded in the multiple corrections, some by master Baldo.[62] In Maassen's description of this collection it is observed that the Collection of Salzburg depends almost entirely on the Collections in Manuscripts of Tours and Verona,[63] both centers whose scriptoria were in contact with the Salzburg archdiocese.[64] One would expect to find collections with such highly theological

---

[56] Fols. 25r-49r. On this MS see K. Forstner, 'Schriftfragmente des 8. und früheren 9. Jahrhunderts in Salzburger Bibliotheken', *Scriptorium* 14 (1960) 251-3; *Die karolingischen Handschr.* 28-30; Mordek, *Kirchenrecht* 248. Addition below, n. 124.

[57] On this MS see my 'The Pseudo-Augustinian *Sermo de conscientia*' 313; and Mordek, *Kirchenrecht* 246.

[58] On this MS see CLA X, pp. xvf., and pl. II.

[59] Between the Salzburg and St. Amand MSS, both of which are heavily annotated, there was very probably a common model. In the Salzburg MS there are some corrections which antedate Baldo, but Baldo himself made marginal corrections perhaps on the basis of the model and also added many of his own invention.

[60] Maassen, *Geschichte* 732.

[61] On this MS see Holter, *Der Codex Millenarius* 152, n. 4; and Mordek, *Kirchenrecht* 43, n. 32.

[62] Fol. 108r. The Insular abbreviation sign for *autem* has been expanded to 'aūt' in the margin.

[63] Maassen, *Geschichte* 732. On the ancient MS of the Collection of the MS of Tours, Paris, B.N. MS lat. 1572, see CLA V no. 530, and Suppl. p. 53. The Verona collection is in Verona, Bibl. cap. MS LVII (55), a later MS.

[64] See L. Jones, 'Two Salzburg Manuscripts and the Influence of Tours', *Speculum* 10 (1935) 288-91. It is well known that some of the best codices of Alcuin's

or Christological orientation in the ancient and well-established centers of Tours and Verona, but the appearance of such a collection in a missionary outpost like Salzburg is somewhat unexpected. Perhaps its Christological portions were of special interest in a region formerly dominated and still in competition with Aquileia, once in schism with Rome in the Three Chapters Controversy.[65] Or perhaps the collection might have supplied ammunition for the battles over the *filioque*. In fact, one of the marginal notations stresses that the Holy Spirit proceeds from the Son as well as the Father.[66] But whatever the reason for its appearance in Salzburg, the well-annotated Collection of Salzburg is evidence for a relatively high degree of theological sophistication in a see often remembered more for its Irish commentaries and arcane texts on antipodes [67] than for its scholars wrestling with the heavy theological issues of Christendom.

Before moving on to the manuscripts from the period of archbishop Adalram, fleeting reference should be made to two early ninth-century codices with canonical fragments, one originating in Mondsee near Salzburg which almost breathes the spirit of Arno's missionary and pastoral concern, and the other from Salzburg which represents Arno's attempts to regulate his clerics and monks. The Mondsee manuscript, Vienna 1370,[68] includes the Creed and canons of Nicea drawn from the *Dionysio-Hadriana* [69] as well as the book on matrimony from the *Collectio Hibernensis* studied

---

works are in Salzburg hands; e.g., Vienna 795, written in Salzburg-St. Amand style, on which see CLA X no. 1490. On the connections between Verona and the Salzburg area see Holter, *Der Codex Millenarius* 182.

[65] On the boundary disputes between Salzburg and Aquileia see Widmann, *Geschichte* 1.109f.; Wodka, *Kirche in Österreich* 41; and G. Schnorr, 'Einfluss und Schicksal des Patriarchates Aquileja im oberen Drautal während des Mittelalters in Beitrag zur Entstehung der Urpfarren Berg und Irschen im Drautal (mit einer Karte)', *Festschrift Nikolaus Grass* 425-47. On the Three Chapters Controversy see R. Schieffer, 'Zur Beurteilung des norditalischen Dreikapitel-Schismas: Eine überlieferungsgeschichtliche Studie', ZKG 87 (1976) 167-201.

[66] Fol. 142r: *in marg.* 'Spm scm a filio procedere sicut a patre'.

[67] See, e.g., H. Löwe, *Ein literarischer Widersacher des Bonifatius: Virgil von Salzburg und die Kosmographie des Aethicus Ister* (Akad. der Wissensch., Mainz, Abh. der Geistes-u. Sozialwissensch. Kl., 1951, 11; Wiesbaden 1951); and *Scriptores Hiberniae minores*, ed. J. Kelly, CCL 108C.

[68] On this MS see Heer, *Missions-Katechismus* 10; Bischoff, *Libri sancti Kyliani* 145; Bischoff, *Schreibschulen* 180; and K. Gamber, *Codices liturgici latini antiquiores* (Spicilegii Friburgensis Subsidia 1; Fribourg/S. 1967) 574, n. 2.

[69] Fol. 71v.

by Dr. Mordek.[70] Arno himself is directly represented by two pieces, a full text of his *Pastoral Instruction*,[71] a fragment of which was noted in the Collection of Diessen, and by his *De catechizandis rudibus*,[72] a manuscript of which is listed in the tenth century as having been given to the Cathedral of Salzburg.[73]

In the Salzburg manuscript, now Wolfenbüttel, Herzogl.-Aug. Bibl. MS 579 (Helmst. 532),[74] there are large numbers of secular legal texts, writings by and to Alcuin, and *excerpta* from the Latin fathers. Intruded into this material is a quaternion containing a letter from Louis the Pious to Arno regarding the Council of Aachen (817), *capitula* from the same council,[75] excerpts from Isidore on the Symbol into which a description of the episcopal grades is inserted,[76] and a folio with a miscellany of canons under the rubric *In canone Aurelianensi*. The first canon is found only in the Coll IIL and the related Collection of Laon, and it was later used in the Council of Worms (868).[77] The other canons include an unusual recension of IV Orléans (541), c.20, also found in the Coll IIL.[78]

---

[70] Fol. 90r. On the MSS containing this book, including Vienna 424, fols. 7r-9v, see Mordek, *Kirchenrecht* 259.

[71] Fol. 53v.

[72] Fol. 1v. On the authorship of this tract see A. Burn, 'Neue Texte zur Geschichte des apostolischen Symbols', ZKG 25 (1904) 145-57; Gamber, CLLA 574; and E. Dahlhaus-Berg, *Nova antiquitas et antiqua novitas*: *Typologische Exegese und isidorianisches Geschichtsbild bei Theodulf von Orléans* (Cologne-Vienna 1975) 102, 253.

[73] Foltz, *Geschichte* 28; and *Mittelalterliche Bibliothekskataloge* 18.

[74] On this MS see C. Beeson, *Isidor-Studien* (Quellen und Untersuchungen zur lateinischen Philologie des Mittelalters 4.2; Munich 1913) 31, 33, 35, 77, 123, n. 1, 125; Siegmund, *Überlieferung* 109; and H. Rochais, 'Defensoriana', *Sacris erudiri* 9 (1957) 245.

[75] MGH Leges 1.201-4, 219-23.

[76] Fol. 91v; *excerpta* from the *Origines* 7.12.4-13 (PL 83.290f.). Later in the MS, fols. 112v-113r, there is a continuation of the definition of the clerical grades, and on fol. 135v there is an Ordinal of Christ, on which see my *Ordinals of Christ* 72, n. 13 (1).

[77] Fol. 93v. See P. Fournier, 'Notices sur trois collections canoniques inédites de l'époque carolingienne: II, La collection de Laon, III, La collection en deux livres', *Revue des sciences religieuses* 6 (1926) 221, 523. The text in the Wolfenbüttel MS is slightly different from those in the Coll. IIL or Laon MS 201, fol. 47v and Leningrad, Publ. Bibl. MS Q.v.II.5, fol. 10r, but it resembles more the Laon text in that it ends with '...sicut in Niceno canones antiqui patres instituerunt'. See addition below, n. 124.

[78] The text is concluded with a threat of excommunication until penance is done.

Adalram period

The volume of extant canon law collections from the period after Arno's death in 821 drops dramatically, but the number of manuscripts with isolated canon law texts and para-canonical material actually increases for this period of Adalram. In fact, if one can judge from the number of marginalia entered by hands of the second quarter of the ninth century into earlier codices of the Arnonian periods, Salzburg scholars seem to have been as keenly interested in canon law as those anywhere in the Carolingian Empire. Moreover, it is in the Adalram period that there was copied the earliest extant codex of the Coll IIL, Paris, B.N. nouv. acq. lat. 452.[79]

It is not absolutely certain that the Coll IIL was compiled in Salzburg, but the sources and textual peculiarities all strongly suggest that it was, and if the Coll IIL was indeed compiled there, it would be one of the few collections native to early ninth-century Salzburg to have enjoyed a reasonably wide geographical distribution from the ninth through the eleventh century. There are extant manuscripts, manuscript fragments, and extracts from the collection from Germany,[80] Switzerland,[81] Austria,[82] and France,[83] and they range in date from the Adalram codex to a nineteenth-century fragmentary copy of the same manuscript among Guglielmo Libri's papers in Paris.[84]

It is unnecessary here to dwell upon the details of the Coll IIL because it has been studied extensively by Paul Fournier.[85] But in this paper it is important to emphasize some of the ties which link the collection with Salzburg.

Book I of the collection, a book of instruction for clerics on theological and liturgical topics, is based on a variety of para-canonical sources, two

---

[79] On this MS see Mordek, *Kirchenrecht* 120.

[80] Vatican MS Pal. lat. 973, on which see B. Bischoff, *Lorsch im Spiegel seiner Handschriften* (Münchener Beiträge zur Mediävistik und Renaissance-Forschung, Beiheft; Munich 1974) 116; and Mordek, *Kirchenrecht* 121, n. 87, and p. 226, n. 56. Professor Bischoff has kindly informed me that the MS is to be dated to s. 2/2 IX, was written in northeastern France under Reims influence, and early travelled perhaps to Germany.

[81] Vatican MS Reg. lat. 407, on which see Mordek, *Kirchenrecht* 120.

[82] Paris, B.N. MS NAL 452.

[83] Basel, Universitätsbibliothek MS N.I.6, nr. 9, on which see Mordek, *Kirchenrecht* 121f., n. 87.

[84] Paris, B.N. nouv. acq. fr. 3264, fol. 72r.

[85] Fournier, 'Notices sur trois collections' 513-26.

of the primary ones being the *De ecclesiasticis officiis* of Isidore and the Ps.-Hieronymian *De vii ordinibus ecclesiae*. The recensions of these texts used in the collection are found in three other contemporary Salzburg codices, Clm 18524b (bearing Baldo's colophon),[86] Clm 14766 (with Baldo's marginalia),[87] and Salzburg, St. Peter Stiftsbibliothek MS a.VIII.32.[88] All three of these manuscripts are, incidentally, sprinkled with isolated canon law and para-canonical texts, such as the *Epistula formatarum*[89] and instructions on the observance of ember days.[90] The arrangement of topics in Book I of the Coll IIL into chapters on the Trinity, the clerical grades, the Mass, and so forth bears striking resemblance to the arrangement of many identical texts in the compendium of theological and liturgical texts of the early Arnonian manuscript, Vienna 1332,[91] annotated by Baldo, or the topics dealt with in the Alcuinian pedagogical tract, *Disputatio puerorum*, which is found in the Salzburg manuscripts Leningrad, Publichnaja Biblioteka MS O.v.I.7, and Vienna 458 with Baldo's colophon.[92]

Book II of the Coll IIL, containing canons from Gallican councils, is introduced with a preface stating that the canons are those missing in the Roman collection, probably a reference to the *Dionysio-Hadriana*.[93] In other words, Book II of the Coll IIL with its particular or local canons was probably intended to do for Bavaria what Dr. Mordek has pointed

---

[86] On this MS see Morin, 'Notes liturgiques' 232, n. 2; Lehmann, *Mitteilungen* 7; Kalff, *De septem ordinibus ecclesiae* 13f.; Lawson, 'Notes on the De ecclesiasticis officiis' 300; Bischoff, 'Paläographische Fragen' 126; and Mordek, *Kirchenrecht* 511.

[87] On this MS see Kalff, *De septem ordinibus ecclesiae* 13; Lawson, 'Notes on the De ecclesiasticis officiis' 300; and Mordek, *Kirchenrecht* 511.

[88] On this MS see Foltz, *Geschichte* 9; Kalff, *De septem ordinibus ecclesiae* 14f.; Forstner, *Die karolingischen Handschriften* 20, 40-2. Cf. Vienna 1051 with a copy of the material in this MS.

[89] Clm 18524b, fol. 203r-v, on which see Kalff, *De septem ordinibus ecclesiae* 13.

[90] See Morin, 'Notes liturgiques' 232, n. 2. Also see Vienna 808, Vatican MSS Reg. lat. 407, and Pal. lat. 973, referred to above, n.53.

[91] Fols. 2r-38v. On this MS see CLA X no. 1501, and Suppl. p. 66.

[92] See below, p. 32. Professor Bischoff, who kindly drew my attention to the Leningrad MS, dates it saec. IX[1]. Other early MSS with the *Disputatio puerorum* or fragments thereof are Vienna 966, 1370 (on which see above, p. 26), Clm 6385 (s. X, on which see N. Daniel, *Handschriften des zehnten Jahrhunderts aus der Freisinger Dombibliothek* [Münchener Beiträge zur Mediävistik und Renaissance-Forschung 11; Munich 1973] 158), 5257 (on which see my *Ordinals of Christ* 8of.), and University of Toronto MS 45, fols. 22/23 (brought to my attention by Mr. William Stoneman and dated by Professor Bischoff as s. 2/2IX [northern France]).

[93] Fournier, 'Notices sur trois collections' 518.

out the Collection of St. Amand seems to have done in northern France [94]—
that is, it acted as a balance or supplement to the universal *Dionysio-Hadriana*. This functional similarity between the Collection of St. Amand and the Coll IIL takes on added meaning when it is discovered that the great majority of canons in Book II of the Coll IIL is also found in the Collection of St. Amand.[95]

In Book II of the Coll IIL there are three major blocks of material, the *Statuta ecclesiae antiqua* (less the *Recapitulatio ordinationis officialium ecclesiae*), miscellaneous Gallican councils, and sections from the *Collectio Dacheriana*. How the block of texts from the *Dacheriana*, largely from its separable preface,[96] is related to the multiple manuscripts of that collection must await Dom Haenni's study,[97] but the other two blocks clearly are in the sphere of influence of the Collection of Diessen. Most, but not all, of the canons of the *Statuta ecclesiae antiqua* are the ones marked by Baldo in the Collection of Diessen, as are the unusual recensions of canons from the Council of Paris of 614 and the Council of Agde.[98]

Between Books I and II of the Coll IIL there is a brief intrusion of several texts which draws the collection sharply into the orbit of Salzburg. The ancient list of provinces and episcopal sees known as the *Notitia Galliarum* has been supplemented in its Germanic sections by the rare addition of the Province of Bavaria with Salzburg and her five suffragan sees.[99] This same recension of the *Notitia Galliarum* with Salzburg also appears in the *Vademecum* manuscript of Grimald, the famous archchaplain of Lewis the German.[100] It cannot be absolutely proven that Grimald's text, now in St. Gall, Stiftsbibliothek MS 397,[101] was borrowed from the

---

[94] Mordek, *Kirchenrecht* 250.

[95] Of the 70 canons in Book II (excluding the *Statuta ecclesiae antiqua*) the Coll IIL and the Collection of the MS of St. Amand have 57 canons in common.

[96] Mordek, *Kirchenrecht* 260.

[97] See G. Haenni, 'La Dacheriana mérite-t-elle une reédition?', RHD 34 (1956) 376-90.

[98] See above, n. 40.

[99] See my 'The Pseudo-Augustinian *Sermo de conscientia*' 313f., n. 5; and on the *Notitia Galliarum* in the MSS of the Coll IIL see K. Werner, 'Die literarischen Vorbilder des Aimoin von Fleury und die Entstehung seiner *Gesta Francorum*', *Medium Aevum vivum, Festschrift für Walther Bulst*, edd. H. Jauss and H. Schaller (Heidelberg 1960) 81, n. 38.

[100] On Grimald see Fleckenstein, *Die Hofkapelle* 1.63, n. 132, p. 65, n. 145, p. 69, 71, 89f., 90, n. 319, p. 105, n. 393, p. 107, 170, 173-6, 179-82, 237.

[101] P. 47. On this MS see B. Bischoff's review of E. Munding, *Die Kalendarien von St. Gallen aus XXI Handschriften*, in *Historisches Jahrbuch* 73 (1954) 499;

Coll IIL, but it must be remembered that there was a constant traffic of manuscripts from Salzburg to the Court of Lewis and that Grimald was also abbot of St. Gall, the vicinity in which our only complete extant manuscript of the Coll IIL was copied.

This St. Gall codex of the Coll IIL, now Vatican MS Reg. lat. 407,[102] is of particular significance not simply because it contains the only complete text of the collection, parts of which have been lost in the mutilated Adalram manuscript, but also because there is an extensive addendum after Book II of para-canonical material met frequently in Salzburg manuscripts, the text on ember days, the Eucharistic sentences attributed to Cyprian, Ambrose, and Hilary, and so forth.[103] All of these para-canonical texts may very well have been in the now mutilated Adalram codex because in another miscellaneous manuscript written in Salzburg or the vicinity in the second quarter of the ninth century, Vienna 1322, these texts are arranged in almost precisely the same sequence in which they appear in the addendum to the Coll IIL in the St. Gall manuscript.[104]

Many miscellaneous manuscripts from the Adalram period containing isolated canonical and para-canonical texts have already been mentioned in connection with the Coll IIL, and therefore it is unnecessary to describe their contents further. But there is a final miscellaneous manuscript, written in the vicinity of Salzburg in the Adalram period, with an isolated canonical text not connected with the Coll IIL. The codex, Budapest, Országos Széchényi Könyvtár MS 316,[105] contains a mutilated text of the *Capitula sancti Augustini*, which served as one of the bases of the canons at the Council of Orange in 529.[106]

B. Bischoff, 'Das Problem der karolingischen Hofschulen', *Versammlung deutscher Historiker* (1956) 51; Fleckenstein, *Die Hofkapelle* 1.173; and my 'The Pseudo-Augustinian *Sermo de conscientia*' 314, n. 5. This famous MS contains a canonical fragment, the *Regula formatarum* (see Maassen, *Geschichte* 400) on p. 37.

[102] On the date and origin of this MS see my 'The Pseudo-Augustinian *Sermo de conscientia*' 313; Mordek, *Kirchenrecht* 120, n. 87. Addition below, n. 124.

[103] Fols. 60r, 70r-71v.

[104] Fols. 63r-75v. Professor Bischoff has kindly notified me that this MS was written in Salzburg or the vicinity s. 2/4-m IX.

[105] On this MS see Lehmann, *Mitteilungen* 5-11; Clavis 664; Gamber, *Codices liturgici latini antiquiores* 404; Lambert, *Bibliotheca Hieronymiana* 641.1; and R. Kottje, 'Hrabanus Maurus – Praeceptor Germaniae?', DA 31 (1975) 541, n. 47.

[106] Fol. 28r-v. On the canons of this council see *Concilia Galliae A. 511-A. 695*, ed. C. deClercq, CCL 148A.53. The MS also contains on fol. 29v the liturgical commentary *Dominus vobiscum* attributed to Alcuin (on which tract see *Amalarii Episcopi Opera liturgica omnia I*, ed. I. Hanssens [Studi e Testi 138; Vatican City 1948] 108-14, 283-338).

Era of Liuphram

It is perhaps going somewhat beyond the chronological limits of the early ninth century to deal with Salzburg canonical manuscripts dating to the middle and second third of the ninth century. But there are three codices from the era of Liuphram which should briefly be mentioned, one because it contains collections not thus far connected directly with Salzburg, and the other two because they are thought to have been written at the direction of Baldo.

The first of these codices, Vienna 522, was studied by Maassen for its two systematic collections,[107] the Collection in 250 Chapters,[108] in reality an *excerptum* from the *Collectio Hibernensis*, and the very disorganized Collection in 400 Chapters.[109] The precise relationship of our Salzburg codex to other manuscripts of the *Hibernensis* and its derivatives and to other manuscripts of the Collection in 400 Chapters must await critical editions and studies of these texts, but it is not without significance that both collections in the Salzburg manuscript are also found in a codex written in the mid-ninth century in southeastern Germany, Clm 4592.[110]

Throughout this description of canon law manuscripts in early ninth-century Salzburg the name of Baldo has been cited with almost monotonous regularity, and it is to this *scholasticus* that the last of our canon law manuscripts are attributed. One of these codices, Vienna 458, is a miscellaneous manuscript with Baldo's colophon and includes liturgico-canonical pieces.[111] Among these is the well-known *Dictatus* of Paulinus of Aquileia,[112] which its editor in the *Monumenta Germaniae historica* connected with the assembly of bishops on the banks of the Danube in 796.[113] The other manuscript, Clm 15821,[114] written slightly after 851 and annotated by Baldo, con-

---

[107] Maassen, *Geschichte* 843. On this MS see Mordek, *Kirchenrecht* 52, 162f., n. 304, and p. 258.

[108] Fols. 57r-113v.

[109] Fols. 113v-92v.

[110] On this MS see Bischoff, *Schreibschulen* 46; and Mordek, *Kirchenrecht* 52, 162f., n. 304, and p. 258.

[111] On this MS, with its letters of Alcuin to Arno, see Levison, 'Die älteste Lebensbeschreibung' 293; Unterkircher, *Die datierten Handschriften* 25, and Abb. 12; and for some of its liturgico-canonical material see my 'The *De officiis vii graduum*: Its origins and early medieval development', *Mediaeval Studies* 34 (1972) 139.

[112] Fols. 179r-86r.

[113] MGH Conc. 2.172-6.

[114] On this MS see Foltz, *Geschichte* 50, n. 1; Unterkircher, *Die datierten Hand-*

tains a canonical collection which a fifteenth-century catalogue entry describes as a *Concordia canonum quam Baldo scribere fecit*.[115] The collection itself, which deserves an independent study, has been described by Levison as an *excerptum* of the *Dionysio-Hadriana* [116] and more recently by Dr. Mordek as being based on the *Breviarium* of Cresconius.[117] In its organization and texts the collection does indeed resemble both these collections, as well as the *excerpta* from the *Dionysio-Hadriana* in the earlier mentioned codex, Salzburg, Carolino-Augusteum Museum MS 2163. But no one seems to have noted the additional relationship of this Baldonian collection to the St. Amand manuscript, Vatican Reg. lat. 1021, and the Coll IIL. The *Concordia*, which may have been in the now lost beginning section of Vatican MS lat. 7222, is also in Vatican MS Reg. lat. 1021.[118] Moreover, after the final *capitula* attributed to Gregory II in the Baldo manuscript there is a rubric, *Haec sunt capitula de diversis canonibus*, and of the three canons following, two are found elsewhere only in the Coll IIL.[119]

Only the tip of canonistic activity in early ninth-century Salzburg has been uncovered in this paper describing the extant manuscripts originating there. As was noted in our introductory remarks, manuscripts and fragments will certainly come to light when the products of the ninth-century scriptoria of Salzburg have been more completely listed.[120] Further, an examination of the holdings of the Salzburg libraries such as Dr. Hofmann did for St. Kilian's Würzburg would undoubtedly increase the number of manuscripts known to have been in Salzburg in the ninth century, but which did not originate there.[121] In fact, the study of St. Kilian's

---

chriften 25; Lehmann, *Mitteilungen* 7; Levison, 'Die älteste Lebensbeschreibung' 293; and Siegmund, *Überlieferung* 70.

[115] Levison, 'Die älteste Lebensbeschreibung' 293; and *Mittelalterliche Bibliothekskataloge* 45.

[116] Levison, 'Die älteste Lebensbeschreibung' 293, n. 1.

[117] Mordek, *Kirchenrecht* 254.

[118] Fols. 1r-14v. The similar *Breviarium ad inquaerendum sententias infra* which Maassen, *Geschichte* 465, thought might be in Vatican MS Reg. lat. 1021 appears in Vienna 737, fols. 161v-94r (on which MS see Foltz, *Geschichte* 28) and the MSS noted by Mordek, *Kirchenrecht* 248.

[119] Clm 15821, fols. 120r-22v; Paris, B.N. nouv. acq. lat. 452, fol. 91r-v; Vatican MS Reg. lat. 407, fols. 37v-38r. These two canons are (1) a text attributed to Augustine's *De civitate Dei*, on which see Fournier, 'Notices sur trois collections' 519; and (2) a heavily reworked version of the *Constitutum Silvestri*, cc. 1, 3, on accusations.

[120] Cf. MGH Conc. 2.51.

[121] See Hofmann, *Libri sancti Kyliani* 61-172.

Würzburg places the intensity of canonistic activity in Salzburg into sharper relief. Of the thirteen manuscripts which reflected for Dr. Hofmann an uncommon interest in canon law from ca. 800-855 in Würzburg, only three originated there.[122] One can easily extrapolate from these figures to see that in Salzburg—represented here by a dozen and a half canon law manuscripts and fragments alone—the level of canonistic activity must have been even higher. But together with the extant canon law manuscripts which originated in the scriptoria or were kept in the libraries of Salzburg, many collections now lost may have been there. For example, it might have been that there were manuscripts or extracts from the *Collectio Vetus Gallica* and *Dacheriana*, the former of which influenced the canons of Arno's Council of Reisbach,[123] and the latter which was partially repeated in the Coll IIL. In sum, when the picture of canonistic activity in early ninth-century Salzburg finally emerges, this metropolitical see of Bavaria will prove to be yet another prominent inselberg in a Carolingian landscape already marked with numerous distinguished centers of canon law.[124]

---

[122] Hofman, *Libri sancti Kyliani* 156.

[123] Mordek, *Kirchenrecht* 103.

[124] After the presentation of this paper in Salamanca Professor Otto Mazal published 'Die Salzburger Dom- und Klosterbibliothek in karolingischer Zeit', *Codices manuscripti* 3.2 (1977) 44-64, esp. 53, noting the possible existence in the early ninth-century Salzburg library of Vienna 2160, a MS written in northern Italy containing the *Collatio legum Mosaicarum et Romanarum*. Professor Mazal's study dramatically illustrated the wide interests and sophisticated tastes of Salzburg scholars not only in canon law, but also in theology, biblical studies, liturgy, and many other areas. Some other publications have come to my attention after this paper was sent to the editors. References should be added to the notes as follows:

(n. 17) F. Unterkircher, *Alkuin-Briefe und andere Traktate (Cod. Vindobonensis 795)* (Codices selecti 20; Graz 1969) 35.

(n. 28) J.-P. Bouhot, 'Extraits du *De corpore et sanguine domini* de Pascase Radbert sous le nom d'Augustin', *Recherches augustiniennes* 12 (1977) 172f.

(n. 56) N.R. Ker, 'A supplement to *Catalogue of manuscripts containing Anglo-Saxon*', in *Anglo-Saxon*, England 5 (1976) 125.

(n. 77) Cf. W. Hartmann, *Das Konzil von Worms 868: Überlieferung und Bedeutung (Abh. Akad. Göttingen*, Dritte Folge 105; Göttingen 1977) 89f.

(n. 102) Cf. R. McKitterick, *The Frankish church and the Carolingian reforms, 789-895* (London 1977) 42.

An unexpected manuscript fragment of the
ninth-century canonical Collection in two books

In 1970 there appeared in the *Harvard Theological Review* an article by the undersigned, 'The florilegium on the ecclesiastical grades in Clm 19414', showing the close connection between an eleventh- or twelfth-century florilegium on sacred orders from Tegernsee with the early ninth-century canonical *Collection in two books* (hereafter Coll IIL). In that article it was surmised that a manuscript of the Coll IIL may have been in southeastern Germany and was used by the compiler of the florilegium.[1] Further research has confirmed that the extant complete or nearly complete ninth-century manuscripts of the Coll IIL were not only in the area of southeastern Germany, but were written there. Through both paleographical and internal textual evidence Paris B.N. nouv. acq. lat. 452 has been shown to have been written in Salzburg and Vatican Reg. lat. 407 to have been written in the vicinity of St. Gall.[2]

How these manuscripts travelled from Salzburg and the vicinity of St. Gall to their present homes in the Paris and Vatican libraries is difficult to trace. There is a possibility that the Salzburg manuscript or one like it had reached France by the middle of the ninth century,[3] but nothing definite is known about either the Paris or Vatican manuscript until the seventeenth century. From a notation on fol. 2r it is clear that the Reginensis manuscript was in Antwerp in 1656, but not in the library of Alexander Petau, which came into Queen Chris-

---

[1] R. Reynolds, 'A florilegium on the ecclesiastical grades in Clm 19414: Testimony to ninth-century clerical instruction', *Harvard Theological Review* 63 (1970) 251 n. 84.

[2] See R. Reynolds, 'The Pseudo-Augustinian *Sermo de conscientia* and related canonical *Dicta sancti Gregorii papae*', RB 81 (1971) 310-17, containing Professor Bischoff's information; H. Mordek, *Kirchenrecht und Reform im Frankenreich: Die Collectio Vetus Gallica, die älteste systematische Kanonessammlung des fränkischen Gallien: Studien und Edition* (Beiträge zur Geschichte und Quellenkunde des Mittelalters; Berlin-New York 1975) 120 n. 87; and my forthcoming 'Canon law collections in early ninth-century Salzburg', in the published Proceedings of the Fifth International Congress of Medieval Canon Law, Salamanca, 21-25 September 1976.

[3] Reynolds, '*Sermo de conscientia*' 310. The ninth-century Basel bifolium of the Coll IIL, which was written in France, is later than the Salzburg manuscript and is textually closer to the Salzburg than the Vatican manuscript. Also Vatican Pal lat. 973, containing an extract from the Coll IIL, was written, according to Professor Bischoff, in northeastern France in the second half of the ninth century under Rheims influence and perhaps early travelled to Germany. Also see K. Werner, 'Die literarischen Vorbilder des Aimoin von Fleury und die Enstehung seiner *Gesta francorum*', *Medium Aevum Vivum: Festschrift für Walther Bulst*, ed. H. Jauss and H. Schaller (Heidelberg 1960) 80 n. 38, where it is noted that the Paris manuscript very probably was in the library of Orléans.

tine's hands.[4] The history of the Paris manuscript is more obscure, but much more intriguing, and it is about one aspect of the history of this manuscript that this note is concerned.

As it now rests in its present home in the Bibliothèque Nationale in Paris, the Salzburg manuscript of the Coll IIL is within the collection of manuscripts which were thought at one time to have been in the possession of Guilielmo Bruto Timoleonte Libri-Carrucci. The depredations in the French libraries of this famous nineteenth-century Florentine scholar are well known and have been described in Delisle's catalogue of the *fonds* Libri,[5] the *Dictionnaire d'archéologie chrétienne et de liturgie* (= DACL),[6] and more recently in a lecture by A. N. L. Munby at Harvard.[7] After removing scores of manuscripts and documents from the French collections he was cataloguing, Libri sold his collection to Lord Ashburnham. Eventually many of the Libri manuscripts were ransomed and sent back to France, and among these was the Salzburg manuscript of the Coll IIL.

In making their claims for manuscripts taken from French libraries, Delisle and his associates could in many cases demonstrate French provenance from evidence in the manuscripts themselves. In some manuscripts, for example, the old reference to Fleury (Floriacum) had been changed by Libri or his accomplices to Florence (Florentia). But in the case of the Salzburg manuscript there does not seem to have been an indication of provenance.[8] Hence, other means were used to show that the manuscript had indeed been in the Libri collection and that it had most likely been taken from a French library.

To demonstrate that the manuscript had been in the Libri collection, one needed simply to point to item no. 80 in the Libri catalogue of manuscripts. This reference could be traced back to papers now in the collection of Libri material kept in the Bibliothèque Nationale. In Paris B.N. nouv. acq. fr. 3279, beginning on fol. 100r, there is a rough draft of the Libri catalogue of manuscripts. On fol. 105r there is an item: 'no. 80. Excerpta de diversis conciliis. Manuscrit sur vélin à longues lignes in 8° du ixe siècle'. This same catalogue entry for the Libri manuscripts also appears in Paris B.N. nouv. acq. fr. 3279, fol. 94r-v; 3260, fol. 99v; and finally in the catalogue of Bourquelot, Bordier, and Lalanne listing 'manuscripts dont d'achat par M. Libri ne s'est trouvé justifié ni par facture ni autrement et dont la possession est par conséquent demeurée suspect' (Paris B.N. nouv. acq. fr. 3286, p. 389).

---

[4] A. Wilmart, *Codices Reginenses latini* 2 (Vatican 1945) 486.

[5] L. Delisle, *Catalogue des manuscrits des fonds Libri et Barrois* (Paris 1888) preface.

[6] H. Leclercq, DACL 9.572-610.

[7] A. Munby, 'The earl and the thief' (The first George Parker Winship lecture under the fund established by the John Barnard Associates, May 1, 1968; Cambridge, Mass. 1968); and A. Munby, 'The triumph of Delisle; a sequel to "The earl and the thief",' *Harvard Library Bulletin* 17 (1969) 279-90. It is an interesting coincidence that the Pontifical Institute of Mediaeval Studies now owns a volume of Delisle, *Catalogue fonds Libri*, whose provenance, as evidenced by his signature and bookplate, is A. Munby.

[8] M. Jean Vezin has kindly written me that there is no provenance noted in the manuscript and that Delisle probably reclaimed the manuscript for what he believed were the French characteristics of the writing. In his various studies on Libri, Delisle was able to suggest provenances for the Paris manuscripts nouv. acq. lat. 448-451 and 453-454, but not for our 452. Cf. Delisle, *Catalogue* xiii; and Leclercq, DACL 9.579, 604.

What proof was there, however, that Libri had taken the Salzburg manuscript? It was known that he had legitimately purchased books, and this could have been one of these. That it was, however, is not likely. On fol. 106v of the Salzburg manuscript Libri or one of his scribes has noted that the codex came from 'Scte Justine de Padua'. This notation appears in many of the manuscripts taken by Libri,[9] and had he legitimately purchased the manuscript, it is unlikely that he would have seen fit to make such an entry.

One piece of evidence which, as far as is known, has not been used to connect Libri with the Salzburg manuscript is in Paris B.N. nouv. acq. fr. 3264. In this manuscript, fol. 71, item 1234, is the famous scrap of white paper with its penciled draft of a false provenance to be entered in some of the manuscripts Libri gave his 'medieval' scribes to correct: 'Hic est liber sci petri de perusio cenobii. Si quis [eum] abstulerit, anathema sit'. As E. K. Rand roguishly noted, Libri must have taken special delight in adding this entry, being 'the only thief in history who wrote his own anathema'.[10] On the next folio, 72, item 1235, there is a white slip of paper which links Libri with the Salzburg manuscript of the Coll IIL. On the verso side of the slip there are lightly penciled a few Latin phrases. On the recto side in black ink are the words:

INCIPIT / IN / NOMINE / DÑI / CAPI
TULAR̄ / LIB̄ / PRIMI / COLLECT̄
DE / LIBRIS / S̄S̄ / PATRUM
LATINORUM

XI	De spiritu sčo
XII	De sča trinitate
XIII	De angelis
XIIII	De nomine beate marie
XV	De ioh̄ baptis
XVI	De apostolis
XVII	De nominibus

If these lines are compared with the Salzburg manuscript of the Coll IIL, it is evident that they are copied from fol. 1r-v. The four lines in capitals are copied from the incipit of the Coll IIL, fol. 1r. The seven *tituli*, written in a cursive hand, are those listed at the top of fol. 1v of the Salzburg manuscript.[11] Why these lines were copied on the white slip of paper is not clear. Nor is it known where the slip was found. But its appearance in Paris B.N. nouv. acq. fr. 3264 indicates that the circumstances of its discovery were such as to lead the compilers of the Libri dossiers to include it among the papers pertaining to the rebinding and restoration of manuscripts carried out under Libri's direction.

One of the fascinating aspects of the Coll IIL is that the manuscripts and fragments of the collection are now geographically far removed from the place of

---

[9] DACL 9.579f. n. 2; and L. Delisle, 'Notice sur des manuscrits du fonds Libri conservés à la Laurentienne', in *Notices et extraits des manuscrits de la Bibliothèque nationale et autres biblicthèques* 33 (Paris 1886) 107.

[10] E. Rand, *A survey of the manuscripts of Tours* 1 (Cambridge, Mass. 1929) 6.

[11] For a list of these *tituli* see P. Fournier, 'Notices sur trois collections canoniques inédites de l'époque carolingienne', *Revue des sciences religieuses* 6 (1926) 525.

38

its compilation. There is a complete manuscript in the Vatican Library, a mutilated manuscript in Paris, and a bifolium in Basel.[12] The white slip from the Libri material in Paris B.N. nouv. acq. 3264 adds a further bit of information about the travels of this intriguing little ninth-century collection of canon law.

VIII

THE PSEUDO-AUGUSTINIAN « SERMO DE CONSCIENTIA » AND THE RELATED CANONICAL « DICTA SANCTI GREGORII PAPAE »

In 1953 Dom Alban Dold published in this review a group of patristic fragments found in bifolium N.I.6 Nr. 9 of the Universitätsbibliothek of Basel. [7] The bifolium, written in France during the middle of the ninth century, [8] contains fragments from three texts. The first is the conclusion of a tract regarding crimes against the Church ; the second is the beginning of a *Sermo de conscientia*, attributed to St. Augustine ; and the third is a portion of the fifth-century *Statuta ecclesiae antiqua*. These fragmentary texts caught Dom Dold's eye for several reasons. First, the *Sermo* attributed to St. Augustine had not, according to Dold's knowledge, been reported. Second, the biblical citations in the *Sermo* and the first fragment had variants differing significantly from Vulgate readings. And third, the text of the *Statuta ecclesiae antiqua* was unlike the one published by Migne in *PL* 56.879f.

---

7. A. Dold, *Alte, teilweise unbekannte Väterfragmente auf dem Doppelblatt NI 6 Nr. 9 der Universitätsbibliothek Basel*, in *Rev. bénéd.* 63 (1953), p. 239-45.
8. *Ibid.*, p. 240, n. 1.

Since Dold's publication of the fragments, they have attracted little attention. The first two fragments are listed in the *Clavis Patrum Latinorum* simply as *sermones anonymi*. [1] They have also been noted in the *Verzeichnis der Sigel* of the *Vetus Latina*, and the Augustinian *Sermo* assigned with reservations to the sixth century. [2] It is the purpose of this article to present the complete texts of the tracts which Dold found in fragmentary form and to place them in their canonical and geographical settings.

Unfortunately nothing regarding the origins of the texts in the Basel bifolium can be deduced from the Basel MS A.XI.49, from which the bifolium was detached. The MS, which has been missing since at least 1934 from the Universitätsbibliothek in Basel, contained theological texts written on paper, and as far as is known, had no connection with the ninth-century bifolium detached from its cover. [3]

In the bifolium itself, however, there are two clues which point to the complete texts of the fragments. First, Dold's third fragment is drawn from the Prologue to the *Statuta ecclesiae antiqua*, a text common to many early medieval canonical collections. [4] Second, the inclusion of the number « *LXII* » before the *Sermo de conscientia* looks suspiciously like a number placed before a text in a canonical collection.

In examining the canonical MSS used by Charles Munier for his edition and study of the *Statuta ecclesiae antiqua*, [5] one discovers that most of the variants of the *Statuta ecclesiae antiqua* in the Basel bifolium are found in VAT. Reg. lat. 407, [6] a MS containing the ninth-century *Collection in Two Books* (hereafter *Coll IIL*). [7] Even closer to the variants of the Basel bifolium are those found in a second MS of the *Coll IIL*, PARIS B.N. n.a.l. 452, [8] a MS not used by Munier. [9] In both MSS of the *Coll IIL* the Prologue of the *Statuta ecclesiae antiqua* is the "third" [10] canon of L. II, immediately preceded by an unusual version of the *Notitia galliarum* [11] and a Pseudo-Augustinian canon, *Omnes*

---

1. E. DEKKERS and A. GAAR, *Clavis Patrum Latinorum*, Editio altera, Steenbrugge, 1961, Nrr. 1162a, b.

2. B. FISCHER, *Verzeichnis der Sigel für Kirchenschriftsteller*, 2. Aufl., Freiburg, 1963, p. 78.

3. Dr M. Steinmann of Basel has provided me with this information.

4. F. MAASSEN, *Geschichte der Quellen und der Literatur des canonischen Rechts im Abendlande bis zum Ausgang des Mittelalters*, I, Graz, 1870, p. 383ff.

5. C. MUNIER, ed., *Les Statuta ecclesiae antiqua*, *Édition-Études critiques*, Paris, 1960, p. 48f.

6. Fol. 32ᵛ-33ʳ.

7. For bibliography on the *Coll IIL*, cfr H. MORDEK, *Die historische Wirkung der Collectio Herovalliana*, in *Zeitschrift für Kirchengeschichte* 81 (1970), p. 225, nn. 25-30.

8. Fol. 92ᵛ-95ʳ.

9. The *Statuta ecclesiae antiqua* is incomplete in the Paris MS, which lacks most of L. II of the *Coll IIL* and contains only the Prologue and what are listed as seventy-one canons of the *Antiqua constituta cartaginensis ecclesiae*.

10. The numbering of canons in L. II is rather strange. The "first" canon listed as such in the table of contents and the body of L. II in both MSS is the first canon of the *Statuta ecclesiae antiqua*. There are, however, clearly three canons before the first canon of the *Statuta*, the third being the Prologue of the *Statuta*.

11. T. MOMMSEN, ed., *Chronica minora saec. IV, V, VI, VII* (*Mon. Germ. Hist. AA*, IX, vol. I), Berlin, 1892, p. 552-612. Mommsen (p. 563) knew of but had not seen VAT. Reg. lat. 407.

causae primitus. [1] At the conclusion of L. I of the *Coll IIL* are two canons, *LXI Dicta sancti gregorii papae*, which is the complete text of Dold's first fragment, and *LXII Sermo sancti augustini de conscientia*, the complete text of Dold's second fragment. [2] Evidently the Basel bifolium was originally detached from a MS of the *Coll IIL*. In the original MS between Dold's first two fragments and the Prologue of the *Statuta ecclesiae antiqua* there would have been the *Notitia galliarum* and the Pseudo-Augustinian canon *Omnes causae primitus.*

The *Dicta sancti gregorii papae* is a tract which first details seven reasons for the criminality of one who assaults the Church and her goods. Following these reasons there are strung together a group of passages from the Old and New Testaments which further emphasize the seriousness of the crime and judgment of those who illegally usurp the goods and offices of the Church.

The *Sermo de conscientia* attributed to St. Augustine is a rambling tract covering such subjects as the secrecy of confession, the dangers of a loose tongue, compassion for one's enemies, and the avoidance of anger. Like the *Dicta sancti gregorii*, the *Sermo* is in large part composed of passages drawn from the Old and New Testaments, often cast in terminology differing from that of the Vulgate. [3]

It is doubtful that either the *Dicta sancti gregorii* or the *Sermo sancti augustini* goes back to the famous doctor to whom it is attributed. The *Dicta* does have some features which sound as if the tract may have been based on Gregory's work. The word *pondus* of the first sentence, for example, was a favorite of Gregory's, [4] and the two passages from *Prov.* 21.27 and *Sir.* 34.24 can also be found in close proximity in Gregory's letter to Bishop Virgil of Arles. [5] But the general impression one gets in reading the tract is that it cannot as a whole go back to Gregory I.

Nor does it seem that the *Sermo de conscientia* was by Augustine. In his original notice of the *Sermo* Dom Dold reported that the Augustinian expert, Dom Cyrille Lambot, had judged the *Sermo* not authentically Augustinian, but of a genre close to the apocryphal *Ad fratres in eremo.* [6] Unfortunately Dom Lambot was never able to publish further on the subject. [7]

---

1. The text, which is said to come from Augustine's *De civitate dei*, later found its way into Burchard's *Decretum* XVI. 23 (*PL* 140, 912) ; the *Collectio canonum* III. 78 of Anselm of Lucca (F. THANER, ed., *Anselmi Episcopi Lucensis Collectio canonum una cum collectione minore*, Innsbruck, 1906, p. 154) ; and the *Collectio canonum* IV. 374 of Cardinal Deusdedit (V. W. VON GLANVELL, ed., *Die Kanonessammlung des Kardinals Deusdedit* I. Bd.: *Die Kanonessammlung*, Paderborn, 1905, p. 581).

2. PARIS *B.N. n.a.l.* 452, fol. 77^v-85^r ; VAT. Reg. lat. 407, fol. 27^r-29^v.

3. In the *Dicta sancti gregorii* the texts from *Prov.* 28.9 and *Sir.* 34.24 differ significantly from the Vulgate readings. In the *Sermo de conscientia* the following passages have readings differing from those of the Vulgate : *Matt.* 5.44, 18.35, 5.23f., 18.21f., and *Jac.* 3.11, 9, 10.

4. Mr. Paul Meyvaert has kindly called this to my attention. Cfr M. WALTHER *Pondus, Dispensatio, Dispositio : Werthistorische Untersuchungen zur Frömmigkeit Papst Gregors des Grossen*, Luzern, 1941, p. 14-71.

5. *Mon. Germ. Hist. Epp.* II, Berlin, 1899, p. 207. On the use of the word *victimare* in Gregory's work and in *Sir.* 34.24, cfr J.F. O'DONNELL, *The Vocabulary of the Letters of St. Gregory*, Washington D.C., 1934, p. 54f.

6. DOLD, *art. cit.*, p. 242.

7. Dom Verbraken has kindly given me this information.

Although I have been unable to locate or give a *terminus ante quem non* for the two tracts, [1] it is possible to give a *terminus a quo* and to suggest several circumstances in which they might have been written in view of their appearance in the *Coll IIL* and related MSS.

Besides the Basel bifolium, which Professor Bischoff has dated to the middle of the ninth century and located in France, the *Dicta* and *Sermo* appear in the two MSS of the *Coll. IIL*, VAT. Reg. lat. 407, originating near St. Gall in the third quarter of the ninth century, and PARIS *B.N.* n.a.l. 452, written in Salzburg late in the episcopate of Adalramnus (821-836). Further, a section of the *Dicta* and the complete text of the *Sermo* appear in other early ninth-century manuscripts from Bavaria. To a canonical manuscript of the first quarter of the ninth century from Salzburg, VAT. lat. 7222, the Master Baldo has added a short piece entitled *De singulis capitulis quos in canonicis libris invenimus*. Within this piece there are listed the seven reasons found in the *Dicta sancti gregorii*. [2] The complete text of the Augustinian *Sermo* can be found in *Clm* 6314, [3] a product of the scriptorium in Freising in the second quarter of the ninth century. [4]

In comparing the text of the *Sermo* in the three MSS and one bifolium in which it appears, it seems that the compiler of *Clm* 6314 and the original compiler of the *Coll IIL* were working from a common exemplar. The Paris MS and Basel bifolium as one family were then copied from the original MS of the *Coll IIL*, and the Vatican MS, with its own variants, later copied from the original MS of the *Coll IIL*.

Since the Augustinian *Sermo* is found in the *Coll IIL*, compiled probably in Salzburg in the early ninth-century, and in the Freising MS, *Clm* 6314, of the second quarter of the ninth century, it is possible to give the *Sermo* and *Dicta* a *terminus a quo* of ca. 836 and to locate the texts as we now have them in the province of Bavaria, erected in 798. [5] Although the two texts may have been

---

1. Both P. FOURNIER, *Notices sur trois collections canoniques inédites de l'époque carolingienne*, in *Rev. des sciences religieuses* 6 (1926), p. 515f., and Dom A. WILMART, *Codices Reginenses Latini*, II, Vatican City, 1945, p. 483, noted these two tracts, but neither author gave any information as to their date or provenance.

2. VAT. lat. 7222, p. 487-8. Professor Bischoff kindly brought this manuscript to my attention. The *De singulis capitulis* follows a group of canons attributed to Pope Gregory II and precedes a short extract from the *De xii abusivis saeculi* attributed to scs gregorius (Cfr *CSEL*, III, p. 152). The incipit of the *De singulis capitulis* is « Unum capitulum quod reus est de sanguine... » The piece reads, with a few exceptions, like the *Dicta sancti gregorii* to the words « ... in conspectu patris sui. » It then ends with the sentence, « Sic ait sanctus hieronimus de loquentibus et pronuntiantibus, plenus est orbis, loquentur quod nesciunt, docent quae non didicerunt, magistri sunt cum discipuli antea non fuerunt. » To what extent the *Dicta* and the *De singulis capitulis* are related is not obvious, but that they are related is clear. In a future study of the canonical *Coll IIL* I hope to deal with the relationship of the *Dicta* and Baldo's addition to VAT. lat. 7222. The *De singulis capitulis* is also found in *Clm* 6355, fol. 259ʳ (s. IX) and *Clm* 5525, fol. 123ʳ (s. IX).

3. Fol. 192ᵛ-194ʳ. Dr. F. Dressler of Munich has kindly provided me with information on the *Sermo* as it appears in this MS.

4. I should like to thank Professor Bischoff for graciously supplying me with information on the origins and dates of these MSS.

5. It is interesting to note that the *Notitia galliarum* of the *Coll IIL* contains the unusual addition of the metropolitical see of Salzburg. Only one other MS

composed in Bavaria itself, it is also possible that they travelled to Bavaria with other materials. [1]

The *Dicta* and *Sermo* were probably included in the *Coll IIL* for the same reasons which induced the compiler to include canons in L. I on penance [2] and canons in L. II on usurpation of ecclesiastical properties and offices by laymen and evil clerics. [3] Both subjects, the sacrament of penance and the usurpation of ecclesiastical properties, were major concerns in the 820's. Public penance was making a comeback in reaction to the penitential system favored by the Irish. [4] Its most obvious manifestation was in the public penance of Louis the Pious at Attigny in 822, occasioned by his anger toward and barbaric treatment of Bernard of Italy. Past and present depredations of ecclesiastical properties, too, were a major concern in the 820's. Agobard of Lyon, for example, reflected this concern in his *De dispensatione ecclesiasticarum rerum* (ca. 824/5). [5] There he requested the return of ecclesiastical properties taken by the predecessors of Louis the Pious, [6] the most notable being Charles Martel, who, under two Pope Gregorys, had appropriated the lands and offices of the Church.

In presenting the texts of the *Dicta sancti gregorii* and the *Sermo de conscientia* here, it has seemed preferable to print them as they appear in the *Coll IIL*, despite the fact that the *Sermo* has an independent existence in *Clm* 6314. Since the Paris MS is the better of the two MSS of the *Coll IIL*, the texts will follow it, and variants in the Vatican and Freising MSS will be noted in the apparatus. Abbreviations have been expanded and standard punctuation marks such as commas, periods, and question marks have been added. [7]

---

reported by Mommsen in his edition of the *Notitia* (*MGH AA*, IX, vol. I, p. 594) contains this addition, ST. GALL MS 397, a MS which Professor Bischoff says was written largely at the court of Louis the German in the ninth century and used by Grimald, the archchancellor of Louis the German, as his *vademecum*. Later the MS was deposited in the library of St. Gall (Cfr *Dict. d'archéol. chrét. et liturg.*, VI. 1, Paris, 1924, coll. *107, 121*, and ST. GALL MS 397, index page^r).

1. The major portion of *Clm* 6314 contains the *Liber scintillarum* attributed to Defensor of Ligugé. The *Coll IIL*, L. II contains canons drawn from several collections, including the *Collection of Diessen*, *Clm* 5508, written in Salzburg with some northern French features (cfr E.A. LOWE, *Cod. Lat. Antiq.* IX, Oxford, 1959, Nr. 1247), and from a northern French collection something like the *Collection of St. Amand*.

2. L. I, cc. 57-59.

3. L. II. cc. 84, 96.

4. A. FLICHE et V. MARTIN, *Histoire de l'Église*, VI, Paris, 1941, p. 214.

5. Cfr A. CABANISS, *Agobard of Lyons : Churchman and Critic*, Syracuse, 1953, p. 50f. ; and E. BOSHOF, *Erzbischof Agobard von Lyon : Leben und Werk*, Köln, 1969, p. 84-101. It is interesting to note that Agobard supported his case on the basis of Gallican canons, exactly the same approach followed by the compiler of the *Coll IIL*.

6. FLICHE et MARTIN, *op. cit.*, V, Paris, 1938, p. 361ff.

7. Three late medieval manuscripts containing the *Sermo de conscientia* have been brought to my attention by J.-P. Bouhot : METZ *Bibl. mun.* 91 (s. XIV), destroyed ; PARIS *B.N.* lat. 18216 (s. XIV), fol. 75^r-^v ; and METZ *Bibl. mun.* 149 (s. XV), fol. 68^v-69^r. In the extant manuscripts from Paris and Metz, the *Sermo* as well as other short texts have been added after the *Speculum*

Paris *Bibl. Nat.* n.a.l. 452 (ix) *Salzburg.*
V: Vatican Reg. lat. 407 (ix) *near St. Gall.*
F: Munich *Staatsbibl.* lat. 6314 (ix) *Freising.*

LXI. DICTA SANCTI GREGORII PAPAE

De eo qui laicus vel adulter clericus ecclesiam dei invasit et abstulit de potestate
sacerdotis et pastoris quam multiplex pondus peccatorum portet. Primo quod
reus est de sanguine animarum quae in illa parrochia sine baptismo defuncti sunt.
Secundo quod homicida est populi qui sine doctrinι et sine fide catholica moriuntur
5 absque paenitentia. Tertio quod sine inpositione manus episcopi sine gratia spiritus sancti moritur populus quod in animam eius redundat. Quarto quod presbiteri
et clerus sine pastore et sine magistro sunt adulteri et erronei et in errore seducunt
populum, ut : *Caecus caecum in foveam perditionis ducat.* Quinto quod cotidie
peccata aliena comedit sive mortuorum sive vivorum qui sua peccata redimentes
10 ecclesiam dei vestierunt de suo. Sexto quod necator et percussor pauperum et
peregrinorum, viduarum et orfanorum, caecorum et claudorum, et omnium mise-
rorum qui frigore vel fame moriuntur aut cruciantur esse probatur, eo quod ipse
sibi tenet unde pauperes christi vivere debuerunt. Septimo quod pessimum est et
horrendum quod ipse errore et caecitate correptus non intellegit se reum esse ante
15 conspectum domini damnatum et quamdiu in hoc peccato iacet nec elymosinae
acceptabiles sunt deo nec orationes purae coram deo, sed sicut psalmigraphus
dixit : *Cum iudicatur exeat condemnatus et oratio eius fiat in peccatum.* Et alibi :
Hostiae impiorum abhominabiles quae offeruntur ex scelere. Et iterum : *Qui despicit
legem dei oratio eius erit execrabilis.* Et item : *Qui dat elymosinam de substantia*
20 *pauperis quasi qui victimat filium in conspectu patris sui.* Quia scriptum est per
spiritum dei : *Qui abstulit patri aliquid vel matri et dicit non est peccatum particeps
homicidae est.* Pater noster deus est ad quem dicimus : *Pater noster qui es in caelis.*
Mater nostra ecclesia est quae nos regeneravit baptismo in sanguine christi. Propterea quicumque pecuniam ecclesiae rapuerit reus erit sanguinis christi : quia
25 ecclesia fabricata est de sanguine christi. Et omnis qui ei fraudem fecerit, ut sanctus
hieronimus dixit : Sacrilegium facit, quia profanat christi sanguinem et homicida
est non unius sed multarum animarum quas mater ecclesia inde nutrire debuit vel
doctrina caelesti vel pane terreno. Et ante tribunal christi reus esse dinoscitur, et
non solum a regno dei separandus sed etiam eterna poena damnandus est. Et iuxta
30 dictum pauli apostoli : *Qui talia agunt digni sunt morte, non solum qui faciunt,
sed qui consentiunt facientibus.*

---

5 impositione *V*   7 errore]   errorem *V*   8 cottidie *V*   15
quandiu *V*   elemosynae *V*   16 psalmigrafus *V*   17 peccatum]
peccato *V*   19 elemosinam *V*   20 victimat] victimet *V*   21 aliquid
patri *inv.* *V*   25 fabricata] fundata *V*   27 eccleia *sic* *V*   29
aetiam *V*   eterno] aeterna *V*   31 sed] et *add.* *V*

---

8 *Matth.* 15, 14 ; *Luc.* 6, 39   22 *Matth.* 6, 9
17 *Psalm.* 108, 7   23 Cfr *I Petri* 1, 3
18 *Prov.* 21, 27   24 Cfr *I Cor.* 11, 27
18-19 *Prov.* 28, 9   28 Cfr *II Cor.* 5, 10
19-20 *Eccli.* 34, 24   30-31 *Rom.* 1, 32
21-22 *Prov.* 28, 24

---

ecclesiae Hugonis cardinalis.   It was, unfortunately, impossible to collate the
Metz and Paris manuscripts with the ninth-century manuscripts before this
article went to the printer.   The collations have now been made, and the only
variants of any significance in the later medieval manuscripts are : 1) the
omission in both manuscripts of the title *De conscientia* and the text *nec vobis
remittetur... dimittimus debitoribus nostris* of ll. 16-18 ; and 2) the omission in
the Paris manuscript of *quia patientia imago est christi* of l. 32.

LXII. SERMO SANCTI AUGUSTINI EPISCOPI DE CONSCIENTIA

Fratres estote fideles in omnibus ut per fidem vestram salvemini. Hodie si tibi aliquis secretum fuerit confessus, serva illud apud te. Audi salomonem dicentem : *Audisti verbum moriatur apud te.* Aut si forte aliqua inimicitia nata fuerit serva
5 secretum. Scis enim quia praeceptum est : *Non occides.* Tu enim si secretum dilataveris occidisti ; forsitan tale secretum est quod ad periculum animae pertineat. Ecce occidisti sed tu securus qui gladio non percutis, fustem non ducis, petra non iactas, calcem non ducis, sed quod peius est lingua occidis. Audi in psalmo lvi**to** : *Filii hominum dentes eorum arma et sagittae et lingua eorum machera acuta.*
10 Et in alio psalmo : *Sagittae acutae cum carbonibus desolatoriis.* Et apostolus iacobus dicit : *Lingua ignis est quae totum corpus incendit.* Ecce cum qualibus gladiis tu occidis ; cum arcu, cum sagittis, et macheris non occidis. Non solum de lingua occidis, sed et incendis. Non debemus haec facere fratres, sed audiamus apostolum dicentem : *Nulli malum pro malo reddentes.* Et iterum : *Si esurierit inimicus tuus*
15 *ciba illum.* Et dominus : *Orate pro inimicis vestris, benefacite his qui vos persecuntur.* Et iterum : *Si non remiseritis unusquisque fratri suo de cordibus vestris nec vobis remittetur.* Nonne in ipsa oratione dominica quid oramus : *Dimitte nobis debita nostra sicut et nos dimittimus debitoribus nostris.* Quomodo nobis habet dimittere si nos non dimiserimus ? Unde et dominus dicit : *Si offeres munus tuum ante altare*
20 *et recordatus fueris quod aliquid habes adversus fratrem tuum, relinque ibi munus tuum et vade reconciliari fratri tuo et sic offeres munus tuum.* Et interrogante apostolo : *Si peccaverit in me frater meus quoties dimittam illi septies ?* Et dominus : *Non dico tibi septies sed septuagies septies.* Et in psalmo lxv**to** quomodo dicit : *Iniquitatem si conspexi in cor meo non exaudiat deus.* Vides quia si iniquitatem retinue-
25 rimus nec exaudiemur sine causa oramus si dolum non dimittamus. Ergo karissimi non expedit ut hoc faciamus. Audi apostolum dicentem : *Benedicite et nolite maledicere.* Et apostolus iacobus : *Non potest de uno foramine aqua dulcis et amara exire.* Ex ipso ore maledicimus homines qui ad imaginem dei facti sunt. Sic age ut ille non sentiat. In ecclesia eum require in processione et pace nuntiata accede
30 ad illum et da ei pacem. Non pro illo facis sed pro te ut dimittantur peccata tua et exaudiatur oratio tua. Omnia quaecumque patimur respiciamus ad christum nihil nobis grave videtur quia patientia imago est christi. Qui vero inpatiens est rixas facit et irascitur. Haec imago diaboli est. Quando vero irascimur mutantur oculi nostri, facies ipsa non rubet, non pallit, dentes non concrepant, labia tremunt.

---

1 LXII *om.* F   sermo] incipit *praem.* F   de conscientia sancti augustini episcopi *inv.* F   3 serva] salva V   4 aut] aud V, ut F 4-5 secretum serva *inv.* V   5-6 dilataveris] delaveris F   6 animae *om.* F   7 gladio] gladium F   petra] petram VF   9 lvi**to**] lvi VF sagitte F   lingua] lingue V   machera acuta] gladius acutus V 11 cum qualibus gladiis tu] tu cum quali gladio F   gladiis] armis V   12 occidis] occides V   sagittis et macheris] sagitta et machera F   13 hec F   15 et] iterum *add.* V   dominus] dicit *add.* V   16 de cordibus vestris *om.* F   19 dimiseremus F   offeres] offers F ante] ad F   20 habes] habebis F   21 offeres] offers F   22 in] im *sic* V   23 lxv**to**] lxv VF   24 cor] corde VF   deus] dominus V   25-26 carissimi V   28 ore ipso *inv.* V   facti] formati V   31 respitiamus F   32 videtur grave *inv.* F   pacientia F   33 hec F   34 pallit] pallet V   concrepant] crepant V

---

4 *Eccli.* 19, 10
5 *Ex.* 20, 13 etc.
9 *Psalm.* 56, 10
10 *Psalm.* 119, 4
11 *Jac.* 3, 6
13 Cfr *ibid.* 10
14 *Rom.* 12, 17
14-15 *Ibid.* 20
15 *Matth.* 5, 44

16-17 *Matth.* 18, 35
17-18 *Matth.* 6, 12
19-21 *Matth.* 5, 23
22 *Matth.* 18, 21
22-23 *Ibid.* 22
23-24 *Psalm.* 65, 18
26-27 *Rom.* 12, 14
27-28 *Jac.* 3, 11
26-28 Cfr *ibid.* 9-10

VIII

35 Haec imago diaboli est. Ergo abiciamus imaginem diaboli et habeamus imaginem christi, ut per ipsam mereamur salvari.

·35 hec *F*   36 salvari] tempore domino nostro ihesu christo cui est honor et laus in saecula saeculorum amen *add. F*

Pseudonymous liturgica in early medieval canon law collections

In his preface to The Name of the Rose Umberto Eco brought to the attention of the reading public at large an early medieval pseudonymous liturgical exposition published in Mabillon's Vetera Analecta[1]. Profusely illustrated with diagrams (see pl. I), the exposition purports to be a revelation given to a bishop Eldefonsus of Spain early in the morning of the seventh day of the tenth month of the year 845; and it deals with the size, shape, and stamping of eucharistic hosts and their distribution on the altar. Since Mabillon's time the tract has often been reprinted and cited by liturgiologists[2]. But because Mabillon had published the tract on the basis of a transcription sent him by Cardinal Bona from an unidentified Vatican manuscript[3], liturgiologists have been unable to verify the text and its illustrations or provide a manuscript context for it. But had they combed the early canon law manuscripts of the Vatican Library, they would have discovered that this pseudonymous piece of liturgica appears in the famous codex of the pseudo-Isidorian Collectio Hispana Gallica Augustodunensis, Vatican, Cod. Vat. lat. 1341[4].

In fact, it is little appreciated by many liturgiologists that early medieval canon law collections are one of the richest sources for pseudonymous liturgical tracts like this Eldefonsine revelation, that their origins are often associated with canon law contexts, and that they owed much of their popularity and diffusion to incorporation within canon law collections.

As anyone knows who has casually paged through the papal and conciliar canons of one of these early medieval canonical collections, either in printed or manuscript form, pseudonymous texts dealing with liturgical questions are

---

1) Umberto Eco, The Name of the Rose, Engl. trs. W. Weaver (1980) p. 2.

2) E. g., Edmund Martène, De antiquis Ecclesiae ritibus libri tres 1 (^{3}1788) p. 140 f.; and Migne PL 106. 881–890.

3) Jean Mabillon, Vetera analecta sive collectio veterum aliquot operum ... cui accessere Mabilonii vita et aliquot opuscula, scilicet dissertatio de pane eucharistico, azymo ac fermentato, ad Eminentiss. Cardinalem Bona. Subjungitur opusculum Eldefonsi Hispaniensis Episcopi de eodem argumento (^{2}1723) p. 548.

4) Foll. 187 v – 188 v.

legion. One need only cite the Pseudo-Isidorian Decretals themselves, which Professor Fuhrmann has pointed out are filled with liturgical regulations[5]. But the pseudonymous liturgica to be studied in this paper are of a slightly different nature because of their expository or interpretive character and also because they made their way from canon law collections into more strictly liturgical compilations, including commentaries and formulaic books such as sacramentaries and pontificals.

To study the full range of these texts in canon law collections would clearly be impossible in a single article and other scholars have adequately studied the appearance in early medieval canonical collections of such liturgico-canonical or canonical texts as the Statuta ecclesiae antiqua[6], Admonitio synodalis[7], and baptismal tracts[8]. Hence, this paper will be limited to an examination of texts on the liturgical ministers and the Mass. In the first part of the paper the character, origins, and attributions in early medieval canonistic manuscripts of these texts will be considered; then some of the possible reasons for their pseudonymity will be suggested; and finally their role in early medieval canon law collections will be sketched.

The earliest texts to be examined here are those on the liturgical ministers, and the oldest of them are the so-called Ordinals of Christ[9]. These little treatises are found in scores of recensions, but common to all of them is a list of the various officers in the ecclesiastical hierarchy together with a deed or saying of Christ giving a dominical sanction for the liturgical function performed by the officer. For example, it is said that Christ was a lector when he read from the book of Isaiah in the synagogue. The oldest example of these texts actually dates back to the patristic Greek Apophthegmata patrum[10], but alternative texts were quickly absorbed into the Latin canonical collections by

5) Horst FUHRMANN, Einfluß und Verbreitung der pseudoisidorischen Fälschungen 1 (MGH Schriften 24.1, 1972) p. 55.

6) Charles MUNIER, Les Statuta ecclesiae antiqua. Édition-Études critiques (Bibliothèque de l'Institut de droit canonique de l'université de Strasbourg 5, 1960).

7) Robert AMIET, Une ‚Admonitio synodalis‘ de l'époque carolingienne. Étude critique et édition, Mediaeval Studies 26 (1964) pp. 41–69.

8) Susan A. KEEFE, Carolingian Baptismal Expositions: A Handlist of Tracts and Manuscripts, in: Carolingian Essays. Andrew W. Mellon Lectures in Early Christian Studies, ed. U.-R. BLUMENTHAL (1983) p. 169 f.

9) On the Ordinals see Roger E. REYNOLDS, The Ordinals of Christ from their Origins to the Twelfth Century (Beiträge zur Geschichte und Quellenkunde des Mittelalters 7, 1978).

10) REYNOLDS, Ordinals p. 18.

the early eighth century[11]. In their earliest canonical forms Ordinals of Christ had no attribution, but by the early twelfth century three authors were given in canonical manuscripts: Isidore, Jerome, and Pope Gaius[12].

Closely associated with the Ordinals of Christ in the canonical collections is a short summary of the duties of the ministers generally called *De officiis septem graduum*[13]. Each of grades in the hierarchy from doorkeeper through bishop (or vice versa) is listed together with a variety of duties. It is said, for example, that the deacon ought to read the Gospel, minister at the altar, and proclaim the word of God to the people. This tract was incorporated into the tenth-century Pontificale Romano-Germanicum, where liturgiologists have traditionally said it had its origins[14], but long before that it was included in the early eighth-century Collectio canonum Hibernensis, where it was paired with an Ordinal of Christ and bore the title *De distantia graduum*[15]. In its many appearances in canonical collections the tract was never attributed to an author, but when it entered liturgical books Isidore of Seville was given credit[16].

Much longer than the Ordinals of Christ or the De distantia graduum is a letter on the ministers called the *De septem ordinibus ecclesiae*[17]. Again, each of

---

11) On their appearance in the Collectio Hibernensis see REYNOLDS, Ordinals p. 61 ff.; and Roger E. REYNOLDS, Unity and Diversity in Carolingian Canon Law Collections: The Case of the Collectio Hibernensis and its Derivatives, in: Carolingian Essays (as in n. 8) p. 127 f.

12) Wolfenbüttel, Herzog August-Bibl. Gud. Lat. 212, fol. 6 v (Collection in Nine Books, attributing the Ordinal to Isidore); Paris, Bibl. Arsenal Lat. 721, foll. 176 v – 177 r (Collection In Nine Books of St. Victor, attributing the Ordinal to Isidore); Munich, Bay. Staatsbibl. Clm 2594, fol. 13 r (the Summa Haimonis, attributing the Ordinal to Isidore); Oxford, Bodl. Lib. Barlow 37, foll. 139 v – 140 r (on this canonistic manuscript, attributing the Ordinal to Jerome, see REYNOLDS, Ordinals p. 142); and Vienna, Österreichische Nationalbibl. Cod. 2178, fol. 52 r (Collection in Ten Parts, attributing a text of Gaius and an Ordinal of Christ to Isidore). On all of these texts see REYNOLDS, Ordinals p. 75, n. 22 (5), 112 f., and 125 f.

13) On this text see Roger E. REYNOLDS, The ‚De officiis VII graduum‘: Its Origins and Early Medieval Development, Mediaeval Studies 34 (1972) p. 113 – 151; Roger E. REYNOLDS, The ‚Isidorian‘ ‚Epistula ad Leudefredeum‘: An Early Medieval Epitome of the Clerical Duties, Mediaeval Studies 41 (1979) p. 254, n. 4; and REYNOLDS, Unity and Diversity (as in n. 11) p. 132.

14) REYNOLDS, De officiis VII graduum p. 114 ff.

15) REYNOLDS, De officiis VII graduum p. 129 f.

16) REYNOLDS, De officiis VII graduum p. 143 ff.

17) ed. Athanasius W. KALFF, Pseudo-Hieronymi De septem ordinibus ecclesiae (1935); and MIGNE, PL Suppl. 2. 265 – 269.

seven grades from gravedigger to bishop is listed with a description of its origins and duties. Although Jerome is usually given in the manuscripts as the author, it is probable that it was composed where the Visigothic liturgical rite was used because at least one of the biblical citations follows the text used in the Mozarabic Antiphonary[18]. Moreover, its earliest appearance is in the sixth-century Visigothic canonical collection known as the Epitome hispanica[19]. But not only is Jerome's authorship in doubt, but also the recipient and title. In some manuscripts the recipient is simply a bishop[20]; and in others it is Rusticus of Narbonne[21], Patrocles of Arles[22], or Pope Damasus[23]. In some instances the tract bears no title at all[24] and in others *De septem*[25], *De sex*[26], or even *De octo ordinibus ecclesiae*[27]. Finally, in at least one canonistic manuscript, it is not Jerome but Pope Silvester who is listed as the author[28].

Also written in Spain or perhaps Catalonia was another letter on the duties of the ministers, the *Epistula ad Leudefredum* generally attributed to Isidore of Seville[29]. Although there is a possibility that Isidore wrote the letter because it resembles his genuine works, the language at times is closer to the Pseudo-Hieronymian De septem ordinibus, and its first appearance is only in ninth-century canon law manuscripts of the canonical Collectio Hispana systematica[30], Collectio Dionysio-Hadriana[31], and the Pseudo-Isidorian

---

18) R. E. REYNOLDS, The Pseudo-Hieronymian ‚De septem ordinibus ecclesiae', Revue Bénédictine 80 (1970) p. 252.

19) Verona, Bibl. Cap. LXI (59), foll. 67 v – 68 r; and Lucca, Bibl. Cap. Feliniana 490, fol. 309 r.

20) E. g., Leiden, Bibl. Rijksuniv. BPL 81, fol. 28 v.

21) E. g., Monza, Bibl. Cap. H. 3. 151, fol. s. n.

22) E. g., Verona, Bibl. Cap. LXI (59), fol. 67 v.

23) E. g., Oxford, Bodl. Lib. Bodl. 311, fol. 62 r.

24) E. g., San Daniele, Bibl. Civ. Guarneriana 203, fol. 144 r.

25) E. g., Vercelli, Bibl. Cap. XV, fol. s. n.

26) E. g., Brescia, Bibl. Civ. Queriniana B. II. 3., fol. 217 r.

27) E. g., Paris, BN Lat. 4280 AA, fol. 302 r.

28) Vatican, Barb. Lat. 679, fol. 298 r.

29) REYNOLDS, Mediaeval Studies 41 p. 252 – 330; and for the possible Catalan origins of this letter see Roger E. REYNOLDS, The Ordination Rite in Medieval Spain: Hispanic, Roman, and Hybrid, in: Santiago, Saint-Denis and Saint Peter, ed. B. REILLY (1985) p. 150 n. 28.

30) Paris, BN Lat. 11709, fol. 254 v.; Paris, BN Lat. 1565, fol. 231 v.

31) Paris, BN Lat. 3838, fol. 167 r, with attribution simply to *pape Hispalensis urbis episcopi*.

Decretals[32], where in several instances the attribution to Isidore is missing entirely.

While our four pseudonymous texts on the ecclesiastical ministers were all compiled before Carolingian times, the expository tracts on the Mass appearing in early medieval canonical collections all had their origins in the Carolingian period. Three of them antedate the celebrated works of Amalarius of Metz, and of them two are called by liturgiologists simply by their incipits. The first, *Quotiens contra se*, makes its oldest appearance in an early ninth-century Lyonese manuscript of the canonical Collectio Dacheriana[33]; and the other, *Primum in ordine*, is in a mid-ninth-century codex from Lorsch with the Collectio Dionysio-Hadriana[34] and a late ninth-century codex from Corbie with Halitgar's penitential[35]. The third early Caroline Mass comentary, the *Dominus vobiscum*, often attributed by liturgiologists to Amalarius himself, in fact almost never bears an attribution in the manuscripts, but in the three instances where it does – in fact, in canonistic manuscripts – it is Jerome[36], Isidore or Alcuin[37].

These three early Carolingian Mass commentaries consist of fairly mundane descriptions and allegorical interpretations of the Mass ordo, but two others are far more extravagant and contain contentious or fanciful explanations of the Mass. One is a correspondence attributed to Pope Damasus and Jerome on a subject the Liber pontificalis tells us was dealt with by the early second-century Pope Telesphorus: the hour of the Mass[38]. In a very short form this correspondence between Damasus and Jerome first appears in a late eighth-cen-

---

32) The earliest manuscripts of the Pseudo-Isidorian Decretals with the Epistula are Yale, Bein. Lib. 442 (s. IX3/4), fol. 240 r; and Rennes, Bibl. Mun. 134 (s. IX/X), p. 224, where the Epistula is attributed simply to a *papae Spalensis episcopi*.

33) Vatican, Reg. Lat. 446, foll. 71 v – 78 r.

34) Vatican, Pal. Lat. 485, foll. 17 v – 27 v.

35) Leningrad, Publ. Bibl. Salt. Shched. Q. v. 1.34, foll. 23 v – 42 v; where our tract written in one ninth-century hand is bound together in the manuscript with the Penitential of Halitgar written in another, foll. 45 r – 88 r; on which see Raymund KOTTJE, Die Bußbücher Halitgars von Cambrai und des Hrabanus Maurus (Beiträge zur Geschichte und Quellenkunde des Mittelalters 8, 1980) p. 33 f.

36) London, BL 16413, fol. 19 r.

37) Budapest, Orsz. Szech. Kön. 316, fol. 29 v (Alcuin); Rome, Bibl. Casan. 2010, fol. 190 v ('Ysidoro episcopo vel ab abbe Albino').

38) Le Liber pontificalis, texte, introduction et commentaire, ed. L. DUCHESNE 1 (²1955) p. 129.

tury manuscript of the canonical Collectio Vetus Gallica[39], but it quickly was augmented with fanciful allegorical interpretations of elements of the Mass liturgy itself and entered into numerous canonical collections of the tenth century and beyond[40]. The other Mass commentary is the Eldefonsine revelation Umberto Eco cited in The Name of the Rose. Besides fanciful illustrative diagrams and descriptions of the size, shape, and stamping of eucharistic hosts, it also is rich with number symbolism. Although probably not of Spanish origin because the date of the revelation is not given according to the Spanish era, the tract was early attributed to an Eldefonsus and attached to the late ninth-century Corbie codex of the Pseudo-Isidorian Collectio Augustodunensis[41]. Later, however, in southern French canonical manuscripts, including one with the penitential of Halitgar[42], no author whatsoever is mentioned.

In all of these texts on the ecclesiastical officers and on the Mass perhaps the most striking characteristic is the variety of authors and titles given in the early canon law manuscripts. But in view of medieval legal compilers' concern for authentication of texts, this cavalier attitude regarding liturgical texts is curious indeed. Let us now look at some of the possible reasons for this.

There are first those tracts like the Ordinals of Christ that are usually anonymous but in a few instances have authors attached to them. The lack of any attribution whatsoever probably is due to the fact that there was a plethora of widely divergent recensions in circulation, and it was almost universally recognized that no single author could have been responsible for the many forms and hence no author was assigned. When Isidore's or Jerome's name was attached, the reason may have been that these authors were widely recognized in the early Middle Ages as the foremost patristic authorities on orders. In cases like the De distantia graduum, canonists very likely were aware of the summary nature of the text and the possibility of varying the list of duties, and they

---

39) Stuttgart, Württ. Landesbibl. HB VI. 113, fol. 103 v; where an early ninth-century hand has added the correspondence.

40) For a list of these see Roger E. REYNOLDS, An Early Medieval Mass Fantasy: The Correspondence of Pope Damasus on a Nicene Canon, in: Proceedings of the Seventh International Congress of Medieval Canon Law, St. John's College, Cambridge 1984, ed. P. LINEHAN (Monumenta Iuris Canonici, Ser. C. Subsidia 8) (in press).

41) Vatican, Vat. lat. 1341, foll. 187 v – 188 v.

42) Paris, BN Lat. 2077, foll. 122 r – 123 r: the text of Halitgar is in a section of the manuscript written in a later hand than that of the Eldefonsine text. In Paris, BN Lat. 2855, foll. 63 r – 68 r, the Eldefonsine text is one part of what was originally three manuscripts since been bound together.

saw no reason to attach a single authority. Hence, it was left to the compilers of liturgical texts to attach Isidore's name, again probably because of his similar genuine works on the liturgical duties of the orders.

An alternative reason for attaching the name of Isidore or Jerome to these same texts might have been that they lay near the genuine works of these fathers – such as is the case of the Collectio Hibernensis[43] – and hence later compilers and scribes simply attached the names of these fathers. This same reason may also account for the attribution to Jerome of the usually anonymous Mass commentary, Dominus vobiscum, which in some manuscripts is close to the genuine works of Jerome or pseudonymous works attributed to him[44].

The De septem ordinibus ecclesiae and Epistula ad Leudefredum are almost universally attributed in canon law manuscripts to Jerome and Isidore respectively. Here, the reason probably was that the theological positions and structures of the texts resembled the genuine works of these fathers. The De septem ordinibus ecclesiae clearly reflects the position in Jerome's biblical commentaries, where he equated the presbyterate and episcopate in their common sacerdotal ordo[45]. And the structure of the Epistula ad Leudefredum with the list of liturgical duties clearly echoes Isidore's treatment of the ecclesiastical hierarchy in his genuine De ecclesiasticis officiis and Origines[46].

In several instances the pseudonymity of our liturgical pieces in canon law manuscripts seems to have been almost fortuitous. For example, the Pseudo-Hieronymian De septem ordinibus ecclesiae is at times attributed to Pope Silvester. There are, of course, the Pseudo-Silvestrian texts that deal with the interstices between the reception of orders and with the hierarchy of clerical accusations[47]; and pehaps the Silvestrian authorship of the De septem ordinibus ecclesiae might have been suggested by these. But much more likely, the attribution comes from the fact that in some manuscripts containing the

---

43) See Collectio Hibernensis I – VII, IX, ed. H. Wasserschleben, Die irische Kanonensammlung (²1885) p. 3 ff.

44) E. g., St. Gall 446, pp. 85 – 105, 303. Many manuscripts containing the Dominus vobiscum have the Damasus-Jerome correspondence, on which see Reynolds, Mass Fantasy (as in n. 40).

45) See Roger E. Reynolds, Patristic ‚Presbyterianism‘ in the Early Medieval Theology of Sacred Orders, Mediaeval Studies 45 (1983) p. 315 ff.

46) Reynolds, Mediaeval Studies 41 p. 272 ff.

47) Reynolds, Ordinals (as in n. 9) p. 30 ff.

hispanic Collection of Novara and the Pseudo-Isidorian Decretals the tract immediately follows the Canones sancti Silvestri, and Silvester's name was attached to the De septem ordinibus ecclesiae, whose recipient and title were notoriously uncertain[48].

The geographical origin or provenance of manuscripts may also have played a role in the pseudonymity of some of our liturgica in early medieval canon law collections. The seemingly strange attribution to Alcuin of the Mass commentary Dominus vobiscum in a canonical manuscript from St. Peter's in Salzburg[49], for example, may have come about because Alcuin, who had also written a simple but very popular exposition on baptism[50], was also in frequent correspondence with scholars and clergy at Salzburg[51], and it seemed fitting to attribute to him a contemporary commentary on the Mass. Likewise, the attribution of the revelation on the size, shape, and layout of eucharistic hosts to an Eldefonsus of Spain may have come about because two of the three manuscripts are from southern France[52] and one of these is written in part in Visigothic script and contains the genuine work of Ildefonse of Toledo[53]. Moreover, the unusual distribution of hosts on the altar undoubtedly suggested the similar practice of the Mozarabic liturgical rite and hence the necessity of assigning a Spanish liturgical expert as author[54].

There is a final and perhaps obvious reason for the pseudonymity of some of our liturgica in canon law collections, an outright attempt to deceive. This seems most obvious in the correspondence on the hour of the Mass between Pope Damasus and Jerome. Although these two fathers did indeed correspond

---

48) Monza, Bibl. Cap. H. 3. 151, fol. s. n.; Brescia, Bibl. Civ. Queriniana B. II. 3., fol. 217 r; Pistoia, Bibl. Cap. C 130, fol. 127 v; Paris, BN Lat. 4280 AA, fol. 302 r; Lucca, Bibl. Cap. 123, fol. 119 r.

49) Roger E. REYNOLDS, Canon law collections in early ninth-century Salzburg, in: Proceedings of the Fifth International Congress of Medieval Canon Law, Salamanca, 21 – 25 September 1976, ed. S. KUTTNER and K. PENNINGTON (1980) p. 31 n. 106.

50) KEEFE, Baptismal Expositions (as in n. 8) p. 184.

51) Alcuin Epp. 265, 266, ed. E. DÜMMLER, MGH Epp. 4 (1895) p. 442 ff.

52) Paris, BN Lat. 2077, foll. 122 r – 123 r (s. X2/2, prov. Moissac); Paris, BN Lat. 2855, foll. 63 r – 68 r (s. X, prov. LePuy).

53) Paris, BN Lat. 2855, foll. 69 v – 159 r.

54) On the distribution of the hosts on the altar in the Mozarabic rite that has continued even into the newly revised rite see Santa Iglesia Catedral PRIMADA, Novus ordo ritus hispano-mozarabici, Misa celebrada solemnemente en la clausura del II Congreso Internacional de Estudios Mozárabes, con motivo del IX Centenario de la Reconquista de Toledo, el 26 de mayo de 1985 (1985) p. 56 f.

on liturgical matters, the fanciful explanations of the Mass in the correspondence are clearly medieval and contradict patristic positions[55]. But it is most important to note that this tract, which is always attributed to Damasus and Jerome in the manuscripts, was embedded in and not simply appended to canonical collections, and hence it was probably felt necessary to assign the tract to a papal authority and his frequent liturgical correspondent.

Having considered some of the reasons for the attributions of our pseudonymous liturgica, let us now look briefly at their role in early medieval canon law collections by examining, first, their position vis-a-vis other canonical material and then their extensive modification in the collections.

The earliest appearance of many of our texts in canon law manuscripts suggests that they were simply addenda. Because they dealt with liturgical procedures in the broad sense, it was thought fitting to append them to manuscripts containing legal procedures enacted largely by popes, bishops, and councils. Such seems to be the case with the early Carolingian commentaries on the Mass[56]. But because of the length of these commentaries or their abundance of allegorizing interpretation they seem never to have been regarded as truly canonistic and hence were never fully integrated into the canon law collections themselves. Other pseudonymous liturgica, however, were clearly seen as canonistic and were used in a variety of ways. In historically arranged collections such as the Pseudo-Isidorian Decretals, texts like the De septem ordinibus ecclesiae and Epistula ad Leudefredum supplemented the otherwise chronologically arranged material[57]. As the texts in these collections were then systematized, our pseudonymous liturgica were incorporated as integral parts of the collections. Thus, the Ordinals of Christ and De distantia graduum were embedded into groups of canons dealing with the ecclesiastical hierarchy[58]. The Epistula ad Leudefredum and the Damasus-Jerome correspondence was used to introduce series of canons on the liturgical ministers and the Mass[59].

---

55) REYNOLDS, Mass Fantasy (as in n. 40).

56) E. g., Vatican, Reg. Lat. 446, with the Collectio Dacheriana and the Mass exposition Quotiens contra se.

57) On the De septem ordinibus ecclesiae in these manuscripts see above n. 48; and on the Epistula ad Leudefredum in these manuscripts see REYNOLDS, Epistula ad Leudefredum (as in n. 13) p. 287 ff.

58) E. g., Collectio Hibernensis VIII, within I–IX, p. 26.

59) The Epistula ad Leudefredum is used as an introductory piece in the Collection in Twelve Parts 2.1, Bonizo of Sutri's Liber de vita christiana 5.71, and Rome, Bibl. Vallic. F 92, fol. 193 v; on which see REYNOLDS, Ordinals (as in n. 9) p. 292 f., 306. The

And the Ordinals of Christ and De distantia graduum came to act as concluding summaries of canons on the ecclesiastical hierarchy[60].

As our texts were incorporated into canon law collections, they were regarded as canonistic pieces and hence came to be altered like other canons deriving from more strictly legislative sources. One of the types of modification was the transformation of a tract into a strictly canonical text. In some canonistic manuscripts, for example, the salutation and exordium of the Epistula ad Leudefredum were suppressed leaving only a stark list of the duties of the grades[61]. Secondly, the texts could be altered in the canonical collections by additions, subtractions, and rearrangement of materials to correspond to developments in liturgy, theology, or canon law. In the De distantia gradum, for example, the grade of acolyte was added by the ninth century thereby reflecting the reality of an eight-grade hierarchy[62]. In recensions of the Epistula ad Leudefredum the grade of psalmist was often omitted, perhaps because in liturgical commentaries the psalmist was often equated with the lector[63]. And in Burchard's Decretum the sequence of grades in the Epistula ad Leudefredum was rearranged to harmonize with the Romano-Gallican sequence of the lower orders from psalmist to acolyte accepted almost universally from the tenth century[64]. A third form of modification of our pseudonymous texts in canonistic manuscripts was abbreviation. The long De septem ordinibus ecclesiae, for example, was severely abbreviated as early as the sixth century and placed in the Epitome hispanica[65]. A fourth and final type of alteration was the dismemberment of longer texts and use of the isolated fragments in canonical collections.

Damasus-Jerome correspondence is used as an introductory piece in the Collection in Five Books 3.212, ed. M. FORNASARI, CC Cont. Med. 6 (1970) p. 413 ff.

60) E. g., Vatican, Vat. Lat. 4317, foll. 102 v – 104 r.

61) Turin, Bibl. Naz. Univ. D. IV. 33, fol. 64 v; Paris, Bibl. Sainte-Geneviève 166, fol. 99 r; Wolfenbüttel, Herzog August-Bibl. Gud. Lat. 212, fol. 8 r; Paris, BN Lat. 10740, fol. 87 r; the Statuta canonum de officio sacerdotum (MIGNE PL 140. 1070); Reims, Bibl. Mun. 675, fol. 36 r; Hereford, Cath. Lib. O. ii. 7, fol. 83 v; Vatican, Vat. Lat. 1348, fol. XLVIIʳ; Vatican, Barb. Lat. 538, fol. 49 v; Rome, Bibl. Vallic. F 54, fol. 130 v; Paris, BN Lat. 4286, fol. 27 r; on which see REYNOLDS, Epistula ad Leudefredum (as in n. 13) p. 293 ff.

62) REYNOLDS, Unity and Diversity (as in n. 11) p. 132.

63) Vatican, Vat. Lat. 1348, foll. XLVIIʳ – XLVIIIʳ. And on the commentaries see Roger E. REYNOLDS, ,At Sixes and Sevens' – and Eights and Nines: The Sacred Mathematics of Sacred Orders in the Early Middle Ages, Speculum 54 (1979) p. 679.

64) REYNOLDS, Epistula ad Leudefredum (as in n. 13) p. 290 f.

65) See n. 19 above.

I. Revelatio of Eldefonsus.
Vatican, Biblioteca Apostolica Vaticana, Vat. lat. 1341, fol. 187ᵛ.

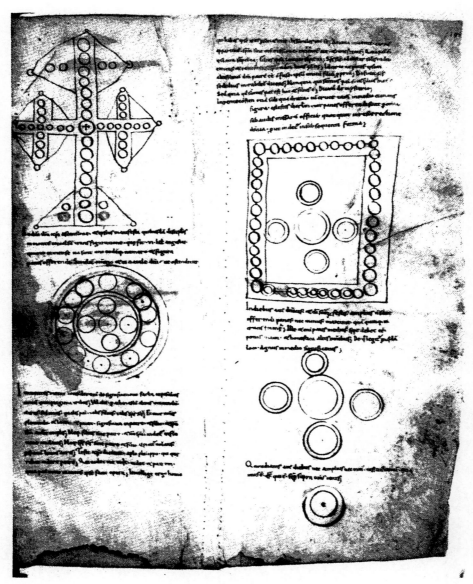

II. Revelatio of Eldefonsus.
Vatican, Biblioteca Apostolica Vaticana, Vat. lat. 1341, fol. 188^r.

Snippets from the Hieronymian De septem ordinibus ecclesiae and Isidorian Epistula ad Leudefredum, for example, are often embedded in other canonistic material[66].

To conclude this paper, let us briefly consider our pseudonymous liturgical pieces in the larger spectrum of medieval forgeries. With the exception of the Hieronymian De septem ordinibus ecclesiae and Damasus-Jerome correspondence on the hour of the Mass, both of which forcefully argue contentious canonistic, theological, or liturgical points, our texts do not seem originally to have been forgeries written to deceive, but rather as simple descriptions or commentaries on liturgical practice. The fact that many of them were originally anonymous and not pseudonymous in early manuscripts is at least partial confirmation of this. But as our tracts moved from appendages to canonical collections into the collections themselves, the need for authentication grew. To assign the texts to a papal or conciliar authority like other canons would clearly not have been fitting in most instances because of their patently descriptive or expository nature. Hence, patristic authorities like Isidore and Jerome were chosen whose genuine works either resembled or touched upon the subjects of the texts. This necessary slide from anonymity to pseudonymity was thus an easy one to make. When compared to such audacious fictions as the Pseudo-Isidorian Decretals, which are often cheek by jowl with them, most of our pseudonymous liturgical texts must be considered the mildest of forgeries in early medieval canonical collections.

---

66) On the addition of snippets from the De septem ordinibus ecclesiae see REYNOLDS, Revue Bénédictine 80 p. 250 f. The addition of snippets from the Epistula ad Leudefredum can be found in Paris, BN Lat. 2449, fol. 135 r; Vatican, Vat. Lat. 3788, fol. 11 r; Vatican, Vat. lat. 1346, fol. 1 v.

X

RITES OF SEPARATION AND RECONCILIATION IN THE EARLY MIDDLE AGES

In his apostolic exhortation of 2 December 1984, *Reconciliatio et Paenitentia* [1], Pope John Paul II emphasized the importance that the theme of reconciliation had played in the recent Year of Jubilee and the fact that reconciliation and penance had been chosen as the theme for the Sixth General Assembly of the Synod of Bishops. This apostolic exhortation with its substantial treatment of these themes represents the position of the Church's magisterium on the subject, but it can also be taken as an invitation for further reflection and study of these themes. It is in the spirit of that apostolic exhortation, then, that this article on the early medieval rites of separation and reconciliation is presented.

In reading the recent apostolic exhortation one cannot fail to be impressed with the number of biblical references to separation and reconciliation and their repetition in the works of the patristic fathers. One would then expect to find these terms used repeatedly in the rituals used in the early medieval western Church. Surprisingly, when one turns to the dictionary of principal liturgical themes by Blaise [2] or to the concordance to the early sacramentaries

---

(1) *Acta apostolicae sedis*, 1985, n. 3 (Vatican City 1985), pp. 185-275.
(2) ALBERT BLAISE, *Le vocabulaire latin des principaux thèmes liturgiques* (Turnhout n.d.), pp. 91, 98.

recently published by Dom Deshusses [3] and looks for these terms, he is confronted with the anomaly that they are rarely represented. Rather, the varieties and gradations of separation and reconciliation are reflected in a host of other terms and a vast complex of rituals and accompanying prayers. To examine exhaustively the complexity of these rites and accompanying signs in a single article would clearly be impossible. Moreover, aspects such as penance, exorcisms, benedictions and the like have been treated extensively elsewhere or in the papers of this Settimana. Hence, this article will concentrate on several representative rites, first of separation and then of reconciliation, and in terms of persons, places, and objects.

Professor Kottje has dealt in this Settimana with the most basic state of personal separation and corresponding rite of reconciliation in the early medieval West, sin and reconciliation through the rite of penance. Beyond this basic state of personal separation in sin, however, was the more serious state of excommunication. To modern man this word conjures up formal, even awesome rites of separation. But in fact, during the early Middle Ages the term could be understood in many ways. In its most modest form it could mean simply ecclesiastical discipline with perhaps no overtones of sin. In the *Ordo Romanus Primus,* for example, the archiparaphonista is threatened with excommunication in the event a different lector should read or a different cantor should sing than the one indicated earlier to the pope [4]. At the other end of the scale excommunication could be used as an alternative term

(3) JEAN DESHUSSES and BENOIT DARRAGON, *Concordances et tableaux pour l'étude des grands sacramentaires,* 3 vols. (Fribourg/S. 1982), III. 4, pp. 30, 217.

(4) c. 39, ed. MICHEL ANDRIEU, *Les Ordines romani du haut moyen âge,* 5 vols. (*Spicilegium sacrum Lovaniense* 11, 23, 24, 28, 29: Louvain 1931-61), II, p. 80.

for anathema and maranatha with their connotations of eternal death and damnation, as the Council of Meaux in 845-46 said [5], or of separation from God, as Benedictus Levita wrote [6]. Between these extremes there could be a variety of degrees of excommunication. For example, the early eighth-century *Collectio Hibernensis* tells us variously that there are three forms of excommunication — ex pace et mensa et missa [7] — or seven forms, including deprivation *a concelebratione, a communicatione mensae, a cohabitatione, a benedictione, a colloquio pacifico, a commeatu, a muneribus* [8]. In a sense, this is not unlike a canon of the Council of Saint-Laurent-lès Mâcon of 855 in which both a moderate and severe sentence of excommunication are developed, the former being exclusion from the threshold of the church and the body and the blood of Christ, and the latter, for those obdurate, including separation from Christian society, exclusion from the Mass, prohibition of living and speaking with Christians, and the eradication of one's name from the *oratio fidelium* [9].

Within this range of excommunications the exclusion itself might be precipitated in several ways. Later canonists would make a distinction between excommunication *de jure* and excommunication *ab homine,* and this distinction did in fact if not in theory obtain in the western Church of the early Middle Ages. That is, excommunication might occur simply in doing or believing something con-

(5) c. 56, ed. WILFRIED HARTMANN, *Die Konzilien der karolingischen Teilreiche 843-859 (Monumenta Germaniae historica, Concilia* III: Hannover 1984), pp. 110-111. Hartmann notes that the designation of anathema as eternal death appears nowhere else.

(6) *Capitula Benedicti Levitae* II. 427, *PL* 97. 801, defines anathema as « ... a Deo separationem ».

(7) XL. 1c, ed. HERMANN WASSERSCHLEBEN, *Die irische Kanonensammlung,* 2nd ed. (Leipzig 1885), p. 153.

(8) XL. 1d, ed. WASSERSCHLEBEN, *op. cit.,* p. 153.

(9) c. 2, ed. HARTMANN, *op. cit.,* pp. 375-376.

demned, or it might occur through a formal rite by which excommunication was imposed on individuals [10].

Anathemas *de jure* go far back into patristic antiquity with condemnations of those who held heretical positions. By 306 the Synod of Elvira had already anathematized those who distributed infamous *libelli* in the Church [11], and synods, popes, and bishops would repeat anathemas of persons and their doctrines in countless decisions enacted during the early Middle Ages. Anathemas *de jure* were also part of such credal statements as the Nicene Creed or the Athanasian *Quicunque vult*. These anathemas were, in a sense, signs of immediate separation from Christian society whatever the degree implied. Beyond these automatic or *de jure* signs of separation, there were rituals to be followed for more formal excommunications. As early as the New Testament, of course, there was the direction regarding evangelical admonition or threefold warning [12], and this New Testament directive was repeated constantly in early medieval synodical decrees and canonical collections as applying to excommunication *ab homine* or formal excommunication [13]. Moreover, it came to be the custom that formal public excommunication was to be used only for notorious sinners. The Synod of Meaux, for example, directs that it be used only for certain and manifest sins and that the more severe

---

(10) A text of Origen that spoke of automatic excommunication even without formal episcopal pronouncement was used in Gratian's *Decretum*, C. XXIV, q. 3, c. 7, on which see FRANÇOIS RUSSO, « Pénitence et excommunication. Étude historique sur les rapports entre la théologie et le droit canon dans le domaine pénitentiel du IXe au XIIIe siècle », in *Recherches de science religieuse*, XXXIII (1946), p. 269.

(11) c. 52, ed. JOSÉ VIVES, *Concilios visigóticos e hispano-romanos* (*España Cristiana*, *Textos* 1: Barcelona-Madrid 1963), p. 10.

(12) Mt. 18. 15-17.

(13) E. g., Regino of Prüm, *Libri duo de synodalibus causis et disciplinis ecclesiasticis* II. 412, ed. F. G. A. WASSERSCHLEBEN (Leipzig 1840), p. 370, and p. 511 for other citations.

anthema could be used only with the consent of the archbishop and co-bishops [14].

By at least the sixth century in the West formal rites of excommunication seem to have been developing. Gregory of Tours, for example, speaks of the relative horribleness of having Psalm 108 read above one's head as opposed to perpetual excommunication [15]. And the Synod of Tours in 567 speaks of the malefactor who not only is excommunicated but is also anathematized by having Psalm 108 read above his head and a malediction pronounced, the results of which are likened to those that befell Judas who stole from the poor [16].

In the ninth century, details of the ritual of excommunication in the western Church begin to be more plentiful. Pope John VIII, for example, is said to have seized the Gospel book and read the excommunication of Photius from a high ambo in a distinct voice [17]. Hincmar of Rheims in admonishing his priests to denounce publically those who are excommunicated says that although excommunications are commonly read after the Gospel during Mass, they should on occasion be read before the Gospel [18]. This was because some malefactors, knowing of the customary practice, were leaving church before the Gospel, thereby avoiding the humiliation of public censure. It is at this same time that a dossier of texts was compiled containing regulations for the excommunication of violators of ecclesiastical properties. These texts, recently studied

---

(14) c. 56, ed. HARTMANN, *op. cit.*, pp. 110-111.

(15) *Historia Francorum* V. 18, ed. Bruno Krusch, *Monumenta Germaniae historica, Scriptores rerum Merovingicarum* I. 1, 2nd ed. (Hannover 1951) p. 223.

(16) c. 25 (24), ed. CHARLES DE CLERCQ, *Concilia Galliae, a. 511-a. 695* (*Corpus christianorum, ser. lat.* 148A: Turnhout 1963), pp. 192-193.

(17) On this reported anathematization, see FRANCIS DVORNIK, *The Photian Schism: History and Legend* (Cambridge 1948), pp. 217-218.

(18) Epistle XVII, *PL* 126. 101.

410

by Horst Fuhrmann [19], contain the first quotations from the Pseudo-Isidorian Decretals together with biblical and canonical material that would be echoed in later excommunication formulae. There are, for example, in the *Collectio de raptoribus* references to the *raptores pauperum*, the fates of Judas, Ananias, and Saphira, a quotation from II John 10, "Nec ave ei dixeris", and a final "Anathema sit". Further, bishops are bidden to inform their people regarding the nature of the anathema and how long it is to last, an obvious encouragement for the malefactor to do penance and be reconciled to the Church [20].

The concern with those who attack the Church so clearly found in this dossier of texts of the second half of the ninth century is reflected in an excommunication formula entered in the well-known late ninth-century Leningrad manuscript of the *Sens Pontifical* [21]. After an introduction deploring the fall of those baptized and stating that they have been properly admonished, their names are read out as persons who are contemptuous of God and his Church. They then are excommunicated and anathematiz-

---

(19) HORST FUHRMANN, *Einfluss und Verbreitung der pseudoisidorischen Fälschungen von ihrem Auftauchen bis in die neuere Zeit*, 3 vols. (*Schriften der Monumenta Germaniae historica* XXIV. 1-3: Stuttgart 1972-74), I, pp. 211-214.

(20) ed. HARTMANN, *op. cit.*, pp. 392-394. It is interesting that the section « Qui abstulerit aliquid patri vel matri... » taken from Pseudo-Anacletus, c. 14, appears even earlier in the *Dicta sancti Gregorii*, used in late eighth- and early ninth-century canonical collections; on which see R. E. Reynolds, « The Pseudo-Augustinian 'Sermo de conscientia' and the related canonical 'Dicta sancti Gregorii papae'», in *Revue Bénédictine*, LXXXI (1971), p. 315; and ROGER E. REYNOLDS, « Canon law collections in early ninth-century Salzburg », in *Proceedings of the Fifth International Congress of Medieval Canon Law, Salamanca, 21-25 September 1976*, eds. STEPHAN KUTTNER and KENNETH PENNINGTON (*Monumenta Iuris Canonici, Series C. Subsidia* 6: Vatican City 1980), p. 23, n. 46.

(21) Leningrad, Gosudarstvennaia ordena Trudovogo Krasnogo Znameni Publichnaia biblioteka imeni M. E. Saltykova-Shchedrina, lat. Q. v. I. 35 (s. IX 3/4), ff. 105v-107r. For the text of this formula see JEAN LUC D'ACHERY, *Spicilegium sive collectio veterum aliquot scriptorum ...*, 3 vols. (Paris 1723), III, pp. 320-321; and ANTONIO STAERK, *Les manuscrits latins du Vᵉ au XIIIᵉ siècle conservés à la Bibliothèque Impériale de Saint-Pétersbourg*, 2 vols. (St. Petersburg 1910), I, pp. 172-173.

ed and various prohibitions are enumerated. The malefactors are to have no contact with Christians and are not to enter the church. No Masses are to be said for them. No oblations, commemorations, or incense are to be accepted on their behalf. Priests are not to attend them at death. And their smelling cadavers are to be cast out without Christian burial. A variety of maledictions is called down on them, after each of which an Amen is said. Moreover, God is called upon to inflict them with poverty, fever, cold, burning, and fire forever. Finally, reflecting the ritual extinguishing of candles at the conclusion of the excommunication ceremonies, it is said that just as this light is extinguished in the eyes of men, so the light of the malefactor is to be extinguished eternally.

The ritual aspects reflected in this excommunication formula from Sens were made much more explicit in a series of excommunication rites gathered together by Regino of Prüm in his canonical *Libri duo de synodalibus causis et disciplinis ecclesiasticis* written ca. 906. Not only ritual directions are found in these but also two allocutions and four excommunication formulae proper with their preface, anathema, and maledictions answered by Amens. Further, it is clear from their titles that there is a definite hierarchy of formulae ranging from an *excommunicatio brevis* to a *terribilior excommunicatio* [22].

The ritual itself [23] begins with a directive, reflecting c. 56 of the ninth-century Synod of Meaux [24], that the excommunication take place only if the crime is certain and manifest. Also, reflecting the customary use reported by Hincmar [25], it is said that the rite, which is here perform-

---

(22) II. 412-417, ed. WASSERSCHLEBEN, *Regino*, pp. 369-376.
(23) II. 412, *ibid.*, pp. 369-371.
(24) See above, n. 14.
(25) See above, n. 18.

ed by a bishop, is to take place after the Gospel with clerics and people in attendance, probably indicating a high Mass on Sundays or feast days.

First, an allocution is read deploring the fact that the person who once renounced the devil and his work in baptism has now been pursuaded by him to devastate the vineyard of Christ, oppress the *pauperes Christi,* and take their goods. Here the teaching, later articulated by canonists, is clear that excommunication can apply only to baptized persons, and there is also a reference to the pressing problem of the ninth century, the violation of ecclesiastical property [26]. The allocution then goes on to say that three times priests have warned the malefactor but he has failed to repent and persists in a spirit of *superbia* or arrogance. Hence, so that one member of Christ's body will not injure the others, the process of evangelical admonition has been followed and the malefactor is now to be considered a heathen, gentile, and pagan. Then, a dossier of New Testament verses regarding separation of malefactors is read, including the "Nec ei ave dixeris" of II John 10. Finally, the member is to be cut off by excommunication lest he infect the rest.

In place of this allocution, an alternative form is provided by Regino, which seems to be directed more to apostates than to violators of churches [27]. It is much shorter and contains a different dossier of New Testament texts, but the result is the same as the first allocution.

Following the allocution there is read, perhaps with some intonation or chant, the formal excommunication itself. In the first of Regino's four forms [28] the bishop

---

(26) On this problem and the texts used to counteract it see FUHRMANN, *op. cit.,* I, pp. 211-214.

(27) II. 414, ed. WASSERSCHLEBEN, *Regino,* pp. 373-374.

(28) II. 413, *ibid.,* pp. 371-372.

again notes that the evangelical admonition has been followed without success and by virtue of the power of the keys he is prohibiting the malefactor from receiving the body and blood of Christ, depriving him of Christian society, and excluding him from the threshold of both the earthly and heavenly Church.   He is then excommunicated, anathematized, and damned with the devil, his angels, and the reprobate to eternal fire.   There is, however, a *nisi* or conditional clause, common to these forms of separation, in which the malefactor is threatened with this punishment unless (*nisi*) he comes to his senses and does penance.

In the second of Regino's excommunication formulae [29] the evangelical admonition is not cited, but the consequences of excommunication are made more specific. The malefactor is forbidden to cross the threshold of the church and to associate with Christians.   Reflecting Pseudo-Calixtus in the Pseudo-Isidorian Decretals [30], no one is to greet or exchange the kiss of peace with him. Priests are directed not to say Mass for him or give him the body and blood of Christ.   Christians, also, are forbidden to consort or to do business with him.   And if they presume to do so, they are also excommunicated, unless their purpose has been to bring the malefactor to satisfaction and penance.

Regino's *terribilior excommunicatio* [31] is specifically directed to the most notorious of criminals — profaners, violators and wasters of property, thieves, plunderers, and murderers — and their names are read out.   Then they are cursed with a series of maledictions based primarily on those in the Old Testament, especially the maledictions

---

(29) II. 415, *ibid.*, p. 374.

(30) PAUL HINSCHIUS, *Decretales pseudo-Isidorianae et Capitula Angilramni* (Leipzig 1863), p. 138.

(31) II. 416, ed. WASSERSCHLEBEN, *Regino*, pp. 374-375.

414

given by Moses in Deuteronomy 27-28. The anathema is then pronounced with the mysterious and terrible maranatha, and Christians are forbidden contact with the malefactor and priests to celebrate Mass for him or give him communion. The malefactor is to be buried in the sepulcher of asses and be regarded as a dung heap on the face of the earth. And anticipating the following ceremony of extinguishing candles, it is said that the light of the malefactor is to be extinguished eternally unless (*nisi*) he should repent and do penance.

Regino's fourth or brief excommunication formula [32] directed to violators of churches simply excludes them from the bosom of the Church and society of other Christians until they repent.

Following the excommunication formula in Regino [33] the ritual continues with all the clerics and people saying "Amen", "Fiat", or "Anathema sit". Then the bishop and twelve priests surrounding him are to throw to the ground the burning candles they have held throughout the ceremony and to trample on them with their feet.

The conclusion to the excommunication rite given by Regino reflects Carolingian canonical usage by directing the bishop to describe exactly what the excommunication entails and to forbid associations with the malefactor lest the people also be excommunicated. Further, letters regarding the excommunication are to be sent to the parishes to be read after the Gospel on Sundays, and neighboring bishops are to be informed so that they might notify their priests.

These rites and formulae given by Regino were to have very wide broadcast throughout the Middle Ages. Not only were they taken over into the enormously popular

(32) II. 417, *ibid.*, p. 375.
(33) II. 413, *ibid.*, p. 372.

Decretum of Burchard of Worms in the early eleventh century [34], but in a slightly modified form they were copied into the *Pontificale Romano-Germanicum* [35]. But alternative formulae continued to be developed in the early Middle Ages that expanded upon these rites. This expansion occurred particularly in the severity of the maledictions and punishments threatened, thereby reflecting perhaps an increasing dependence on this form of ecclesiastical discipline in the face of rising violence in the tenth and early eleventh century.

One of these alternative rites came to be placed in the *Pontificale Romano-Germanicum* itself [36] and was attributed to a pope Leo, who, according to Lester Little [37], was probably Leo VII (936-39). Other versions of this same rite are reported at St.-Benoit-sur-Loire and St.-Martin of Tours, and since the general version of the *Pontificale Romano-Germanicum* singles out the servants of St. Peter, it was perhaps directed to Cluny itself. Although cast in the form of a letter, the *Excommunicatio Leonis papae* clearly is an excommunication formula to be used ritually because of the Amen responses after the maledictions and threats. The major differences between this formula and those given by Regino are the invocation of the Trinity, Peter, Mary, the angels, apostles, martyrs and others in the excommunication and the virulence of the maledictions and threats. Not only is the punishment of Judas threatened, but also that of the Old Testament rebels Dathan and

---

(34) XI. 2 (rubric), 3-7, PL 140. 856-860.

(35) LXXXV-LXXXIX, eds. CYRILLE VOGEL and REINHARD ELZE, *Le Pontifical romano-germanique du dixième siècle*, 3 vols. (*Studi e Testi* 226, 227, 269; Vatican City 1963, 1972), I, pp. 308-314.

(36) XC, *ibid.*, I, pp. 315-317.

(37) LESTER K. LITTLE, « Formules monastiques de malédiction aux IXe et Xe siècles », in *Revue Mabillon*, LVIII (1975), pp. 383-384.

Abiron. The number of maledictions, too, has been extended, and the biblical basis for most of them is still clear.

Another alternative form with yet more violent language is entered into a tenth-century codex from Leyre containing the works of St. Jerome [38]. Here the punishments of several ancient secular reprobates are cited, including Julian the Apostate and Nero. And the fury of the punishments and maledictions is intensified tenfold. The malefactors' seed is condemned; their days are to be short and evil; misery and pestilence are to be their companion. Their malediction is to endure day and night at all hours: as they sleep, as they are awake, as they fast, eat, drink, speak, touch, and walk inside or out. Their eyes are to be blinded, their ears stopped, their mouths dried out, their tongues cleave to the roofs of their mouths, and so forth. Their grave is to be with the dogs and asses and their cadavers devoured by wolves.

Finally, a yet more fearsome alternative formula was printed by Martène from a Fécamp codex, which the Abbe Martimort has not been able to identify, but which would appear to date to the late tenth century [39]. In this example, St. Stephen and St. Ouen of Rouen have been added to the worthies whose aid is invoked, and the names of Korah, Decius, Herod, Valerian, and Simon Magus added to the list of ancients who were punished with the same penalties the malefactor will also be. In the maledictions particular attention is paid to the various parts of the body.

---

(38) Rouen, Bibl. mun. A. 425, f. 2v. On this manuscript see GENEVIÈVE NORTIER, *Les bibliothèques médiévales des abbayes bénédictines de Normandie* (Paris 1971), p. 142; and BERNARD LAMBERT, *Bibliotheca hieronymiana manuscripta: La tradition manuscrite des œuvres de Saint Jérôme*, 4 vols. (*Instrumenta patristica* IV: Steenbrugge 1969-1972), I, p. 270. The text is found in EDMOND MARTÈNE, *De antiquis ecclesiae ritibus*, 4 vols. (Venice 1763-1764), II, p. 325.

(39) AIMÉ-GEORGES MARTIMORT, *La documentation liturgique de dom Edmond Martène: Étude codicologique* (*Studi e Testi* 279: Vatican City 1978), p. 422. MARTÈNE, *op. cit.*, II, p. 322.

The ferocity of penalties in these formulae of excommunication also appears in another but closely related formula of separation widely used from the middle of the ninth century throughout the early Middle Ages, the malediction. This form, currently being studied by Lester Little [40], was often confused with excommunication and anathema because those two terms often occurred in the maledictions themselves.   Moreover, like the excommunication formulae, maledictions could be read out in Mass after the Gospel or Credo, and as the neumes in a late ninth-century Limoges codex indicate [41], they could be intoned or chanted.

Undoubtedly, the best known of these maledictions is one appearing in the Farfese *Liber tramitis* [42], but perhaps the most interesting one is from St.-Wandrille.   A copy of its frequently printed text is now found in a sixteenth-century codex from Rouen [43], but it clearly goes back to the mid-ninth century or before [44].   Most of the formulae of malediction in this manuscript are like those of our excomunication formulae, but it is the ritual surrounding them together with elements not found in excomunications that make this *Tenor maledictionis* particularly interesting.   The malediction formula itself is said after the Gospel at Mass on Sundays and other days with the priest standing before the altar.   After the malediction, the bells

---

(40) See LESTER K. LITTLE, « La morphologie des malédictions monastiques », in *Annales: Economies, Sociétés, Civilisations*, XXXIV (1979), pp. 43-60.   Several interesting maledictions in connection with oaths have recently been published by FERNANDO VALLS TABERNER, *Los Usatges de Barcelona: Estudios, comentarios y edición bilingüe del texto* (Barcelona 1984), pp. 126-130.

(41) Paris, BN lat. 5/II, f. 220v.

(42) ed. PETER DINTER, *Liber tramitis aevi Odilonis Abbatis* (*Corpus Consuetudinum Monasticarum* 10: Siegburg 1980), pp. 247-248.

(43) Rouen, Bibl. mun. Y 208, on which see MARTIMORT, *op. cit.*, p. 419.

(44) See LITTLE, « Formules », p. 383.

418

of the monastery are sounded and Psalms and prayers are said. The Psalms and psalmic *preces* are drawn, as one might expect, from the penitential Psalms and such texts as Psalm 108. The prayers derive from in the Gelasian sacramentaries of the eight century, some of which were included in the Supplement to the *Gregorian Sacramentary* by Benedict of Aniane. In these prayers two themes are especially stressed: the clamor made to God by humble but afflicted sinners, and the *superbia* or arrogance of those who afflict them.

These two themes of the malediction are also found in the closely related rite of separation called the *clamor* [45]. It is often stated that this rite was a monastic one and served for monks as the equivalent of the episcopal or secular rite of excommunication. This is in part true, but as Canal has argued [46], it could also be used in cathedrals or other churches served by groups of clergy. The rite itself, which has elements resembling the excommunication of places or interdict, to be treated later, may go back at least to the mid-eighth century, as Bauerreis has shown [47]. And it is clear that it could take a variety of forms ranging from the minor *clamor* to the great *clamor* and that several alternative formulae could be used.

The minor *clamor*, whose ritual setting closely resembles the malediction, is rarely found in manu-

---

(45) On the *clamor* see ADOLPH FRANZ, *Die Messe im deutschen Mittelalter: Beiträge zur Geschichte der Liturgie und des religiösen Volkslebens* (Freiburg/Br. 1902), pp. 206-211; JOSEPH A. JUNGMANN, *The Mass of the Roman Rite: Its Origins and Development (Missarum Sollemnia)*, trs. FRANCIS A. BRUNNER, 2 vols. (New York 1951-1955), II, p. 292, n. 87; ROMUALD BAUERREISS, « Der 'Clamor', eine verschollene mittelalterliche Gebetsform und das Salve Regina », in *Studien und Mitteilungen zur Geschichte des Benediktiner-Ordens und seine Zweige*, LXII (1949-1950), pp. 26-33; JOSÉ MARIA CANAL, *Salve Regina Misericordiae: Historia y Leyendas en torno a esta antifona* (*Temi e Testi* 9: Rome 1963), pp. 159-170; and the *Liber tramitis, op. cit.*, p. 1v.

(46) CANAL, *op. cit.*, p. 164.

(47) BAUERREISS, *op. cit.*, p. 26.

scripts [48]. It was performed at Mass, not after the Gospel or Credo, but after the Pater noster and before the *Pax domini*. While all present prostrated themselves, the priest, holding the consecrated host, genuflected before the altar and the deacon read the minor *clamor* in the form of a prayer. Thereafter Psalm 24 was said, the bells were rung, several *capitula* were said together with the collect *Hostium nostrorum*. Then it is specified that all present were to say Amen in a loud voice, indicating perhaps that the earlier formulae were read in a low or humbled voice.

An intermediate but more severe form of *clamor* can be found in the Farfese *Liber tramitis* [49]. Here, at the principal Mass of the day after the last petition of the Pater noster, "Libera nos a malo", a rough cloth was put on the pavement before the altar. A crucifix, Gospel book, and relics were then placed on it. All the clerics prostrated themselves and sang Psalm 73 in a low or humble voice and the bell was rung twice. Thereafter, a priest stood before the consecrated host and relics and said with a loud voice the formula of *clamor* frequently found in medieval manuscripts entitled *in spiritu humilitatis*. This prayer mentions violators of ecclesiastical property and emphasizes the humility of those praying. It is specifically directed to Jesus, whose corpus is both on the altar and on the humiliated crucifix and whose word in the Gospels lies on the rough cloth. The saints too, whose relics also lie humiliated, are invoked. Jesus is asked to rise up (*Exurge*) and break the *superbia* or arrogance of the malefactors. After the formula, the relics are returned to their place and the priest continues in a low voice with the embolism of the Pater noster, "Libera nos quaesumus domine".

(48) MARTÈNE, *op. cit.*, II, p. 321, based on the *Consuetudines ecclesiae beati Martini Turonensis* of ca. 1227, on which see MARTIMORT, *op. cit.*, pp. 419, 224-227.

(49) 174, ed. DINTER, *op. cit.*, pp. 244-247.

420

A ritual very much like this but entitled the great *clamor* is reported in a text from St.-Martin of Tours, which Patrick Geary [50] has dated to an early period but which in reality is from the Customaries of Tours of 1227 [51]. Despite its late date, it contains elements that clearly go back to rituals of the early medieval period. The text is very confused in its order and perhaps intentionally reflects the disorder of the office and Mass it presents. For example, the Mass is said as a private one in a low voice despite the fact that it is the principal Mass of the day; the subdeacon and deacon wear surplices to read the Epistle and Gospel; candles are lit and then extinguished; and the antiphons are read without music. But most interesting in all of this disordered ritual is the humiliation of relics with spines or thorns.

The ceremony is not limited simply to the Mass but begins very early after the office of Prime. In this ritual a silver crucifix and reliquaries are humiliated on the floor between the choir stalls. A wooden crucifix covered with thorns is placed in the nave of the church. Then the reliquary of St. Martin itself is covered with thorns. Moreover, all the doors of the church, save a small one, are barred with thorns. This practice of humiliation of relics of saints with thorns after the violation of church property can be found as far back as the sixth century. Gregory of Tours, for example, reports that a bishop went to the tomb of St. Mitrius, and after prostrating himself before it and declaring that neither light could be burned nor Psalms sung there, he threw thorns over the tomb and closed the doors of the church [52].

(50) PATRICK GEARY, « L'humiliation des saints », in *Annales: Economies, Sociétés, Civilisations*, XXXIV (1979), pp. 29-33.

(51) MARTIMORT, *op. cit.*, pp. 419, 224-227; MARTÈNE, *op. cit.*, II, p. 321.

(52) WILHELM RICHTER, *De origine et evolutione interdicti usque ad aetatem Ivonis Carnotensis et Paschalis II, I. Scriptores, Epistolae, Concilia* (Rome 1934), p. 14.

These rituals of separation in excommunication, malediction, and *clamor* could be directed against persons of any sort. But there were other rites of separation directed against specific classes or person with particular callings. Representative of these is the rite of clerical degradation. In the later Middle Ages these rites, resembling a military degradation, were well developed and have been studied extensively by Bernhard Schimmelpfennig [53] and Marc Dykmans [54]. In these later ceremonies the bishop as he read a condemnation ceremonially removed the symbols and instruments that had been given to the members of each ecclesiastical grade as they had been ordained, even to removing with a glass or knife the place of unction on the hand and the corona of the tonsured cleric. Unfortunately, the detail provided in the later ritual is lacking for the early Middle Ages, but through various canon law texts, we know that a similar practice existed in the early Middle Ages. At the Council of Nîmes in 886, for example, two bishops were degraded by having their vestments removed, their crosiers broken over their heads, and their episcopal rings removed from their fingers [55]. And the Council of Limoges of 1031 laid down regulations for the degradation of a presbyter. First, the bishop orders that the sacerdotal vestments be removed from the offender. Then he takes from him the maniple and the chasuble. Thereupon, he demotes the presbyter to the diaconate by rearranging the stole worn in presbyteral fashion around his neck to the diaconate position [56].

---

(53) BERNHARD SCHIMMELPFENNIG, « Die Absetzung von Klerikern in Recht und Ritus vornehmlich des 13. und 14. Jahrhunderts », in *Proceedings of the Fifth International Congress of Medieval Canon Law*, pp. 517-532.

(54) MARC DYKMANS, « Le rite de la dégradation des clercs d'après quelques anciens manuscrits », in *Gregorianum*, LXIII (1982), pp. 301-331.

(55) MANSI, XVIII. 46.

(56) MANSI, XIX. 540.

Beyond these rites of separation involving the removal of clerical insignia, there were other signs of clerical degradation specified in the canons. Among these might be the removal of the cleric's name from the *matricula* or *tabula clericorum*. Further, *litterae commendatitiae* might be denied the cleric, and this was tantamount to excommunication or deprivation of communion with his fellow clerics. Clearly as the Council of Limoges indicated, there might be a partial degradation only — in that case from the presbyterate to the diaconate — but more severe forms could mean that the cleric would no longer be able to occupy a place in the church with the clerics; he might be deprived of his revenues; and perhaps even status as a cleric might be denied him [57].

During the early Middle Ages excommunication or separation of persons had a parallel in the excommunication of places. Later canonists would define this as an interdict — local or particular, depending on its extent — but in the early Middle Ages a variety of alternative terms was used, including excommunication and censure. As was the case with excommunication, the extent of the interdict might vary greatly. It might be simply a closing of a single church or a part of a church for the celebration of Mass or other divine services. On the other extreme, an entire territory might be placed under an interdict, such as was suggested at the Synod of Limoges in 1031 after certain princes around Limoges has violated the *Pax dei* [58]. Among the many dramatic signs and effects of the interdict were: only clerics, paupers, pilgrims, and infants under two could

---

(57) E. VACANDARD, « Déposition et dégradation des clercs », in *Dictionnaire de théologie catholique*, IV. 1 (Paris 1924), coll. 455-456.

(58) MANSI, XIX. 541-542. On the related *Treuga dei* with its rites of separation, see ROGER E. REYNOLDS, « Odilo and the *Trevga Dei* in Southern Italy: A Beneventan Manuscript Fragment », in *Mediaeval Studies*, XLVI (1984), pp. 450-462.

receive Christian burial; altars were to be stripped of their ornaments to indicate the mourning of Good Friday; altars were to be recovered only at Mass, which was to be celebrated behind closed doors; no marriages or ordinations were to take place; the kiss of peace was not to be given; and only Lenten foods were permitted.

As was the case in personal excommunication, so with interdicts there might be a simple declaration of the fact *de jure*. But more dramatic rites could accompany the declaration, and these might closely resemble the ones we have met in the ritual of *clamor*. Already the case of the thorns on the tomb of St. Mitrius reported by Gregory of Tours has been mentioned [59], but there are others like it, many of which have been gathered together in Richter's dossier of texts on the interdict [60]. For example, at Agde after ecclesiastical land had been usurped, the bishop entered the church, prostrated himself before the relics of St. Andrew throughout the night in deep sorrow, and on the next day smashed the lamps and declared that no light should burn — that is, no services take place — until God avenged the crime and the property of the church was restored [61]. And in the life of St. Eligius of Noyon a story is told of how he went to the basilica of St. Columba after a theft of ornaments and threatened to place thorns over the doors of the church to prohibit the veneration of the saint until the ornaments were restored [62].

The last rites and signs of separation we shall deal with here are connected with things, and we shall look briefly at representative examples connected with animals, devils, and objects. Specialists in all the early medieval vernacular

---

(59) See above, p. 420.
(60) RICHTER, *op. cit.*
(61) *ibid.*, p. 13.
(62) *ibid.*, pp. 14-15.

424

literatures are acquainted with various forms of charms against sickness, disease, and noxious animals. The early medieval western Church had a similar device in various rites used to drive away or separate the evil thing from the petitioner. One of these rites, interestingly enough, appears directly after the excommunication formula in the *Sens Pontifical* described earlier. It is called a *Carmen* and is appropriately neumed and is directed against a dragon or snake. First, the Pater noster is said, ending with its "Libera nos a malo". Then there is a plea to the members of the Trinity to encircle the petitioner. Finally, there is a threefold cry, "Fuge inimice, fuge inimice, fuge inimice" [63]. This is not entirely unlike the so-called excommunication of flies reported in the life of St. Bernard by William of Saint-Thierry [64].

The dragon in the Sens *Carmen* may, of course, be the devil, and in fact in a number of exorcisms and orations that go back to the Gelasian sacramentaries of the eighth century there is similar terminology. In the *Gellone Sacramentary*, for example, there is a long series of exorcisms to be said over a Christian vexed with a demon [65], and these were later used in the Supplement to the *Gregorian Sacramentary* as catechumenal exorcisms [66]. It has been argued by Bartsch in his extensive study that medieval exorcisms should not be understood in the modern sense of driving the devil or devils away, but rather in the sense of abjuration or "Beschwörung" [67]. In part this

---

(63) The text of this is printed in STAERK, *op. cit.*, I, p. 173.

(64) See H. D'ARBOIS DE JUBAINVILLE, « Les excommunications d'animaux », in *Revue des questions historiques*, V (1868), p. 277.

(65) 2402-2413, ed. A. DUMAS, *Liber sacramentorum Gellonensis*, 2 vols. (*Corpus christianorum ser. lat.* 159, 159A: Turnhout 1981), I, pp. 353-359.

(66) *Ibid.*, II, p. 108.

(67) ELMAR BARTSCH, *Die Sachbeschwörungen der römischen Liturgie: Eine liturgiegeschichtliche und liturgietheologische Studie* (Münster/W. 1967).

may be true, but clearly the terminology of separation appears repeatedly in these prayers and exorcisms: *repelle, exiat, recedat, abscede, discedere, mittere, proiecit, effuge, separassit, vade,* and so forth. In short, exorcisms such as these contain some of the clearest and most powerful images of separation in the early Middle Ages.

There is, finally, separation connected with objects. Long before the early Middle Ages, curses, threats of separation, and anathemas were attached to a variety of objects, and in the early Middle Ages they were used on anything from tombs to tomes. On a seventh-century tomb in Merida, for example, there is a threat to profaners with language almost precisely like that of excommunications and maledictions: "... sit anathema, percussus lebra Gezie perfruatur et cum Juda traditore abeat portionem et a leminibus [*sic*] eclesie separetur..." [68]. With regard to books, anyone who works with manuscripts is familiar with such threats as "Quicumque istum librum rapuerit aut furaverit vel aliquo malo ingenio abstulerit ab aecclesia S. Caeciliae sit perpetua damnatione damnatus et maledictus nisi reddiderit vel emendaverit. FIAT FIAT AMEN AMEN" [69].

This article has dealt only with the rites and signs of separation thus far, and it is no accident that these have occupied the majority of our time because in liturgical books they generally occupy far more space and are far more elaborate than corresponding rites and signs of reconciliation. One thinks, for example, of the *Pontificale Romano-Germanicum,* where ten pages of the edition of Reinhard Elze and the lamented Cyrille Vogel are devoted to excom-

---

(68) CH. MICHEL, « Anathème », in *Dictionnaire d'archéologie chrétienne et de liturgie* I. 2 (Paris 1924), col. 1935.

(69) W. WATTENBACH, *Das Schriftwesen im Mittelalter,* 4th ed. (Graz 1958), p. 531.

426

munication rites but only four to the corresponding rite of reconciliation of excommunicates [70]. This is not to say, however, that reconciliation was neglected, because the object of these rites and signs of separation was to bring about reconciliation. Repeatedly we have encountered the *nisi* clause attached to the formulae clearly urging the malefactor to emendment of life, penance, and reconciliation.

In the formulae for excommunication of persons one of the first points earlier stressed was that the person had been baptized, and in some of the earliest rites reported in the West of the reconciliation of persons separated from the Church this point is reiterated. For example, a canon from the First Council of Arles in 314 [71], often repeated in early medieval canonical collections [72], directs that on receiving a heretic into the Church, he be questioned about the Creed, asked if he was baptized in the name of the Trinity, and if so, hands be laid on him to receive the Holy Spirit. Moreover, we have seen in the excommunication allocutions that the excommunicate was to be considered as a heathen, gentile, and pagan, and by least the eighth century we find prayers in the sacramentaries for the reconciliation of heretics and pagans. In the *Gellone Sacramentary*, for example, there are prayers for the reconciliation of heretics, a benediction for those returning from heresy [73], and a reconciliation for persons returning from paganism in which the Holy Spirit is called down [74].

(70) eds. VOGEL and ELZE, *op. cit.*, I, pp. 308-321.

(71) c. 9 (8), ed. CHARLES MUNIER, *Concilia Galliae, a. 314-a. 506 (Corpus christianorum, ser. lat.* 148: Turnhout 1963), pp. 10-11.

(72) See, for example, the *Collectio vetus gallica* LVII. 3, ed. HUBERT MORDEK, *Kirchenrecht und Reform im Frankenreich. Die Collectio vetus gallica, die älteste systematische Kanonessammlung des fränkischen Gallien: Studien und Edition (Beiträge zur Geschichte und Quellenkunde des Mittelalters* 1: Berlin 1975), pp. 582-583.

(73) Nr. 347, ed. DUMAS, *op. cit.*, I, pp. 348-349.

(74) Nr. 350, *ibid.*, I, pp. 350-351.

Moreover, there are in the Gelasian sacramentaries of both types and the *Gregorian Sacramentary* Mass sets and rituals whose prayers refer to those who have repented of their sins and have returned to the Church [75]. These prayers would eventually be added to a ritual of reconciliation given in Regino's *Libri duo de synodabilus causis* immediately following the variant forms of excommunications earlier discussed.

In Regino's rite of reconciliation [76] it is particularly interesting to see how the effects and rites of excommunication and malediction are reversed. The rite begins with the repentant excommunicate before the doors of the church, that is, before the threshold he has earlier been forbidden to cross. The same bishop who excommunicated him is there ready to reconcile him, standing with twelve priests in a circle. The bishop then asks the excommunicate if he wishes to do penance and the excommunicate prostrates himself in the gesture of humility the clergy took in the rite of *clamor*. If the excommunicate indicates that he is willing to do penance, the bishop takes him by the right hand, leads him across the threshold of the church [77], and returns him to the communion and society of Christians denied him in the original excommunication. Letters are then directed to the parishes and other bishops who had previously received notification of the excommunication that the person has been taken back into Christian society.

(75) See, for example, Nrs. 1384, 861, 851, and 1327 of the supplemented *Gregorian Sacramentary*, ed. JEAN DESHUSSES, *Le Sacramentaire grégorien: ses principales formes d'après les plus anciens manuscrits* (*Spicilegium Friburgense* 16: Fribourg/S. 1971), pp. 453, 315, 313, and 440.

(76) II. 418, ed. WASSERSCHLEBEN, *Regino*, pp. 375-76.

(77) It is interesting that there was a penitential portal on the north side of medieval churches, on which see O. K. WERCKMEISTER, « The Lintel Fragment Representing Eve from Saint-Lazare, Autun », in *Journal of the Warburg and Courtauld Institutes*, XXXV (1972), pp. 20-23, a reference kindly drawn to my attention by M. Eric Palazzo.

The rite of absolution itself, which is added to Regino's ceremonial in the *Pontificale Romano-Germanicum* [78], consists of a series of Psalms, several of which are from the penitential Psalms and which parallel those used in the maledictions. Brief *preces* from the Psalms, which have their opposites in the *preces* of the maledictions, are then read. These are followed by a longer series of prayers taken from the Gelasian and Gregorian sacramentaries, which have their opposites in the prayers taken from these ancient sacramentaries in the malediction ceremonies. Following this in the *Pontificale Romano-Germanicum* is an absolution for several excommunicates in which forgiveness is declared and benediction given, after each of which there is an Amen, paralleling the Amens of the maledictions in the earlier excommunication. The reconciled malefactors are then asperged with holy water and receive the odor of incense, counteracting, presumably, the stench of their bodies specified in the earlier excommunication formulae. Finally, paralleling the "Exurge domine" used in the excommunication and malediction formulae, the reconciled persons are exhorted, "Exurge qui dormis, exurge a mortuis", and, balancing the extinguishing of candles in the excommunication rite, the reconciliation ceremony ends with the words, "et illuminabit te Christus".

A rite similar to this was also used by Burchard in his *Decretum* [79] but the order was changed, placing some of the prayers before the entrance into the church, and several of the prayers themselves were modified or were replaced with different forms.

The principles of symbolic restoration of what was lost and the use of balancing gestures and texts in the rite of

---

(78) XCI. 6-18, eds. VOGEL and ELZE, *op. cit.*, I, pp. 318-321.
(79) XI. 8, *PL* 140. 860-861.

reconciliation of excommunicates is also found in the early medieval rites of reconciliation of degraded clerics. Again, evidence for the rites and formulae themselves is scant for the early Middle Ages, but there is enough to see that these principles of symbolic restoration and textual balance applied then also. A canon often repeated in early medieval canonical collections from the Fourth Council of Toledo of 633 deals with the case of unjustly condemned clerics [80]. If the cleric is a bishop, he is to be restored by receiving a stole, ring, and staff; if a presbyter, a stole and chasuble; if a deacon, a stole and alb; if a subdeacon, a paten and chalice; and if the lower grades, whatever was given at the original ordination.

This symbolic restoration was certainly accompanied by statements of reconciliation and prayers, as we know from several late eleventh-century sources. In the manuscript Paris, BN lat. 820, for example, the deacon is addressed with the words, "Recipe istud orarium ut habeas licentiam legendi evangelium", and the presbyter with the words, "Recipe hanc planetam ut possis legaliter celebrare missam"[81]. A pontifical from Kotor written in Beneventan script at the very end of the eleventh or early twelfth century elaborates on this with a full rite for the reconciliation of a lapsed presbyter or other clerics [82]. It is particularly interesting for its close resemblance to the reconciliation of excommunicates. After penance, the presbyter stands near the altar dressed in an alb and cincture. The bishop and other clerics stand around him in a circle. After the presbyter prostrates himself and seven Psalms and

---

(80) c. 28, ed. VIVES, *op. cit.*, pp. 202-203.
(81) On this manuscript see MARTÈNE, *op. cit.*, II, p. 319, and MARTIMORT, *op. cit.*, Nr. 858, p. 418.
(82) RICHARD GYUG, *An Edition of Leningrad MS. BAN f. 200: The Lectionary and Pontifical of Kotor* (diss. Toronto 1983), pp. 58, 293.

430

litanies have been sung, the bishop takes by the right hand this one who is specified as having been « excommunicated », lifts him up with the words, "Surge frater", and notes how his evil acts have been instigated by the devil. The presbyter is then to stand erect, and as one of the *milites Christi* he is to receive the arms of Christ. First, a stole is put around his neck and the words used in his first ordination are repeated. Then the chasuble and maniple are restored, again with the words of the first ordination. A prayer is said, again dwelling on the deceits of the devil and the return of that which was lost. Finally, there is a renewal of the laying on of hands by the bishop.

The last representative rite of reconciliation to be treated in this article is one concerning places and objects, the reconciliation of violated churches, holy places, cemeteries, and altars. Unlike the rite for the reconciliation of degraded clerics, there is abundant evidence from the early Middle Ages with both the ritual itself and the prayers. In the eighth-century *Gellone Sacramentary*, for example, there are two formulae under the rubric *Reconciliatio altaris ubi humicidium [sic] perpetratur* [83], and these two formulae would eventually provide the foundation for later rituals. The first of these formulae, entitled "Deus indultorem", dwells on the treachery of the devil, the corruption of the place, and the need for restoration. The second, "Deus cuius bonitas", speaks of the reasons for the violation: negligence, violence, drunkenness, or obscenity. Celestial grace is asked for to rid the place and the altar of the infection of the devil. Finally, restoration is asked for in terms of pure simplicity, luster of innocence, and glory.

These two prayers were taken into the tenth-century

---

(83) 2398, 2399, ed. Dumas, *op. cit.*, I, pp. 351-352.

Claudius Pontifical [84], which according to D. H. Turner shows no influence of the continental *Pontificale Romano-Germanicum* and which he believes to be the oldest surviving true English pontifical [85]. In this pontifical the rubric for the rite indicates that the reconciliation is not only for the altar polluted by homicide, but also for any holy place polluted by the shedding of blood. More interesting is the fact that the brief reconciliation of these two prayers is accompanied by a Mass of reconciliation for churches with a set of prayers whose constant theme is purification from the filthiness caused by barbarian deeds done in the place. This custom reported in the *Claudius Pontifical* of combining both reconciliation rite and Mass was picked up in a number of other early medieval English pontificals, which embellish both the prayers and provide ritual directions. The *Lanalet Pontifical* [86], for example, adds a third prayer of reconciliation mentioning the cemetery and asking for the purity of paradise. And the Mass has been augmented with a series of benedictions taken from diverse episcopal benedictions in the Supplement to the *Gregorian Sacramentary*. The *Benedictional of Archbishop Robert* adds to this actual directives. In the reconciliation itself the bishop asperges the holy place three times with holy water as he circles it and says the three prayers. And a complete Mass text is given including not only the elements in the *Lanalet Pontifical* but also the antiphons, responsories, and lessons [87].

---

(84) ed. D. H. TURNER, *The Claudius Pontificals (from Cotton MS. Claudius A. iii in the British Museum) (Henry Bradshaw Society* 97: Chichester 1971), p. 66.

(85) *ibid.*, p. xxviii.

(86) ed. G. H. DOBLE, *Pontificale Lanaletense (Bibliothèque de la Ville de Rouen A. 27. Cat. 368) A Pontifical formerly in Use at St. Germans, Cornwall (Henry Bradshaw Society* 74: London 1937), pp. 21-22.

(87) ed. HENRY A. WILSON, *The Benedictional of Archbishop Robert (Henry Bradshaw Society* 24: London 1903), pp. 110-113.

432

On the Continent, the ritual directions of the *Robert Benedictional* are much more abundant in the *Pontificale Romano-Germanicum,* which provides only a reconciliation ceremony, not a Mass [88]. In the additional ritual and texts of the *Pontificale* the principles of symbolic restoration and textual balance are very much in evidence. For example, the relics are replaced, resembling the interment of relics at the original consecration. Gregorian water with its salt, wine, and ashes is used to asperge the church during the threefold circuit of the bishop, again paralleling the original consecration. And in the opening ceremony before the doors of the church, a prayer borrowed from the ancient *Oratio in sacrario* [89] bids the devil to flee, thereby providing access for the angel of peace. It is this same devil who has entered those doors that in their consecration were to be conduits of peace [90].

It is appropriate to conclude this article by referring again to the recent apostolic exhortation *Reconciliatio et paenitentia.* In that document there was a progressing description of the matter and consequences of sin, the recognition of sin, and finally reconciliation. The pope, following the teaching of Thomas Aquinas, spoke of sin as a disorder, a rupture in man's relation to God and his fellow man. And in distinguishing the varieties of sin, the pope spoke of mortal sins or sins that lead to spiritual death and separation from God. The representative rites of separation and reconciliation we have examined in this article certainly applied to these sins whose consequences involved grave social disorder — violation of ecclesiastical property, violence, theft, and the like. In attempting to bring

---

(88) L, eds. VOGEL and ELZE, *op. cit.,* I, pp. 182-185.
(89) See, for example, the *Gellone Sacramentary,* 2861, ed. DUMAS, *op. cit.,* I, p. 453.
(90) See the *Pontificale Romano-Germanicum* XL. 19, 21, eds. VOGEL and ELZE, *op. cit.,* I, p. 133.

about order, the rites of separation were a public and ordered recognition of the sin, even though in such rituals as the *clamor* there was an intentional or symbolic disorder. In recognizing the sin publically and separating the sinner from God in the anathemas and from Christian society in the excommunications, the rites were not solely punitive. Rather, they contained a medicinal element in their invitations to reconciliation. This appeared in the *nisi* clauses encouraging emendation of life and repentance. Because the offenses were public and the rites of separations had been public, so too were the rites of reconciliation public. To bring about reconciliation the rituals themselves were structured so as to restore symbolically those things that had been lost and the prayers compiled so as to balance those of the corresponding rites of separation. In short, early medieval rites of reconciliation, like those of separation, were crafted to bring about the same end — order out of disorder, harmony from dissonance.

ODILO AND THE *TREVGA DEI* IN SOUTHERN ITALY: A BENEVENTAN MANUSCRIPT FRAGMENT*

F ROM her beginnings the Church has been involved in the making and maintenance of both war and peace, and in the course of the eleventh century she was a leader in both causes. The First Crusade preached by Pope Urban II late in the century is the prime example of the Church's promotion of war. Fully as important were her efforts to promote peace in the violence of the early decades of that same century, and the instruments through which this was attempted were the Peace and Truce of God.[1]

From their origins in southern France at the turn of the millennium, the ideas of the Peace and Truce of God spread rapidly, and by the 1040s the idea of the Truce of God or the *Treuga Dei* seems to have reached Italy. In chronicles and miscellaneous documents from the vicinity of Milan, Turin, and Aosta, we know of its entrance into that part of Italy closest to southern France.[2] Two documents have usually been singled out by historians as the most important witnesses for the early entrance of the *Treuga Dei* into Italy. The first and longer of these was printed in the eighteenth century by Martène and Durand in

---

* I am grateful to the Biblioteca Vallicelliana, Rome for permission to publish the text of this fragment and to Dr. M. Vivarelli for the photograph.

[1] The most important recent work on the Peace and Truce of God is that of Hartmut Hoffmann, *Gottesfriede und Treuga Dei* (Schriften der Monumenta Germaniae historica 20; Stuttgart, 1964). For additional bibliography see L. E. Boyle, 'Peace of God', *New Catholic Encyclopedia* 11 (New York, 1967), pp. 45 f.; H. E. J. Cowdrey, 'The Peace and Truce of God in the Eleventh Century', *Past and Present* 46 (1970) 42-67; R. Bonnaud-Delamare, 'La paix de Touraine pendant la première croisade', *Revue d'histoire ecclésiastique* 70 (1975) 749-58, with extensive references to his earlier work on the topic; Thomas N. Bisson, 'Une paix peu connue pour le Roussillon (A.D. 1173)' in *Droit privé et institutions régionales. Études historiques offertes à Jean Yver* (Publications de l'Université de Rouen, Sér. juridique 31; Paris, 1976), pp. 69-76; Jean-Pierre Poly, *La Provence et la société féodale (879-1166): contribution à l'étude des structures dites féodales dans le Midi* (Paris, 1976), pp. 194-202, who takes issue with Hoffmann on the date of the origins of the *Treuga Dei*; and Thomas N. Bisson, 'The Organized Peace in Southern France and Catalonia', *American Historical Review* 82 (1977) 290-311.

[2] Hoffmann, *Gottesfriede*, pp. 82, 85 f.

Reprinted from *Mediaeval Studies*, 46 (1984), pp. 450-462, by permission of the publisher. © 1984 by the Pontifical Institute of Mediaeval Studies, Toronto.

the *Thesaurus novus anecdotorum*.[3] Later it was edited in the *Monumenta Germaniae historica* under the title *Treuga Dei archidioecesis arelatensis (c. 1037-1041)*.[4] This document is a letter directed to the bishops and clergy of Italy from a group of bishops in the province of Arles, including Raimbald of Arles, Benedict of Avignon, and Nithard of Nice, and from Abbot Odilo of Cluny. In the letter the origins and regulations of the *Treuga Dei* are laid out, and both spiritual benefits and punishments are specified for those who keep or fail to keep them. The second document, also edited in the *Monumenta Germaniae historica* and there entitled *Treuga Dei lombardica (c. 1040-1050)*,[5] is one which Carl Erdmann connected with the Synod of Pavia in 1046.[6] This document also lays out the regulations for the *Treuga* and concludes with an extensive malediction for truce breakers and benediction for truce keepers.

In his fundamental study of the Peace and Truce of God, Hartmut Hoffmann considered all of this evidence for the entrance of the *Treuga Dei* into Italy.[7] He made the important observation that the *Treuga* entered Italy probably because of the connections of the bishops of the province of Arles and Abbot Odilo with northern Italy and with Rome itself. Raimbald was at the Synod of Pavia in 1046 where peace was discussed; Benedict visited Rome; and Nithard's diocese bordered on northwest Italy. Further, Odilo's prestige was great throughout Italy. In the third decade of the eleventh century he had made journeys to the Campania and Monte Cassino, and late in his life while visiting Rome and recovering there from a fall from his horse he was in contact with such southern Italian bishops as Lawrence of Amalfi.[8] As Jacques Hourlier has pointed out, it is difficult to evaluate exactly the role of Odilo in the promotion of the *Treuga Dei*, but 'en tous cas la diffusion de l'idée lui doit beaucoup.'[9]

Despite Odilo's contact with southern Italy and his presence in Rome, Hoffmann could point to only one piece of evidence for the extension of the *Treuga Dei* into central and southern Italy between the 1040s and the end of the century. This evidence is in the famous confession in Old Italian: 'Me accuso de la sancta treua k io noll obseruai siccomo promisi', found in Rome, Biblioteca

---

[3] Ed. Edmond Martène and Ursin Durand, 1 (Paris, 1717), cols. 161-63.

[4] MGH *Legum sectio IV. Constitutiones et acta* 1 (Hanover, 1893), pp. 596 f. n. 419.

[5] ibid., p. 598 n. 420.

[6] Carl Erdmann, *The Origin of the Idea of Crusade*, trans. Marshall W. Baldwin and Walter Goffart (Princeton, 1977), p. 65 n. 18.

[7] Hoffmann, *Gottesfriede*, pp. 81-85.

[8] See Jacques Hourlier, *Saint Odilon, abbé de Cluny* (Bibliothèque de la Revue d'histoire ecclésiastique 40: Louvain, 1964), pp. 86 f., 112; and *Chronica monasterii casinensis* 2.54, ed. Hartmut Hoffmann, *Die Chronik von Monte Cassino* (MGH SS 34; Hanover, 1980), pp. 66-68.

[9] Hourlier, ibid., p. 109.

Vallicelliana MS. B 63, fol. 231v.[10] On the basis of Pirri's study of manuscripts from Sant'Eutizio presso Norcia, Hoffmann dated the text to 1037-89 and placed it in that important Benedictine house.[11] Although Pirri's dating of the manuscript is open to question,[12] Hoffmann's surmise is probably correct that the *Treuga Dei* very likely worked its influence in the hinterlands of Italy, where Cluniac influence was great, by the mid-eleventh century.[13] The present note is intended to contribute a further piece of evidence connected with an Abbot Odilo to support Hoffmann's suspicion. This evidence is to be found in another codex of the Biblioteca Vallicelliana that seems to have been unduly neglected by scholars.

The codex itself, C 45, contains a variety of shorter manuscripts of different sizes and of disparate dates. Of special interest here are the first 73 folios. The first 64 folios, measuring 145×225 mm. and bearing the ex libris of the Certosa of St. Bartholomew at Trisulti near Frosinone,[14] is a palimpsest codex, whose upper text is a collection of letters and excerpta from St. Jerome.[15] The lower text, written at right angles to the upper text, is a beautiful missal in two columns (each being of 88×235 mm. with 28 lines) copied by a Beneventan hand of the tenth or eleventh century. The second part of the manuscript, fols. 65-72, is again a palimpsest codex, measuring 140×200 mm., and also bears the ex libris of the Certosa di Trisulti. The upper text deals with the election of bishops, continence, marriage, abstinence, and miscellaneous matters, and the lower text, nearly illegible but written in the same direction as the upper text, is again in Beneventan hands of the tenth or eleventh century.

Bound around this second part of the codex (fols. 65-72) is a very rough and venous piece of parchment numbered as fol. 73, with writing on one side only

[10] This text is edited in Pietro Pirri, *L'abbazia di Sant'Eutizio in Val Castoriana presso Norcia e le chiese dipendenti* (Studia anselmiana 45; Rome, 1960), p. 47, and for a facsimile of the folio see pl. 5.

[11] Hoffmann, *Gottesfriede*, p. 86.

[12] Although the first folio (fol. 220) of the section in the codex that contains the calendar on which Pirri based his dating does indeed come from Sant'Eutizio and is written in an eleventh-century hand, the remainder of the codex to fol. 283v, a palimpsest manuscript, is in a hand that Edward B. Garrison, 'Saints Equizio, Onorato, and Libertino in Eleventh- and Twelfth-Century Italian Litanies as Clues to the Attribution of Manuscripts', *Revue bénédictine* 88 (1978) 306, has dated to the first quarter of the twelfth century. Immediately before this section of the manuscript, on fols. 217-218, there are in two different hands extracts taken from the canonical *Collection in Five Books* in a recension like that in a manuscript that was at Sant'Eutizio (on which see below, p. 454). Hartmut Hoffmann, 'Die Briefmuster des Vallicellianus B 63 aus der Zeit Paschalis' II.', *Deutsches Archiv* 19 (1963) 130, without recognizing these extracts, pointed out that this section of the manuscript seems to have no particular connection with Sant'Eutizio.

[13] Hoffmann, *Gottesfriede*, p. 86.

[14] fols. 1r (cf. fols. 64r and 74r with the same ex libris) and 64r.

[15] See Bernard Lambert, *Bibliotheca hieronymiana manuscripta: la tradition manuscrite des œuvres de Saint Jérôme* (Instrumenta patristica 4B; Steenbrugge, 1972), p. 134.

and whose text has been clipped at top and bottom probably to make it fit the present dimensions of the manuscript. As a result of this mutilation, the measurements of fol. 73 are now 152 mm. in width at the top, 235 mm. on the side, and 145 mm. at the bottom. The text, which is faded and in poor condition through water-marking, folding, rubbing, and mutilation, can be seen on both fol. 73r and on the long, thin, triangular-shaped strip folded toward fol. 65r. Like the lower texts of the first two parts of the codex, this text on fol. 73r is in Beneventan script. Although the folio does not bear the ex libris of the Certosa di Trisulti, it is possible that it did come from there together with its enveloping fols. 1-158. Given the fact that a number of other manuscripts written in Beneventan script came to the Biblioteca Vallicelliana from the Certosa,[16] it would not be surprising if this single folio also has St. Bartholomew as its provenance.

The date of the script of our folio is difficult to determine. There are characteristics that might suggest a twelfth-century date such as the heavy use of uncial *a* at the beginning of words, the regular closing of the loop of *b*, a *g* whose lowest horizontal stroke is fairly straight or turned down slightly,[17] and the regular use of the twelfth-century abbreviations of forms of *omnis*.[18] Nonetheless, the overall impression given is a hand of the first part of the eleventh century. It is roundish, not angular,[19] and has such early eleventh-century characteristics as the tall, thin shaft (with serifs) for the ascenders of *b* and *h*,[20] single points for punctuation,[21] and the eleventh-century liturgical abbreviation for *suis*.[22] Hence, although a twelfth-century date is possible, an eleventh-century date is to be preferred.[23] In any event, the somewhat

---

[16] Among these manuscripts are: (1) Rome, Biblioteca Vallicelliana B 59, on which see E. A. Loew, *The Beneventan Script: A History of the South Italian Minuscule*, 2nd enlarged edition prepared by Virginia Brown (Sussidi eruditi 33; Rome, 1980), 2.127, to which may be added four binding fragments on fols. 116v, 117v-118r, 119r, and 121v from codices in Beneventan script (all new Beneventan items cited in this article will be listed and briefly described by Virginia Brown, 'A Second New List of Beneventan Manuscripts (II)', forthcoming in *Mediaeval Studies*). The text on fol. 79v of MS. B 59 is related to another codex not in Beneventan script, namely, Rome, Biblioteca Vallicelliana F 64, fol. 151v; (2) B 66 (on which see Loew-Brown 2.127); (3) C 39 (on which see Loew-Brown 2.128); (4) C 63 (on which see Loew-Brown 2.128); and (5) C 70 (on which see Loew-Brown 2.128).

[17] See Loew-Brown 1.133-35.

[18] ibid. 1.174.

[19] For examples of the roundish script of the eleventh century antedating the developed style of the Desiderian period and beyond, see E. A. Lowe, *Scriptura beneventana. Facsimiles of South Italian and Dalmatian Manuscripts from the Sixth to the Fourteenth Century* 2 (Oxford, 1929), pls. LV-LXVI.

[20] See Loew-Brown 1.134 f.

[21] ibid. 1.227.

[22] ibid. 1.93.

[23] The final *r*, so critical in dating Beneventan manuscripts, is found only occasionally in our

undeveloped and uncalligraphic style of the hand suggests that the scribe was working in a small or isolated location, away from such major centers as Monte Cassino, Benevento, Cava, or Naples.[24] Moreover, features such as the heavy use of uncial *a* suggest that the scribe may have been writing in an area bordering on one where Carolingian script was used, not unlike the case of Rome, Biblioteca Vallicelliana T. XVIII.[25]

The significance of fol. 73r is twofold. First, it contains a text on the *Treuga Dei*, which, like the northern Italian *Treuga Dei archidioecesis arelatensis*, mentions an Abbot Odilo and a number of bishops and clerics. Second, the text is written in a Beneventan hand, a script that was restricted almost exclusively to southern Italy and Dalmatia from the mid-eighth to the sixteenth century.[26] Beneventan script could, of course, be written outside the zone of Beneventan influence by itinerant scribes — witness the marginalia with Beneventan characteristics in Rome, Biblioteca Vallicelliana B 11,[27] the important codex of the canonical *Collection in Five Books*,[28] written at and almost certainly coming from Sant'Eutizio presso Norcia[29] — but such a phenomenon seems to have

---

manuscript (*applicuerunt, stabilierunt, martyrum*), but is somewhere between a short and long form. In the *-ri-* ligature the shaft of the *r* descends below the line (cf. Loew-Brown 1.137).

[24] For the major centers of Beneventan writing see Loew-Brown 1.67-77.

[25] Caterina Tristano, 'Scrittura beneventana e scrittura carolina in manoscritti dell'Italia meridionale', *Scrittura e civiltà* 3 (1979) 115, 146, suggests that this famous canonistic manuscript with its Carolingian script and a Beneventan hand with Carolingian influence was written on the northern confines of Beneventan-script territories with strong ties in Lazio on one hand and Monte Cassino on the other; on this article see Rosaria Pilone, 'Scrittura beneventana e scrittura carolina a proposito di un recente saggio', *Benedictina* 30 (1983) 203-208. Also on this manuscript see Paola Supino Martini, 'Carolina romana e minuscola romanesca. Appunti per una storia della scrittura latina in Roma tra IX e XII secolo', *Studi medievali*, 3rd Ser., 15.2 (1974) 783 n. 29. Besides fols. 31r-33v with their Beneventan script noted by Tristano, Supino Martini, and Loew-Brown 2.131, there are other instances in the manuscript where Beneventan hands appear: on fol. 47r, lines 1-6 were copied by a second Beneventan hand resembling that of fol. 31r; much later in the manuscript (fol. 187vb3-4) there are several words written in Beneventan script by a third hand in the midst of Carolingian script, and the scribe then breaks into Beneventan script for a rubric and a text of can. ccxlv, only to return to Carolingian script on fol. 188ra.

[26] See *Montecassino e la cultura scritta: XV centenario della nascita di san Benedetto* (Assessorato alla cultura regione Lazio, Teatro di Roma, n.d.), p. 24; and Virginia Brown, 'The Survival of Beneventan Script: Sixteenth-Century Liturgical Codices from Benedictine Monasteries in Naples' in *Monastica. Scritti raccolti in memoria del XV centenario della nascita di S. Benedetto (480-1980)* 1 (Miscellanea cassinese 44; Monte Cassino, 1981), p. 237.

[27] A Carolingian hand has correctly used the Beneventan *-ti-* ligatures on fols. 21v and 52r (53r). On fol. 60r (61r) there is a marginal entry using uncial *a*'s but the Beneventan *e*, correct *-ti-* ligatures, and unions of *ec* and *en*.

[28] On this collection see most recently *Collectio canonum Regesto farfensi inserta*, ed. Theo Kölzer (Monumenta iuris canonici, Ser. B: Corpus collectionum 5; Vatican City, 1982), pp. 48-55.

[29] It is, of course, possible that the codex was loaned for a time to another scriptorium in the Beneventan-script zone, where the marginalia with their Beneventan features were added, and

been fairly rare. Hence, our single folio would appear to prove almost beyond doubt that the *Treuga Dei* was known, as Hoffmann suspected, even in the southern hinterlands of Italy prior to the end of the eleventh century.

Beyond its importance as a witness to the *Treuga Dei* in southern Italy by the twelfth century, our text is interesting for its parallels to the northern Italian texts of the *Treuga Dei* and to elements of French, Catalan, and even German formulae of excommunication and malediction from the ninth to the eleventh century. As to its content, our text, printed at the end of this note, has several major sections.

The first section is unfortunately mutilated, but what is clear is that Abbot Odilo with bishops and clerics is presenting a mandatum regarding the *Treuga Dei*. Like Rodulf Glaber and Hugh of Flavigny, who reported on the establishment of the *Treuga*,[30] and the *Treuga Dei archidioecesis arelatensis*,[31] our document first connects the *Treuga* with a *pax* or *pax firma*. And like the *Treuga Dei archidioecesis arelatensis*, our text says it was made with the concurrence of Odilo, presumably of Cluny, and other bishops and clerics.[32] The mandatum itself, like the 'mandatum novum et bonum e coelo' mentioned by Landulf of Milan in his report of the *Treuga*,[33] begins by saying that the *Treuga Dei* was instituted not by men but by heavenly powers. Both Hoffmann and Horst Fuhrmann have seen behind reports of the supernatural origins of

---

then later returned to Sant'Eutizio. Against this, however, are several indicia in the codex itself. First, there are numerous eleventh- and twelfth-century additions to the manuscript in Carolingian hands resembling the copyists at Sant'Eutizio, and these indicate the continued presence of the manuscript at Sant'Eutizio. Second, had the manuscript been loaned for some time to a scriptorium in the Beneventan-script zone, one might expect more additions in the script than the few extant marginal notations. That the *Collection in Five Books* was connected with the Beneventan-script zone and hence of special interest to scholars and scribes who wrote in the script is seen in the facts: (1) that one of the other two relatively complete codices of the collection, Monte Cassino 125, is written in a Beneventan script of the second quarter of the eleventh century; (2) that the other manuscript from Narni, Vatican Library Vat. lat. 1339, although written in a Carolingian hand, has Beneventan interrogation-signs throughout and the Insular-Beneventan sign for *enim* on fol. 308v; and (3) that a number of canon law collections deriving from the *Collection in Five Books* are written in Beneventan script (e.g., Rome, Biblioteca Vallicelliana F 2, F 8, F 54), are copied from Beneventan-script models (e.g., Rome, Biblioteca Vallicelliana R 32, fol. 50r-v), or have Beneventan-script symptoms (e.g., Vatican Library Vat. lat. 4317, fols. 26v. 27r, 28r, 103v, 121v, 180r with correctly used Beneventan ligatures for -*ti*-, or Naples, Biblioteca Nazionale XII A 28 [olim 96], fol. 197r with its Insular-Beneventan sign for *enim*).

[30] 'Anno ipso [1041] treva Dei primum statuta est et firmata, et pax ipsa treva Dei appellata' (*Chronicon Hugonis* 2.30 [MGH *SS* 8; Hanover, 1848], p. 403).

[31] '... sit firma pax et stabilis treuva' (MGH *Constit. et acta* 1.597).

[32] '...necnon et venerabili abbate domno Odilone una cum omnibus episcopis et abbatibus et cuncto clero ...' (ibid. 1.596). The possibility should be held open, of course, that the Odilo here is not the famous abbot of Cluny but another Odilo.

[33] *Landulfi Historia mediolanensis* 2.30 (MGH *SS* 8.67).

the *Treuga Dei* the so-called *Himmelsbrief*, a heavenly letter used to add authority to certain ideas and institutions;[34] and indeed in our document, like the reports of Rodulf Glaber,[35] Hugh of Flavigny,[36] Landulf of Milan,[37] and the *Treuga Dei archidioecesis arelatensis*,[38] the notion of a heavenly origin is repeated. In a sense, our document with its litany of the heavenly and saintly founders of the *Treuga* contradicts the *Treuga Dei lombardica*, which pointed out that it was a group of religious and secular dignitaries, including *marchiones*, who instituted the *Treuga*.[39]

After the material on the origins of the *Treuga Dei*, our text exhorts its readers to keep the truce and then begins to detail the advantages of so doing. This is cast in the form of an absolution from sins and is highly reminiscent of the text in the *Treuga Dei archidioecesis arelatensis*, which says:

> Quicumque hanc pacem et treuvam Dei observaverint ac firmiter tenuerint, sint absoluti a Deo patre omnipotente et filio eius Iesu Christo et Spiritu sancto et de sancta Maria cum choris virginum et de sancto Michaele cum choris angelorum et de sancto Petro principe apostolorum cum omnibus sanctis et fidelibus cunctis nunc et semper et per omnia saecula saeculorum.[40]

or the benediction in the *Treuga Dei lombardica*:

> Set qui has treuuas Dei bene observaverint et qui conscilium et adiutorium fractoribus non dederint, nisi ut emendent ut constitutum est, benedicti sint a Deo Patre et Filio et Spiritu sancto et a sancta Maria virgine et de omnibus angelis et archangelis, patriarchis et prophetis, apostolis, martyribus, confessoribus, monachis, virginibus, heremitis et omnibus sanctis Dei; et omnes benedictiones quae sunt scriptae in libris, descendant super eos. Fiat, Fiat, Fiat.[41]

After an assurance of absolution to those who maintain the *Treuga*, our text, like the *Treuga Dei archidioecesis arelatensis*,[42] goes on to mention a specific

---

[34] Hoffmann, *Gottesfriede*, pp. 82 f.; and Horst Fuhrmann, *Einfluss und Verbreitung der pseudoisidorischen Fälschungen von ihrem Auftauchen bis in die neuere Zeit* (Schriften der Monumenta Germaniae historica 24.1; Stuttgart, 1972), p. 100.

[35] 'Quae non solum humanis praesidiis, sed et divinis confirmata est terroribus' (*Chronicon Hugonis* 2.30 [MGH *SS* 8.403]).

[36] '... et ut eam susciperent, quia voluntas Domini erat, et a Deo non ab homine decretum hoc processerat ...' (ibid. 8.403).

[37] '... mandatum novum et bonum e coelo ...' (*Landulfi Historia mediolanensis* 2.30 [MGH *SS* 8.67]).

[38] 'Credimus namque istam causam a Deo nobis coelitus inspiratam divina opitulatione, quia apud nos, ut credimus, nihil boni agebatur, quando a Deo populo suo transmissa est' (MGH *Constit. et acta* 1.597).

[39] 'Fideles episcopi et abbates et sacerdotes atque marchiones convenientes, divina pietate illos inspirante, constituerunt treuuas Dei ...' (ibid. 1.598).

[40] ibid. 1.597.

[41] ibid. 1.598.

[42] ibid. 1.597; and see below, p. 457.

promise or *promissa* to keep the *Treuga Dei*; and to those who for such reasons as ignorance, drunkenness, and the like, break their promise, a variety of penances is assigned. In the *Treuga Dei lombardica* a penance of bread and water is mentioned,[43] but our text speaks of corporal punishment, not unlike the historians who speak of corporal punishment for those who break the *Pax Dei*.[44]

The final section of our document is perhaps the most interesting not only because it threatens the most dire excommunication and malediction on those who willingly break the *Treuga* or who counsel its violation, but also because some elements bear a striking resemblance to texts from the ninth to the eleventh century in Italy and beyond. First, in our document there is the threat of excommunication in the name of the Trinity, Mary, angelic hosts, apostles, and a variety of saintly worthies. Then, the malediction, anathema, and excommunication are related to Old and New Testament and even secular precedents. Third, the truce breaker is cursed with a litany of maledictions in all of his physical states of being. And finally, there is an indication of mercy if there are signs of true repentance.

In the northern Italian texts on the *Treuga*, namely, the *Treuga Dei archidioecesis arelatensis* and the *Treuga Dei lombardica*, some of the elements of this final section of our document also appear. In the former there is first a simplified form of excommunication in the name of the Trinity and the saints:

> Qui vero treuvam promissam habuerint et se scientibus infringere voluerint, sint excommunicati a Deo patre omnipotente et filio eius Iesu Christo et Spiritu sancto et de omnibus sanctis Dei sint excommunicati;

then a malediction that mentions the historical precedents:

> maledicti et detestati hic et in perpetuum, et sint damnati sicut Dathan et Abiron et sicut Iudas qui tradidit Dominum, et sint dimersi in profundum inferni sicut Pharao in medio maris;

and finally a call for emendation of life: 'si ad emendationem non venerint sicut constitutum est.'[45] In the *Treuga Dei lombardica* the malediction is an extension of the excommunication form in the *Treuga Dei archidioecesis arelatensis*:

> Maledicti sint a Deo Patre et Filio et Spiritu sancto et a sancta Maria virgine et de angelis et archangelis, patriarchis et prophetis, apostolis, martyribus et confessoribus, eremitis, virginibus et de omnibus sanctis Dei.[46]

---

[43] '... et unum annum summat ibi poenitentiam, stans in pane et aqua et extra domum positus' (ibid. 1.598).

[44] Hoffmann, *Gottesfriede*, pp. 55, 84.

[45] MGH *Constit. et acta* 1.597.

[46] ibid. 1.598.

Although the northern Italian texts on the *Treuga Dei* with their threats of excommunication and malediction bear a distinct resemblance to the final section of our document, other excommunication and malediction formulae from beyond Italy have elements that are sometimes even closer to our text. In both the early tenth-century *Libri duo de synodalibus causis* of Regino of Prüm and the early eleventh-century *Decretum* of Burchard of Worms there is a malediction referring to Old Testament precedents together with an exhortation to emend one's ways:

> ... veniantque super eos omnes illae maledictiones, quas Dominus per Moysen in populum divinae legis ... nisi forte resipuerint, et ecclesiae Dei, quam laeserunt, per emendationem et condignam poenitentiam satisfecerint.[47]

This was repeated in the *Pontificale romano-germanicum*, represented in Monte Cassino MS. 451 and Rome, Biblioteca Vallicelliana MS. D 5 (both in Beneventan script)[48] and in the excommunication of Baldwin of Flanders.[49] Further, the *Pontificale romano-germanicum* has several excommunication formulae that repeat these statements in expanded forms. In the *Excommunicatio Leonis papae* (Leo VII?, 936-939) the excommunication is pronounced in the name of the Trinity, angels, and saints; Old Testament precedents are cited; and emendation of life is called for in a way not unlike the final section of our text:

> Quapropter ex auctoritate Dei patris omnipotentis et filii eius domini nostri Iesu Christi et spiritus sancti paracliti, atque ex vice beati Petri apostoli; necnon et beatae Mariae matris domini; et per beatos angelos, apostolos, martires, confessores, ac virgines, excommunicamus eos atque maledicimus, qui .... Sit pars eorum cum Dathan et Abiron, quos terra pro sua suberbia vivos absorbuit, et cum Juda proditore .... Sintque maledictiones illae, quas dominus super filios Israhel per Moysen promulgavit .... Si autem ad penitentiam et emendationem venerint et secundum modum culpae fructus dignos penitentia fecerint ....[50]

From Urgel in Catalonia there is a formula for excommunication against those who would steal from the Church that also bears a striking resemblance to the excommunication form in our document:

> ... excommunicamus eos ad Patrem et Filium et Spiritum sanctum et per omnes ordines angelorum et archangelorum et omnes virtutes coelorum, sive per omnes

---

[47] Regino, *Libri duo* 2.416, ed. F. G. A. Wasserschleben (Leipzig, 1840), pp. 374 f.; Burchard, *Decretum* 11.6 (PL 140.860).

[48] See Michel Andrieu, *Les Ordines romani du haut moyen âge*, vol. 1: *Les manuscrits* (Louvain, 1931), p. 197 and *Le pontifical romano-germanique du dixième siècle*, ed. Cyrille Vogel and Reinhard Elze (Studi e Testi 226, 227, 269; Vatican City, 1963-72), 1.314.

[49] Étienne Baluze, *Capitularia regum francorum* 2 (Venice, 1773), col. 464.

[50] Monte Cassino, Archivio della Badia 451, pp. 165 f.; and Vogel-Elze, *Pontifical romano-germanique* 1.315-17.

Patriarchas et Prophetas, et per omnes Apostolos et Martyres vel Confessores, et per omnes sanctos Dei sic eos excommunicamus et anathematizamus atque abominamus et alienamus eos ....[51]

And in the *Tenor maledictionis ferendae* and *Modus exequendi huiusmodi maledictionem* published by Martène the Old and New Testament and secular precedents are rehearsed:

> Auctoritate omnipotentis Dei .... Cum Chorà, Dathan et Abiron qui descenderunt in infernum viventes. Cum Juda ... et Nerone ... Fiat, Fiat. ... Omnipotens Deus qui solus respicis ... ignis perpetui cruciatus cum Dathan et Abiron, Juda atque Pilato ... et Nerone, cum quibus cruciatu perpetuo ....[52]

Here there is the interesting reference (also made in our document, in the *Treuga Dei archidioecesis arelatensis*, and in the *Excommunicatio Leonis papae*) to Dathan and Abiron, a biblical reference widely found in the maledictions of charters and documents from the eighth to the eleventh century.[53]

A combination of both the excommunications and extension of maledictions to the physical state of the accursed found in our text also goes back to a variety of documents from the ninth century and beyond. In the ninth-century manuscript, Paris, Bibliothèque Nationale lat. 5/II, for example, such an excommunication and malediction is threatened:

> Sint maledicti et excommunicati et anathematizati a consorcio omnium fidelium christianorum dei. *Veniat super eos malediccio* omnium sanctorum dei. Maledicant illos angeli et archangeli dei. Maledicant illos patriarche et prophaete. Maledicant illos omnes apostoli et omnes martires et omnes confessores et omnes virgines .... Maledicti sint stantes et sedentes. Maledicti sint iacentes et ambulantes. Maledicti sint dormientes et vigilantes. Maledicti manducantes et bibentes ... *infernum* et cum *datan et abiran.*[54]

Norman manuscripts from the tenth century and beyond echo these threats:

> Damnentur cum Juda traditore .... Pereant cum Datiano et Nerone. Judicet illos Dominus, sicut judicavit Dathan et Abiron, quos terra vivos absorbuit ... maledicti sint dormientes et vigilantes, maledicti jejunantes et manducantes et

---

[51] Baluze, *Capitularia*, col. 470.

[52] Edmond Martène, *De antiquis ecclesiae ritibus libri* 2 (Antwerp, 1736), cols. 900-902, lib. III, cap. 3, ordo iii. This text is found in a late manuscript, Rouen, Bibliothèque Municipale 1228 (Y. 208), on which see Aimé-Georges Martimort, *La documentation liturgique de Dom Edmond Martène: étude codicologique* (Studi e Testi 279; Vatican City, 1978), p. 419.

[53] See Lester K. Little, 'Formules monastiques de malédiction aux ixe et xe siècles', *Revue Mabillon* 58 (1975) 384, and references therein.

[54] fol. 220r-v, ed. Little, ibid., 386 f.

bibentes; maledicti sint loquentes et tacentes .... Maledicti stando, jacendo, sedendo ....[55]

... sit cruciatus cum Chore, Datan, et Abiron, Juda atque ... Nerone ... Herode .... Maledicti sint dormientes, et vigilantes. Maledicti sint stantes, et jacentes .... Maledicti edentes et bibentes. Maledicti loquentes et tacentes ....[56]

And finally a formula of excommunication that Baluze connected with the earlier formula from Urgel in Catalonia calls down a most violent malediction in an extensive litany of curses highly reminiscent of our document:

... ut aeternis suppliciis cruciandus mancipetur cum Dathan et Abiron .... Maledictus sit vivendo, moriendo, manducando, bibendo, esuriendo, sitiendo, jejunando, dormitando, dormiendo, vigilando, ambulando, stando, sedendo, jacendo, operando, quiescendo, mingendo, cacando, flebotomando.[57]

By at least the second half of the eleventh century the 'overkill' of anathemas was being called into question by such eminent churchmen as Peter Damian, and as a result maledictions like these and ours had largely fallen into disuse by the twelfth century.[58] When in the late eleventh century, then, the *Treuga Dei* was promulgated by such popes as Urban II in southern Italian councils like that in Troia (1093),[59] excommunication and malediction were threatened, but the violence of the threats found in our southern Italian document had largely disappeared.

*
**

[55] Ed. Martène, *De antiquis ecclesiae ritibus*, col. 911, lib. III, cap. 4, formula vi, from Rouen, Bibliothèque Municipale 453 (A. 425), on which see Martimort, *La documentation*, p. 422.

[56] Martène, ibid., cols. 911 f., formula vii, from a Fécamp manuscript, on which see Martimort, ibid., pp. 422 f.

[57] Baluze, *Capitularia*, cols. 469 f.

[58] Little, 'Formules', 384 f. and cf. Lester K. Little, 'La morphologie des malédictions monastiques', *Annales: économies, sociétés, civilisations* 34.1 (1979) 48.

[59] 'c. 2. Si quis treviam Dei fregerit, usque tertio ad satisfactionem ab episcopo moneatur. Quod si nec tertio satisfacere consenserit episcopus, vel cum metropolitani consilio, aut cum duobus, aut uno vicinorum episcoporum, in rebellem anathematis sententiam dicat, et per scripturam episcopis circumquaque denunciet. Si excommunicatum episcoporum nullus in communionem suscipiat; immo, scriptura suscepta, sententiam quisque confirmet. Si quis aliter praesumpserit, ordinis sui periculo subjacebit', ed. G. D. Mansi, *Sacrorum conciliorum nova et amplissima collectio*, 31 vols. (Florence, 1759-98), 20.790. Cf. the Council of Melfi (1089) (Mansi 20.724 f.) and the account of Lupus Protospatharius in the Annales ad an. 1089 (MGH *SS* 5; Hanover, 1844), p. 62. It is on the basis of these documents that G. A. Loud, 'The Church, Warfare and Military Obligation in Norman Italy' in *The Church and War*, ed. W. J. Sheils (Studies in Church History 20; Oxford, 1983), p. 35, has recently argued that 'The Peace and Truce of God came late to southern Italy under papal auspices....'

In presenting the text of our document here, paragraphs have been introduced to emphasize the different sections of our text. Pointed brackets have been used where the text is obscured either by the tightness of the binding or by the fading of the ink on the rough and water-marked single sheet of parchment. Where the partially obscured letter or letters can be read with some certainty, they have been inserted between the pointed brackets, but where this is not possible, conjectural readings have been added in the apparatus. Abbreviations have been expanded and the spelling of the manuscript maintained. Punctuation has been in part modernized but maintained insofar as possible.

< ... > et <   >ᵃ <   >ᵇ nunc <   >ᶜ pax firma pro treugua Dei <   >ᵈ pre <   >ᵉnus Odil<   >ᶠs abbas cum ceteris episcopis et cum sanctis clericis mandat vobis, non ex part<e>   regis terreni, non ex parte ma < r > chionis, non ducis, non comitis, non al<   >ᵍius pa<r>tis (*sic*) persone, sed ex parte Dei et omnium sanctorum, angelorum, et archangelorum, et omnium celestium virtutum, et omnium sanctorum, patriarcharum, et prophetarum, apostolorum, et martyrum, confessorum, atque virginum et omnium electorum sanctorum Dei.

Nec <   >ʰtet aliqui < s > ⁱhoc eos vel esse sed illi prout possibile est in pace persistentibus hosⁱ <   >ʲ dies predictos deifice pacis omnimodo datos per treuguam Dei applicuerunt et omnibus Christianis custodiendam in perpetuum stabilierunt.

Quicumque istam treuguam Dei cum pace et humilitate firmam tenuerint et bene observaverint, sint absoluti a culpis et a peccatis suis a Deo Patre omnipotente et a Filio eius Iesu Christo et a piritu (*sic*) sancto et a sancta Maria regina celi cum omni choro virginum, et a sancto Michaele cum omni exercitu angelorum, et a sancto Petro cum omni ordine apostolorum, martyrum, confessorum, virginum, et orthodoxis viris, nunc et semper et in secula seculorum. Amen.

Qui vero istam treuguam Dei promissam habuerit et si in ea< > ᵏ inciderit nescienter aut per ignorantiam aut per ebrietatem aut forte per iracundiam, in

---

ᵃ   illeg.: space for approximately 4 letters.
ᵇ   illeg.: *pro*?
ᶜ   illeg.: space for 2-3 letters.
ᵈ   illeg.: *quam* ?
ᵉ   illeg.: *clarus domi-*?
ᶠ   illeg.: space for 1 letter.
ᵍ   illeg.: *-ter-* ?
ʰ   illeg.: *pu-*?
ⁱ   *hoc eos ... persistentibus hos*: syntax and meaning unclear.
ʲ   illeg.: space for 2-3 letters.
ᵏ   illeg.: *m* ?

ipso die subito traat ad penitentiam et veniam accipiat, ter virgis cesus et si in secunda die produxerit novem peniteat et novem virgis cesus et permaneat inlesus.

Et < >[1] < > [m]tem et sponte fregerit illam aut frangere consiliatus fuerit < > [n] excommunicatus a Deo Patre omnipotente et a Filio eius Iesu Christo et a Spiritu < > [o] a sancta Maria regina celorum digna cum omni choro virginum, et a sancto Michaele cum omni exercitus (*sic*) angelorum, et a sancto Petro cum omni ordine apostolorum, martyrum, confessorum, virginum et ab omnibus electis Dei, episcopis, presbyteris, abbatibus, fideles (*sic*) clericis, et orthodoxis viris. Sit maledictus et anathematizatus et excommunicatus, detestabilis et abominatus modo et in perpetuum; sit condampnatus et absorbeat eum mater terra sicut Dathan et Abiron, s < i > t demersus in profundum inferni cum Nerone et Herode et Iuda traditore. Et quandiu vixerit in isto seculo, sit maledictus et ana < th > ematizatus, ambulando, stando, sedendo, iacendo, dormi < en > do, vigilando, manducando, bibendo, loquendo, tacendo. Sit maledictus in omni opere suo. Nullus eum adiuvet nec etiam < > [p]c < > [q] mandatum fregit sit misertus ei. Iste et omnes maledictiones que (*sic*) sub Moysen et Aaron percussa est Egiptus veniat (*sic*) super eos qui hanc treuguam Dei fregerit. Et si in sanctam trinitatem et veram pacem recognosce < > [r] erit et si emendationem et condignam penitentiam contrito cor < de > et < h > umiliato spiritu venerit et accipiat penitentiam sicut illis < ... >

---

[l]   illeg.: *q*?
[m]   illeg.: *per volunta-*?
[n]   illeg.: *sit*?
[o]   illeg.: *sco et*
[p]   illeg.: space for 3-4 letters.
[q]   illeg.: space for 3 letters.
[r]   illeg.: space for 4-8 letters.

Rome. Biblioteca Vallicelliana ms. C 45.
fol. 73r and facing strip to fol. 65r
(Photograph: Dr. M. Vivarelli)

XII

A SOUTH ITALIAN LITURGICO-CANONICAL
MASS COMMENTARY*

* For references to several manuscripts and secondary literature I am grateful to Professors
Raymund Kottje and Robert Somerville.

Reprinted from *Mediaeval Studies*, 50 (1988), pp. 626-670, by permission of the publisher. © 1988 by the
Pontifical Institute of Mediaeval Sudies, Toronto.

Introduction

IN his *Disquisitiones criticae* published in 1836, the canonist Augustin Theiner printed an ancient text regarding the hour of Mass.[1] Theiner's text begins with a correspondence between the fourth-century Pope Damasus I, who asks at what hour Mass should be celebrated, and a response by St. Jerome, who reminds his papal interrogator that the First Council of Nicea had declared that Mass was not to be celebrated after the third hour on Sundays and between the third and ninth hour on other days. Theiner's text then continues with what is one of the most remarkable and fanciful commentaries on the Mass produced in the early Middle Ages. After the correspondence between Damasus and Jerome the text explains at great length why Mass should not be said after the third hour, why the priest is to celebrate with two other persons, and why he should wear seven vestments. Then seven 'trinities' in the order and celebration of the Mass are explained: (1) the lights used at Mass with their wax, wick, and flame; (2) the incense with its odor and fire; (3) the bread, wine, and water; (4) the tersanctus; (5) the triform nature of the term for the celebrant as *sa-cer-dos* and *pres-bi-ter*; (6) the tripled corporal on the altar and over the chalice and oblation, and the cover on the chalice; and (7) the threefold Agnus Dei. The text then concludes with an admonition to priests to celebrate as directed in the commentary.

Theiner's text is found in many manuscripts written in Beneventan script or with Beneventan-script symptoms and in manuscripts with south Italian connections. In fact, his own text was based on the codex Biblioteca Apostolica Vaticana Vat. lat. 1339 (V5 below), with Beneventan-script symptoms. But if the texts in these manuscripts are compared with Theiner's, it is clear that his is defective in several ways. Most important, it lacks significant introductory material found in the manuscripts explaining that the correspondence between Damasus and Jerome had been occasioned by a controversy in Rome as to when Mass should be said.

Theiner's defective text has been reproduced as recently as 1974 in the supplement to Migne's *Patrologia latina*[2] together with a list of manuscripts said to contain the text. But, strangely, the texts in these manuscripts are all a vastly reduced version in which there is simply: (1) the question Damasus put to Jerome; (2) Jerome's response that the Council of Nicea had forbidden solemn Mass to be said after the third hour on Sundays and from the fifth to the eighth on other days; and (3) a short, almost ungracious response by Damasus that Jerome is

---

[1] *Disquisitiones criticae in praecipuas canonum et decretalium collectiones seu Sylloges Gallandianae dissertationum de vetustis canonum collectionibus continuatio* (Rome, 1836), pp. 301-303.

[2] PLS 5.396 f.

correct. This reduced version of the text was printed without comment as long ago as 1899 by Aloisius Knoepfler in a footnote to his edition of the *Liber de exordiis* of Walafrid Strabo.[3]

A decision on the hour of the Mass attributed to the Council of Nicea and connected with Damasus has long been known to modern scholars, at least back to the time of Baronius in the sixteenth century, and is reported in Mansi's *Sacrorum conciliorum nova et amplissima collectio.*[4] Moreover, references to the long form of the text not unlike Theiner's had appeared in a variety of incipit lists of canons in early medieval canonical collections.[5] Occasionally in more recent secondary literature brief references have been made to the text in either Theiner's long or Knoepfler's short forms.[6] But it was not until 1970 that a reasonably accurate critical edition of Theiner's long form was printed by Mario Fornasari in his partial edition of the south Italian canonical *Collection in Five Books.*[7] Unfortunately, this new edition is at odds not only with Theiner's text but also with all of the manuscripts of this collection. Further, in Fornasari's *Initia canonum* listing the occurrences of the text in early medieval canonical collections, our text is cited as appearing only in the *Collection in Five Books.*[8]

In view of this somewhat haphazard treatment and editing of the text, it is appropriate that a more systematic examination of its origins and development be undertaken and that its various forms be critically edited. New evidence largely from manuscripts from southern Italy or with south Italian connections dramatically illustrates how layer by layer the text grew into at least eleven recensions in almost three dozen manuscripts. Using this new material, this study will focus on

---

[3] *Liber de exordiis et incrementis quarundam in observationibus ecclesiasticis rerum*, 2nd edition (Munich, 1899), pp. 70 f.

[4] Caesar Baronius, *Annales ecclesiastici* (Angers, 1866), 5.493: 'Prohibitum etiam ex praescripto (ut ibi ponitur) Nicaeni canonis, ne ante horam tertiam diebus festis Missae canerentur, aliis vero diebus a media hora quarta usque ad nonam facere liceret.' On the citation in Mansi 3.642, see Raymund Kottje, *Studien zum Einfluss des Alten Testamentes auf Recht und Liturgie des frühen Mittelalters (6.-8. Jahrhundert)*, 2nd edition (Bonner historische Forschungen; Bonn, 1970), p. 59.

[5] e.g., PL 138.413 (III.45); Theiner, *Disquisitiones*, p. 304.

[6] Franz Zimmermann, *Die Abendmesse in Geschichte und Gegenwart* (Vienna, 1914), pp. 108 f., noting what is presumably the text known to Baronius; Michel Andrieu, *Les Ordines romani du haut moyen âge* 1 (Spicilegium sacrum lovaniense. Études et documents 11; Louvain, 1931), p. 342, citing Knoepfler's edition and listing manuscripts with the short correspondence alone; E. Dekkers, 'La messe du soir à la fin de l'antiquité et au moyen âge: notes historiques', *Sacris erudiri* 7 (1955) 117 n. 5, citing Theiner's text and what he calls an extract of it in our ninth-century codex G below; *Clavis patrum latinorum*, ed. Eligius Dekker and Aemilius Gaar, 2nd edition (Steenbrugge, 1961), no. 633b; and Bernard Lambert, *Bibliotheca hieronymiana manuscripta: la tradition manuscrite des oeuvres de saint Jérôme* 3A (Steenbrugge, 1970), no. 355, noting Theiner's edition and listing manuscripts of several versions of the correspondence only.

[7] *Collectio canonum in v libris (lib. i-iii)* (CCM 6; Turnhout, 1970), pp. 413-15.

[8] *Initia canonum a primaevis collectionibus usque ad Decretum Gratiani*, vol. 1: *A-G*, ed. M. Fornasari (Monumenta Italiae ecclesiastica, Subsidia 1; Florence, 1972), no. 1635[1].

the curious correspondence between Damasus and Jerome and the accompanying Mass commentary by tracing its spectacular growth and diffusion in its liturgical, canonical, codicological, and historical contexts. To be sure, some of the lines of development to be sketched here are conjectural and may be modified as other manuscripts come to light. But the text as a whole has been neglected far too long by scholars; and now that sufficient manuscript evidence has been found to illustrate its development, the text deserves to be singled out for more extensive analysis and to be edited critically in its various recensions.

I

DATE OF THE CORRESPONDENCE AND MASS COMMENTARY

It has long been recognized that although the text as a whole is attributed to Damasus and Jerome, the long Mass commentary, whose colorful contents will be described in more detail later, is clearly not from the patristic period. It is far too fanciful and too far-fetched. But could the simple, brief correspondence between Damasus and Jerome on the hour of the Mass be authentic? Damasus and Jerome certainly did correspond on many matters, some liturgical, but there appears to be no evidence of a controversy in fourth-century Rome over the hour at which Mass could be celebrated and certainly no canon of the First Council of Nicea on such a subject. By at least the early sixth century, however, there might indeed have been more concern over the hour of the Mass, perhaps in Rome itself. Evidence for this is found in the *Liber pontificalis*, where one of the early second-century popes, Telesphorus, is said to have directed that aside from Christmas, no Masses were to be said before the cursus of the third hour:

> Hic constituit ut ... natalem Domini noctu missas celebrarentur; nam omni tempore, ante horae tertiae cursum nullus praesumeret missas celebrare, qua hora Dominus noster ascendit crucem....[9]

Here the *cursus* of the third hour may simply mean the third hour or about 9 a.m., but since the term *cursus* also has liturgical overtones, the term may also mean the divine office celebrated at the third hour, perhaps something like the office of terce celebrated as a type of foremass in the early Middle Ages.[10] If this were the case, the text attributed to Telesphorus may indicate that there should normally be no Mass before the office of terce at about 9 a.m., and that the Mass thereafter should be celebrated during the time of Christ's sacrifice.

---

[9] *Le Liber pontificalis: texte, introduction et commentaire* 1, ed. L. Duchesne, 2nd edition (Paris, 1955), p. 129.
[10] Joseph A. Jungmann, *The Mass of the Roman Rite: Its Origins and Development (Missarum Sollemnia)* 1, trans. Francis A. Brunner (New York, 1951), pp. 247 f.

Legislation or quasi-legislation on the hour of the Mass continued to be reported in various early medieval sources. In the *Bobbio Missal*, for example, written perhaps as early as the late seventh or early eighth century in northern Italy,[11] there is a corrupt text, perhaps copied from an older exemplar, with a regulation on the hour of the Mass justified again with events in Christ's life:

INCEPIT INQUISITIO DE LEGE. AD MESAM CELEBRARE.
Si necesitas fuerit ad galurum cantu lecet sacerdutes traderem et consacrare sacrificium et de ora nonam usque ad uesperum septema et octauam ora nun es iustum consacrare sacrificium as autem duas oras quas christus in crocem pendit tenebre facte s<unt> he duas horas in qua sul et lona et omniam sidira tenebrecati sunt et os ualleum racientem christo perdederunt nec sacreficium ofererint non lecet set elas et elam septema firia com eueneret autem diaem paxe mesa in eo diae non celebr<e>tur idio et elas doas oras omnebus diaebus septema et hoctauam misa cantare non lecet quia tenebre uocate sunt e pependentem christo dei filium in crucem elimenta trimuerunt in uigilias enim pahe corus misit in media noctes et pus inplere debet quia media noctem christo de sepulcrum surexit citeris diaebus a deluculum diae usque ad crepuscolum noctes per sumptas duas oras licet sacreficium tradere et consecrare.[12]

It is perhaps significant that this text is adjacent to an Ordinal of Christ with its dominical sanctions[13] and not far removed from the Pseudo-Hieronymian *De omnes cursus* (sic)[14] on the hours of the divine office in which it is pointed out that at the third hour Christ was crucified and the Holy Spirit descended to the apostles, and at the sixth hour Christ ascended the cross.

By the late eighth and ninth centuries the decision attributed to the second-century Pope Telesphorus was being widely circulated in a variety of forms beyond the *Liber pontificalis*. These different forms seem to reflect some confusion as to what exactly was meant by the decision. Walafrid Strabo in his *De exordiis*, for example, simply repeated the text of Telesphorus, but added a theme that would later appear in the Mass commentary attached to the correspondence between Damasus and Jerome, namely, that there was to be no fasting on Sundays and feast days:

[11] Klaus Gamber, *Codices liturgici latini antiquiores* 1, 2nd edition (Spicilegii friburgensis subsidia 1; Fribourg, 1968), p. 168.

[12] *The Bobbio Missal. A Gallican Mass-Book (MS. Paris. Lat. 13246)*, ed. E. A. Lowe (Henry Bradshaw Society 58; London, 1920), pp. 177 f.

[13] Roger E. Reynolds, *The Ordinals of Christ from Their Origins to the Twelfth Century* (Beiträge zur Geschichte und Quellenkunde des Mittelalters 7; Berlin-New York, 1978), p. 58.

[14] ibid., p. 73 n. 15; and on the use of this text in related manuscripts, see Jonathan Glenn Black, *The Daily Cursus, the Week, and the Psalter in the Divine Office and in Carolingian Devotion* (Diss. Toronto, 1987), pp. 285-89.

Nam Telesphorus papa constituit, ut nullo tempore ante horae tertiae cursum ullus praesumeret missas celebrare, qua hora Dominus noster secundum Marci evangelium crucifixus asseritur. Inter haec notandum neque ieiunandum in dominicis et festis maioribus, ubi non cogit necessitas, sicut et canones ostendunt, ...[15]

Amalarius of Metz in his *Liber officialis* repeated the account of Telesphorus, but then without any reference to the *cursus* said that it was fitting to say Mass at the third hour:

Memoratus papa Telesforus scripsit quo tempore primo diei liceret missam caelebrare. Legitur in Gestis episcopalibus dixisse memoratum papam ut ante horae tertiae cursum nullus praesumeret missas caelebrare, qua hora Dominus noster ascendit in crucem. Si enim propterea aptum est iuxta memoratum papam tempus horae tertiae caelebrationi missae, quia in eo legitur secundum Marcum crucem Christum ascendisse ....[16]

Finally, the forgers of the Pseudo-Isidorian Decretals reported Telesphorus as saying that Mass was not to be said before the third hour of the day, because Christ had ascended the cross at that hour and also because the Holy Spirit had descended on the apostles:

Reliquis enim temporibus missarum caelebrationes ante horam diei tertiam minime sunt caelebrandae, quia eadem hora et Dominus crucifixus et super apostolos Spiritus Sanctus descendisse legitur.[17]

In the Pseudo-Isidorian Decretals all reference to the *cursus* of the third hour has disappeared, perhaps reflecting the tendency in the second half of the ninth and early tenth centuries for the vesting prayers and so-called accession prayers to replace the office of terce as the rites of preparation for the Mass.[18]

Given this seeming confusion in the ninth century as to what the second-century Pope Telesphorus had meant, it is perhaps not surprising to find the author of our correspondence state that in the fourth century another pope, Damasus, the great western father, Jerome, and also the first ecumenical council of the Church had all said that Mass was not to be celebrated after the third hour. The general confusion reflected in the texts as to whether Mass was to be celebrated before, at, or after the third hour suggests that our correspondence between Damasus and Jerome was compiled sometime between the sixth-century *Liber pontificalis* and the late eighth century and probably not long before it was entered in a corrupt

---

[15] ed. Knoepfler, pp. 70 f.

[16] *Liber officialis* 3.42.1 f.; *Amalarii episcopi Opera liturgica omnia* 2, ed. Jean Michel Hanssens (Studi e testi 139; Vatican City, 1948), pp. 378 f.

[17] *Decretales pseudo-isidorianae et Capitula Angilramni*, ed. Paul Hinschius (Leipzig, 1863), pp. 110 f.

[18] On this see Roger E. Reynolds, 'Mass, Liturgy of the' in *Dictionary of the Middle Ages* 7.184.

form by an early ninth-century hand into a late eighth-century Stuttgart manuscript (S below) of the canonical *Collectio Vetus Gallica.*[19]

II

PLACE OF ORIGIN OF THE CORRESPONDENCE BETWEEN DAMASUS AND JEROME

As is clear from the dates of the manuscripts containing the text in any form, the oldest contain only the correspondence, suggesting that the Mass commentary was a later accretion. But do the origins of these early manuscripts with the correspondence alone shed any light on the place of origin of the text? Southern Germany or the Rhaetian Alps might be suggested since the three earliest codices were written in the vicinities of Chur (S), St. Gall (G), and Regensburg (Pr) respectively.[20] Nonetheless, this same version with minor variants can be found in a codex in Beneventan script of the eleventh century; and a slightly different text of the correspondence with a longer conclusion is heavily represented in Bene-ventan-script codices from the tenth century and beyond [Text 2 below]. Thus, although the earliest manuscripts of the corrrespondence suggest an origin in regions far removed from southern Italy, it is not beyond the realm of possibility that even the correspondence itself originated in southern Italy and was taken north in the late eighth century.

III

FORMS OF THE CORRESPONDENCE

Thus far four distinct forms of the short correspondence between Damasus and Jerome have been found, and these are edited below as Texts 1 through 4. Text 1, the shortest form and the one found in the oldest manuscripts, is curious in that the concluding reply by Damasus appears to be a somewhat crude addition, probably intended to give papal approval to Jerome's citation of the canon attributed to Nicea. As it stands, it is unclear if this was the original conclusion or an abbreviation or summary of the longer and more gracious reply by Damasus reported in Text 2, found in the southern Italian manuscripts of the tenth century and later. In its oldest witness, MC1, the longer conclusion of Text 2 is corrupt,

[19] Hubert Mordek, *Kirchenrecht und Reform im Frankenreich. Die Collectio Vetus Gallica, die älteste systematische Kanonessammlung des fränkischen Gallien. Studien und Edition* (Beiträge zur Geschichte und Quellenkunde des Mittelalters 1; Berlin-New York, 1975), pp. 294 f.
[20] ibid., noting that the first part of S is related to Italian collections.

and possibly northern copyists, unable to make sense of the longer conclusion, simply omitted it.

The longer correspondence forms in Texts 3 and 4 are interesting in their expansion of the Nicene decision to include additional hours on ordinary days when Mass can be said, an expansion that is in some ways reminiscent of the text on the hour of the Mass in the *Bobbio Missal* noted above. In the Long Correspondence Form with Short Conclusion [Text 3] it is specified that on (feast?) days it is not licit to say Mass from the fifth to the seventh hour; and on ordinary days it is licit to say Mass from early morning to the fourth hour and from the eighth to the twelfth hour. According to the Long Correspondence Form with Long Conclusion [Text 4] on ordinary days it is licit to celebrate Mass from early morning through every hour to the twelfth. The difference in these hours in the two manuscripts probably reflects the continuing uncertainty beyond the ninth century as to exactly when Mass could be said, a phenomenon also found in the variants of Text 2, where in MC1 it is stated that Mass is not to be said on other days from the fifth to the eighth hour, while other manuscripts limit the celebration of Mass from the fifth to the seventh hour.

Although Texts 2 through 4 appear to contain a more complete form of the correspondence between Damasus and Jerome, it was nonetheless the truncated form of the very early Stuttgart, St. Gall, and Prague manuscripts that had the widest broadcast, especially in liturgical codices. In these liturgical manuscripts, the short form of the correspondence is often placed next to other texts dealing with aspects of the Mass that would be treated in the longer Mass commentaries. Among the texts contiguous with our brief correspondence are the *Capitula* of Theodulf of Orléans, the *De exordiis* of Walafrid Strabo, the *Liber officialis* of Amalarius of Metz, and other well-known eighth- and ninth-century Mass commentaries, including one beginning with the salutation *Dominus vobiscum*. Several witnesses with the truncated form, written during the ninth century and later, were copied in southern Germany, but at least by the early eleventh century (and probably before) the texts in them were being included in south Italian liturgical and canonical manuscripts by scribes writing in Beneventan script, as is seen in L below.[21]

---

[21] On south German elements in L see Mordek, ibid., pp. 104 f. For the vast liturgico-canonical florilegium in L see Letha Mahadevan, 'Überlieferung und Verbreitung des Bussbuchs "Capitula Iudiciorum"', *Zeitschrift der Savigny-Stiftung für Rechtsgeschichte*, kan. Abt. 72 (1986) 24-28. It is interesting that this codex contains the second epistle of Clement with additions in a recension like that found in the Beneventan-script fragment of Goslar, Stadtarchiv S. N. (see above, p. 600). It also contains the Mass commentary *Dominus vobiscum*, attributed to Jerome, on which see Roger E. Reynolds, 'Pseudonymous liturgica in early medieval canon law collections' in *Fälschungen im Mittelalter. Internationaler Kongress der Monumenta Germaniae Historica, München, 15.-18. September 1986* (Schriften der Monumenta Germaniae Historica 33.2; Hanover, 1988), n. 36.

That either Text 1 or 2 survived beyond the ninth century at all was due probably not so much to the intrinsic validity or usefulness of the text itself as to its routine inclusion in series of other texts, such as the closely related manuscripts V1, V2, V3, and W1[22] with Text 1, or C, Ma1, and P1 with Text 2 embedded in a vast south Italian florilegium.[23] In fact, the validity and authenticity of the correspondence forms could be and probably were questioned on two grounds by at least the tenth century. First, as has been seen, the correspondence could be taken to contradict the Telesphorus text, a text widely known and copied by the early tenth century in scores of canonical and liturgical manuscripts, including many containing the correspondence between Damasus and Jerome.[24] Second, by at least the early tenth century it must have been noticed that the correspondence contained a reference to a decision of the First Council of Nicea nowhere to be found in the normative text of twenty canons of that council. There was, of course, a tradition in the West well into the ninth century that the Council had enacted some seventy canons,[25] and perhaps it might early have been thought that the reference in our correspondence was to one of the fifty 'lost' canons of Nicea. But this tradition of fifty 'lost' Nicene canons had been severely attacked in the mid-ninth century in the celebrated controversy between the two Hincmars, and hence any so-called 'lost' Nicene canons, including ours, would probably have been considered tainted by the tenth century.

IV

GROWTH OF THE MASS COMMENTARY

Despite the questionable nature of our correspondence, it did survive, but as the foundation for layer upon layer of commentary on the meaning of the eucharistic liturgy. Such layers would seem to have developed in southern Italy since testimony

---

[22] B, V1, V2, V3, W1 and M are all vast florilegia of canonical and liturgical texts, including Mass commentaries and the *Ordines romani*, whose relationships have been treated extensively by Andrieu, *Les Ordines romani*, pp. 84-89, 238-40, 294-300.

[23] C, Ma1 and P1 contain a vast miscellany of texts often studied individually or as a whole. See, e.g., Reynolds, *Ordinals of Christ*, pp. 91 f. for bibliography, and Herbert Bloch, 'Der Autor der "Graphia aurea urbis Romae"', *Deutsches Archiv* 40 (1984) 150 n. 259, citing the Harvard dissertation on the florilegium by Elizabeth Susan Lott. Our text in MC1 is embedded in a florilegium and followed by the explanation of the parts of the Creed according to their apostolic origin.

[24] The Telesphorus canon appears, e.g., in the *Collectio canonica ambrosiana* 2.233 (*Collezioni canoniche milanesi del secolo xii*, ed. Giorgio Picasso [Pubblicazioni dell'Università Cattolica del S. Cuore, Saggi e Ricerche, 3rd Ser., Scienze storiche 2; Milan, 1969], p. 247).

[25] Horst Fuhrmann, *Einfluss und Verbreitung der pseudoisidorischen Fälschungen von ihrem Auftauchen bis in die neuere Zeit* (Schriften der Monumenta Germaniae Historica 24.3; Stuttgart, 1974), pp. 680 f., 702 f.

to them is found largely in codices written in Beneventan script or with Beneventan-script symptoms and in codices related in some way to the south Italian canonical *Collection in Five Books* or the *Collection in Nine Books.* The initial strata of transformation of the correspondence into Mass commentary may go back perhaps to the early tenth century because it has been argued on textual grounds that the *Collection in Nine Books,* which contains the longest version of our Mass commentary, was compiled by the early tenth century.[26] Moreover, the earliest manuscript to contain any version of the correspondence and Mass commentary, V7, is dated to *c.* 1000, and the text bears some resemblance to that in the *Collection in Nine Books.*[27]

The process of transforming the early brief correspondence into the Mass commentary probably began when its potential conflict with the widely known Telesphorus canon was noted. As a result, two changes in the correspondence itself were introduced. First, a brief prologue was added to explain that the entire Roman Church was embroiled in controversy over the hour of the Mass and hence Damasus had written to Jerome for advice. Then, the letter of Damasus was altered and improved upon slightly, and Jerome's reply was also augmented slightly with the statement that on ferial days Mass was not to be celebrated from the third to the ninth hour. With these rather minor modifications in place, imaginative liturgical commentators then began to graft onto this stock of the correspondence their own colorful explanations of the elements of the eucharist.

V

SHORT PENITENTIAL FORM

The first transformation of the correspondence into a Mass commentary proper appears in texts mutually related by an intruded penitential canon, and hence this group is placed under the general rubric of Penitential Forms. Although the first form is found in twelfth-century manuscripts, its brevity probably indicates that it represents the earliest stratum in the growth from simple correspondence to Mass commentary. In this Short Penitential Form [Text 5] the commentator completely replaces the conclusion of the Correspondence Forms of Texts 1 through 4 with a longer description of the reception of Jerome's response in Rome where it was verified that the 318 Fathers, inflamed as they were by the Holy Spirit, had indeed made the decision in the presence of the emperor Constantine that anyone who

---

[26] Paul Fournier and Gabriel Le Bras, *Histoire des collections canoniques en occident depuis les Fausses Décrétales jusqu'au Décret de Gratien* 1 (Paris, 1931), p. 346.

[27] On the date of V7 see Paola Supino Martini, *Roma e l'area grafica romanesca (secoli x-xii)* (Biblioteca di Scrittura e civiltà 1; Alessandria, 1987), p. 74.

might dare say Mass after the third hour on Sunday would be anathematized. Then the commentator explains why Mass cannot be said after the third hour on Sunday. Strangely, he uses one of the very points Telesphorus in the Pseudo-Isidorian Decretals had raised in objecting to Mass being said before the third hour, namely, that it was at the third hour that the Holy Spirit had descended on the apostles, whose successors were the 318 Fathers. Then, borrowing further from an idea in Walafrid Strabo's text of Telesphorus, the commentator adds that fasting and abstinence are also forbidden on Sundays from the third hour on. To enforce this he uses a penitential canon, something like that in the *Penitentialia Vallicelliana I* and *II*,[28] threatening with penance for seven days anyone who through negligence fasts on Sundays. Returning to the confused problem as to when the sacrifice may be offered, the commentator further says that on ferial days the sacrifice may not be offered 'a media hora tertia usque in horam nonam', because it was at that time that Christ had made his own sacrifice on the cross. To conclude his text, the commentator takes up a theme found neither in the correspondence between Damasus and Jerome nor in the Telesphorus and Walafrid material but one debated extensively in the eighth and ninth centuries, namely, how many persons are necessary to celebrate Mass.[29] The commentator agrees heartily with his ninth-century forebears that it is improper for a priest to celebrate alone, but his reason is not the usual ninth-century argument that a single priest cannot give the salutation *Dominus vobiscum* without at least one other person present. Rather, the commentator argues that when Christ made his sacrifice, he did so not alone, but between two thieves.

VI

INTERMEDIATE PENITENTIAL FORM

The next accretions to the correspondence and Mass commentary are found in an eleventh-century codex, Va1, written in Beneventan script which contains other liturgical commentaries, including Amalarius' *Expositio I* with separable preface,[30] and the early Carolingian *Dominus vobiscum*. In this Intermediate Penitential

---

[28] 1.108, 'Qui in die dominica per negligentiam jejunaverit et opera fecerit aut si valneaverit, vii dies peniteat, si pro damnatione diei dominicae hoc facit, abominabitur ab ecclesia catholica sicut judeus', and 2.75, 'Qui jejunat in die dominico sponte, anathema sit; qui operatur in die dominico, vii dies peniteat; qui contemnit indictum ab ecclesia jejunium, xl dies peniteat' (*Die Bussbücher und die Bussdisziplin der Kirche nach handschriftlichen Quellen dargestellt*, ed. Herm. Jos. Schmitz [Mainz, 1883], 1.325, 385).

[29] See Jean M. Hanssens, 'Fungiturne minister missae privatae diaconi et subdiaconi vicibus?', *Ephemerides liturgicae* 48 (1934) 410-12.

[30] On which see Roger E. Reynolds, 'Unity and Diversity in Carolingian Canon Law Collections: The Case of the *Collectio Hibernensis*' in *Carolingian Essays: Andrew W. Mellon Lectures in Early Christian Studies*, ed. Uta-Renate Blumenthal (Washington, D. C., 1983), p. 126.

Form [Text 6] the references to the Council of Nicea and the inflaming Holy Spirit seem to have provided the impetus for expanded trinitarian and pneumatological commentary on the parts of the Mass. Indeed, in the margin of the manuscript, there is a gloss on the trinity at the crucifixion, Christ and the two thieves, where the malefactors are identified as Aspalorga and Alaban, not the usual Gestas, Dismas, Limas, or the like. The commentator seems to have felt that the case against a single priest at Mass should be bolstered, and this he did with four arguments. First, he introduces the argument from the salutation *Dominus vobiscum* and improves upon it by saying that two additional ministers must be present at Mass because if only one were present, the priest's salutation would be *Dominus tecum*, not *Dominus vobiscum*. Second, the commentator argues that two ministers with the priest must be present for there to be a perfect reflection of the Trinity in the Mass. Third, Christ himself had said, 'Where two or three are gathered in my name, there am I in the midst of them'.[31] Finally, in the Scriptures it is said that on the testimony of three witnesses matters are confirmed before God and men (1 Jo 5:7-8).

Yet another stratum is added to the text as the commentator lists the seven vestments a priest must wear or carry at Mass: the alb, cincture, amice, stole, chasuble, maniple, and towel. Although in later versions of the text the towel or sudarium is glossed as a corporal [Text 7 and Text 10, MC2], it appears here to be a strange doublet for the maniple. No reason for the septiformity of vestments is given, and the doublet of both maniple and towel suggests that the traditional six vestments have been expanded to seven for a reason not expressed. In any event, 'et trilicem', perhaps referring to a triple-fiber or triple-folded towel or sudarium used to place the sacrifice on the altar, is connected with the Trinity.

Having dealt with the septiformity of vestments, the commentator turns to a trinitarian scheme wherein each of three objects necessary in the Mass is seen as having a trinity within itself. First, light is necessary at Mass because otherwise the sacrifice would be like that of a blind man. But the light must be lit with a flame for there to be a trinity, that is, in the oil or wax, in the wick, and in the flame. Again, one suspects that these three objects should have been compared directly to the three persons of the Trinity, but here for reasons unknown the comparisons have been omitted. Second, incense is necessary at the sacrifice because, when the angels of Satan fell to earth, they made such a stench that the priest must cense the altar so that the devil will flee and the odor of incense can rise to God.[32] But

---

[31] Cf. Theodulf of Orléans, *Capitula I*, c. 7, ed. Peter Brommer (MGH *Leges, capitula episcoporum* 1; Munich, 1984), p. 108.

[32] For similar arguments in later commentaries, see Lothar of Segni (Innocent III), *De sacro altaris mysterio libri sex* 2.17, 58 (PL 217.808, 834) and William Durandus, *Rationale* 4.10.5 (*Prochiron, vulgo Rationale divinorum officiorum, Gulielmo Durando, I. V. D. celeberrimo, mimatensi episcopo, authore* [Lyons, 1551], fol. 63v).

like the light at the sacrifice, the incense must be lit with flame for there to be a trinity: in the incense itself, in the odor, and in the fire. The third trinity of objects at the Mass, according to the commentator, is in the oblata, the bread, wine, and water. If solely bread were used, only the Father would be present; if bread and wine alone were used, only the Father and Son would be present. So all three, the bread of the Father, the wine of the Son, and the water of the Holy Spirit, are necessary in the Mass.

VII

THE TORTOSA FORM

Three of the explanations that seem to be missing in the Intermediate Penitential Form are supplied by yet another, long recension of the correspondence and Mass commentary in a codex of the chapter library of the cathedral at Tortosa [Text 7]. This codex was written in Beneventan script perhaps of the tenth or eleventh century, but in the early twelfth century the text was erased and replaced by a number of liturgical commentaries, including ours.[33] As it now stands in the Tortosa manuscript, the text of our Mass commentary is corrupt; although it lacks the penitential canon common to the Penitential Forms, it is related to them. Moreover, it contains some of the explanations missing in the Short and Intermediate Penitential Forms and hence is of significant value in reconstructing the text as a whole. The first of these explanations is an expansion of the argument that Mass should not be celebrated 'a media hora tercia usque in mediam horam octavam' because Christ was on the cross at those hours. The commentator adds that therefore the angels cannot acccept the priest's sacrifice at those hours. The second expansion deals with the vestments; it is clearly stated that the seven vestments, including the 'corporalem triplicem', refer to the seven gifts of the Holy Spirit. The third expansion explains that in the trinity of the burning light the wax represents the Father, the wick the Son, and the fire the Holy Spirit. In the Tortosa version this third expansion seems to have been misplaced,[34] and while later texts would omit the specific comparison of the wax to the Father, the wick to the Son, and the fire to the Holy Spirit, the general comparison of the light to the Trinity would remain, still misplaced.

In addition to these expansions of the earlier Penitential Forms the Tortosa Form continues by enlarging the trinity of objects in the Mass to a septiformity.

---

[33] See Roger E. Reynolds, 'South Italian *Liturgica* and *Canonistica* in Catalonia (New York, Hispanic Society of America MS. HC 380/819)', *Mediaeval Studies* 49 (1987) 484; and for the same Mass exposition as that appearing before ours see Jean-Paul Bouhot, 'Les sources de l'*Expositio missae* de Remi d'Auxerre', *Revue des études augustiniennes* 26 (1980) 157.

[34] This reference to the light is placed after the fourth trinity of the tersanctus, but it fits more properly with the discussion of the light in the first of the trinities.

First, there is an obvious trinity in the tersanctus: Sanctus Sanctus Sanctus. Second, in the terms for the priest himself there is a trinity. In one of these terms, *sa-cer-dos*, there are clearly three elements: *sa-* signifying the Father, *cer-* signifying the Son, and *-dos* signifying the Holy Spirit. Moreover, in the term *pres-bi-ter* there is also a trinity: *pres-* signifying the primary person of the Trinity, the Father; *bi-* signifying the binary person of the Trinity, the Son; and *-ter* obviously signifying the tertiary person of the Trinity, the Holy Spirit. The Tortosa commentator then adds enigmatically that a trinity is also signified by the tripled corporal on the altar, but he fails to elucidate this point. As the seventh trinity in the Mass the commentator finally points out that in the threefold Agnus Dei the Trinity is clearly present. There is then a brief conclusion supported by Christ's words in Mt 15:14 and Lc 6:39, which urges priests to celebrate Mass as has been explained. Appended to the commentary in the Tortosa Form are two texts. The first, urging the priest to celebrate in a state of cleanliness, would come to be reflected in the Mass commentary itself. The other, a text regarding the necessity of two ministers and the celebrant at Mass, is based on a canon attributed to Pope Sother and can be found in P2, the manuscript of the canonical *Collection in Four Books* following Text 3.

VIII

THE NEAPOLITAN PENITENTIAL FORM

Most of the commentary in the Tortosa manuscript is found in N, an early twelfth-century Neapolitan codex with Beneventan-script symptoms containing a fragment of Burchard's *Decretum*, to which several additional canons, including our Mass commentary, have been added by a different hand.[35] As in the other Penitential Forms, the penitential canon is intruded after the prohibition of fasting on Sundays and feast days, but four new elements have been added in the Neapolitan Form [Text 8]. First, there is a puzzling statement in the section on the light at Mass that this is a 'sententia sanctae trinitatis', or signification of the Holy Trinity. Second, after the misplaced general comparison of the burning light to the Trinity found in the Tortosa Form, there is added an admonition to priests, reflected in the texts attached to the Tortosa Form, to celebrate in cleanliness and chastity. Third, the strange reference in the Tortosa manuscript to the trinitarian significance of the corporal on the altar is elucidated: it is the tripled (corporal?) on the altar and over the chalice and oblata, and the cover (pall?) over the chalice that signify the Trinity. Fourth, the enigmatic reference earlier to the 'sententia

---

[35] On this manuscript see Hubert Mordek, 'Handschriftenforschungen in Italien: I. Zum Überlieferung des Dekrets Bischof Burchards von Worms', *Quellen und Forschungen aus italienischen Archiven und Bibliotheken* 51 (1971) 647, 649 n. 56.

sanctae trinitatis' is clarified when it is specified that there are in the Mass commentary seven trinitarian significations representing the seven gifts of the Holy Spirit: the light, incense, oblata, tersanctus, priest with his triform names, corporal on the altar and over the chalice and oblata, and the cover over the chalice, and threefold Agnus Dei. Finally, the conclusion has been expanded, but Christ's words have been omitted.

IX

THE EXTENDED PENITENTIAL FORM

The longest form of the Mass commentary [Text 9] is used as c. xlvi of L. III of the south Italian *Collection in Nine Books*, a collection unique to the eleventh-century codex V4 in Beneventan script. The text here is substantially like that in the Neapolitan Penitential Form, although there is the tripled corporal on the altar with no reference to the oblata and cover on the chalice. The most important difference, however, is that instead of the rather simple trinitarian explanations of the terms for the priest there is a fantastic word-letter trinitarian explanation of the abbreviation for the terms *sacerdos* and *presbiter*. First, the letters P, F, and double S are said to represent the Father, Son, and Holy Spirit, and the intercalated letters S, C, and D, being the abbreviated form of the word *sacerdos*, represent three operations of the persons of the Trinity. Then the letters P and F signify the Father and Son, and the double S the operation of the Holy Spirit. The intercalated letters P, B, and T, as the abbreviated form of the word *presbiter*, signify the operations of the Trinity. The consummation of all this comes when the letters of the abbreviation of *sacerdos* and *presbiter* are equated directly with the three persons of the Trinity.

X

THE VULGATE FORM

This form of the correspondence and Mass commentary [Text 10] has the widest circulation and appears in at least ten manuscripts. It very much resembles the Neapolitan and Extended Penitential Forms, but there are several differences. First, the Vulgate Form lacks the penitential canon. Second, like the Tortosa Form the Vulgate Form notes that Mass may not be said during the time that Christ hung upon the cross because during this time the angels in heaven are occupied in accepting his sacrifice. But the Vulgate Form adds to this a question, 'Ergo quid prodest illud sacrificium?' Third, the trinitarian equivalences of the terms *sacerdos* and *presbiter* as found in the Neapolitan Form are repeated. Fourth, the explanation of the trinity of the tripled corporal on the altar and above the chalice and oblata, and the cover over the chalice found in the Neapolitan Form appears here.

Whereas the earlier recensions of the correspondence and Mass commentary, such as those of the Penitential and Tortosa Forms, are to be found usually in single, isolated manuscripts, the Vulgate Form appears in at least ten codices. The reason for the relatively wide distribution of the Vulgate Form lies in the fact that it was included in the *Collection in Five Books*, which the Roman law expert, Carlo Guido Mor, forty years ago dubbed as the vade-mecum of central and southern Italian canonists of the eleventh and twelfth centuries.[36] The *Collection in Five Books* is, indeed, a canon law collection, and hence it is understandable that the correspondence of Damasus and Jerome dealing with a Nicene decision should be included if only for the sake of canonistic completeness. But the *Collection in Five Books* is more than a canon law collection. It is one of the richest patristic and liturgical florilegia of the early Middle Ages—a fact generally overlooked by patristic, canon law, and liturgical scholars alike. Hence, it was also appropriate that a correspondence attributed to two of the great fathers of the Western Church, together with liturgical Mass commentary, be included in a florilegium of this type.

Whether or not the *Collection in Five Books* was the vade-mecum for Italian canonists of the eleventh and early twelfth centuries, as Mor said it was, is somewhat problematical (as any scholar will attest who has lugged one of the heavy folio-sized volumes from desk to desk at the Vatican, Vallicelliana, and Monte Cassino libraries). Rather, the collection seems to have been a vast and well-ordered reference tool in such monastic libraries as Monte Cassino, Sant'Eutizio in Val Castoriana, and perhaps Narni and Farfa.[37] Nonetheless, manuscripts of the derivatives of the *Collection in Five Books* are indeed of vade-mecum or at least saddlebag size and were scattered throughout central and southern Italy and even Catalonia. The reason for the inclusion of our text in these derivative collections lies probably in the fact that, within the *Collection in Five Books* itself, it was the first text in the section devoted to the subject of the Mass[38] and thus served as an introduction or interpretative preface to subsequent canons dealing with the objects, persons, and elements of the eucharistic liturgy. Further, it is not surprising to find our text included in such liturgical florilegia as that of the Farfese *Multiloquiorum* of the manuscript V6 or the Tortosa codex, given the attempt in these manuscripts to collect a number of liturgical commentaries.

---

[36] 'La reazione al *Decretum Burchardi* in Italia avanti la riforma gregoriana', *Studi gregoriani* 1 (1947) 201.

[37] Theo Kölzer, *Collectio canonum Regesto Farfensi inserta* (Monumenta iuris canonici, Ser. B, Corpus collectionum 5; Vatican City, 1982), pp. 48-55, has argued that a copy of the collection served as the source of his collection in the Farfa Register.

[38] In the collection the title of our text in 3.212 (Fornasari, *Collectio*, p. 413) serves as the divisional rubric for the subsequent canons on the Mass.

XI

ABBREVIATED VULGATE FORM

Although the manuscript errors of this form in manuscript V7 are often like those in the Extended Penitential Form in the *Collection in Nine Books*, compiled perhaps in the tenth century, the Abbreviated Vulgate Form [Text 11] is clearly based on the Vulgate Form. It contains the question 'Ergo quid prodest illum sacrificium?' and in an abbreviated fashion the trinitarian significance of *sa-cer-dos* and *pres-bi-ter*.[39] Moreover, the abbreviations in the earlier witness, V7, are both more and less extensive than in the later manuscript, NY, which shows that there were at least two versions of the abbreviation in circulation.

V7 is highly significant for the date and location of the Mass commentary and the Vulgate Form. The manuscript itself was written in Rome perhaps as early as A.D. 1000;[40] this shows that the Vulgate Form of our commentary was in circulation and had been abbreviated probably even before the compilation sometime between 1014 and *c.* 1025 of the *Collection in Five Books*. Further, although written in normal minuscule and 'romanesca', there are numerous Beneventan-script symptoms, even to the typical interrogation marks in the question 'Ergo quid prodest illum sacrificium?', which suggests a south Italian model.[41] Finally, the Bedan martyrology in the codex has additions of a Beneventan type.[42]

The other codex of the Abbreviated Vulgate Form, NY, although from a house of canons regular at Santa Maria del Estany southwest of Vic in Catalonia, is also closely related to a south Italian tradition and to the Roman codex V7.[43] Our Mass commentary here follows a text on the origins of Septuagesima that appears elsewhere in a Beneventan-script codex.[44] Following the commentary are texts similar to those found in the *Collection in Five Books*, but resembling more closely those in V7. Several liturgico-canonical pieces subsequent to our commentary are related to texts circulating in eleventh-century Roman manuscripts with Beneventan-script connections.[45]

* *

[39] In the codex V7 the scribe presented the explanation of *sa-cer-dos*, wrote *Pater*, and then left a blank on the page of a size necessary to write the explanation for *pres-bi-ter*. NY lacks completely the explanation for *pres-bi-ter*.

[40] Supino Martini, *Roma e l'area*, p. 74.

[41] Reynolds, 'South Italian *Liturgica*', 485 n. 24.

[42] Henri Quentin, *Les martyrologes historiques du moyen âge. Étude sur la formation du martyrologe romain* (Paris, 1908), pp. 39-42.

[43] Reynolds, 'South Italian *Liturgica*', 480.

[44] Thomas Forrest Kelly and Herman F. Holbrook, 'Beneventan Fragments at Altamura', *Mediaeval Studies* 49 (1987) 466-71.

[45] Reynolds, 'South Italian *Liturgica*', 483-92; to which should now be added the observations of Supino Martini, *Roma e l'area*, pp. 88-98, 122.

All the forms of the correspondence between Damasus and Jerome and the appended Mass commentary appear in manuscripts written from the turn of the millennium to the early twelfth century. Then the text seems to have fallen out of favor. In the dates and origins of the codices there is a possible explanation for the rise and decline in popularity of the text; it is precisely this period in which the *Collection in Five Books*, its sources, and derivatives were widely copied and circulated.[46] Beginning in the late eleventh and early twelfth centuries, however, developments in the areas of canon law, liturgy, and theological study were taking place that would render our text obsolete. In canon law Gratian's *Decretum* would make prior collections such as the *Collection in Five Books* and its derivatives largely out of date. In the area of liturgical commentary a new style came into vogue, epitomized in the *Micrologus* of Bernold of Constance, in which the florid but questionable explanations of the liturgy found in our text were downplayed and attempts were made at a more sober, historical analysis.[47] Finally, in the area of sacramental theology there came into being in the late eleventh and early twelfth centuries the new type of florilegium, the sentence collection, drawing together patristic and early medieval texts on liturgical matters under intense debate at that time: the reality of Christ's presence in the bread and wine, the sacramental character of the various liturgical rites of the Church, and so forth. Because of the questionable authenticity of our correspondence between Damasus and Jerome with its reference to a dubious Nicene decision, and because of the fantasy of the Mass commentary, it is no wonder that our text had fallen out of favor by the mid-twelfth century, and indeed no wonder that modern canonistic and liturgical historians have paid scant attention to it since. Nonetheless, in its exuberance, color, and imagination the correspondence and commentary attributed to Pope Damasus and St. Jerome affords us a precious insight into the spiritual and allegorical understanding of elements in the eucharistic liturgy of the early Middle Ages.

XII

TEXTS

Several conventions have governed the presentation of the edition of the eleven recensions of the Mass commentary below. The manuscripts do not often exhibit the texts as divided into paragraphs or parts, so an effort has been made to illustrate the evolution and growth of the text by isolating the correspondence itself between Damasus and Jerome and by placing the salutations and titles in small capitals. The

---

[46] For a list of manuscripts and fragments see Roger E. Reynolds, 'Law, Canon: to Gratian' in *Dictionary of the Middle Ages* 7.408-10.

[47] See Reynolds, 'Liturgy, Treatises on' in *Dictionary of the Middle Ages* 7.624-33.

fanciful commentary on the Mass following the correspondence has been divided into paragraphs so as to emphasize the development and structure of the sometimes obscure text.

For individual recensions, the text of the oldest surviving witness has generally been followed. The orthographic peculiarities of that witness have been preserved, although in some cases angle brackets indicate editorial additions. It is important to emphasize here that grammatical and syntactical errors and occasionally gibberish have been retained in the texts because these readings were often incorporated into later versions and thus can provide useful evidence regarding textual transmission. Purely orthographical variants are usually not reported. Modern conventions of punctuation and capitalization have been employed in place of the highly erratic punctuation and capitalization in the manuscripts. Textual variants are reported according to chronological sequence.

Further information is given at the beginning of each text for peculiar problems. Manuscripts containing each text are listed together with date and origin or provenance when known.

1. *Short Correspondence Form with Brief Conclusion*

This version is found in the following manuscripts:

S = Stuttgart, Württembergische Landesbibliothek HB VI 113 (s. vIII/IX, Chur), fol. 103v

G = St. Gall, Stiftsbibliothek 446 (s. $IX^3/_3$, St. Gall), p. 204

Pr = Prague, Státní knihovna ČSR Tepla 1 (*c.* 828-876, vicinity of Regensburg; prov. Kloster Oberaltaich), pp. 204-205

B = Bamberg, Staatliche Bibliothek Lit. 131 (A.II.53) (s. x), fol. 76r-v

L = London, British Library Add. 16413 (s. xı, south Italy), fols. 6v-7r

V1 = Vatican City, Biblioteca Apostolica Vaticana Vat. lat. 1146 (s. xı, central Italy), fol. 34r

W = Vienna, Österreichische Nationalbibliothek 914 (s. xı), fols. 32v-33r

M = Munich, Bayerische Staatsbibliothek Clm 14581 (s. xI/xII, St. Emmeram), fols. 77v-78r

V2 = Vatican City, Biblioteca Apostolica Vaticana Vat. lat. 1147 (s. xI/xII, central Italy), fol. 36v

V3 = Vatican City, Biblioteca Apostolica Vaticana Vat. lat. 1148 (s. xII, central Italy), fol. 35r.

The text printed here is based on G because the text in S, the oldest witness, contains a number of corruptions and lacks the important *non* in l. 10. The text of G has been collated with S, Pr, B, L, V1, W, M, and V2. Grammatical and syntactical errors such as *qualis* (l. 3) and *alias ... has* (l. 10) have been preserved.

As for the relationships of the manuscripts, it appears that G and S derive from a common form and that B is related to G. The text of L, written in Beneventan script, clearly reflects a south Italian tradition. V1 and V2, both from central Italy, are clearly related, although V2, like the related Pr and W, has omitted several words in ll. 8 f. M shares readings with V1 and V2, as well as with L.

The correspondence of Damasus and Jerome, together with c. 24 of Theodulf of Orléans' *Capitula I* (MGH *Leges, Capitula episcoporum* 1.121), has been entered by an early ninth-century hand on a blank folio of S. It is perhaps significant that the correspondence and Theodulf's *Capitula* also appear in the central Italian V1.

INQUISITIO BEATI DAMASI PAPE URBIS ROMAE A HIERONIMO PRESBITERO

Frater et conpresbiter noster Hieronimae, quid tibi videtur de die sancto dominico qualiter sollemnia missarum agere debemus, aut de aliis diebus qualis horis est licitum celebrare?

5   RESPONDIT HIERONIMUS

Domine et dulcissime pater, tibi veritas minime est absconsa. Synodo Niceni concilii, cum ccc x et viii patres, qualiter apud ipsos est inventum quod in die dominico nullus post horam diei terciam sollemnia missarum agere presumat, et denuntiaverunt quod qui presumat anathema sit; et aliis vero diebus v vi vii viii hora
10 non celebrentur sollemnia missarum; alias vero has licitum est.

Papa dixit, Rectum est quod dixisti.

---

1 Ieronimo Presbitero *ante* Inquisitio ... Rome *W*   Ad Hieronimum *L V1 M* (Ab Hieronimo *corr. V1*)   Urbis Romae *om. Pr*   Presbiterum *V1 M* (Presbitero *corr. V1*)   2 Fratri *L* compresbiter *Pr*   noster conpresbiter *S*: conpresbitero nostro *L*   Hieronimo *L Pr*   quid] quod *B W*   3 qualiter] qua hora *L*   missarum sollempnis *L*   de *om. L*   qualis] quibus *L M*: qualibus *V1 V2 W*   4 lititium *Pr*   5 Responsio *V1 M V2 W*   6 Domne *Pr*   et *om. L* dulcissime] sanctissime *L*   est *om. B*   Synodo *om. L*: Sinado *S*   7 ccc xx et viii *Pr*   patribus *L*   apud] aput *S*: ab *L*   ipsis *L*   quod in] ut *L*   8 tertiam oram diei *L*   8-9 et ... presumat *om. V2 W*   9 quod ... sit] ut qui presumpserit anathematizetur *L*   et] de *add. L*: *om. L*   diebus *om. Pr*   10 non *om. S*   celebretur *L*   sollempnitas *L*   aliis *L M V1 V2 W*   has] horis *L M V1 V2 W*   lititum *Pr*   11 Papa] Damasus *add. L*   quod] ut *L*

2. *Short Correspondence Form With Long Conclusion*

This form appears in the following manuscripts:

MC1 = Monte Cassino, Archivio della Badia 384 (s. X, south Italy), p. 135
C = Cava dei Tirreni, Biblioteca del Monumento Nazionale dell'Abbazia della SS. Trinità
    3 (s. XI, south Italy), fol. 313r-v
Ma1 = Madrid, Biblioteca Nacional 19 (s. XII), fol. 157r
P1 = Paris, Bibliothèque Nationale lat. 7418 (s. XIII/XIV, Italy), fols. 205v-206r.

The text printed here is based on its oldest witness, MC1, which is written in Beneventan script. The following spelling, grammatical, and syntactical errors have been retained: *diem sanctam dominicam quam* (ll. 2-3); *consilii* (l. 6), *Damasius* (l. 11), *tue terris* (l. 12), and *homi* (l. 12). The corruption *tue terris* of l. 12 instead of *tuearis* suggests scribal misunderstanding of the exemplar. C is written in Beneventan script; Ma1 contains Beneventan interrogation signs and has material related to the south Italian canonical *Collection in Five Books*.

Because of its title the text of MC1 appears to be related to the Short Correspondence Form with Brief Conclusion in the Beneventan-script codex L.

INQUISITIO DAMASII PAPE AD HIERONIMUM PRESBITERUM

Fratri et conpresbitero nostro Hieronimo. Quid tibi videtur de diem sanctam dominicam quam hora missarum sollemnia agere debemus, aut aliis diebus quibus horis licitum est celebrare?

RESPONDET HIERONIMUS

5

Domine sanctissime pater, tibi veritas minime est absconsa. Niceni consilii ccc x et viii patres qualiter et ab ipsis est institutum ut die dominica nullus post tertiam horam missarum sollemnia agere presumat, et denuntiaverunt ut qui presumserit,

---

1 Inquisitio] Epistola *C*: Epistula *Ma1 P1*   Damasi *C Ma1 P1*   Presbiterum *om. C Ma1 P1*: De die dominica qua hora celebratur *add. P1*   2 Damasus papa *ante* Fratri *C Ma1 P1*   die *C Ma1 P1*   sancta *C Ma1 P1*   3 dominica *C Ma1 P1*   qua *C Ma1 P1*   sollempnia *C Ma1 P1*   quibus] qui *C*   4 est licitum *C Ma1 P1*   5 Hieronimus respondit *C*: Hieronimus respondet *Ma1 P1*   6 consilii] concilii recordare ubi *C Ma1 P1*   7 qualiter] adunati fuerunt *add. C Ma1 P1*   tertiam] ausus esset *add. C Ma1 P1*   8 horam *om. C Ma1 P1*   sollempnia *Ma1 P1*   presumat *om. C Ma1 P1*   presumserit] presumpserit *C Ma1 P1*

anathematizetur; et de aliis diebus v et vi vii viii hora non celebretur sollemnitas
10 missarum; aliis vero horis licitum est.

Papa Damasius, Rectum est quod dixisti; dextera tua erigat, virtute confirmet,
potestate tue terris aecclesie tue sanctisque altaribus cum homi desiderata prosperi-
tate restituas. Amen.

---

9 et² *om. C Mal Pl*   viii *om. C Mal Pl*   9-10 missarum sollempnitas *C Mal Pl*
11 Damasius] Damasus dixit *C Mal Pl*   erigas *C Mal Pl*   confirmes *C Mal Pl*   12 tue
terris] tuearis *C Mal Pl*   homi] omni *C Mal Pl*   desiderata *om. C Mal Pl*   13 Amen *om.*
C Mal Pl

3. *Long Correspondence Form with Short Conclusion*

This form is in P2 (Paris, Bibliothèque Nationale lat. 9631 [s. xii], fol. 46r).
Its conclusion demonstrates that this text is related to the Short Correspondence
Form with Brief Conclusion. On the same folio containing our commentary there
are canons regarding the number of celebrants in the Mass that are attributed to
Pope Leo ('Auctoritate apostolica interdicimus ut nullus presbiterorum missas
solus celebrare presumat nisi cum duobus aut tribus clericis ...') and to Pope Sother
('Statutum est ut nullus presbiterorum missarum sollempnia celebrare presumat
nisi duobus presentibus sibique respondentibus ut ipse tercius habeatur ...'). This
latter text is appended to the Tortosa Form (Text 7 below).

INTERROGATIO DAMASI PAPE

Frater et conpresbiter noster Iheronime, quid tibi videtur de die dominica et de
aliis diebus quibus et qualibus horis licitum est missarum sollempnia agere et
celebrare?

5

RESPONSIO IHERONIMI

Domino nostro beatissimo et sacratissimo pape Damaso Iheronimus. Tibi
veritas minime est absconsa, et synodus Niceni concilii quomodo et qualiter apud
illos cccxviii patres est inventum ut nullus in dominico die post horam terciam
ipsius diei presumat missam celebrare secundum institutionem canonicam, et qui
0 presumit, anathema sit; et aliis diebus hora v et vi et vii non est licitum missam
celebrare secundum institutionem canonicam; et aliis horis in cotidianis diebus

licitum est missam celebrare iuxta canones, hoc est, mane hora i et ii et iii et iiii
et post meridiem hora viii et viiii et x et xi et xii.

Beatus Damasus dixit, Rectum est quod dicis et omnibus nobis placet.

4. *Long Correspondence Form with Long Conclusion*

This form is printed from Wo (Wolfenbüttel, Herzog-August-Bibliothek Cod.
Guelf. 69 Weissenburg [s. x/xi, prov. Weissenburg]), in which the text is entered
perhaps as a *probatio pennae* on fol. 1r. The manuscript contains the works of
Paulinus of Aquileia and the *Vita* and *Regula* of Pachomius. Like P2, the text here
is related to the Short Correspondence Form with Brief Conclusion in S, G, and
Pr. The misspelling of *Nicaemi* (l. 5) has been preserved.

INTERROGATIO DAMASI PAPAE DE MISSARUM CELEBRATIONE

Frater et prespiter noster Hieronimus, quid tibi videtur de die dominico, et de
aliis diebus quibus et qualibus horis licitum est missarum sollemnia celebrare?

RESPONDIT HIERONIMUS

5   Tibi domine papae veritas minime absconsa est. Et quomodo sinodus Nicaemi
concilii, quomodo et qualiter apud ccc x et viii patrum inventum est, ut nullus in
dominico die post horam tertiam ipsius diei presumat missam celebrare. Et qui
presumpserit, anathema sit a Deo et hominibus; et aliis festis diebus hora v vi et
vii non est licitum missam celebrare secundum canones, et ceteris horis in
10 cotidianis etiam diebus licitum est missam celebrare mane hora i ii iii iiii v vi vii
viii viiii x xi et xii in nomine Dei summi et in honorem sancte Mariae, et similiter
omnium qui in caelis sunt et in terra. AMEN.

5. *Short Penitential Form*

This form is found in the following manuscripts:

P3 = Paris, Bibliothèque Nationale lat. 3187 (s. XII), fols. 131v-132v
Ta = Tarragona, Biblioteca Provincial 26 (s. XII, Catalonia), fol. 224r.

The text here is printed from P3, and the misspelled *Misce* (l. 1), *qorum* (l. 18),
and *missa* (l. 20) have been preserved. It is noteworthy that in Ta a very extensive

part of the text has been omitted, including the last part of Jerome's reply and the beginning of the explanation after the reply had been received in Rome.

P3 also contains the canonical *Collection in Four Parts*, the last of whose canons ends on fol. 121v. Another hand continues on fol. 123r with various texts. Our Mass exposition bears the number 'lxxii' in P3, which suggests that it may have been drawn from a canonical collection; following the exposition is the celebrated canon, noted as 'lxxiii', attributed to Pope Gregory VII[48] on the office, the same canon which precedes the Mass exposition in Ta.

Ta, the so-called *Pontifical of San Ramón*, is a liturgico-canonical manuscript containing the canonical *Liber Tarraconensis* and a variety of liturgical pieces.[49] A different hand has entered our Mass commentary at the end of the Gregorian canon.

Epistula Damasii pape ad Hieronimum presbiterum de ora misce LXXII

Cum quadam diae resideret sanctissimus papa Damasus in sede beati Petri apostoli, intentio orta est in tota aecclesia Romana de sacrificio qua hora licet sacrificium sacerdoti offerre, et non inveniebant. Tunc transmisit aepistulam suam
5 ad beatum Hieronimum presbiterum Hierosolimis ita.

Damasus papa Hieronimo presbitero in Domino aeternam salutem

Dirigimus vestrae fraternitati quia intentio orta est in tota aecclesia Romana de sacrificio qua hora licet sacrificare et non invenimus et inde finem. Dirigat nobis sanctitas vestra vos quia omnia scrutamini quomodo exinde agamus.

10   #### Hieronime

Pater sanctissime, veritas nobis minime est absconsa. Recordare concilii Niceni in quo ccc decem et octo patres sancti congregati fuerunt. Constitutum est enim

---

1 Ad Hieronimum ... lxxii *om. Ta*   2 residet Damasus sanctissimus papa *Ta*   5 presbiterum *om. Ta*   6 in Domino *post* salutem *Ta*   7 fraternitate *Ta*   8 nobis *om. Ta*   11 vobis *Ta*   12 in quo *om. Ta*

[48] On this text see Ch. Dereine, 'La prétendue règle de Grégoire VII pour chanoines réguliers', *Revue bénédictine* 71 (1961) 111.
[49] Reynolds, 'South Italian *Liturgica*', 484.

650

ab eis quod siquis diae dominicae resurrectionis post horam tertiam ausus fuerit canere missam, anathematizetur; aliis vero diebus a tertia usque ad horam nonam,
15 similiter anathematizaetur; aliis vero horis licitum est sacrificare.

Cumque fuisset relecta aepistula, invenerunt in concilio scriptum a ccc decem et octo patribus sanctis qui inflammati fuerunt de Spiritu Sancto quomodo in Nicea qoram Constantino magnifico et catholico ac sanctissimo imperatorae scripserunt et constituerunt: siquis die dominico sacrificare ausus fuerit post horam tertiam aut
20 ausus fuerit canere missa, in dampnatione eius sit et anathematizaetur.

Pro eo quod Spiritus Sanctus hora tertia descendit ad apostolos, ideo non est licitum post horam tertiam die dominico nec sacrificare nec ieiunare nec ullam abstinentiam habere. Siquis pro neglectu ieiunaverit, vii dies peniteat in pane et aqua. De aliis vero diebus a media hora tertia usque in horam nonam, similiter
25 anathematizetur pro eo quod ista hora Christus in passione in patibulo crucis stetit pro nostra salute.

Et ipsa sacrificia quando sacri<fi>caverit sacerdos, non presuma<t> solus sacrificare quia Christus quando sacrificium pro totius mundi salute se immolare permisit, duo latrones in cruce fuerunt cum eo.

---

13 dominica die *Ta*   13-19 resurrectionis ... siquis die dominico *om. Ta*   19 aut] aud *Ta*
20 fuerit *om. Ta*   missas *Ta*   23 abstenenciam *Ta*   24 in] mediam *add. Ta*
27 sacrificaverit *Ta*   presumat *Ta*   28 sacrificaverit *Ta*   imolare *Ta*

6. *Intermediate Penitential Form*

This form is found in Va1 (Rome, Biblioteca Vallicelliana B 66, fols. 75v-78r [s. xi, south Italy]). The following grammatical and syntactical errors have been preserved: *patres sancti* (ll. 12, 16), *missa* (ll. 13, 19), *Alii* (l. 23), *amictu* (l. 40), and *illud odorem* (l. 49). Fols. 89-152 of the codex were copied in the twelfth century and bear the ex-libris of S. Bartolomeo di Trisulti.[50]

AEPISTULA IERONIMI PRESBITERI DE SACRIFICIO

Dum resideret sanctissimus papa Damasus in sede beati Petri apostoli, intentio orta est in ecclesia Romana de sacrificio qua hora sacerdoti licet offerre, et non

---

[50] On the Beneventan-script codices from S. Bartolomeo di Trisulti, see Roger E. Reynolds, 'Odilo and the *Treuga Dei* in Southern Italy: A Beneventan Manuscript Fragment', *Mediaeval Studies* 46 (1984) 453 n. 16.

inveniebat exinde finem. Tunc misit aepistulam ad beatum Ieronimum Ierusolimis
5 ita.

DAMASUS PAPA IERONIMO IN DOMINO SALUTEM

Dirigimus vestrae fraternitatis quia intentio orta est in Romana aecclesia de
sacrificio qua hora sacerdos sacrificaret et non inveniemus exinde finem. Dirigat
nobis sanctitas vestra quomodo inde exigamus.

10   IERONIMUS

Pater in Domino sanctissime, veritas tibi minime est absconsa. Recordare
concilium Niceni ubi a cccx et viii patres sancti affixum et constitutum est, siquis
sacerdos die dominico supra tertia hora presumpserit missa canere, anathematizetur: aliis vero diebus si a tertia et usque in nonam praesumpserit, similiter
15 anathematizetur; aliis vero horis licitum est sacrificare.

Cumque lecta fuisset epistula, invenerunt in concilio scriptum a cccxviii patres qui
inflammati fuerunt de Spiritu Sancto, qualiter in Nicenam coram Constantino
magnifico et catholico ac sanctissimo imperatore scripserunt et constituerunt,
siquis sacerdos die dominico supra hora tertia presumpserit missa canere, anathe-
20 matizetur.

Pro eo quod Spiritus Sanctus hora tertia descendit ad apostolos, ideo non est
licitum post horam tertiam die dominico nec sacrificare nec ieiunare. Siquis per
neglegentiam ieiunaverit, vii dies poeniteat in pane et aqua. Alii vero diebus a
media hora iiii usque in media hora viii qui sacrificaverit, similiter anathematizetur,
25 pro eo quia in ista hora Christus in patibulo crucis stetit pro nostra salute.

Et quando sacrificaverit sacerdos, non praesumat sacrificare solus quia Christus
quando sacrificium pro totius mundi saluta immolari se permisit, duo latrones
immolati sunt cum eo. Ergo si solum sacrificaverit, cui dicit, Dominus vobiscum?
Melius est illi dicere, Dominus mecum et cum spiritu meo. Ecce satis blasphemat
30 si duo vel tres non habet ministros. Et si hoc habet, sana fide potest dicere
Dominus vobiscum et illi respondentes, Et sic nobis optasti ut Deus esset
nobiscum, et nos optamus ut sit Dominus cum spiritu tuo. Et si solus sacrificaverit,
videtur esse Pater solus nec Filium nec Spiritum Sanctum in Trinitate esse. Si cum
ministro uno sacrificaverit, ergo dicit, Dominus tecum. Ab illo sit longe. Si cum

---

27 latrones] nomina latronum, Aspalorga et alio Alaban *in marg. Val*

35 duobus ministris sacrificat, videtur in eo esse perfecta Trinitas. Et aliter, ergo cum
sacrificat habeat secum duos ministros. Sic Salvator in evangelio dicit, Ubi duo vel
tres congregati fuerint in nomine meo in medio eorum sum (Mt 18:20). Et in alio
loco, tres testimonia apud Deum firmata sunt (1 Jo 5:7-8?). Et si plus fuerint
melius sunt apud Deum et homines.

40 Et habeat secum sacerdos quando sacrificat linea et cingulum et amictu et orarium
et planeta, et in manu teneat mappulam et sudarium et trilicem in honore sancte
Trinitatis propter sacrificium ponenda super altare.

Et in nullo permittimus sine lumine sacrificare quia qui sine lumine sacrificat
videtur esse sacrificium cecum. Absit! Non permittat Deus ut hoc fiat sacrificium
45 a Christianis quia si lumen accensum habet perfecta Trinitas ibi videtur habere
virtutem quia oleum aut cera et papirum et flamma Trinitatem significant.

Et habeat incensum sacerdos quia angeli Satane quando ceciderunt de caelo in
terram in fetore ceciderunt. Cum autem odorem incensi facit sacerdos ad altare,
mox fugit diabolus et illud odorem incensi ante Deum ascendit, et incensum et
50 odorem et ignem Trinitatem significat.

Et quando offerens Deo in altare, si solum panem ponit videtur Pater non habere
Filium, et si panem et vinum ponit videtur esse Pater cum Filio non habere
Spiritum Sanctum. Si panem et vinum et aquam adunatim, videtur esse Patrem et
Filium et Spiritum Sanctum.

7. *Tortosa Form*

This form is found in To (Tortosa, Biblioteca Capitular 122 [s. x/xi, south Italy;
s. xii, Catalonia], fols. 42v-43v) and is printed here with the puzzling abbreviation
for Mt 18:20 (l. 39), probably denoting something like 'congregati fuerint in
momine (*sic*) meo i. (*sic*) sum in medio.' Errors such as *toto* (l. 3) have been
preserved.

DE HORA SACRIFICANDI

Cum quadam die resideret sanctissimus papa Damasus in sede beati Petri apostoli,
intentio orta est in toto ecclesia Romana de sacrificio qua hora debet et liceret
offerre, et non inveniebatur. Tunc transmisit epistulam suam ad beatum Iheroni-
5 mum presbiterum Iherusolimis ita dicendo.

DAMASUS PAPA IERONIMO PRESBITERO IN DOMINO ETERNAM SALUTEM

Dirigimus sanctitati atque fraternitati vestre quia intentio orta est in tota ecclesia Romana de sacrificio qua hora licet offerre et non invenimus eundem finem. Dirigat nobis sanctitas vestra vos qui omnia scrutamini quomodo exinde agamus.

10   IHERONIMUS

Pater sanctissime, veritas vobis minime est absconsa. Recordare concilium Nicenum ubi a trecentis decem et octo patribus affixum et constitutum est ut siquis die dominico post horam terciam ausus fuerit missam canere, anathematizetur; aliis vero diebus a tercia usque ad horam nonam si praesumpserit, similiter anathemati-
15 zetur.

Cumque perlecta fuisset epistula, invenerunt in concilio scriptum a trecentis decem et octo patribus sanctis qui imbuti erant Spiritu Sancto quod in Nicea coram sancto Constantino magnifico et catholico viro ac sanctissimo imperatore scripserunt et constituerunt ut siquis die dominico post horam terciam ausus fuerit missam
20 canere, in dampnatione anathematizentur.

Pro eo quod Spiritus Sanctus hora tercia descendit ad apostolos, ideoque non licet post horam terciam die dominico sacrificare nec ieiunare nec ullam abstinenciam habere. De aliis vero diebus a media hora tercia usque in mediam horam octavam, qui hoc praesumpserit anathemate feriatur pro eo quod in istas horas Christus in
25 passione et in patibulo crucis stetit pro nostra salute. Ideoque si in istas horas praesumpserit sacerdos sacrificare, angeli non suscipiunt sacrificium ad offerendum maiestati.

Ipsa vero sacrificia quando sacerdos sacrificat, non praesumat solus sacrificare quia Christus quando sacrificium pro totius mundi salute immolari se permisit, duo
30 latrones cum eo in cruce fuerunt. Si ergo solus sacrificaverit sacerdos, cui dicit, Dominus vobiscum? Certe melius est dicere, Dominus mecum et ipse respondeat, Et cum spiritu meo. Si duo autem tres habet ministros, sana fide dicere potest, Dominus vobiscum et illi respondeant, Sicut tu nobis optasti vero Deus esset nobiscum, et nos similiter optamus ut sit Dominus cum spiritu tuo. Si solus et enim
35 sacrificat, videtur Pater esse solus sine Filio et Spiritu sancto. Si autem cum uno ministro sacrificaverit, cui detur, Dominus vobiscum? Melius est ergo dicere, Dominus tecum aut nobiscum. At si cum duobus ministris sacrificaverit, videtur esse perfecta Trinitas. Ergo qui sacrificat habeat secum duos ministros sicut dicit in evangelio, Ubi duo vel tres c. f. i. m. i. s. i. m. eorum (Mt 18:20).

40 Sacerdos vero habeat quando sac<ri>ficat amictum, camisum, cingulum, manipulum, stolam, planetam, corporalem triplicem in honore Trinitatis ad sacrificandum septem dona Spiritus Sancti.

In nullo permittimus sine lumine sacrificare quia qui sine lumine sacrificaverit
videtur illum esse cecum sacrificium quia absit ut fiat sacrificium cecum apud
45 Christianos, quia si lumen accensum habet, perfecta Trinitas ibi videtur habere
virtutem quia in oleo sive cera et papiro et flamma Trinitas significatur.

E contra sententia sancte Trinitatis quia lumen pro vice Christi ponitur. Omnis
sacerdos quando sacrificat lumen habeat quia ipse dixit, Ego sum lux mundi (Jo
8:12). Habeat ergo incensum quia angeli quando de celo ceciderunt in terram cum
50 fetore ceciderunt. Cum vero sacerdos incensum facit ad altare, praesentaliter fugit
diabolus et ille odor per angelos ante Deum accenditur, et per incensum et odorem
et ignem Trinitas significatur.

Quando autem sacerdos offert Domino sacrificium, id est panem et vinum et
aquam, ibi adesse debent quia si solum panem ponit, videtur Pater non habere
55 Filium. Si panem et vinum, videtur Pater esse cum Filio sed non habere Spiritum
Sanctum. Sed si panem et vinum et aquam intersunt, videtur Pater esse cum Filio
et Spiritu Sancto.

Inde est enim quod dicimus, Sanctus Sanctus Sanctus tribus vicibus ad honorem
individue Trinitatis. Et si solum ignem habeat ad sacrificandum, videtur etiam Pater
60 non habere Filium nec Spiritum Sanctum quia in lumine tria sunt, cera papirus et
ignis, per quos Trinitas intelligi quod etiam et presbiter: per cera Pater, per
papirum Filium, per ignem Spiritum Sanctum.

Sacerdos et enim T<ri>nitatem eandem interpretatur: Pater sa-, Filius cer-,
Spiritus Sanctus -dos. Unde sacerdos Trinitas intelligitur quod etiam et presbiter:
65 Pater pres-, Filius bi-, Spiritus Sanctus -ter. Ecce sacerdos et presbiter Trinitas
intelligi potest.

Similiter etiam corporale triplici positum in altari eodem modo Trinitas figuratur.

Tribus etiam vicibus Agnus Dei propter sanctam Trinitatem figurative dicimus.

Quicumque sacerdotum quam ut supradiximus praesumptionem aliter sacrificare
70 praesumpserit, nec sibi lumen nec aliis lucem praestat sicut alibi legitur in
eva<n>gelium, Si cecus cecum duxerit nonne ambo in foveam cadunt? (Mt 15:14,
Lc 6:39)

Unusquisque presbiter hostiam sanctam et immaculatam Domino offerre licet
absque sorde semper debet et cum magno timore coram Deo humiliter custodire
75 ut non ipsius negligentia quoquomodo maculetur. Hoc quoque ut a sanctis patribus

constitutum est, Nullus illorum missarum sollempnia solus celebrare praesumat nisi duobus sibique respondentibus, id est tercius habeatur quia pluraliter ab eo dicitur in secretis, Orate pro me fratres ut meum ac vestrum sacrificium acceptum sit omnipotenti Deo.

76-79 Nullus illorum ... omnipotenti Deo: cf. Burchardum, *Decretum* 3.74 (PL 140.689) et Gratianum, *De consec.* 1.61 et fontesque eius (Friedberg 1.1311).

8. *Neapolitan Penitential Form*

This form is found in N1 (Naples, Biblioteca Nazionale, Vindob. lat. 23 [s. XII, central Italy], fol. 94v). In the text printed below the following incorrect spellings and grammatical and syntactical errors have been preserved even though many of these have been corrected in the manuscript: *toto* (l. 7), *concili* (l. 11), *patres* (l. 17), *solum* (ll. 27, 29), *mappula* (l. 42), *trilice* (l. 42), *paperunt* (l. 47), *poni* (l. 55), *sorte* (l. 61), *Trinitate* (l. 66). N1, which has Beneventan-script symptoms, has an ex-libris on fol. 3v: 'Liber monachorum congregationis S. Iustine de padua deputatus monasterio S. Severini de Neapoli signatus numero 26'.

EPISTULA DAMASI AD IERONIMUM PRESBITERUM

Dum quadam die resideret sanctissimus papa Damasus in sede beati Petri apostoli, intentio orta est in tota ecclesia Romana de sacrificiis qua hora licet sacrificium sacerdoti offerre, et non inveniebant. Tunc transmisit epistulam suam ad beatum
5 Hieronimum presbiterum Hierosolimis ita.

DAMASUS PAPA HIERONIMO PRESBITERO IN DOMINO AETERNAM SALUTEM

Dirigimus vestrae fraternitati quia intencio nunc orta est in toto ecclesia Romana de sacrificio qua hora licet sacrificare et non invenimus exinde finem. Dirigat nobis sanctitas vestra vos qui omnia scrutatis quomodo exinde exigamus.

---

6 Damasus ... salutem *in marg. N1*   9 scrutatis *ex* scrutamini *corr. N1*

Pater sanctissime, veritas vobis minime est absconsa. Recordare concili Niceni ubi ccc decem et viii patres sancti erant, et affixum et constitutum est ab eis: siquis die dominico resurrectionis super hora tertia ausus fuerit canere missam, anathematizetur; aliis diebus a quarta usque in horam nonam, similiter anathematizetur;
15 aliis vero horis licitum est sacrificare.

Cum relecta fuisset epistula, invenerunt in concilio scriptum a ccc decem et viii patres sanctis qui inflammati fuerunt de Spiritu Sancto, quomodo in Nicea coram Constantino magnifico et catholico ac sanctissimo imperatore scripserunt et constituerunt, siquis dominico die super horam tertiam ausus fuerit canere missam,
20 in dampnatione anathematizetur.

Pro eo quod Spiritus Sanctus ora tertia descendit ad apostolos, ideo non est licitum post horam tertiam die dominico nec sacrificare nec ieiunare nec ullam abstinentiam habere. Siquis per neglectum ieiuniaverit, vii dies peniteat in pane et aqua. De aliis vero diebus a media hora quarta usque in mediam horam nonam, similiter
25 anathematizetur pro eo quod istas horas Christus in patibulo crucis stetit pro nostra salute.

Et ipsa sacrificia quando sacrificaverit sacerdos, non presumat solum sacrificare quia Christus quando sacrificium pro totius mundi salute se immolari permisit, duos latrones in cruce fuerunt cum ipso. Ergo si solum sacrificaverit, cui dicet,
30 Dominus vobiscum? Melius est illi dicere, Dominus mecum et cum spiritu meo. Ecce satis blasphemat si duos vel tres non habet ministros. Et si hoc habet, sana fide potest dicere, Dominus vobiscum. Illi ei respondentes dicant, Et tu sicut nobis obtasti ut Deus esset nobiscum, et nos obtamus ut sit Dominus cum spiritu tuo. Quia si solus sacrificat videtur esse Pater solus, Filium nec Spiritum Sanctum in
35 Trinitate esse. Si cum ministro uno sacrificat, ergo dicit, Dominus tecum. Absit. Si cum duobus ministris sacrificat, videtur esse in eo perfecta Trinitas. Et aliter, ergo cum sacrificat habeat secum duos ministros, sicut evangelium dicit, Ubi duo vel tres steterint in nomine meo in medio eorum sum (Mt 18:20). Et in omni loco tria testimonia apud Deum firmata sunt (1 Jo 5:7-8?). Et si plus sunt, ecce quam
40 melius sunt apud Deum et hominem.

Et habeat sacerdos secum quando sacrificat lineam et cingulum et amictum et orarium et planetas, et in manu teneat mappula et sudorum trilice in honore sanctae Trinitatis propter sacrificium ponendum super altare.

---

12 patribus *ex* patres *corr. N1*   27 solus *ex* solum *corr. N1*   29 solus *ex* solum *corr. N1*
32 Dominus vobiscum *in marg. N1*   34 Filium] neque credit *s.s. N1*

Et in nullo permittimus sine lumine accenso sacrificare. Qui sine lumine accenso
45 sacrificaverit videtur esse sacrificium cecum. Absit hoc. Non permittat Deus ut hoc
fiat sacrificium cecum esse apud Christianos quia si lumen accensum habet,
perfecta Trinitas ibi videtur habere virtutem quia oleum aut cera et paperunt et
flamma Trinitatem significat.

Ecce alia sententia sanctae Trinitatis quia inde lumen pro vice Christi sicut ipse
50 dixit, Ego sum lux mundi (Jo 8:12). Et habeat incensum quia quando angeli
Sathane ceciderunt de caelo in terram in fetore ceciderunt. Cum odorem incensi
facit sacerdos ad altare, praesentialiter fugit diabolus et ille odor per angelos ante
Deum ascendit, et incensum et odorem et ignis Trinitatem significat.

Et quando offert Domino in altare, non solum panem quia si solum panem ponit
55 videtur Pater non habere Filium. Si panem et vinum poni, videtur esse Pater cum
Filio et non habere Spiritum Sanctum. Si panem et vinum et aquam adunatim,
videtur esse Pater et Filius et Spiritus Sanctus.

Unde dicimus, Sanctus Sanctus Sanctus ter in honorem sancte Trinitatis. Et si
solum ignem habet ad sacrificandum, videtur esse Pater et non habere Filium quia
60 lumen accensum Trinitatem sanctam in se significat.

Quia qui sacrificat non in sorte adulterii sed mundus ab omni coinquinatione
adulterii sacrificaverit quia sacerdos Trinitatem interpretatur: Pater sa-, Filius cer-,
Spiritus Sanctus -dos. Pater pres-, Filius bi-, Spiritus sanctus -ter. Ergo sacerdos
et presbiter Trinitatem intellegere potest.

65 Ergo per trilicem positam in altare et desuper calicem cum oblatione et operi-
mentum super calicem similiter sancta Trinitate figuratur.

Ecce sicut diximus iii vicibus Agnus Dei propter sanctam Trinitatem.

Ecce septem sententie sancte Trinitatis in honorem septiformis Spiritus Sancti
gratiae.

70 Ergo non praesumat sacerdos aliud facere quando sacrificat nisi quomodo supra
diximus ut inluminet se et animas Christianorum illuminet. Et si aliter facere
praesumpserit, nec sibi lumen nec aliis Christianis lumen prestat. Sed ille cecus et
alios in cecitatem post se trahit.

---

47 paperunt *ex* paperui *corr. N1*   55 ponere *ex* poni *corr.* N1   56 habere *ex* haberer *corr.*
N1   57 Pater *ex* Patrem *corr. N1*   Filius *ex* Filium *corr. N1*   Spiritus Sanctus *ex* -tum -tum
corr. N1   61 sorte *ex* sorde *corr. N1*   64 Trinitas *ex* -tem *corr. N1*

9. *Extended Penitential Form*

This form is found in V4 (Vatican City, Biblioteca Apostolica Vaticana Vat. lat. 1349 [s. XI, south Italy], fols. 81r-82v). The text printed here preserves such spelling, grammatical, and syntactical errors as: *sacerdos* (l. 3), *epistula sua* (l. 4), *vestrae fraternitatis* (l. 7), *vestras* (l. 9), *absconse* (l. 11), *missa* (l. 13), *fuisse* (l. 17), *patres sancti* (ll. 17-18), *hora tertia* (l. 22), *Alii* (l. 23), *solum sacrificaret* (l. 26), *salutem* (l. 27), *habent* (l. 30), *Si* (l. 33), *fuerit* (l. 36), *ammitum* (l. 40), *planeta* (l. 41), *sudario* (l. 41), *lumen accensus* (l. 43), *sorte* (l. 59), *aduteriis* (l. 60), *sacrifices* (l. 60), *trilicemcem* (l. 70), *posita* (l. 70), and *si* (l. 72).

EPISTULA BEATI DAMASI PAPE AD IERONIMO PRESBITERO DE ORDI<NE> MISSARUM XLVI

Dum quadam die resideret sanctissimus papa Damasus in sede beati Petri apostoli, intentio orta est in tota aecclesia Romana de sacrificio qua hora licet sacerdos offerre, et non inveniebant exinde finem. Tunc transmisit epistula sua ad beatum
5 Hieronimum Hierusolimis ita.

DAMASUS PAPA HIERONIMO PRESBITERO IN DOMINO SALUTEM

Dirigimus vestrae fraternitatis quia intentio orta est in tota ecclesia Romana de sacrificio qua hora sacrificaret et non invenimur exinde finem. Dirigat nobis sanctitas vestras vos qui omnia scrutasti quomodo exinde exigamus.

10   HIERONIMUS

Pater sanctissime, veritatis vobis minime est absconse. Recordare concilium Niceni ubi cccxviii patres sancti: affixum et constitutum est ab eis, siquis die dominico sacerdos supra hora tertia ausus fuerit canere missa, anathematizetur; aliis diebus a tertia usque in nona, similiter anathematizetur; aliis vero horis licitum
15 est sacrificare.

Cumque lecta fuisse epistula, invenerunt in concilio scriptum a cccxviii patres sancti qui inflamati fuerunt de Spiritu Sancto quomodo in Nicena coram Constantino magnifico et catholico ac sanctissimo imperatore scripserunt et constituerunt, siquis die dominico sacerdos supra tertia ausus fuerit canere missam,
20 in damnatione anathematizetur.

Pro eo quod Spiritus Sanctus hora tertia descendit ad apostolos, ideo non est licitum post hora tertia die dominico nec sacrificare nec ieiunare. Siquis per neglectum ieiuniaverit, vii dies peniteat in pane et aqua. Alii vero diebus a media hora iiii usque in media hora viii, similiter anathematizetur, pro eo quod ista hora
25 Christus in patibulo crucis stetit pro nostra salute.

Et ipsa sacrificia quando sacrificaverit sacerdos, non praesumat solum sacrificaret quia Christus quando sacrificium pro totius mundi salutem immolari permisit, duo latrones immolari cum eo. Ergo si solum sacrificaverit, cui dicet, Dominus vobiscum? Melius est illi diceret, Dominus mecum et cum spiritu meo. Ecce satis
30 blasphemat si duo vel iii non habet ministros. Et si hoc habent, sana fide potest dicere, Dominus vobiscum et illi respondentes, Et tu sic nobis optasti ut Deus esset nobiscum, et nos optamus ut sit Deus cum spiritu tuo. Quia si solus sacrificaverit, videtur esse Pater solus, nec Filium, nec Spiritum Sanctum in Trinitate esse. Si cum ministro uno sacrificat, ergo dicet, Dominus tecum. Ab illo sit longe. Si cum duo
35 ministros sacrificaverit, videtur in eo esse perfecta Trinitas. Et aliter, ergo cum sacrificat habeat secum duos ministros. Si ergo dicit, Ubi duo vel tres fuerit in nomine meo in medio eorum sum (Mt 18:20). Et in alio loco, tres testimonia apud Deum firmata sunt (1 Jo 5:7-8?). Et si plures sunt, quam melius sunt aput Deum et hominem.

40 Et habeat sacerdos secum quando sacrificat lineam et cingulum et ammitum et orarium et planeta, et in manu teneat manipulum et sudario trilicem in onore Trinitatis propter sacrificium ponendo super altare.

Et in nullo permittimus sine lumen accensus sacrificare quia si sine lumen accensus sacrificaverit, videtur esse sacrificium cecum. Absit. Non permittat Deus ut hoc fiat
45 sacrificium cecum esse Christianos quia si lumen accensus habet, perfecta Trinitas sibi videtur habere virtutem quia oleum aut ceram et papirum et flamma Trinitate significat.

Ecce alia sententia significat Trinitatem, qui inde lumen pro vice Christi sicut ipse dixit, Ego sum lux mundi (Jo 8:12). Et habeat incensum quia quando angeli Satane
50 ceciderunt de caelo in terra, in fetore ceciderunt. Et cum odore incensi facit sacerdos ad altare, praesentialiter fugit diabolus et illum odorem per angelos ante Deum ascendit. Et incensum et odorem et ignem Trinitatem significat.

Et quando offerunt Domino in altare, non solum panem quia si solum pane poni, videtur esse Pater cum Filio non haberet Spiritum Sanctum. Si panem et vinum et
55 aqua adunatim, videtur esse Patrem et Filium et Spiritum Sanctum.

---

36 secum *ex* secundos *corr.* V4   43 accensus *ex* -sum *corr.* V4

Unde dicimus, Sanctus Sanctus Sanctus iii vicibus in honorem sanctae Trinitatis. Et si solum ignem habet ad sacrificandum, videtur esse Patrem non aberet Filium nec Spiritum Sanctum quia lumen accensum Trinitatem significat.

Quia qui sacrificat non sorte adulteriis sed mundus ab omni coinquinatione aduteriis sacrifices quia sacerdos Trinitas imperat:

Pater sanctificat, Filius clarificat,
P S F C
Spiritus Sanctus de Patre procedens, et Filio benedicens
S S D P P F B
sanctificans sacrificium taliter consumatur Pater, Filius,
S S T ERGO S C
Spiritus Sanctus, Pater, Filius, Spiritus Sanctus.
D ET P B T
Trinitas intellegi potest.

Ergo trilicemcem posita in altare et desuper ponit sacerdos calicem, similiter sanctam Trinitatem figuratur.

Ecc<e> si diximus iii vicibus Agnus Dei propter sanctam Trinitatem in honore septiforme Spiritus Sancti gratiae.

Ergo non praesumat sacerdos aliut facere quando sacrificat nisi quomodo supradiximus, ut illuminet se et animas Christianorum illuminet. Et si aliter facere praesumpserit, nec sibi lumen nec aliis Christianis lumen praestat. Sed ille cecus et aliud in cecitati post se trait.

---

57 Filium *ex* Filius *corr.* *V4*

10. *Vulgate Form*

This form appears in the following manuscripts:

Collection in Five Books

MC2 = Monte Cassino, Archivio della Badia 125 (s. $\text{XI}^2/_4$?, Monte Cassino), pp. 155-157

V5 = Vatican City, Biblioteca Apostolica Vaticana Vat. lat. 1339 (s. XI med., prov. Narni), fols. 135v-136v

Va2 = Rome, Biblioteca Vallicelliana B 11 (before 1087, Sant'Eutizio in Val Castoriana), fols. 129v-131r.

Derivatives of the Collection in Five Books

F = Florence, Biblioteca Riccardiana 300 (s. XI, central Italy), fols. 94v-96v

T = Toledo, Biblioteca Capitular 22-32 (s. XI, central Italy, prov. Viterbo), pp. 212-219

A = Rome, Biblioteca Angelica 1447 (s. XI, central Italy), pp. 46-48
Va3 = Rome, Biblioteca Vallicelliana F 92 (s. XI ex., Sant'Eutizio in Val Castoriana), fols. 190v-192r
Ma2 = Madrid, Biblioteca Nacional 373 (s. XI/XII, south Italy), fols. 61r-64r
N2 = Naples, Biblioteca Nazionale XII A 28 (s. XI/XII, central Italy), fols. 69r-72r
V6 = Vatican City, Biblioteca Apostolica Vaticana Vat. lat. 4317 (s. XI/XII, Farfa?), fols. 151v-153v.

The text printed here is taken from MC2, the oldest manuscript of the south Italian *Collection in Five Books*, and has been collated with the other manuscripts listed above. Glosses in the codices have been reported in the first apparatus since some glosses have been incorporated into the text (e.g., *scrutati estis*, 1. 9 in A). Textual variants are reported according to chronological sequence with those in the *Collection in Five Books* first and then those in the derivative collections.

It should be noted that the text in MC2 is at variance with all the others at several points beyond purely erroneous readings: *questio* (ll. 3, 7), *quibus horis* (1. 8), and *et qui hoc praesumpserit* (ll. 23-24). The great number of variant readings in ll. 23-24 is reported in full. Shared readings indicate that Va2 and Ma2 are very close and that T and N2 bear some resemblance. These four witnesses all have Beneventan-script symptoms.

MC2 has generally been dated to *c.* 1025, although the abbreviations have suggested to some that it might have been written somewhat later.[51]

V5 was written around the middle of the eleventh century in 'romanesca', but was clearly based on a Beneventan-script model, as its Beneventan-script symptoms show.[52] It has often been stated that the manuscript originated at Farfa, but more recently a Narni origin has been suggested. Even this suggestion, however, remains a hypothesis, although it is clear that the codex was once in Narni.[53]

Va2 was written at Sant'Eutizio in Val Castoriana in part by Ubertus, a monk and later abbot there, whose death is recorded by at least 1087.[54] Although the manuscript is written in 'romanesca', it exhibits Beneventan-script symptoms; textually it is often closer to MC2 than to V5.

F contains a celebrated *ordo missae*[55] together with a canonical collection in

---

[51] See E. A. Loew, *The Beneventan Script. A History of the South Italian Minuscule*, 2nd enlarged edition prepared by Virginia Brown, 2 vols. (Sussidi eruditi 33-34; Rome, 1980), 1.211, 213, 344; and Mordek, *Kirchenrecht*, p. 100 n. 15.

[52] Reynolds, 'South Italian *Liturgica*', 488 n. 25; and Supino Martini, *Roma e l'area*, pp. 226 f. and n. 69.

[53] Supino Martini, ibid., p. 229.

[54] ibid., p. 205.

[55] See Adalbert Ebner, *Quellen und Forschungen zur Geschichte und Kunstgeschichte des Missale Romanum im Mittelalter: Iter Italicum* (Freiburg i. Br., 1896), pp. 300-302.

seventeen books called the *Collectio Riccardiana.* L. VIII deals with the eucharist and contains our Mass commentary.

Although copied in an inelegant eleventh-century minuscule, T has numerous Beneventan-script symptoms. The canonical collection in this codex, the *Collectio Toletana,*[56] is derived largely from the *Collection in Five Books* and Burchard's *Decretum.* The collection itself is farraginous, and our Mass commentary has been inserted helter-skelter after canons from Burchard's *Decretum* and before canons from L. IV of the *Collection in Five Books.*

A contains the *Collectio Angelica* in thirteen books, which is based largely on the *Collection in Five Books* with material also from the *Collection in Seventy-Four Titles.*[57] Our Mass commentary is c. 77 of L. IV and precedes a number of canons on the eucharist.

Va3, like Va2, was written at Sant'Eutizio but somewhat after the time of Ubertus. Besides liturgical material, the codex has a canon law and penitential section that draws on the *Decretum* of Burchard of Worms and the *Collection in Five Books.* As might be expected from its origin, our text in this manuscript is related to that in Va2.

The portion of Ma2 containing our text is written in both normal minuscule and Beneventan script. The collection in four books, in which our text appears as c. 32 of L. IV, is clearly dependent on the *Collection in Five Books.*

N2, a codex written in ordinary minuscule, also displays Beneventan-script symptoms. It contains a canonical collection based on the *Collection in Five Books* and is divided into five parts. Our commentary, c. 83 of L. III, introduces a group of canons on the eucharist.

V6 contains the *Liber multiloquiorum in Seven Books* written in the late eleventh or early twelfth century in 'romanesca' but with Beneventan-script symptoms. The codex itself has been attributed perhaps to Farfa or vicinity on the basis of its reference on fol. 1r to Abbot Berardus II and a text from Pope Sylvester to Hugh of Farfa.[58] Recently, on the basis of the script, decoration, and a fourteenth-century note giving its provenance as a monastery 'sancti Benedicti', Paola Supino Martini has placed the origin of the codex not in Farfa itself but in a Benedictine house with Farfese connections.[59] The *Liber multiloquiorum* derives largely from the *Collection in Five Books,* a codex of which is thought to have been at Farfa; our Mass commentary appears as c. 39 of L. IV, a book that also contains such other liturgical commentaries as the *Dominus vobiscum.*

---

[56] Reynolds, 'Law, Canon: to Gratian', 408.

[57] ibid.

[58] Roger E. Reynolds, 'The "Isidorian" *Epistula ad Leudefredum*: An Early Medieval Epitome of the Clerical Duties', *Mediaeval Studies* 41 (1979) 306.

[59] Supino Martini, *Roma e l'area,* pp. 297 f.

CCXXXV INCIPIT ORDO QUOMODO SACERDOS DEBET SACRIFICARE

Dum quadam die resideret sanctissimus papa Damasus in sede beati Petri apostoli,
questio orta est in tota ecclesia Romana de sacrificio quibus horis liceret sacerdos
sacrificium offerre, et non inveniebatur. Tunc transmisit epistulam suam ad beatum
5 Hieronimum presbiterum Hyerosolimis ita.

DAMASUS PAPA HIERONIMO PRESBITERO IN DOMINO AETERNAM SALUTEM

Dirigimus vestrae fraternitati quia questio orta est in tota ecclesia Romana de
sacrificio quibus horis licet sacrificare et non invenimus exinde finem. Dirigat nobis
sanctitas vestra vos qui omnia scrutatis quomodo exinde agamus.

10   HIERONIMUS

Pater sanctissime, veritas in vobis minime est absconsa. Recordare concilium
Nicenum ubi a ccctis x et viii patribus sanctis affixum et constitutum est, siquis die
dominico resurrectionis post horam tertiam ausus fuerit canere missam, anathematizetur; aliis vero diebus a tertia usque in horam nonam si praesumpserit,
15 similiter anathematizetur; aliis vero horis licitum est sacrificare.

_____

2 Dum] .i. quando *MC2*   resideret] .i. sedere *MC2*   sanctissimus] .i. beatissimus *MC2*
3 orta] .i. nata *MC2*   4 Tunc] .i. Deinde *MC2*   5 ita] .i. sic *MC2*   7 Dirigimus] .i.
Mandamus *MC2*   8 Dirigat] .i. Mandet *MC2*   9 scrutatis] .i. estis *MC2*   agamus] .i. faciamus
MC2   12 affixum] .i. confirmatum *MC2*: .i. affirmatum *V5 A*   constitutum] .i. habeis *MC2*

_____

1 ccxxxv] clxiii *V5*: clxxiii *Va2*: lxxvii *A*: xxxii *Ma2*: lxxxiii *N2*: xxxviiii *V6*: om. *F T Va3*
Incipit ... sacrificare] In Christi nomine incipit celebrationis misse *T*: De horis dierum in quibus
sacrificare oportet *V6*   Quomodo] Quod *V5 Va2 Va3 N2*: Quando *F*   Debeat *A*   2 die om.
Va3   resisteret *Va3*   Damascus *T*   sedem *Va2 F N2*   beatissimi *V6*   3 questio] intentio
V5 Va2 F T A Va3 Ma2 N2 V6   toto *T*   Romana ecclesia *Va3*   qua hora *V5 Va2 F T A Va3
Ma2 N2 V6*   licet *T A*   sacerdos] ad add. *V5*: om. *Va3*: sacerdoti *V6*   4 offeri *T*
inveniebatur] -bant *N2*: -bat *V6*   epistulas suas *V5 Va2 F T A Va3 Ma2 N2 V6*   5 Hieronimus
presbiter *Va3*   Hierusolimis *V5*: Hierusolymis *Va2*   6 Damascum *T*   eterna *T*   7 Dirigi-
mus] Diligimus *N2*   fraternitatis *T*   questio] intentio *V5 Va2 F T A Va3 Ma2 N2 V6*   toto
T   Romana ecclesia *Va3*   8 qua hora *V5 Va2 F T A Va3 Ma2 N2 V6*   licet] liceat *V6*:
sacerdos add. *T*   fine *Va2 F*   9 vestra] vestras *T*   vos om. *V6*   scrutatis] scrutasti *T*: scrutati
estis *A*: scrutamini *V6*   10 Hieronime *T*: Hieronimi Responsio *A*   11 vobis] nobis *T V6*   est
om. *T*   absconsa est *Va3*   concilium] domine add. *N2*   12 a om. *Ma2*   patres *Va2 Ma2*
sanctis] est add. *A*: sancti *Va2 T Ma2*   adfixum *Va2 F Ma2 N2*   est om. *A*   13 resurrectio
Va2 Ma2   hora *Va2 T Ma2 N2*   tertia *Va2 T Ma2 N2*   missa *Va2 T Ma2*   14 alii *Va2*
aliis ... 15 anathematizetur om. *Ma2*   vero om. *Va2 F Va3 A*   diebus] si sacrificaverit add.
A   hora *Va3 T*   nona *V5 Va2 T*   si om. *A*   praesumpserit om. *A*   15 similiter om. *T*
hores *N2*

Cum relecta fuisset epistula, invenerunt in concilio scriptum a ccctis x et viii
patribus sanctis qui inflammati fuerunt de Spiritu Sancto quomodo in Nicena sancti
coram Constantino magnifico et catholico et sanctissimo imperatore scripserunt
et constituerunt, siquis die dominico post horam tertiam ausus fuerit canere
20 missam, in dampnatione anathematizetur.

Pro eo quod Spiritus Sanctus hora iiia descendit ad apostolos, ideo non licet post
horam iiia die dominico sacrificare nec ieiunare nec ullam abstinentiam habere. De
aliis vero diebus a media hora iiiia usque in media hora viiia, et qui hoc
praesumpserit, similiter anathematizetur pro eo quod istis horis Christus in
25 passione et patibulo crucis stetit pro nostra salute. Ideoque si in istis horis
praesumpserit sacrificare, angeli non recipiunt sacrificium ad offerendum maiestati.
Ergo quid prodest illud sacrificium?

Et ipsa sacrificia quando sacrificaverit sacerdos, non praesumat solum sacrificare
quia Christus quando sacrificium pro totius mundi salute immolari se permisit, duo

---

17 inflammati] .i. accensi *MC2*   21 ideo] .i. propterea vel idcirco *MC2*   26 praesumpserit]
.i. ausus fuerit *MC2*

---

16 Cum] Cumque *V5 Va2 F A Va3 N2 V6*   conciliis *N2*   17 sanctis patribus *V6*   patres
Va2 Ma2   sancti *Va2 F Ma2*   sanctis patribus *V6*   imflamati *Va3*   Sancto Spiritu *Ma2*
quomodo *om. Va3*   in Nicena] inicena *N2*   Nicena] Nica *Va3*: Nicea *A*   sancti *om. T*
sancto *Ma2*   18 Constantino] magno et *add. Ma2*   catholica *Ma2*   et²] ac *V5 Va2 F A T*
Va3 V6: a *N2*   inperator *T*   19 siquis] in *add. A*   hora *F T V6*   tertiam] tertia *V5 Va2*
F T Ma2 V6   20 missas *V5 Va2 F Ma2 N2 V6*: missa *T*   in *om. T*   dampnatione *om. T*
damnatione *V5 Va2 F Ma2 V6*   21 horam *V6*   tertiam *V6*   ad] super *F*   licet] die
dominico *add. Va3*   22 hora *T N2*   iiia] tertiam *Va2 F A Va3 Ma2 V6*: nec *add. Va3*   die]
diem *F*: *om. Va3*   dominico *om. Va3*   abstinentia *N2*   habere] nisi a malo tantum *add. A*
De] In *A*   23 vero diebus ... hora viiia] vero diebus a media hora iiia usque ad aliam mediam horam
iiiiam a quarta in mediam horam octavam *V5*: vero diebus a media hora iiia usque alia media hora
iiiia a quarta in media hora octaba *Va2*: vero diebus a media hora tertia usque ad aliam mediam hora
iiiia a iiiia in mediam horam octabam *F*: vero diebus a media hora iiia usque ad alia mediam hora
iiiia similiter anathematizetur a iiiita usque in mediam horam viiita *T*: vero diebus sacrificet a media
hora tertia usque ad mediam horam iiiitam a quarta media usque in horam viiiiam si sacrificaverit *A*:
vero diebus a media hora tertiam usque ad aliam mediam horam quartam a quarta in media hora
octava *Va3*: vero diebus a media hora iii usque alia media hora iiii a quarta in media hora viii *Ma2*:
vero diebus a media hora tertia usque ad aliam media hora iiiia a iiiia in mediam horam viii *N2*: vero
diebus a media hora tertia usque alia mediam horam iiiia a quinta in mediam horam viiia *V6*
23-24 et ... praesumpserit *om. V5 Va2 F T A Va3 Ma2 N2 V6*   24 ista hora *V5 Va2 F T A Va3*
Ma2 N2: istas horas *V6*   25 et] in *Va2 F A Va3 Ma2*: in *add. V5 T N2 V6*   stetit] stent *T*
salutem *T*   si *om. T*   in *om. Va2 F T A Va3 Ma2 N2 V6*   istas horas *V5 Va2 F Va3 Ma2*
N2 V6: ista hora *T*   26 maiestatis *Va2 T*   27 Ergo quid ...29 sacrificium? *om. T*   Quid ergo
A   quid] quod *N2*   illud] illum *Va2 F Ma2 N2*   28 ipsa] ipsum *T*: ipso *N2*   sacrificium
T Ma2   sacrificaverint *Va3*   solus *V5 Va2 F T A Va3 Ma2 N2 V6*   29 salutem *T N2*
inmolari *T*   duos *V5 Va2 A Ma2*

30 latrones in cruce fuerunt cum eo. Ergo si solus sacrificaverit sacerdos, cui dicit,
Dominus vobiscum? Certe melius est illi dicere, Dominus mecum et ipse respondeat, Et cum spiritu meo. Ecce satis blasphemat si duos vel tres non habet
ministros. Et si habet, sana fide potest dicere, Dominus vobiscum et illi ei
respondentes, Et tu sicut nobis optasti ut Deus esset nobiscum, et nos optamus ut
35 sit Dominus cum spiritu tuo. Quia si solus sacrificat, videtur Pater esse solus,
Filium et Spiritum Sanctum in Trinitate non esse. Si cum uno ministro sacrificaverit, ergo cui dicit, Dominus vobiscum? Melius est ei dicere, Dominus tecum vel
nobiscum. Absit. Si cum duobus ministris sacrificat, videtur esse perfecta Trinitas.
Et aliter, ergo qui sacrificat habeat secum duos ministros sicut Dominus in
40 evangelio dicit, Ubi duo vel tres steterint in nomine meo in medio eorum sum (Mt
18:20). Et in omni loco, tres testimonia apud Deum firmata sunt (1 Jo 5:7-8?).
Et si plus sunt, ecce quam melius sunt apud Deum et hominem.

Et habeat sacerdos secum quando sacrificat lineam et cingulum et amictum et
orarium et planetam, et in manu teneat manipulum et sudarium trilicem in
45 honorem sanctae Trinitatis propter sacrificium ponendum super altare.

Ecce una sententia sanctae Trinitatis, Et in nullo permittimus sine lumine accensum sacrificare quia qui sine lumine accensum sacrificaverit, videtur esse sacrificium caecum. Absit hoc. Non permittat Deus ut fiat sacrificium caecum esse apud

---

31 *in marg.* Nota Dominus vobiscum *A*   36 *in marg.* Nota minus quanties ministri *A*
37 tecum] .i. ab illos sit longe *MC2*   40 dicit] .i. ait *MC2*   40 sum] ego *A*   44 *in marg.* Nota
vestimenta sacerdotis *A*   lineam] .i. *MC2*   cingulum] .ii. *MC2*   amictum] .iii. *MC2*
45 orarium] .iiii. *MC2*   planetam] .v. *MC2*   manipulum] .vi. *MC2*   sudarium] .vii. *MC2*
in marg. sudarium unde lingua rustica dicitur corporale *MC2*   49 caecum] .i. obscurum *MC2*
Absit] .i. Non fiat *MC2*

---

30 cum eo fuerunt *A*   31 est *om. N2*   illi *om. A N2*   32 pblasphemat *Va2*   duo *Va2*
Va3 Ma2 N2   33 illi] ille *F:* ile *T*   34 respondeant *A*   esset] esse *T*   35 si *om.* V6
sacrificaverit *Ma2*   esse Pater *Va3*   36 Filium] Filius *T A*   Spiritus Sanctus *T A*   in Trinitate
non esse] non esset cum illo in Trinitate *T*   37 est *om. A*   ei *om. F A Va3 N2*   vel] idest *T*
38 nobiscum] nobis *T*   Adsit *V6*   ministros *V6*   sacrificaverit *N2*   esset *T*   perfecta
esse *A*   39 qui] si *N2*   duo *Va3*   40 dicit] ait *T*   duos *Va2*   steterunt *T*   41 tres]
tria *V5 T A Va3*   firmata sunt apud Deum *Va3*   42 si *om. V6*   sunt] est *Va2 T Ma2*
44 linea *Va2 F Va3 Ma2 N2*   cinculum *Va3*   45 planeta *N2*   manum *Va2*   mappulam
V5 Ma2 V6: mappula *Va2 F Va3 N2*   trilice *F Va3*   in] propter *Va3*   46 honore *V5 T A*
Ma2 N2 propter] ad *Va3*   47 Ecce ... Trinitatis *om. T*   sententiam *Va2*   nullo] ullo *Va3:*
nulla *T*   lumen *Va2 Ma2*   accenso *V5 F T A Va3 N2 V6*   48 lumen *Va2 Ma2*   accenso
V5 F A Va3 N2 V6   49 permittat] ergo *add. T*   ut *om. A*   fiat *om. A*   cecum esse]
sacrificium *V5:* esse caecum *A:* esse *om. T Ma2 V6*

50 Christianos, quia si lumen accensum habet, perfecta Trinitas ibi videtur habere virtutem, quia in olei et cere et papiri flamma Trinitas significatur.

Ecce alia sententia sanctae Trinitatis, Quia inde lumen pro vice Christi ponitur. Omnis sacerdos lumen habeat quando sacrificat quia ipse dixit, Ego sum lux mundi (Jo 8:12). Et habeat incensum quia quando angeli Satanae caeciderunt de caelo in

55 terram in faetore caeciderunt. Cum odorem incensi facit sacerdos ad altare, praesentialiter fugit diabolus et ille odor per angelos ante Deum ascendit, et per incensum et odorem et ignem Trinitas significatur.

Et quando offert Domino in altare, non ponat solum panem quia si solum panem ponit videtur Pater non habere Filium. Si panem et vinum ponit, videtur esse Pater

60 cum Filio non habere Spiritum Sanctum. Si panem et vinum et aquam adunatum ponit, videtur esse Pater et Filius et Spiritus Sanctus.

Unde dicimus, Sanctus Sanctus Sanctus iii vicibus in honore sanctae Trinitatis. Et si solum ignem habet ad sacrificandum, videtur esse Patrem, non habere Filium nec Spiritum Sanctum quia lumen accensum Trinitatem significat.

65 Qui sacrificat non in sorde adulterii sed mundus ab omni inquinatione adulterii sacrificet quia sacerdos Trinitas interpretatur: Pater sa- et Filius cer- et Spiritus Sanctus -dos; Pater pres-, Filius bi-, Spiritus Sanctus -ter. Ecce sacerdos et presbiter Trinitas intelligi potest.

---

53 *in marg.* Nota sacerdos lumen et incensum habet quando sacrificat *A*   54 Satanae] .i. diaboli *MC2*   caeciderunt] .i. caderunt *MC2*   55 *in marg.* Nota incensi et ignem et odorem *A* 59 *in marg.* Nota panem et vinum et aquam *A*   65 sorde] .i. inquinato vel contaminatio sive pollutio *MC2*   66 *in marg.* Nota sacerdos presbiter *A*

---

50 accenso *T Va3T*   habent *N2*   ibi] sibi *T:* ubi *N2*   51 in *om. Va2 Ma2*   oleum *Va2 Ma2*   et[1]] aut *Va2 Ma2*   cera *Va2 Ma2*   papirum *Va2 Ma2*   flammas *Va2 Ma2*   Trinita *T*   significat *Va2 Ma2*   52 sanctae Trinitatis sententia *F*   quia] qui *Va2 F A Ma2* 54 incensum habeat quando sacrificat *A*   quia] qui *T*   angeli Satanae quando *T*   55 terra *Va2 T Ma2 N2*   fetorem *A*   odore *T Va3*   56 praesens taliter *T:* presentaliter *Ma2*   ille odor] illum odorem *Va2 Ma2*   angelum *T*   per[2] *om. Va2 Ma2*   57 odore *T*   igne *T*   significat *Va2 Ma2*   58 offertur *Va3*   altari *A*   panem[1]] pane *Va3*   si] qui *Ma2*   59 Patrem *Va3* non *om. T*   habere] abent *T*   esse] esset *T: om. Va3 A*   60 habere] habet *T*   Spiritum Sanctum] -tu *T:* -to *T*   aqua *F T N2*   adunatum *om. T*   60-61 ponit adunatum *A*   esset *T*   Patrem *Va2 Va3 Ma2*   Filium *Va2 F T Va3 Ma2*   Spiritum *Va2 F T Va3 Ma2*   Sanctum *Va2 F T Va3 Ma2*   62 iii] tribus *V5 A Va3 N2 V6*   63 solus *T*   esse *om. V5 T A Ma2 N2 V6*   Pater *T*   habere] abet *T*   Filium *om. F*   nec] et *A*   63-64 nec Spiritum Sanctum *om. V5 Va2 F T Ma2 N2 V6*   64 Trinitas *Va2 Ma2:* Trinitate *T*   significat] Et *add. A* 65 Qui] Quia *N2*   sorte *T*   sed ... adulterii *om. N2*   sed] set *T*   66 sacrificat *Va3*   quia] qua *Va3*   interpretatur] significatur *N2*   et[1] *om. T A*   cer- ... 67 Filius *om. Va3*   et[2] *om. T*   67 bi-] et *add. Va3*   68 presbiteri *N2*   intellegi *Va2 T Va3 N2*

Ergo trilicem positam in altare et desuper calicem cum oblatione et operimento
70 super calicem similiter sancta Trinitas figuratur.

Ecce sicut diximus tres Agnus Dei propter sanctam Trinitatem.

Ecce septem sententiae sanctae Trinitatis in honorem septiformis Spiritus Sancti
gratiae.

Ergo non praesumat sacerdos aliud facere quando sacrificat nisi quomodo supra-
75 diximus ut illuminet se et animam Christianorum. Et si aliter facere praesumpserit,
nec sibi lumen nec aliis Christianis praestat. Sed ille caecus est et alios in
caecitatem post se trahit. Audi Christum dicentem, Si caecus caecum duxerit ambo
in foveam cadunt (Mt 15:14, Lc 6:39).

---

69 *in marg.* Nota trilicem *A*

---

69 Ergo] per *add. A*: et *add. N2*   posito *T*: posita *N2*   in altare positam *Va3*   oblationem
T: oblata *Ma2*   operimentu *A*   70 figurantur *N2*   71 tres] vicibus *add. Va2 Ma2*
72 septem] viiei *V5*: septiae *add. N2*   sententiae *om. N2*   honore *T A Ma2*   septiformes *Va2*:
septiusforme *T*   Sanctus *Ma2*   Sancti Spiritus *A*   74 Ergo] Ego *T*   quando] quam *T*
75 et] etiam *N2*   animam] -mas *T A V6*: *om. N2*   76 alios] alius *F*: aliis *N2*   77 cecitate *T*
Va3   trait *T Va3 N2*   caecus] cecum *T N2*   caecum] cecum ducatu prebeat *add. A*   duxerit
om. A

11. *Abbreviated Vulgate Form*

This form appears in the following manuscripts:

V7 = Vatican City, Biblioteca Apostolica Vaticana, Archivio di San Pietro H 58 (s. XI in.,
    Rome), fols. 45v-47r

NY = New York, Hispanic Society of America HC 380/819 (s. XI, Catalonia), fols.
    106v-108r.

The text printed here from V7 contains numerous spelling, grammatical, and
syntactical errors such as: *Sacrificaret* (l. 2), *residere* (l. 3), *sedem* (l. 3), *sacerdos*
(l. 5), *aeterna* (l. 7), *fraternitatis* (l. 8), *vestras* (l. 10), *sanctitissime* (l. 12),
resurrectio (l. 14), *missa* (l. 14), *alii* (l. 15), *fuissed* (l. 17), *inverunt* (l. 17),
trecenti ... patres (ll. 17-18), *sancti*[1, 2] (l. 18), *Niceam* (l. 18), *hora tertia* (l. 20),
equod (l. 25), *duo ministro* (l. 38), *linea* (l. 43), *manum* (l. 44), *sudari trilice* (l.
44), *lumen accensum* (ll. 46, 47), *sacrificarire* (l. 47), *pemittat* (l. 48), *sibi* (l. 49),
angelo (l. 55), *haberet* (l. 58), *mundum* (l. 64), *trilicem posita* (l. 67), *est* (l. 67),
honororae septiformes (l. 70), *alius Christianus* (l. 73), and *cecum*[1] (l. 73).

668

INCIPIT EPISTULA SANCTI DAMASI PAPE HIERONIMO PRESBITERO HIERUSOLIMIS TRANSMISSA QUOMODO SACERDOS DEBET SACRIFICARET

Dum quadam die residere sanctissimus papa Damasus in sedem beati Petri apostoli, intentio horta est in tota ecclesia Romana de sacrificio qua hora licet
5 sacerdos sacrificium offerre, et non inveniebat. Tunc transmisit epistulas suas ad beatum Hieronimum presbiterum Hierusolimis ita.

DAMASUS PAPA HIERONIMO PRESBITERO IN DOMINO AETERNA SALUTEM

Dirigimus vestrae fraternitatis quia intentio horta est in tota aecclesia Romana de sacrificio qua hora licet sacrificari et non inveniemus exinde finem. Dirigat nobis
10 sanctitas vestras vos qui omnia scrutatis quomodo exinde agamus.

HIERONIMO

Pater sanctitissime, veritas in vobis minime est absconsa. Recordare concilium Niceni ubi trecenti decem et octo patres sancti affixum et constitutum est ab eis, siquis die dominico resurrectio post hora tertia ausus fuerit canere missa, anathe-
15 matizetur; alii diebus a tertia usque in hora octava si praesumpserit, similiter anathematizetur; aliis vero horis licitum est sacrificare.

Cumque relecta fuissed epistula, inverunt in concilio scriptum a trecenti x et octo patres sancti qui inflammati fuerunt de Spiritu Sancto quomodo in Niceam sancti coram Constantino magnifico hac sanctissimo imperatore scripserunt et constitue-
20 runt, siquis die dominico sacrificare post hora tertia ausus fuerit canere missas, in dampnatione anathematizetur.

Pro eo quod Spiritus Sanctus hora tertia descendit ad apostolos, ideo non licet post hora tertia die dominico nec sacrificare nec ieiunare nec ullam abstinentiam abere.

---

1 Sancti *om. NY* Pape] Directa *add. NY* Hierusolimis Transmissa *om. NY* 2 Quomodo] Qualiter Vel Quibusmodis *NY* Sacrificare Debeat *NY* 3 resideret *NY* sede *NY* 4 liceat *NY* 5 sacerdoti *NY* misit *NY* 6 beatissimum *NY* Hierosolimis *NY* 7 aeternam *NY* 8 fraternitati *NY* 9 liceat *NY* invenimus *NY* 10 vestra *NY* vos *om. NY* qui] quae *NY* scrutatur *NY* 11 Iheronimae *NY* 12 sanctissime *NY* veritas] enim *add. NY* minime] nulla *NY* Recordamini *NY* concilii *NY* 13 trecenti] fuerunt *add. NY* sancti] quomodo *add. NY* fixum *NY* 14 resurrectionis *NY* horam *NY* terciam *NY* missam *NY* 15 aliis *NY* in] ad *NY* horam *NY* octava] nonam *NY* 17 fuisset *NY* invenerunt *NY* 18 patribus *NY* sanctis *NY* inflamati *NY* Nicena *NY* 19 magnifico] et catholico *add. NY* constituerunt] ut *add. NY* 20 horam *NY* terciam *NY* fuerit] aut *add. NY* missam *NY* 22 horam *NY* terciam *NY*

De aliis vero diebus a media hora tertia usque alia media hora quarta in media hora
25 hoctava, similiter anathematizetur pro equod ista hora Christus in passione in
patibulo crucis stetit pro nostra salute. Ideoque si istam horam presumpserit
sacrificare, angeli recipiunt sacrificium ad offerendum maiestatis. Ergo quid
prodest illum sacrificium?

Et ipsa sacrificia quando sacrificaverit sacerdos, non praesumat solum sacrificare
30 quia Christus quando sacrificium pro totius mundi salute immolari se permisit, duo
latrones in cruce fuerunt cum eo. Certe melius est illi dicere, Dominus mecum, et
ipse respondeat, Et cum spiritu meo. Ecce satis blasphaemat si duo vel tres non
habet ministros. Et si abet, sana fide dici potest, Dominus vobiscum et illi ei
respondeat, Et tu sicut nobis optasti Deus esse nobiscum et ut nos optamus ut sit
35 Dominus cum spiritu tuo. Quia si solum sacrificat, videtur Pater esse solus, Filium
nec Spiritum Sanctum in Trinitate non esse. Si cum uno ministro sacrificaverit,
ergo cui dicit, Dominus vobiscum? Melius ei dicere, Dominus tecum vel nobiscum.
Absit. Si cum duo ministro sacrificat, videtur esse perfecta Trinitas. Et aliter, ergo
qui sacrificat habeat secum duos ministros sicut Dominus dicit in evangelio, Ubi
40 duo vel tres steterint in nomine meo in medio eorum sum (Mt 18:20). Et in omni
loco, tres testimonia apud Deum firmata sunt (1 Jo 5:7-8?). Et si plus sunt, ecce
quam melius sunt apud Deum et hominem.

Et abeat sacerdos secum quando sacrificat linea et cingulum et amictum et orarium
et planetam, et in manum teneat mappulam et sudari trilice in honore sancte
45 Trinitatis propter sacrificium ponendum super altare.

Ecce una sententia sanctae Trinitatis, Et in nullo permittimus sine lumen accensum
sacrificarire quia qui sine lumen accensum sacrificaverit, videtur esse sacrificium
cecum. Absit hoc, et non pemittat Deus ut fiat sacrificium cecum esse aput
Christianos quia si lumen accensum habet, perfecta Trinitas sibi videtur havere
50 virtute quia oleum aut cera et papyrum flammas Trinitas significat.

Ecce alia sententia sanctae Trinitatis, Qui inde lumen pro vice Christi ponitur.
Omnis sacerdos lumen habeat quando sacrificat quia ipse dixit, Ego sum lux mundi

---

24 usque] ad *add. NY*   aliam *NY*   mediam *NY*   hora] horam *NY*   quarta] terciam *NY*
25 equod] eo quod *NY*   ista *NY*   hora *NY*   27 angeli] non *add. NY*   maiestati *NY*
28 sacrifitium illud *NY*   29 ipsa sacrificia *om. NY*   solus *NY*   30 quando] in *add. NY*
imolari *NY*   31 Ergo si solus sacrificaverit sacerdos, cui dicit, Dominus vobiscum? *add. NY*   illi
om. NY   32 duos *NY*   33 potest dicere *NY*   33-34 et illi ei ... esse nobiscum *om. NY*
34 ut *om. NY*   35 solum] solus *NY*   36 Si] vero *add. NY*   37 Melius] est *add. NY*
38 duobus *NY*   ministris *NY*   Et aliter *om. NY*   40 tres] tria *NY*   43 lineam *NY*
44 manu *NY*   mapulam *NY*   sudarium *NY*   46 lumine *NY*   accenso *NY*   47 sacrificare
NY   lumine *NY*   accenso *NY*   48 et *om. NY*   permittat *NY*   esse *om. NY*   apud *NY*
49 sibi] ibi *NY*   50 virtutem *NY*   aut] et *NY*   cerae *NY*   et] aut *NY*   papiri *NY*
flamma *NY*   Trinitatem *NY*   significant *NY*   51 Qui] Et *NY*   52 ipse] Dominus *add. NY*
habeat *NY*

(Jo 8:12). Et habead incensum quia quando angeli Sathanae ceciderunt de caelo in terra, in fetore caeciderunt. Cum odore incensi facit sacerdos ad altare, 55 praesentialiter fugit diabolus et illo odore per angelo ante Deum ascendit, et incensum et odorem et ignem Trinitas significat.

Et quando offert Domino in altare, non solum panem quia si solum pane poni videtur Pater non haberet Filium. Si panem et vinum poni, videtur Pater esse cum Filio non habet Spiritum Sanctum. Si panem et vinum et aquam adunatum poni, 60 videtur esse Patrem et Filium et Spiritum Sanctum.

Unde dicimus, Sanctus Sanctus Sanctus iiibus vicibus in honore sanctae Trinitatis. Et si solum ignem habet ad sacrificandum, videtur esse Patrem non haberet Filium quia lumen accensum Trinitas significat.

Qui sacrificat, non in sordide adulterii sed mundum ab omni inquinatione adulterii 65 sacrificaverit quia sacerdos Trinitas interpretatur: Pater sa- et Filius cer- et Spiritus Sanctus -dos. Pater. Ecce sacerdos et presbiter Trinitas intellegi potest.

Ergo trilicem posita altare et desuper calicem cum oblatione est et operimento super calicem similiter sancta Trinitas figuratur.

Ecce sicut diximus iiies Agnus Dei propter sanctam Trinitatem.

70 Ecce sanctae Trinitatis in honororae septiformes Spiritus Sancti gratiae.

Ergo non presumat sacerdos alius facere quando sacrificat nisi quomodo supra-diximus ut illuminet se et animas Christianorum. Et si aliter facere presumpserit, nec sibi lumen nec alius Christianus praestat. Audi Christum dicentem, Si cecum cecum duxerit ambo in foveam cadunt (Mt 15:14; Lc 6:39).

---

54 terram *NY*   Cum] vero *add. NY*   odorem *NY*   altarem *NY*   55 ille *NY*   odor *NY* angelos *NY*   56 odor *NY*   ignis *NY*   Trinitatem *NY*   significant *NY*   57 offert] sacerdos *add. NY*   altari *NY*   solum] offert *add. NY*   solus *NY*   panis *NY*   poni] ponatur *NY* 58 habere *NY*   panis *NY*   poni] ponatur *NY*   59 Filio] et *add. NY*   habere *NY*   poni] ponitur *NY*   60 esse *om. NY*   62 habere *NY*   63 Trinitatem *NY*   64 sordibus *NY* mundus NY   65 sacrificet *NY*   66 Pater *om. NY*   intellegi *NY*   67 trilice *NY*   posita] in *add. NY*   altari *NY*   est] aetiam *NY*   69 Ecce sicut] Et *NY*   dicimus *NY*   iiies] ter *NY* 70 Ecce] septem sententiae *add. NY*: *in marg.* septem *add. V7*   honore *NY*   septiformis *NY* 71 aliud *NY*   73 aliis *NY*   Christianis *NY* praestat] Sed ille caecus est et alios in cecitatem post se trahit *add. NY*   cecum] caecus *NY*

XIII

THE GREEK LITURGY OF ST. JOHN CHRYSOSTOM
IN BENEVENTAN SCRIPT:
AN EARLY MANUSCRIPT FRAGMENT*

THE influence of Greek liturgical culture in the areas where Beneventan script was written has long been known and well documented. For example, the renowned Barberini codex, Vatican, Biblioteca Apostolica Vaticana (hereafter BAV) Barb. gr. 336, written in Greek in the late eighth or early ninth century and bearing the earliest surviving text of the Liturgies of SS. Basil and John Chrysostom, has long taken pride of place among the scores of liturgical manuscripts from southern Italy.[1] Greek liturgical rolls written in southern Italy, although somewhat rare, are not uncommon,[2] and their influence on Latin liturgical *rotuli* of the region has often been stressed.[3] The liturgy of the Roman rite, written in Greek in southern Italy, the so-called Liturgy of St. Peter, has been intensively analyzed;[4] and there are multiple studies of the Latin translations by Leo Thuscus and Nicholas of Otranto of the so-called *Missa graecorum* in the late twelfth and early thirteenth centuries.[5]

* For permission to publish photographs of the fragment and for help in the preparation of this article I am grateful to the manuscript librarian of Bryn Mawr College, Pennsylvania, Leo Dolenski. Research for this article on 'monumenta liturgica beneventana' was done with the help of a grant from the Social Sciences and Humanities Research Council of Canada.

[1] On this codex and its origin, see Anselm Strittmatter, 'The "Barberinum s. Marci" of Jacques Goar', *Ephemerides Liturgicae* 47 (1933) 329-67; André Jacob, 'L'evoluzione dei libri liturgici bizantini in Calabria e in Sicilia dall'viii al xvi secolo, con particolare riguardo ai riti eucaristi' in *Calabria Bizantina. Vita religiosa e strutture amministrative (Atti del primo e secondo incontro di Studi Bizantini)* (Reggio Calabria, 1974), p. 51; and A. Jacob, 'La tradition manuscrite de la liturgie de Saint Jean Chrysostome (viiiᵉ-xiiᵉ siècles)' in *Eucharisties d'Orient et d'Occident*, 2 vols. (Lex Orandi 46-47; Paris, 1970), 2.109-138.

[2] See, e.g., André Grabar, *Les manuscrits grecs enluminés de provenance italienne (ixᵉ-xiᵉ siècles)* (Paris, 1972), p. 47.

[3] See, e.g., Gerhard B. Ladner, 'The "Portraits" of Emperors in Southern Italian *Exultet* Rolls and the Liturgical Commemoration of the Emperor', *Speculum* 17 (1942) 181-200; and Guglielmo Cavallo, *Rotoli di Exultet dell'Italia meridionale* (Bari, 1973), pp. 32-35.

[4] See the bibliography on this in Roger E. Reynolds, 'St. Peter, Liturgy of' in *Dictionary of the Middle Ages*, ed. Joseph R. Strayer, 12 vols. (New York, 1988), 10.620-21; to which may be added Klaus Gamber, 'Die griechisch-lateinischen Mess-libelli in Süditalien' in *La chiesa greca in Italia dall'viii al xvi secolo: Atti del Convegno storico interecclesiale (Bari, 30 apr.- 4 magg. 1969)*, 3 vols. (Padua, 1973), 3.1299-1306.

[5] Anselm Strittmatter, '"Missa Grecorum", "Missa Sancti Iohannis Crisostomi". The Oldest

Reprinted from *Mediaeval Studies*, 52 (1990), pp. 296-302, by permission of the publisher. © 1990 by the Pontifical Institute of Mediaeval Studies, Toronto.

In his recent important study of the Old Beneventan chant Thomas Forrest Kelly has noted numerous instances in which Greek liturgical practice was used in the area where Beneventan script was written, and he has demonstrated that elements of the Greek liturgy were taken into the liturgical rite celebrated in Benevento itself. In some instances the Greek text was transliterated into Latin characters to be used on several of the most significant feasts in the liturgical rite there.[6] The present article draws attention to another extraordinary Greek liturgical text transliterated into Latin characters with rubrics in Latin, both written in Beneventan script of the late tenth or early eleventh centuries.

The fragment with this Greek liturgical text is now in the manuscript collection of the Bryn Mawr College Library and bears the provisional shelfmark Goodhart Collection, Fragment 2. It was the third fragment in a bound collection of fragments of Greek manuscripts given to the library by Howard Lehman Goodhart in 1943. The fragment came to the attention of John Mitchell of the University of East Anglia, who generously notified Virginia Brown of its existence.

The fragment of text is written on a single piece of somewhat brittle and rough vellum measuring about 203 x 137 mm. For the lines, crude prick marks of both holes and slits are visible on the right-hand margin. The folio was originally ruled on the flesh side with a stylus, which has left a yellowish stain. There are twenty horizontal lines ruled about 8 mm. apart, and these are run through by vertical lines to form margins enclosing a horizontal writing space of about 108 mm.

The writing on the folio does not follow the original rulings. Instead the folio was folded to make a bifolium, and text was entered on only one side (now unnumbered fol. 1r-v) at right angles to the original ruling.

The script is in a black ink with red/orange rubrics. Although in some places of the Greek transliterated text on fol. 1r, the script appears to be in a pale brown ink that has been gone over with a stronger black ink, the black has in fact been rubbed off.

After the text was completed the bifolium was bound, presumably with other bifolia containing texts before and after it. There are three sets of binding holes: the lowest set, 7 mm., is 11 mm. from the bottom of the bifolium; the middle set, 3.5 mm., is 67 mm. from the bottom of the bifolium; and the top set is now lost owing to tearing of the upper centre of the bifolium, caused presumably by wear or when the bifolium was torn from attached bifolia.

It would seem that the surviving bifolium was part of the last quire of a *libellus* with two or more quires attached because its text falls late in the liturgical rite it

Latin Version Known of the Byzantine Liturgies of St. Basil and St. John Chrysostom', *Traditio* 1 (1943) 79-137. On the notion and misuse of the term *Missa greca*, see Bernice M. Kaczynski, *Greek in the Carolingian Age: The St. Gall Manuscripts* (Cambridge, Mass., 1988), p. 102.

    [6] Thomas Forrest Kelly, *The Beneventan Chant* (Cambridge, 1989), pp. 203-218.

represents. Thus, quires before our bifolium would have contained the first and largest part of the liturgical rite, and a bifolium or bifolia bound into our bifolium after fol. 1v would have contained the remainder of the liturgical rite. The blank parts of our bifolium, fol. 2r-v, would have been the outside cover of the last quire of the liturgical *libellus*.

With the exception of the rubric 'PH<B>ON ' (a shortened form of Ekphonos?), a Greek *zeta* and what resemble the Greek *mu*'s, the writing is entirely in Latin characters. The text written in black ink is the transliterated form of the end of the precommunion and beginning of the communion of the Liturgy of St. John Chrysostom. Further, with the exception of the words 'Proschome', which is rubricated, and 'Ta agia tis agiis,' on fol. 1v, this Greek transliterated text is in an uncalligraphic Beneventan hand. These words and the rubrics for the text in Latin on fol. 1r-v are written in a calligraphic Beneventan hand. It is always risky to date a text on the basis of the few letters in our fragment, but its open character, the lack of a descender on the final *r*, and the *n* and *m* with feet rather than lozenges suggest that the text was written in the late tenth or early eleventh centuries.[7] It is not in Bari-type Beneventan script[8] and therefore was written probably not in Puglia but somewhere else in the lower or central part of southern Italy.[9]

In the examples of transliterated Greek text in Professor Kelly's study, the writing in the manuscripts is in a sure Beneventan hand, probably signifying that there was a long tradition of copying such transliterated texts. In our fragment, however, there appear to be two distinct methods of writing, the calligraphic and uncalligraphic types. The former is used for the Latin and a few Greek words on fol. 1v. That one scribe was responsible for both this writing and the uncalligraphic sections of the transliterated Greek text is likely if the forms of such letters as *a, c, e,* and *r* are compared. Why the scribe would have used these two types is unclear. It is possible that the scribe was generally accustomed to writing in Latin, and when called upon to transliterate from a Greek text he became unsure and switched into the uncalligraphic style. For example, at times his *m*'s are in proper Beneventan script; at other times they resemble a Greek *mu*. But if the scribe were uncertain when he came to Greek text, why did he write on fol. 1v in the

[7] See E. A. Loew, *The Beneventan Script. A History of the South Italian Minuscule*, 2nd enlarged edition prepared by Virginia Brown, 2 vols. (Sussidi eruditi 33-34; Rome, 1980), 1.137 and plates I and II.

[8] On the relation between Greek and Beneventan scripts in Puglia see Alessandro Pratesi, 'Influenze della scrittura greca nella formazione della beneventana del tipo di Bari' in *La chiesa greca* 3.1095-1109.

[9] There are now indications that Beneventan script was written in Basilicata (see Virginia Brown, 'A New Commentary on Matthew in Beneventan Script at Venosa', *Mediaeval Studies* 49 [1987] 443-65), but there is no substantial evidence that it was written in Calabria, although it is most likely that it was. It is, of course, possible that our scribe was a traveller who wrote in Beneventan script at some place distant from southern Italy.

uncalligraphic script the *nomina sacra* 'Isu xps', which he would certainly have known from Latin? Perhaps, the uncalligraphic script is an attempt to imitate the Greek script of his examplar, but one cannot be certain of this. In any event, all of this suggests that the scribe was not copying from a previously transliterated text but was writing *de novo* from 1) a text in Greek, 2) one he knew by heart, or 3) one being dictated to him.

Which was it? There are indications of all three. For a written copy made by a scribe who was acquainted with Greek are the *phon, zeta*, accents (sometimes misused), and the *m*'s that in some instances resemble the Greek *mu*. On the other hand, the orthography of the Greek transliterated text may indicate an oral or memory source. Why, for example, would our scribe, if following a written Greek source, change a Greek *kappa* to a Latin *c* in some places but maintain it in others? Moreover, the sign 7 is used for a Greek accent, for an *iota*, and for *uio, ei*, and *h*. One indication that our scribe was transliterating from a text he knew by heart in Greek but may have had before him a written source or a dictated source appears in the last word of fol. 1r. The scribe originally wrote *apu* and then over this wrote *el*. The former word comes from one text of the Liturgy of St. John Chrysostom represented in variant manuscripts printed in the classic text by Goar[10] and in such manuscripts as the famous twelfth-century Rossano codex, Vatican, BAV Vat. gr. 1970,[11] but not in the renowned Barberini text of about 800. The text subsequent to the word *apu* emended to *el*, however, is from the Barberini text. That is, the scribe recognized the appropriate form found in the Barberini text, but began unthinkingly to write the later variant, probably from memory. In short, the scribe knew both Greek and Latin. He may have been transliterating from a Greek text — hence the uncalligraphic form of the transliteration — but he also was transliterating from what appears to have been dictation or memory.[12] That such might happen in the early Middle Ages has been brilliantly demonstrated by Ann Freeman, who has shown that in the composition of the *Libri Carolini*, Theodulf of Orléans used common Latin Psalter texts but the memory of his native Visigothic liturgical use intruded into the writing of the biblical text.[13]

Because our text appears on such a poor piece of parchment, it might be thought that it is a *probatio pennae*. This is unlikely, however, because of the utilitarian

---

[10] On the manuscripts used by Goar, see Strittmatter, 'The "Barberinum s. Marci" of Jacques Goar', 330 f.

[11] On this manuscript see Giovanni Mercati, 'L'Eucologio di S. Maria del Patire con un frammento di Anafora greca inedita', *Revue bénédictine* 46 (1934) 224-40; and Jacob, 'La tradition manuscrite de la liturgie de Saint Jean Chrysostome (viiie-xiie siècles)', 127.

[12] On this phenomenon see Jacob, 'La tradition manuscrite de la liturgie de Saint Jean Chrysostome (viiie-xiie siècles)', 111.

[13] See Ann Freeman, 'Theodulf of Orléans and the Psalm Citations of the "Libri Carolini"', *Revue bénédictine* 97 (1987) 195-224.

rubrics and because it begins and ends in mid sentences. Thus, it seems to have been part of a more extensive text of the Liturgy of St. John Chrysostom. Our scribe, knowing both Latin and Greek, was thus probably writing the text for a Latin-speaking priest who could not read Greek characters but who had to serve a Greek-speaking community using the Liturgy of St. John Chrysostom. That a Latin-speaking priest might offer the Eucharist according to the Greek rite rather than the Roman or Beneventan might seem extraordinary, until it is remembered that in southern Italy there were frequent liturgical interchanges by Greek and Latin communities,[14] and that prior to the Schism of 1054 between the Greek and Latin churches this probably would not have been considered unusual or uncanonical in southern Italy.

The poor quality of the bifolium and its writing suggest that the *libellus* to which it belonged was not made for deluxe or continuous usage such as other extant grand Greek manuscripts and *rotuli* of the Liturgy of St. John Chrysostom[15] or the imposing Latin manuscripts from Benevento with their transliterated Greek elements.[16] We know, for example, of occasional services at Monte Cassino on a portable altar being celebrated in Latin and Greek in the tower of St. Benedict[17] and if it were a Greek Mass, there might simply have been a Greek translation of the Latin rite such as is found in later manuscripts.[18] But it is not beyond the realm of possibility that at Monte Cassino and elsewhere the Greek liturgy celebrated in these occasional joint services might have been that of St. John Chrysostom and that an unprepossessing *libellus* such as ours might have been used.

Beyond its importance in showing the liturgical interplay between Latins and Greeks in southern Italy, our text is extraordinary for the development of the Greek liturgy itself. As has been noted, the oldest texts of the Liturgies of SS. Basil and John Chrysostom appear in the eighth- or ninth-century Barberini codex in Greek described by Cardinal Pitra: 'Le plus ancien et le plus beau des nos manuscrits liturgiques assurément l'inestimable *Euchologe* du viii⁰ siècle, que les princes Barberini ont heureusement conservé dans leur riche bibliothèque.'[19] There are then few witness of these liturgies until the thirteenth century,[20] and hence, our

---

[14] Kelly, *Beneventan Chant*, p. 204.
[15] E.g., see above note 2.
[16] Kelly, *Beneventan Chant*, pp. 206-217.
[17] ibid., 205.
[18] See Strittmatter, '"Missa Grecorum", "Missa Sancti Iohannis Crisostomi"', 79-137.
[19] Jean B. Pitra, *Hymnographie de l'Eglise grecque* (Rome, 1867), p. 56.
[20] Jacob, 'La tradition manuscrite de la liturgie de Saint Jean Chrysostome (viiiᵉ-xiiᵉ siècles)' lists the following manuscripts of the Liturgy of St. John Chrysostom from c. A.D. 800 to the thirteenth century. The Italo-Greek type are: Vatican, BAV Barb. gr. 336 (s. viii/ix); Leningrad, Gosudarstvennaia publichnaia biblioteka imeni M. E. Saltykova-Shchedrina gr. 226 (the *Euchologion* of Porphyre Uspenskij) (s. x); Grottaferrata, Biblioteca della Badia F. β. VII (s. x); F. β. IV (s. x2/2) Z. δ. II

fragment from the late tenth or early eleventh centuries is precious indeed. If the text is compared with the Liturgies of SS. Basil and John Chrysostom in the Barberini codex,[21] most of it could, in fact, have derived from either, but the first few words on fol. 1r are found only in the Liturgy of St. John Chrysostom.[22]

Our text is further significant in that it reflects the Liturgy of St. John Chrysostom in transition in southern Italy from what André Jacob calls the Italo-Greek or Calabrese tradition to the Constantinopolitan tradition.[23] The text largely follows the Italo-Greek or Calabrese form, but in several cases variants from later Constantinopolitan witnesses to the Liturgy of St. John Chrysostom appear. The emended 'apu' at the bottom of fol. 1v is an instance of this,[24] as is the 'Enite to ko' at the bottom of fol. 1v, which appears in variant manuscripts reported by Goar.[25] Also it is interesting that the prayer 'khari tu...' concludes in the tradition of the Liturgy of the Presanctified found both in the Barberini manuscript[26] and in the eleventh-century Liturgy of St. John Chrysostom,[27] but not in the Barberini text of the Liturgy of St. John Chrysostom.[28]

The transliterated text of our fragment is printed below in the left-hand column. The orthography of the fragment is maintained, and Latin abbreviations such as 'Sec sacer' and 'Can com' are kept because their expansion into 'Secreto sacerdos' or 'Cantus communionis' is uncertain. Also the sign 7 has been maintained because it was used to transliterate a variety of accents, diphthongs, and letters. In the right-hand column below, the Greek text of the Barberini codex is printed as it is found in Swainson's edition (B), with variants in our fragment as reported in 1) the Liturgy of the Presanctified (P) from that same codex, 2) the eleventh-century Liturgy of St. John Chrysostom (E), 3) the Codex Rossanensis (R), and 4) the communion chant (Ps 148:1).

(1090). The Constantinopolitan type are: Moscow, Gosudarstvennaia biblioteka SSSR imeni V. I. Lenina gr. 27 (s. x); Mt. Sinai, St. Catherine's Monastery gr. 958, 959 (s. xi); 961, 962 (s. xi-xii); 1036 (s. xii-xiii); Vatican, BAV gr. 1970 (the Rossano codex) (s. xii); and Jerusalem, Patriarchal Library, Stavrou 109 (*rotulus* of s. x).

[21] For these texts see F. E. Brightman, *Liturgies Eastern and Western Being the Texts Original or Translated of the Principal Liturgies of the Church*, vol. 1: *Eastern Liturgies* (Oxford, 1896), pp. 340 f.

[22] ibid.

[23] Jacob, 'L'evoluzione dei libri liturgici bizantini in Calabria e in Sicilia', 61, and 49, where he notes that in the Calabrese *Euchologion* there are parts noted for other participants beyond the *sacerdos* (as is the case in our fragment), while in the Constantinopolitan *Euchologion* the parts are for the *sacerdos* alone.

[24] See above, p. 299.

[25] Jacobus Goar, *Euchologion sive Rituale Graecorum* (Venice, 1730), pp. 65, 76.

[26] C. A. Swainson, *The Greek Liturgies Chiefly from Original Authorities* (Cambridge, 1884), p. 97.

[27] ibid., 136.

[28] ibid., 93.

BRYN MAWR FRAGMENT

\<recto\>
\<i\>atros ton psicho\<n\>
imon ke to somato\<n\>.
Φον sacer: khari tu ku
ke hictirmis ke 7 filan-
thropian tu monoge-
nu su 7u meth u eblogi-
tos 7 sin to panagio
ke agatho ke zoopio
su pneumati nin ke
a7 ke is tus eonas ton
eonon. *Sec sacer*:
Prosche kyrie Ihesu Christe
O theos imon ex agiu-
catik7tiriu ke el- \<eras. apu\>

\<verso\>
\<th\>e is to agiase imas
\< \> ano to patri sincathi-
menos, ke ode imin ao-
ratos sinon, ke cata-
xioson ti cratea su
chiri, metadune imin
ke di imon panti to
lau su. *Leva\<t\> ipsa munera
ad celos et dicat diaconus*:
Proschome. Et sacer:
Ta agia tis agiis. *Populus*:
Is agios is kurios Ihesu Christus

doxan theu patros. Amin.
Can com: Enite to ko

GREEK TEXT

\<B\>ἰατρὸς τῶν ψυχῶν
καὶ τῶν σωμάτων ἡμῶν
χάριτι \<τοῦ κυρίου\>
καὶ οἰκτιρμοῖς καὶ φιλαν-
θρωπίᾳ τοῦ. \<P \> μονογε-
νοῦς σου Υἱοῦ, μεθ᾽ οὗ εὐλογη-
τὸς εἶ σὺν τῷ παναγίῳ
καὶ ἀγαθῷ καὶ ζωοποιῷ
\<σου\> Πνεύματι, νῦν \<E\> καὶ
ἀεί, καὶ εἰς τοὺς αἰῶνας τῶν
αἰώνων.
\<B\> Πρόσχες, Κύριε ᾽Ιησοῦ Χριστέ,
ὁ Θεὸς ἡμῶν, ἐξ ἁγίου
κατοικητηρίου σου καὶ ἐλ-
\<R ἀπὸ θρόνου τῆς...\>

\<B\> θὲ εἰς τὸ ἁγιάσαι ἡμᾶς,
ὁ ἄνω τῷ Πατρὶ συγκαθεζό-
μενος καὶ ὧδε ἡμῖν ἀό-
ρατος συνών κατα-
ξίωσον τῇ κραταιᾷ σου
χειρὶ μεταδοῦναι ἡμῖν
καὶ δι᾽ ἡμῶν παντὶ τῷ
λαῷ σου.

Πρόσχωμεν.
Τὰ ἄγια τοῖς ἁγίοις.
Εἷς ἄγιος, εἷς Κύριος ᾽Ιησοῦς Χρισ-
τός, εἰς
δόξαν Θεοῦ Πατρός. \<᾽ Αμήν\>
\<Ps 148:1\> Αἴνειτε τόν κύριον

XIII

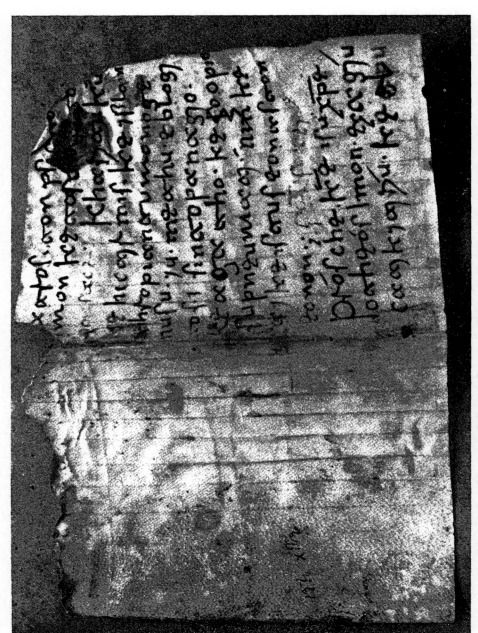

1. Bryn Mawr College Manuscript Collection, Provisional Shelfmark, Goodhart Collection, Fragment 2, folio 2v 1r

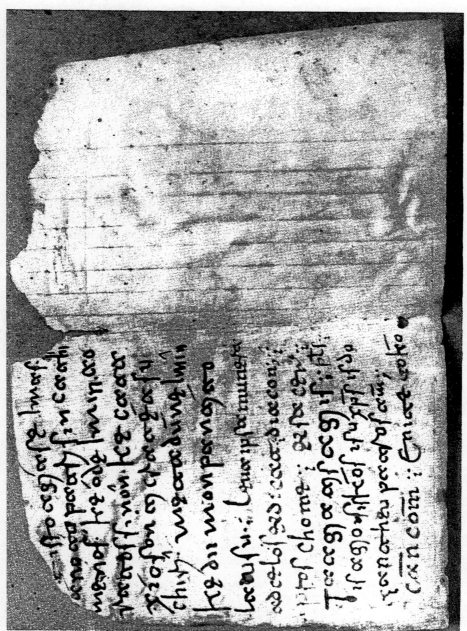

2. Bryn Mawr College Manuscript Collection, Provisional Shelfmark, Goodhart Collection, Fragment 2, fols. 1v-2r.

XIV

THE SOUTH-ITALIAN CANON LAW
COLLECTION IN FIVE BOOKS
AND ITS DERIVATIVES:
NEW EVIDENCE ON ITS ORIGINS,
DIFFUSION, AND USE

I N an article entitled 'La reazione al "Decretum Burchardi" in Italia avanti la
riforma gregoriana', Carlo Guido Mor contrasted the aims and diffusion of the
Decretum of Burchard of Worms to those of indigenous Italian canon law
collections before the Gregorian reform.[1] After characterizing Burchard's *Decretum*, Mor described various indigenous collections circulating in the Italian
peninsula from the late ninth to the early eleventh century. Of special importance
in central and southern Italy was what he styled the vade-mecum of canonists of
that region, the *Collection in Five Books* (hereafter *5L*),[2] which Mor observed
would remain the vade-mecum well into the Gregorian era.

Mor's characterization of the *5L* as the vade-mecum of Italian canonists of the
eleventh century is curious indeed because, as he knew, there exist only three
manuscripts of this collection, and all three are of substantial size and weight. Yet
Mor's designation of the *5L* as a vade-mecum was apt in another sense because
despite the physical cumbersomeness of the extant codices, the *5L* spawned a host
of derivative compilations that in their size and content seem indeed to have been
the handbook of many an eleventh- and even twelfth-century Italian canonist.

Since the publication in 1970 of Mario Fornasari's useful but flawed edition of
the first three books of the *5L*,[3] much has been written in reviews, articles, and
books about not only the origins but also the character of the collection.[4] It is the

---

[1] *Studi gregoriani* 1 (1947) 197-206.

[2] ibid., p. 201.

[3] *Collectio canonum in v libris (lib. i-iii)* (CCCM 6; Turnhout, 1970) [hereafter F]; on which
see Gérard Fransen, 'Principes d'édition des collections canoniques', *Revue d'histoire écclésiastique*
66 (1971) 125-36; and Hubert Mordek, 'Anzeigen', *Zeitschrift der Savigny-Stiftung für Rechtsgeschichte, kan. Abt.* 60 (1974) 477-78.

[4] The more specialized literature will be dealt with below, but an example of a more recent
general consideration of the collection may be found in Johannes Laudage, *Priesterbild und
Reformpapsttum im 11. Jahrhundert* (Cologne-Vienna, 1984), pp. 78-83.

Reprinted from *Mediaeval Studies,* 52 (1990), pp. 278-295, by permission of the publisher. © 1990 by the
Pontifical Institute of Mediaeval Studies, Toronto.

modest purpose of this article to assemble some of this material and to reexamine it in light of 1) new evidence, largely codicological and palaeographical, regarding its origins; 2) the hitherto suspected but unsubstantiated extensive diffusion of the collection; and 3) the character of the collection and its derivatives.

I. Origins: Codicological and Palaeographical Evidence

First, as to its origins, it is useful to summarize the conclusions of Fornasari and reactions to them. According to Fornasari the collection was probably compiled between 1014 and 1023 at Farfa for the priest Lupus, who is named in one of the prefaces.[5] Although it had traditionally been said that the major indigenous source for the *5L* was the early tenth-century *Collection in Nine Books*, Fornasari claimed, rather, that it was the even earlier *Collection of Vallicelliana T. XVIII*.[6] Probably the earliest codex of the *5L*, according to Fornasari, was the renowned eleventh-century Vatican codex, Biblioteca Apostolica Vaticana (hereafter BAV) Vat. lat. 1339, which he claimed was written at Farfa.[7] A direct copy of this manuscript was made, according to Fornasari, at Monte Cassino (now Archivio della Badia 125) during the early abbacy of Theobald; and it was mentioned in the *Chronica Casinensis* of 1023.[8] Probably dependent on this Cassino manuscript is the eleventh-century central Italian codex, Rome, Biblioteca Vallicelliana B 11.[9]

Fornasari's statements regarding the origins of the codices and their relationships were soon challenged and augumented by various scholars. Gérard Fransen was quick to point out that long ago the authors of the *Bibliotheca Casinensis* had associated Fornasari's priest Lupus with a travelling monk at Monte Cassino named in a colophon of the Monte Cassino codex.[10] Moreover, Fransen suggested that the Vallicelliana codex was probably closer than any other to the original collection because 1) it preserves most clearly within the books the divisional rubrics that Fornasari often relegated to his apparatus; 2) the Vallicelliana codex is shorter than the other two manuscripts; and 3) the Vallicelliana codex does not contain the multiple interlinear glosses found in the Vatican and Monte Cassino manuscripts.[11]

---

[5] F, pp. xvii-xix.
[6] F, pp. xiii f.
[7] F, pp. vii f.
[8] F, p. ix.
[9] F, pp. ix f.
[10] 'Principes', 130 f.
[11] 'Principes', 131-36.

Hubert Mordek then contributed several valuable pieces of information regarding the origins of the manuscripts of the collection.[12] First, he drew attention to the work of the art historian, E. B. Garrison, who had suggested that the famous Vatican manuscript was written at Narni in the second to third quarter of the eleventh century on the basis of a lost Farfese exemplar. Further, Mordek noted again the *Chronicon Casinensis* of 1023, which said that the abbot Theobald had made a *Liber canonum* for the poorly stocked library at Monte Cassino. But most important was Mordek's reference to the *Commemoratorium* of 1019 mentioning a *Liber canonum* which Theobald had had copied for the monastery of San Liberatore near Chieti as its provost before returning to Monte Cassino to become abbot there.

These contributions of Mordek were further developed by Theo Kölzer with several tantalizing suggestions.[13] First, Kölzer speculated that there was a lost manuscript of the *5L* at Farfa, on which his own *Collection of the Farfa Register* was based.[14] Moreover, he tentatively suggested that Theobald's *Liber canonum* at San Liberatore may even have been a copy of the *5L* which was carried to Monte Cassino to be used there as an exemplar for the extant Monte Cassino manuscript 125.[15] And finally, Kölzer drew attention to the south Italian rather than Farfese origins of the *5L* by showing that one of the texts of Gregory I in the *5L* has readings of a Monte Cassino tradition.[16]

In light of additional palaeographical and codicological evidence, let us look at some of these observations regarding the origins of the collection. First, regarding the indigenous sources. Arguments have been made that both the *Collection of Vallicelliana T. XVIII* and the *Collection in Nine Books* of Vatican City, BAV Vat. lat. 1349 were sources of the *5L*, but it is unlikely that either manuscript could have been the direct source because both codices have been dated to the eleventh century[17] — although the collections they contain are certainly earlier. Further, Fornasari's designation of the *Collection of Vallicelliana T. XVIII* as the source of the *5L* was based on the narrow evidence of a few Roman law texts;[18] and it is clear

---

[12] Mordek, 'Anzeigen', 477-78; and *Kirchenrecht und Reform im Frankenreich. Die Collectio Vetus Gallica, die älteste systematische Kanonessammlung des fränkischen Gallien. Studien und Edition* (Beiträge zur Geschichte und Quellenkunde des Mittelalters 1; Berlin-New York, 1975), p. 100, notes 14 f.

[13] *Collectio canonum Regesto Farfensi inserta*, ed. Theo Kölzer (Monumenta iuris canonici, Ser. B, Corpus collectionum 5; Vatican City, 1982).

[14] ibid., p. 54. It is possible, of course, that the *Collection of the Farfa Register* was based not on a complete manuscript of the *5L*, but on an excerptum of that collection.

[15] ibid., p. 54, note 128.

[16] ibid., pp. 50, note 111, and 222.

[17] See E. A. Loew, *The Beneventan Script. A History of the South Italian Minuscule*, 2nd enlarged edition prepared by Virginia Brown, 2 vols. (Sussidi eruditi 33-34; Rome, 1980), 2.131, 145.

[18] F, p. xiv.

that the *5L* contains numerous texts beyond these which are found in the *Collection in Nine Books* but not in the Vallicelliana collection. But here it is significant that the versions of a number of texts found in both the *5L* and *Collection in Nine Books* are much closer to recensions in yet another collection written in a manuscript pre-dating the *5L* by almost a quarter century, the *Collection of Vatican Archivio San Pietro H 58*, written *c.* 1000.[19] In short, the indigenous sources of the *5L* are more varied than any scholar has suspected. But what is perhaps most interesting is that the manuscripts of all these suggested sources are connected with southern Italy. The manuscript of the *Collection in Nine Books* is written in the Beneventan script of south Italy; the *Collection of Vallicelliana T. XVIII* was written in both Carolingian and Beneventan scripts probably not far south of Rome.[20] And even the codex Vatican, BAV Archivio San Pietro H 58, written in Rome itself, is filled with Beneventan-script symptoms and was clearly based on a south Italian exemplar.[21]

From the sources of the *5L* we now turn to the manuscripts of the collection itself. First, it must be stressed that none of the three extant manuscripts is a copy of either of the others. Although it has long been recognized that the collection is in two versions, a long and a short (and there is disagreement as to which manuscript contains which form[22]), there is a plethora of variants which make suspect any claim that one of the codices is a 'direct' copy of the others or even of an 'original' manuscript of the collection. Moreover, even though the Vallicelliana manuscript is shorter than the other two, it contains texts that the others lack.

That any of the extant manuscripts was a direct copy of the others is even more unlikely because of their very disparate origins — although admittedly they could have been taken from place to place. While there is no controversy regarding the script of the Monte Cassino manuscript, there is a problem about its date. On the basis of the reference to a *Liber canonum* in the *Chronica Casinensis* and because of its ornamentation, the codex is generally dated to the early eleventh century or *c.* 1023.[23] E. A. Lowe, however, long ago pointed out that the abbreviations are

---

[19] Roger E. Reynolds, 'A South Italian Liturgico-Canonical Mass Commentary', *Mediaeval Studies* 50 (1988) 642.

[20] Roger E. Reynolds, 'Odilo and the *Treuga Dei* in Southern Italy: A Beneventan Manuscript Fragment', *Mediaeval Studies* 46 (1984) 454, note 25.

[21] See Roger E. Reynolds, 'South Italian *Liturgica* and *Canonistica* in Catalonia (New York, Hispanic Society of America MS. HC 380/819)', *Mediaeval Studies* 49 (1987) 487, and Paola Supino Martini, *Roma e l'area grafica romanesca (secoli X-XII)* (Biblioteca di *Scrittura e civiltà* 1; Alessandria, 1987), p. 74.

[22] E.g., Paul Fournier, 'Un groupe de recueils canoniques italiens des xᵉ et xiᵉ siècles', *Mémoires de l'Institut national de France. Académie des inscriptions et belles-lettres* 40 (1916) 163 (rpt. in Paul Fournier, *Mélanges de droit canonique* ed. T. Kölzer, 2 vols. [Aalen, 1983], 2.213-331), holds that the Vatican and Vallicelliana manuscripts have the longer form; but Fransen, 'Principes', 136, says the Vallicelliana manuscript has the shorter version.

[23] E.g., Mordek, *Kirchenrecht,* p. 100, note 15.

more like those of the later eleventh century;[24] and with the general upward dating of Beneventan-script codices by Virginia Brown,[25] it is possible that this manuscript may have been written later than the 1020s.[26]

There is, moreover, the renowned illustrated Vatican codex of the *5L*, Vatican, BAV Vat. lat. 1339. Fornasari's theory that the codex originated at Farfa has recently been bolstered by art historians who have compared the style of the copious illustrations preceding the collection itself to remnants of frescoes at Farfa.[27] As Horst Fuhrmann has suggested, however, the unnumbered quire on which these illustrations appear might not have been made for the present manuscript.[28] They may have been made for another manuscript of the *5L* or a similar compilation. More importantly, it is now the considered opinion of most

---

[24] Loew, *Beneventan Script* 1.211, 213.

[25] This has come about for several reasons. First, it is now known that the script was written well into the sixteenth century rather than ending in the fourteenth, and hence many of the codices that Lowe squeezed into earlier dates to fit his scheme must be dated later (see Virginia Brown, 'A Second New List of Beneventan Manuscripts (II)', *Mediaeval Studies* 50 [1988] 585). Second, Lowe did not take into account the results of musical palaeography, and specialists in Beneventan notation tend to date the codices in that script later than did Lowe. Third, it is clear now that Beneventan script was a very conservative one, in part because it was preeminently a liturgical one (see the review by Roger E. Reynolds of J. Mallet and A. Thibaut, *Les manuscrits en écriture bénéventaine de la Bibliothèque Capitulaire de Bénévent: Tome I, manuscrits 1-18* [Paris 1984] in the *The Journal of Ecclesiastical History* 36 [1985] 487), and hence manuscripts that appear to be early may in fact be later. E.g., it is interesting that Lowe dated to the twelfth century the Caiazzo (now Vatican) manuscript containing the Office of Corpus Christi composed by Thomas Aquinas after 1264; see E. A. Lowe, 'A New List of Beneventan Manuscripts' in *Collectanea vaticana in honorem Anselmi M. Card. Albareda a Bibliotheca Apostolica edita*, 2 vols. (Studi e testi 219-220; Vatican City, 1962), 2.218.

[26] For a more precise date we await the study of Francis Newton on the scribes of Monte Cassino.

[27] Charles B. McClendon, *The Imperial Abbey of Farfa. Architectural Currents of the Early Middle Ages* (Yale Publications in the History of Art 36; New Haven, 1987), pp. 80-82, 164 f., notes 21-23. Despite what he sees as the Farfese connections of the illuminations and frescoes, McClendon notes that Vat. lat. 1339 'seems to have been made for use in the neighboring town of Narni, and it may have been produced at one of Farfa's many dependencies there'. There is the alternative, of course, that the impressive illustrations on the quaternion fols. 7r-14v, bearing no quire number, were executed at Farfa and added to the remainder of the manuscript that was written in or near Narni.

[28] Horst Fuhrmann, 'Eine im Original erhaltene Propagandaschrift des Erzbischofs Gunthar von Köln (865)', *Archiv für Diplomatik* 4 (1958) 32, note 94. It should be added that in the four-bifolia quire containing the illustrations the measurements of the double-column are not quite as wide as they are elsewhere in the manuscript and that the vertical frame is shorter. On the illustrations themselves, see Roger E. Reynolds, 'Rites and Signs of Conciliar Decisions in the Early Middle Ages' in *Segni e riti nella Chiesa altomedievale occidentale* (Settimane di studio del Centro italiano di studi sull'alto medioevo 33; Spoleto, 1987), 215-21, and figs. 8-16. According to *A Catalogue of Canon and Roman Law Manuscripts in the Vatican Library, vol. I, Codices Vaticani latini 541-2299* (compiled under the direction of Stephan Kuttner and Reinhard Elze [Studi e testi 322; Vatican City, 1987], p. 74), drawings of the fallen heretics were added to the conciliar illustrations in the fourteenth century, but an inspection of the codex shows that these were drawn over the faded original drawings of the fallen heretics.

palaeographers that the manuscript was probably written not at Farfa but in or near Narni in typical 'romanesca' script about the middle of the eleventh century.[29] Further, it is also clear that the codex was based on a south Italian Beneventan-script exemplar because it is filled with abbreviations and punctuation marks of that script.[30] Moreover, it is interesting that in the quire with a patristic florilegium preceding the collection itself, there is a text which also appears in a Beneventan-script section of the codex Vallicelliana T. XXI.[31]

The third extant codex of the *5L*, Rome, Biblioteca Vallicelliana B 11, has received the least attention from canonistic scholars, yet it is perhaps the most intriguing of the manuscripts from a palaeographical and codicological standpoint. First, we know exactly where it was written and the name of one of the major scribes. It was written at Sant'Eutizio in Val Castoriana not far from Norcia by Ubertus, a very productive scribe and then abbot of that Benedictine house, whose death is recorded by at least 1087.[32] His promotion from scribe to abbot may explain such features of the manuscript as its incompleteness and the virtual lack of the interlinear glosses that characterize the other codices of the *5L* and its derivatives.[33] Perhaps just as interesting, a close codicological and palaeographical examination suggests that the manuscript may be made up of two codices of the *5L*, the first of which contains fragments of the prefaces and the *capitulatio* for the first book of the collection.[34] This takes on added significance since the earliest

---

[29] Supino Martini, *Roma,* p. 229. Despite this palaeographical evidence, there remains the possibility that a scribe from Narni itself or nearby executed this deluxe codex in or for Farfa itself. (It is interesting that the other two 'complete' extant manuscripts of the *5L* were made for the major Benedictine abbeys of Monte Cassino and Sant'Eutizio in the Val Castoriana.) Later the manuscript might have been taken to Narni where the notations for its provenance of Narni were entered on fols. 1r, 6r, 205v, and 315r.

[30] Reynolds, 'South Italian *Liturgica*', 488, note 25.

[31] fol. 53v; and cf. Vat. lat. 1339, fol. 6r.

[32] Supino Martini, *Roma,* p. 205.

[33] The Vallicelliana manuscript does have some glosses. The prefaces of books 3, 4, and 5, fols. 99r, 154r, and 234r, all have copious glosses; and in the first few canons of book 2, fols. 58r-59r, the scribe has begun to enter glosses like those of the Vatican and Cassino manuscripts. (It is interesting here that the Vallicelliana and Cassino glosses are closer than the Vallicelliana and Vatican glosses.) It almost appears as if the original intention was to gloss the canons, but that the scribe for some reason — loss of interest, other duties, promotion from scribe to abbot, or whatever — failed to complete his task.

[34] The first codex is represented in fols. 1r-3v of the Vallicelliana manuscript. Although Supino Martini (*Roma,* p. 205, note 14) sees the hand of Ubertus, the primary scribe of the remainder of the manuscript, in fols. 1r-3v, the hand appears to be different. Ubertus wrote in a blackish-brown ink and used orange for his rubrics. His letters, bold and large, include a distinctive 3-shaped *z*, a round-bottomed *g*, and a suprascript *s* for the final *s* of a word. But the most distinctive feature of his hand are letters on the bottom lines of folios that Fornasari described as being influenced by charter styles, but that might also be called 'dripping' letters because they descend into the lower margin. The dripping letters themselves are an eccentricity particularly of the scriptorium of S. Eutizio from the second to fourth quarter of the eleventh century (on which see E. B. Garrison, *Studies in*

twelfth-century inventory of books at Sant'Eutizio speaks of a *Liber canonum* and a *Liber alius canonum*.[35] This second reference may, of course, be to one of several

the History of Mediaeval Italian Painting, 4 vols. [Florence, 1953], 2.121 f.), but Ubertus' are especially noticeable because they end in a curve or sickle-shape. The scribe responsible for fols. 1r-3v with the *capitulatio* of book 1 of the *5L* has a distinctive *r-i* ligature very close to that of Ubertus, but he used minuscule, not uncial *d*'s. Nor did he use 'dripping' letters. Further, the ink used is a much lighter brown than that in the major portion of the manuscript (although this, of course, does not in itself indicate a different hand).

As the Vallicelliana manuscript now exists, the first two paper fly-leaves inserted at the Biblioteca Vallicelliana bear the modern title and contents of the manuscript. The title on fol. IIr reads *Collectio canonum in quinque libros divisa sancto Isidoro episc. hispalen. falso tributa cum praefatione eiusdem s. Isidori auctore anonymo graeco-italo noni vel decimi seculi I. C. Qui monachum se prodit in suis praefationibus*; and the monastic reference makes one wonder if this is an allusion to the *frater* of the preface of the collection now cut away from the manuscript. After the two paper leaves, there are three parchment folios with the *capitulatio* of book 1 written by a hand similar to but different from that of Ubertus. The *capitulatio* breaks off with c. 202, not c. 164, as does the Vatican manuscript of the *5L*. Originally the first quire of the Vallicelliana codex consisted not of three parchment folios but of three, or perhaps four, bifolia. What may have been the first of these four bifolia is now a small rectangular piece of parchment attached to what remains of the second bifolium. This bifolium is in turn a very narrow v-shaped strip, the left-hand portion of which is bound around or before the two modern paper folios, and the right-hand portion of which, originally containing the remainder of the *capitulatio* of book 1, is glued to support what is left of the third bifolium. What was the third bifolium is now a single folio, the left-hand portion of which is bound around or before the two paper folia, and the right-hand portion of which is now fol. 3. The fourth or innermost bifolium of the original first quire of the manuscript now makes up fols. 1-2 of the manuscript. What remains of this mutilated first quire of the Vallicelliana manuscript is of special importance for several reasons. On the recto side of the original left-hand section of the second bifolium (i.e., the small v-shaped strip now bound before the two paper leaves and glued as a support for the present fol. 3), there are still visible parts of three large letters. At the top of the thin strip there is an 'I' written on what was probably the first line, corresponding in the *5L* to 'In Christi nomine' or 'Incipit prologus libri canonum' of Fornasari's Prefatio or I. – Praephatio. (F, p. 13). Below this there is the curve of a letter rubricated in orange, probably corresponding to the 'O' of 'Oportuni' (Fornasari's I. – Praephatio; F, p. 13). And two thirds of the way down the strip is a curved part of another rubricated letter, probably corresponding to the 'C' of 'Cernimus' (Fornasari's II. – Praephatio; F, p. 14). Given the length of this preface, it is probable that the text covered the remainder of this folio and the succeeding folio (the left-hand strip of the existing fol. 3, now bound around the two paper leaves), and was then followed on the present fols. 1-3 by the *capitulatio* for book 1 of the collection. The second significant feature of this mutilated first quire is that the numbers assigned to the *capitula* in the *capitulatio* do not correspond to those in book 1 of the collection. They are, in fact, consistently off by one number. Such numerical disparity between canons in *capitulationes* and books of a collection in the early Middle Ages is not at all uncommon. There is, however, another possibility suggested by the fact that the scribe of this first quire appears to have written only this portion of the manuscript; to wit, that this first quire was made for a now lost manuscript of the *5L*, which was perhaps either a model for or a copy of our codex, and was later attached to the remainder of the manuscript written by Ubertus and other scribes. This first quire, written by the different hand, could have been used to replace a worn-out first quire, which probably bore the signature 'i'. (The first signature in the manuscript, 'iii' on fol. 18v, is for the quire fols. 11-18. The signature 'ii' for the quire beginning on fol. 4 would have been on a now missing folio making up a bifolium whose left-hand section is fol. 4 and whose right-hand section consists of two tiny fragments after fol. 10v).

[35] Rome, Biblioteca Vallicelliana T. I, fol. viii' (on which see Pietro Pirri, *L'abbazia di Sant'*

derivative collections of the *5L*, which, as we shall see, were written at Sant'Eutizio. It is also possible that it refers to a second copy of the *5L*, part of which was joined to the section of the manuscript written by Ubertus.

While the south Italian connections of the Monte Cassino and Vatican manuscripts of the *5L* are abundantly clear, traces of these connections also are found in the Sant'Eutizio codex. There are texts in this manuscript that appear in the Monte Cassino codex and not in the Vatican manuscript.[36] Perhaps more importantly, the scribe who added marginalia to the Sant'Eutizio manuscript also used a number of Beneventan conventions.[37]

There is, finally, a fragment of a manuscript, seemingly hitherto unnoticed in the literature on the *5L*, that may be a witness to a lost codex of the collection. This single folio is buried in a volume of Hebrew, Greek, and Latin fragments in Rome, Biblioteca Vallicelliana R 32.[38] The fragment contains not only consecutive canons from the *5L* (1.212-19, 220-24), but also a divisional rubric like one found in the Vallicelliana manuscript of the *5L* (1.213: 'Incipit de iudicio in primis'). Further, it contains virtually all of the interlinear glosses of the Vatican and Monte Cassino manuscripts of the *5L*. Although it may be that this folio comes from a derivative collection of the *5L*, there are several other indicia that suggest a manuscript of the *5L* itself. First, the folio, even though cropped, is a large one,[39] more like the manuscripts of the *5L* than its derivatives, which are often smaller.[40] Secondly, its extensive texts and glosses are virtually identical to those in the extant full manuscripts of the *5L*. Thirdly, this fragment has preserved a divisional rubric characteristic of the complete manuscripts. And fourthly, there are in the cropped margins of the folio traces of chapter numbers which bear a distant resemblance to those of the Vatican manuscript of the *5L*.[41] Although this single folio is written in a central Italian script and has numerous parallels to the complete Vatican and Vallicelliana manuscripts of the *5L*, it also bears traces of south Italian influence.

Eutizio in Val Castoriana presso Norcia e le chiese dipendenti, 2nd edition [Studia Anselmiana 45; Rome, 1960], pp. 347 f.).

[36] E.g., the Vallicelliana and Cassino manuscripts have an additional preface (*De confirmatione*), which Fornasari reported in the former but not in the latter codex (F, pp. 18, 4).

[37] This Carolingian hand has correctly used the Beneventan *ti* ligatures on fols. 21v and 52r (53r). On fol. 60r (61r) there is a marginal entry using normal uncial *a*'s but the Beneventan *e*, correct *ti* ligatures, and unions of *ec* and *en*.

[38] fol. 50 (32u and 52u).

[39] 269 x 190 mm.

[40] The abbreviated derivative of the *5L* in Naples (Biblioteca Nazionale Vittorio Emanuele III, XII A 28), for example, is a mere 195 x 120 mm. (140 x 100 mm.).

[41] E.g., next to the rubric *De personis eligendis ad iudicium* (F, p. 132) there remains an *xx* that is closer to the *cxxviiii* of Vat. lat. 1339, fol. 54r, than the *cxcviiii* in Vallicelliana B 11, fol. 45v; and next to the rubric *De eo quod iudicia* (F, p. 133) there is half an *x* together with *xi*, which is closer to the *cxxx* of Vat. lat. 1339, fol. 54r than the *cc* of the Vallicelliana codex, fol. 45v.

There are Beneventan abbreviations and conventional signs,[42] and the misspelling of several words probably arose from misreadings of a Beneventan-script model with its strangely formed letters and ligatures.[43]

* * *

In the late nineteenth and early twentieth centuries, the origins of the *5L* were established largely according to internal criteria. Gaudenzi, for example, argued for Ravenna on the basis of the canons in the collection attributed to the German emperor, Henry II.[44] Fournier suggested the triangle of Monte Cassino-Benevento-Naples because of its dependency on the *Collection in Nine Books*, generally said to be from the Naples-Benevento area.[45] Fornasari, using palaeographical evidence, then located the origins of the collection in Farfa. Thus far it will have been seen that the palaeographical and codicological evidence strongly suggests Italy south of Rome. It may be that Fournier's points of the triangle have to be changed from Monte Cassino-Benevento-Naples to one encompassing the area south of Rome to Chieti to Monte Cassino, but in any event palaeographical evidence suggests that the origins are to be found in south Italy.

II. DERIVATIVES OF THE *COLLECTION IN FIVE BOOKS*: PAST RESEARCH AND NEW EVIDENCE

For Fournier the surest sign of the importance of the *5L* in the history of canon law was its influence on later collections; and he was able to list over a dozen, each in a single codex.[46] It would be superfluous here to rehearse his descriptions of the

---

[42] E.g., there are such Beneventan-Insular uses as the suprascript ' for a final *s* (see Loew, *Beneventan Script* 1.213) and *f* for *secundum* (see Loew, *Beneventan Script* 1.193). The conventional sign)-(, an Insular abbreviation somewhat like the legal)) of Beneventan script meaning *contra*, is also used, and the scribe has found it necessary to gloss it (cf. Loew, *Beneventan Script* 1.160).

[43] E.g., the text reads *malorum* for *maiorum* probably because the scribe mistook the I-longa of his Beneventan model for an *i*. (see Loew, *Beneventan Script* 1.302, 308 f.). Our text also reads *qui nato modo* rather than *quinto modum*, a mistake that could have arisen from a misreading of a Beneventan model with its union of the letters *nt* (see Loew, *Beneventan Script* 1.139, 149). Also perhaps a model with a Beneventan-Insular sign 7 for *et* (see Loew, *Beneventan Script* 1.180) led the scribe to write such curiosities as *zanimis* for *et animis* or *zalibi* for *et alibi*.

[44] A. Gaudenzi, 'Lo svolgimento parallelo del diritto longobardo e del diritto romano', *Memorie della R. Accademia delle scienze dell'Istituto di Bologna, classe di scienze morali, Sezione giuridica, Ser. I* (1908), 61 f.

[45] Fournier, 'Un groupe', 152, 188.

[46] Paul Fournier's most extensive treatments of these derivatives are found in 'Un groupe', 190-208 and 'De l'influence de la collection irlandaise sur la formation des collections canoniques', *Nouvelle revue historique de droit français et étranger* 23 (1899) 64-71; and Paul Fournier and Gabriel Le Bras, *Histoire des collections canoniques en occident depuis les Fausses Décrétales jusqu'au Décret de Gratien*, 2 vols. (Paris, 1931-32), 1.444-54 and 2.116-27.

borrowings from the *5L* in each derivative, but it is useful to analyze their major structural characteristics and the types of combinations made with material from the *5L* and other collections.

The most easily recognized type of derivative collection is one in which the *5L* is combined with material from Burchard's *Decretum*. This point was noted in the article cited above by Carlo Guido Mor, who stressed that very quickly after the compilation of the *5L*, parts of it were combined with the *Corrector* of Burchard in particular and to a lesser extent with material from other books in the *Decretum*.[47] Mor did not adequately stress, however, the extent of this blending. Of the more than a dozen derivative collections described by Fournier, nine contain extracts from Burchard,[48] and seven of these borrow from the *Corrector*.[49] The *5L* itself had extensive sections dealing with penance, but it appears that the usefulness of the selection of canons in the *Corrector* was seen as superior or more complete than the *5L*, and thus the *Corrector* was used in southern and central Italy to augment the penitential sections of the *5L*.

Another category of derivative collection described by Fournier might be styled as an abbreviated type, and there are two forms of this type. In the first, the number of canons taken from the *5L* is fewer, but they are maintained basically in the sequence followed in the *5L*. Thus, the small codex, Naples, Biblioteca Nazionale Vittorio Emanuele III, XII A 28, is a collection in five books with the number of canons from the *5L* vastly reduced.[50] In the other abbreviated form, the canons are spread over more than five books and are often arranged according to the divisional rubrics in the *5L* itself. For example, the Florentine *Collectio Riccardiana* is a compilation whose seventeen books or parts are divided largely according to the divisional rubrics of the *5L*.[51]

A third category of derivative collection described by Fournier might be called a farraginous type or one in which canons from the *5L* are thrown together helter-skelter or combined with canons from other collections in no discernible order. An example of this would be the south Italian *Collection of Veroli*.[52]

---

[47] Mor, 'La reazione', 202 f.

[48] Florence, Biblioteca Medicea Laurenziana 4, sin. 4; Florence, Biblioteca Riccardiana 300; Monte Cassino, Archivio della Badia 216; Rome, Biblioteca Vallicelliana F 2, F 8, F 92; Vatican, BAV Vat. lat. 3830, 4977, 8487.

[49] Florence, Biblioteca Riccardiana 300; Monte Cassino, Archivio della Badia 216; Rome, Biblioteca Vallicelliana F 2, F 8, F 92; Vatican, BAV Vat. lat. 3830, 4977.

[50] On the size of this codex see above, note 39.

[51] Florence, Biblioteca Riccardiana 300. The seventeen books or parts were so designated in J. Lamius, *Catalogus codicum manuscriptorum qui in Bibliotheca Riccardiana Florentina adservantur* (Livorno, 1756), pp. 129-33, but they are not actually numbered in the manuscript. The canons collected under the divisional rubrics, however, might be styled as books or parts.

[52] Rome, Biblioteca Vallicelliana B 32, especially fols. 154r-158v.

That the influence of the *5L* penetrated even the collections of the Gregorian reform is seen in a fourth type of compilation. In the small codex, Rome, Biblioteca Vállicelliana F 54, the *Collection in 74 Titles* is augmented by a vast florilegium of patristic texts and canons from the *5L*, the latter largely from the 'penitential' books of the *5L*.[53]

Finally, among the derivative collections described by Fournier, it is noteworthy that three are associated with liturgical material. Thus, the *Collectio Riccardiana* has an *ordo missae*,[54] the *Collection of Vallicelliana F 2* an *expositio missae*,[55] and the *Collection of Vallicelliana E 62* a missal-ritual combined with extracts from book 5 of the *5L*.[56]

In his major study of these derivative collections, Fournier stressed that they all had their origins in the area from Umbria southward to Naples.[57] Later, however, he pointed to what he thought was the influence of the *5L* in the north of Italy, specifically in the *Collectio Veronensis*.[58] Peter Landau has more recently demonstrated that the *5L* was not used in this collection,[59] but the influence of the collection may have reached northern Italy inasmuch as Giorgio Picasso's *Collectio Ambrosiana II* contains several concordances of canons also found in the *5L*.[60]

In concluding his major study of the derivatives of the *5L* Fournier acknowledged that his enumeration was far from complete and invited further investigation.[61] Indeed, more recent discoveries have virtually doubled Fournier's number of derivative collections. The types of these additional collections also resemble those Fournier has described.

The combination of the *5L* and Burchard's *Decretum*, especially the *Corrector*, is represented in the small *Collectio Toletana*, edited recently by John Douglas Adamson.[62] This manuscript was long classified in Toledo simply as a theological one, but it was Antonio García y García who noted its canonistic character,

---

[53] fols. 67r-169v.

[54] On the *ordo missae* in the Riccardiana codex, see Adalbert Ebner, *Quellen und Forschungen zur Geschichte und Kunstgeschichte des Missale Romanum im Mittelalter: Iter Italicum* (Freiburg i. Br., 1896), pp. 300-302.

[55] fols. 101v-102v; and cf. Fournier, 'Un groupe', 198.

[56] See Fournier, 'Un groupe', 199.

[57] Fournier, 'Un groupe', 209.

[58] Verona, Biblioteca Capitolare LXIV (62); and see Fournier and Le Bras, *Histoire* 2.117 f.

[59] 'Die *Collectio Veronensis*', *Zeitschrift der Savigny-Stiftung für Rechtsgeschichte*, kan. Abt. 67 (1981) 85 f.

[60] *Collezioni canoniche milanesi del secolo xii* (Pubblicazioni dell'Università Cattolica del S. Cuore, Saggi e ricerche, 3rd Ser., Scienze storiche 2; Milan, 1969), pp. 32, 95, 110, 112 f., 115, 117 f., 122, 140 f.

[61] Fournier, 'Un groupe', 209.

[62] Toledo, Biblioteca Capitular 22-32, now edited by John Douglas Adamson, *The Collectio Toletana* (M.S.L. Report; Toronto, 1987).

especially the Burchardian material.[63] Much more numerous are the canons borrowed from the *5L*, 232 out of 376, the majority from books 4 and 5.

Two newly identified collections are examples of the two sub-forms of the abbreviated derivatives of the *5L*. First the manuscript of the *Collection of Rieti*[64] is mutilated at the beginning and the end, but what remains — extracts from books 3 and 4 of the *5L* — tends to indicate that this collection largely followed the arrangement of the *5L* itself. The other new collection, the Roman *Collectio Angelica*,[65] is also mutilated at beginning and end, but it contained at least thirteen books. The canons are generally presented in the order in which they are found in the *5L*, but occasionally the compiler has reordered them, often according to their divisional rubrics in the *5L*. Perhaps the most striking thing about the canons drawn from the *5L* in this collection, however, is that at times their readings and inscriptions follow none of the extant manuscripts of the *5L*. For example, a canon attributed to the German emperor, Henry II, in the extant manuscripts of the *5L* is attributed in the *Collectio Angelica* to Charlemagne and contains a text longer than the one presently known.[66] Moreover, added to the famous canon of Henry II on shipwrecks is a further canon attributed to the emperor that does not appear in any of the extant manuscripts of the *5L*.[67]

The third type of derivative collection, the farraginous variety, is represented in yet another section of Vallicelliana T. XXI, this time apparently connected with Sant'Eutizio.[68] In this derivative the excerptor skips freely about the *5L* for his

---

[63] Antonio García y García, 'Canonistica Hispanica (II)', *Traditio* 23 (1967) 504 f.

[64] Rieti, Archivio Capitolare 5, on which see Roger E. Reynolds, 'Basil and the Early Medieval Latin Canonical Collections' in *Basil of Caesarea: Christian, Humanist, Ascetic. A Sixteen-Hundredth Anniversary Symposium*, ed. Paul Jonathan Fedwick (Toronto, 1981), 528.

[65] Rome, Biblioteca Angelica 1447.

[66] Rome, Biblioteca Angelica 1447, p. 94: 'De eo qui pignus auri vel argenti vel domum acceperit de ornamentis ecclesiae. Karolus Rex'; cf. *5L* 4.283; ed. Ludwig Weiland, *MGH Constitutiones et acta publica imperatorum et regum* 1 (Hanover, 1893), p. 62, taken from Vat. lat. 1339, fol. 216; 4.283.

[67] Rome, Biblioteca Angelica 1447, pp. 202-203. There is first the canon 'Siquis de naufragio post evasionem maris. Ex iudicio Enrici regis cxxvi' (= *5L* 3.211: F, pp. 412 f.), after which comes 'cxxvii. De incendiis domorum. Idem ipse Enricus, Unde supra. Simili damnatione constringantur ... maneat innodatum'.

[68] fols. 284r-302v. Supino Martini (*Roma*, pp. 305 f.) designates this section of the manuscript among her 'MSS non localizzati', although she notes similarities with manuscripts and texts from Sant'Eutizio. Among the more important palaeographical features common to this manuscript and those of Sant'Eutizio are the 'dripping letters'. In T. XXI these are not of the type used in Vallicelliana B 11 and its close associates, but more like those of Rome, Biblioteca Vallicelliana B 4 and C 10, pt. 2, fols. 139r-279v, both manuscripts from Sant'Eutizio and dating to the end of the eleventh century. In these manuscripts the dripping letters end not with the sickle-shaped curve, but with a graceful sinuous flourish, which at times loops over itself. Beyond the palaeographical features, there is also internal evidence in the texts of the quires containing our excerptum that links them to Sant'Eutizio or perhaps one of her dependencies. The quires contain both the canonical excerptum, beginning in the middle of the second quire (fol. 284r) and running to the end of the fourth quire (fol. 302v), and what the modern catalogue calls 'litanies', running from fol. 271r to 283v. Actually

sources: a few from book 1, several from book 3, back to book 1, then book 4, and so forth. In most cases the number of canons from the *5L* does not extend beyond three or four in sequence. Whether the excerptor depended on a manuscript of the *5L* itself or another farraginous collection of canons is not clear. In any case, the variants are similar to those of the extant Vallicelliana manuscript of the *5L* from Sant'Eutizio, although glosses, different inscriptions, and canons not found in this latter codex indicate that it could not have been the direct source.

Related to this farraginous collection in Vallicelliana T. XXI are two small farraginous excerpta in yet another manuscript written at Sant'Eutizio, Rome, Biblioteca Vallicelliana B 63.[69] In one section of the codex a scribe has entered a number of canons from book 3 of the *5L*.[70] In another section a different scribe has copied yet another section from book 3 as well as a number of glosses apparently drawn from canons in book 5 of the *5L*.[71] In the canons from book 3 a recension of the *5L* like the extant Sant'Eutizio codex was used, but the glosses could not have been borrowed from that source.

Perhaps most surprising among the newly identified derivatives of the *5L* is the number involving combinations of extracts from the *5L* and the *Collection in 74 Titles*. Fournier identified only one manuscript of this type of combination,[72] but to this four more can be added.[73] In three cases canons from the *5L* have simply

these 'litanies' are an abbreviated martyrology, and it is in their contents that the connections of the quires with Sant'Eutizio are clear. In this martyrology the scribe has capitalized a number of his entries or has underlined them in yellow. Among these are Eutizio (with yellow underlining; added later in a small hand; fol. 276r) and a number of feasts of Spoleto (capitalized; fol. 283v), in whose diocese Sant'Eutizio lay. Also on fol. 283r, a scribe has added in large black letters the name of 'Thomas Abbot' (of Farfa, *c*. 680-720), who was venerated at Sant'Eutizio. Garrison (*Studies* 2.124 and 4.165 f., 218, 237, 251) has pointed out that such entries as these can be found in a number of central Italian liturgical books not originating at Sant'Eutizio. But the case for an origin at Sant'Eutizio is strengthened if our martyrology in T. XXI is compared with a longer one in Rome, Biblioteca Vallicelliana E 59, whose contents Pirri (*L'abbazia*, pp. 359 f.) has described among his manuscripts from Sant'Eutizio and where the dedication of the basilica of Sant'Eutizio is noted in large rubricated letters on fol. 59v. In Vallicelliana E 59, the hand is not far removed from those at Sant'Eutizio at the end of the eleventh century, and as in our quires of T. XXI, there is the suprascript *s* for the final *s* and dripping letters occasionally with a 'flaming letter' rising into the upper margin (see Garrison, *Studies* 2.122). If the long martyrology of Vallicelliana E 59 is compared with the shorter one in our T. XXI, there are a few differences, but the correspondences are even more striking. Among these are the names of Eutizio, which is both capitalized and rubricated, and Thomas Abbot, whose *depositio* is placed on 10 December. Also there are the Spoleto entries in both martyrologies.

    [69] Supino Martini, *Roma*, pp. 201-223.
    [70] fol. 218r-v.
    [71] fol. 217r-v. These were written by the same hand that was responsible for additions on fols. 218v-219r.
    [72] Rome, Biblioteca Vallicelliana F 54 (see Fournier, 'Un groupe', 191 f.).
    [73] El Escorial, Real Biblioteca de San Lorenzo Z.III.19, fols. 79v-116r; Monte Cassino, Archivio della Badia 522, pp. 179-95; Rome, Biblioteca Angelica 1447, pp. 210-12; and Rome, Biblioteca Casanatense 2010, fols. 142v-172r.

been included in florilegia of patristic canons appended to manuscripts used by John T. Gilchrist for his edition of the *Collection in 74 Titles*,[74] with perhaps a recognition that the *74 Titles* was too narrow in its scope and had to be augmented with canons from an older source. In the other case, the *Collectio Angelica* just described, canons from the *74 Titles* have been appended to a derivative of the *5L*,[75] this time perhaps a recognition that the older *5L* was too narrow and had to be updated with new material from a Gregorian reform collection.

The combination of canons from the *5L* with liturgical material is also represented in the recently identified derivatives. In one case, canons from book 1 of the *5L* have been combined to form an ordination allocution that is inserted into a Pontifical of Chieti, Vatican City, BAV Vat. lat. 7818.[76] And in this connection, it should be remembered that Theobald, who was abbot of San Liberatore near Chieti, may have had a *Liber canonum* made in his monastery there before the *Liber canonum* he had made later for his abbey of Monte Cassino. In another case, canons from the *5L* have been used with large numbers of liturgical expositions and theological and patristic texts to form a *Liber multiloquiorum in Seven Books*, written perhaps in or near Farfa or a Farfese dependency.[77]

Just as significant as the large number of derivatives of the *5L*, both those described by Fournier and those more recently identified, are their origins and connections with the extant manuscripts of the *5L*. Fournier stressed that those he knew originated largely from Umbria southward to Naples; but he failed to emphasize fully the extent of their connections with south Italy. Of the manuscripts known to him, Fournier noted only one as being written in Beneventan script.[78] In reality six of his are written in this script.[79] The Neapolitan abbreviated derivative, moreover, is filled with Beneventan-script symptoms, and the *Collection of Vat. lat. 3830*, despite its having been written in north central Italy, contains a number of texts from the southern part of the peninsula.[80] When we turn to our recently identified derivatives, the connections with southern Italy continue to be striking. Four of the manuscripts, in whole or in part, were written in Beneventan

---

[74] The three manuscripts cited in note 73, with the exception of Biblioteca Angelica 1447. See *Diversorum patrum sententie sive Collectio in LXXIV titulos digesta* ed. John T. Gilchrist (Monumenta iuris canonici, Ser. B, Corpus collectionum 1; Vatican City, 1973), pp. xxxii-xxxiv, xliii f., xlvi f.

[75] These correspond to *74T* 1.1-11; Gilchrist, *Diversorum patrum*, pp. 19-25.

[76] For an edition and study of this allocution in Vatican, BAV Vat. lat. 7818, see Roger E. Reynolds, 'A South Italian Ordination Allocution', *Mediaeval Studies* 47 (1985) 438-44.

[77] On the *Liber multiloquiorum* see Reynolds, 'A South Italian Liturgico-Canonical Mass Commentary', 662.

[78] Rome, Biblioteca Vallicelliana F 54 (cf. Fournier, 'Un groupe', 191).

[79] Madrid, Biblioteca Nacional 373; Monte Cassino, Archivio della Badia 216; Rome, Biblioteca Vallicelliana B 32, F 2, F 8, F 54.

[80] Cf. Supino Martini, *Roma*, pp. 315 f. and Stephan Kuttner, 'The Council of Carthage 535: A Supplementary Note', *Zeitschrift der Savigny-Stiftung für Rechtsgeschichte, kan. Abt.* 73 (1987) 347, note 6.

script,[81] while an additional two have Beneventan-script symptoms.[82] In short, over half of the twenty-five derivatives identified thus far were written in the south Italian Beneventan script or contain symptoms thereof.

Connections with the abbey of Sant'Eutizio and the region around Farfa, which both produced extant manuscripts of the *5L*, are also strong in the derivatives. Fournier knew that one of his derivatives came from each of these locations.[83] Of the recently identified derivatives, two came from or were associated with Sant'-Eutizio while one originated in Farfa or the vicinity.[84]

III. THE CHARACTER OF THE *COLLECTION IN FIVE BOOKS* AND ITS DERIVATIVES

As with most collections compiled in the eleventh century, the *5L* has traditionally been understood primarily in relation to the so-called Gregorian reforms. As such, it has been styled a reforming collection before the reform, a collection with many of the same aims as the *Decretum* of Burchard but distinctively Italian in character. Without disputing this traditional view, this article will conclude by suggesting several other possible characterizations of the collection and its derivatives in light of more recent scholarship.

First, it must be stressed that the formats of the three extant manuscripts of the collection suggest that from the beginning the *5L* was acknowledged to be in the process of growth, with augmentation possible. In the Vallicelliana manuscript, for example, spaces have been left at various points, where later hands have at times added canons and texts of various types.[85] The scribe of the Vatican manuscript systematically left blank spaces after divisions of canons almost as an invitation for further additions.[86] Second, while it is undeniable that the *5L* is preeminently a collection of canons, it can also be regarded as another type of textual florilegium, particularly of patristic texts. In part, this came about because one of the ultimate sources of the collection, the Irish *Collectio canonum hibernensis*, was itself filled with extracts from the patristic fathers, and these were incorporated into the *5L*.

---

[81] El Escorial, Real Biblioteca de San Lorenzo Z.III.19; Monte Cassino, Archivio della Badia 522; Rieti, Archivio Capitolare 5; and Vatican, BAV Vat. lat. 7818.

[82] Toledo, Bibioteca Capitular 22-32 and Vatican, BAV Vat. lat. 4317.

[83] Rome, Biblioteca Vallicelliana F 92, and Vatican, BAV Vat. lat. 8487; Fournier, 'Un groupe', 195, 204.

[84] Rome, Biblioteca Vallicelliana B 63, and T. XXI and Vatican, BAV Vat. lat. 4317.

[85] Blank spaces are found on fols. 12r-v, 56v-57v, 75r-v, 99r-v, 104v, 153v, 162r-v, 188v-189r, 189r, 192r, 233v, 235r-v. It could, of course, have been that the scribe was simply reproducing the blank spaces of the archetype.

[86] fols. 25v, 40r, 52r, 69r, 104r-105r, 108r, 113r, 113v, 129v, 141v, 143r, 144v, 151v, 157r, 160v, 177r, 184r, 189r, 195v, 201v, 207v, 208r, 210v, 212r, 214v, 221r, 223r, 224r, 241r, 243v, 250v, 253r, 275v, 297v, 301r, 302v, 304v, 305r, 309r.

The compilers of the *5L* also included many additional patristic texts, both authentic and pseudonymous, which were circulating in southern Italy. Thus, we find in the *5L* texts attributed to John of Constantinople,[87] Basil,[88] the desert fathers,[89] Jerome and Damasus,[90] and so forth.

Because the *5L* was regarded as a patristic florilegium, it attracted to itself further patristic texts. Thus, the Vatican manuscript of the *5L* has substantial sections of patristic florilegia, largely of a non-canonical nature, added before the collection.[91] And Paola Supino Martini has recently suggested on palaeographical and codicological grounds that an additional quire with these patristic texts was made specifically to be added to the *5L* in that manuscript.[92]

The *5L* was regarded also as a florilegium of liturgical texts, and in several instances liturgical canons which are only tangentially disciplinary were used within the collection.[93] As in the case of the patristic florilegia, so the *5L* attracted liturgical texts to itself. Thus, at the conclusion of the Vatican manuscript of the *5L* a penitential *ordo* and an excerpt from a sacramentary have been added[94] — again on folios made specifically to go with the rest of the manuscript.[95] Attached to the Casanatense codex of the *74 Titles* and excerpta from the *5L*, moreover, is the Mass exposition *Dominus vobiscum* attributed to Isidore or Alcuin.[96]

That the *5L* was regarded in its own day as a rich patristic and liturgical florilegium is indicated by its use in the derivative collections. We have seen, for example, how canons from the *5L* were mixed with patristic texts and added to manuscripts such as those containing the *Collection in 74 Titles*.[97] Derivatives of the *5L* had various liturgical *ordines* added to them[98] or used liturgical texts from the *5L* itself to supplement such vast liturgical florilegia as the Farfese *Liber multiloquiorum*.[99]

---

[87] See, e.g., *5L* 5.149 (Vat. lat. 1339, fol. 289v); 5.155.2 (Vat. lat. 1339, fol. 290v); 5.156 (Vat. lat. 1339, fol. 291r); 5.158 (Vat. lat. 1339, fol. 291r); and 5.160 (Vat. lat. 1339, fol. 291v).

[88] On which see Reynolds, 'Basil', 527.

[89] E.g., *5L* 3.272 (F, pp. 448 f.).

[90] See Reynolds, 'A South Italian Liturgico-Canonical Mass Commentary'.

[91] fols. 1r-6v.

[92] Supino Martini, *Roma*, p. 228.

[93] E.g., the pseudonymous correspondence between Damasus and Jerome and the accompanying Mass commentary as cited above in note 90.

[94] fols. 311r-317v, on which see *A Catalogue of Canon and Roman Law Manuscripts in the Vatican Library, vol. I*, p. 73.

[95] Supino Martini, *Roma*, p. 228.

[96] Roger E. Reynolds, 'Pseudonymous Liturgica in Early Medieval Canon Law Collections' in *Fälschungen im Mittelalter. Internationaler Kongress der Monumenta Germaniae Historica, München, 16.-19. September 1986. Teil II. Gefälschte Rechtstexte. Der bestrafte Fälscher* (MGH Schriften 33.2; Hanover, 1988), p. 71, note 37.

[97] See above, note 74.

[98] See above, notes 54 f.

[99] See above, note 77.

In recent important articles, Theo Kölzer suggested that canonical collections compiled before and during the period of the Gregorian reform should be examined for their monastic character;[100] and certainly this is appropriate for the *5L*, which in several senses may be considered a monastic collection. First, it has been shown that at least two of the extant manuscripts of the collection were produced in monasteries. These derivative collections compiled in monasteries suggest that there were other copies of the *5L*, now lost, that were monastic in origin. Simply because a collection was copied or kept in a monastic setting, however, does not *ipso facto* make it monastic. Rather, the contents must display at least a modicum of interest in specifically monastic questions. While not overwhelmingly monastically oriented, there are sections of the *5L* devoted to religious men and women,[101] thereby suggesting that it could be intended to be used in a monastic setting. In recent literature a great deal has been made of the Ps.-Bonifatian (JE +1996) and Ps.-Gregorian (JE +1366, +1951) canons regarding the privileges of monks as demonstrating monastic dispositions of a collection or manuscript.[102] Indeed, the Vallicelliana manuscript of the *5L* from Sant'Eutizio does contain the Ps.-Bonifatian canon.[103] Further, the derivative collections frequently have these canons.[104] Beyond these, one of the derivatives, the *Collection of Vallicelliana F 2*, contains a canon on the election of an abbot,[105] and the *Collectio Toletana* includes a canon originally directed to clerics but altered so as to pertain to monks.[106]

There is a final characteristic of the *5L* which is clear in its preface and in the ways it was used in the derivative collections, but has perhaps been obscured by the edition of only the first three books by Fornasari. That is, the *5L* is highly penitential in nature. It was written, according to the preface, for the remedy of a

---

[100] Theo Kölzer, 'Die Farfenser Kanonessammlung des Cod. Vat. lat. 8487 (Collectio Farfensis)', *Bulletin of Medieval Canon Law* N.S. 7 (1977) 97; and 'Mönchtum und Kirchenrecht. Bemerkungen zu monastischen Kanonessammlungen der vorgratianischen Zeit', *Zeitschrift der Savigny-Stiftung für Rechtsgeschichte, kan. Abt.* 69 (1983) 121-42. Also see Giorgio Picasso, '"Sacri canones et monastica regula" nella cultura del monachesimo subalpino (sec. XI)' in *Dal Piemonte all'Europa: Esperienze monastiche nella società medievale (Relazioni e comunicazioni presentate al XXXIV Congresso storico subalpino, Torino, 27-29 maggio 1985)* (Turin, 1988), pp. 199-211.

[101] E.g., 2.107-202; F, pp. 253-95.

[102] E.g., Kölzer, *Collectio canonum*, p. 54; and John Gilchrist, 'The Influence of the Monastic Forgeries attributed to Pope Gregory I (JE +1951) and Boniface IV (JE +1996)' in *Fälschungen im Mittelalter*, pp. 263-87.

[103] fol. 162r-v.

[104] E.g., El Escorial, Real Biblioteca de San Lorenzo Z.III.19, fols. 10v-11r (JE + 1366), 111r-112r (JE + 1996); Monte Cassino, Archivio della Badia 216, pp. 173-178 (JE + 1366), 181-183 (JE + 1996); Rome, Biblioteca Casanatense 2010, fols. 187v-188v (JE + 1996); Rome, Biblioteca Vallicelliana F 92, fols. 192v-193v (JE + 1996).

[105] fol. 92r.

[106] Cap. 144; on which see Adamson, *Collectio Toletana*, p. 7.

diversity of sins,[107] and books 4 and 5 are heavily penitential in nature. Contemporaries quickly discovered this and drew heavily from these books, combining them often with the *Corrector* of Burchard.[108]

* * *

In sum, our vade-mecum of south and central Italy in the eleventh century was many things to many people — to canonists, compilers of patristic florilegia, liturgists, monks, and confessors. Although full copies of the *5L* itself are rare, its importance and richness are reflected in its many and diverse derivatives.

---

[107] This was stressed by Fournier ('Un groupe', 166).
[108] See above, notes 49 and 62.

XV

SOUTH ITALIAN *LITURGICA* AND *CANONISTICA* IN CATALONIA (NEW YORK, HISPANIC SOCIETY OF AMERICA MS. HC 380/819)*

FOR the past few years a remarkable codex in the library of the Hispanic Society of America in Manhattan has caught the attention of medievalists in a variety of fields. Written in the eleventh century and kept at least into the last century at Santa María del Estany, a house of canons regular southwest of Vic noted for its Romanesque cloister, the codex was briefly described there by Jaime Villaneuva.[1] By the first decade of this century the manuscript had found its way to the Leipzig antiquarian Karl W. Hiersemann,[2] from whom it was acquired by the Hispanic Society of America and given its present shelf mark.

Recently the contents of MS. HC 380/819 were catalogued by Charles B. Faulhaber,[3] and since then several items in the codex have attracted scholars. The text of the Council of Troyes (878) has been the special concern of Hubert Mordek, who, shortly before the appearance of Faulhaber's catalogue, had published an edition of the text of that council but without benefit of the Hispanic Society witness.[4] Peter Brommer noted several of his Carolingian *capitula episcoporum* in this manuscript, dated it to the beginning of the twelfth century, and located its *Schriftheimat* perhaps in England.[5] For its *ordo canonicorum* Luc

* I am grateful to the Trustees of the Hispanic Society of America for permission to publish material from this manuscript, whose existence was kindly brought to my attention a decade ago by J. N. Hillgarth, my colleague and member of the Society.

[1] *Viage literario a las iglesias de España*, vol. 7: *Viage a la iglesia de Vique año 1806* (Valencia, 1821), pp. 234-36.

[2] See Roger E. Reynolds, 'The Ordination Rite in Medieval Spain: Hispanic, Roman, and Hybrid' in *Santiago, Saint-Denis, and Saint Peter: The Reception of the Roman Liturgy in León-Castile in 1080*, ed. Bernard F. Reilly (New York, 1985), p. 150 n. 34.

[3] *Medieval Manuscripts in the Library of the Hispanic Society of America: Religious, Legal, Scientific, Historical, and Literary Manuscripts*, 2 vols. (New York, 1983), 1.8 f., 19 f., 23 f., 38 f., 79, 87, 119-21, 131-34, 138-41 and 2, pls. 1 and 2.

[4] Hubert Mordek and Gerhard Schmitz, 'Papst Johannes VIII. und das Konzil von Troyes (878)' in *Geschichtsschreibung und geistiges Leben im Mittelalter: Festschrift für Heinz Löwe zum 65. Geburtstag*, ed. Karl Hauck and Hubert Mordek (Cologne-Vienna, 1978), pp. 179-225.

[5] *Capitula episcoporum*, ed. Peter Brommer (MGH *Leges, capitula episcoporum* 1; Munich, 1984), especially p. 86.

Reprinted from *Mediaeval Studies*, 49 (1987), pp. 480-495, by permission of the publisher. © 1987 by the Pontifical Institute of Mediaeval Studies, Toronto

Jocqué of the Corpus Christianorum has begun a study of the last folios of the manuscript (which may not originally have been a part of it). Miquel dels Sants Gros Pujol, director of the Museu Episcopal in Vic, has been concerned with the place of the codex in the history of his diocese.

Other parts of the manuscript, particularly the texts regarding Hilary of Poitiers,[6] deserve the attention of scholars, but there is one section that should be of special interest to students of south Italian texts. This part (fols. 106r-109v) may well have included the first item of what Villanueva, on his visit to Santa María del Estany, described as 'Fragmentos de consueta antigua de este monasterio'[7]—a reference noted by Charles Dereine in his catalogue of rules of canons regular in Spain.[8] Written by a scribe Faulhaber designates as Hand A, the four leaves follow the texts on Hilary of Poitiers and precede the *ordo canonicorum*. In his description Faulhaber specified only four texts in this section, and for only one did he provide parallel texts or sources.[9] There are, however, seven distinct liturgical and canonical pieces, of which several are closely related to texts used in southern Italy and written in Beneventan script. These seven texts will be discussed and edited below, where the orthography of the manuscript will be maintained and modern punctuation and paragraphs will be introduced. The use of (*sic*) denotes erroneous or difficult readings.

I

The first text deals with the liturgical season of Septuagesima, the rationale for the word, and its origins. That this was a topic of concern as early as the ninth and tenth centuries where Beneventan was written is illustrated by the renowned Monte Cassino calendric and computistic manuscript, whose provenance is Benevento itself, namely, Rome, Biblioteca Casanatense 641.[10] On fol. 82r of this tenth-century codex, there is a text on Septuagesima entitled *Ratio Septuagesimae et Sexagesimae et Quinquagesimae et Quadragesimae* which incorporates a snippet of Alcuin's well-known *Epistula* 143 on Septuagesima[11] and is followed on fols.

---

[6] It may be of significance that east of Santa María del Estany and southeast of Vic there is still the medieval town of Sant Hilari Sacalm, which bears the name of the Poitevin saint; see Paul H. Freedman, *The Diocese of Vic: Tradition and Regeneration in Medieval Catalonia* (New Brunswick, N. J., 1983), p. 5.

[7] Villaneuva, *Viage literario*, p. 236.

[8] 'Coutumiers et ordinaires de chanoines réguliers', *Scriptorium* 5 (1951) 109, item 12.

[9] *Medieval Manuscripts* 1.141, item 138, citing the Ordinal of Christ and material provided by the author of the present article, who also provided bibliographical information for item 137.

[10] On this codex see E. A. Loew, *The Beneventan Script. A History of the South Italian Minuscule*, 2 vols., 2nd edition prepared by Virginia Brown (Sussidi eruditi 33-34; Rome, 1980), 2.122.

[11] MGH *Epp.* 4 (Berlin, 1895), pp. 224-27.

82v-83v by Charlemagne's letter to Alcuin on the matter.[12] Another tract on Septuagesima written in Beneventan script has now been discovered at Altamura by Thomas Forrest Kelly and is published on pp. 466-71 above by Herman F. Holbrook.[13] It is a version of this tract which is also found in the Catalan manuscript.

*   If the Altamura and Catalan versions are compared, several differences emerge. First, the Catalan text is divided into three sections by rubrics. The first part, like the Altamura version, discusses why the term Septuagesima signifies not seven weeks or seventy days but sixty-four days (ll. 1-5). While the Altamura text with its corrupt listing of numbers is beyond meaning, the Catalan version is comprehensible. Septuagesima is comprised of sixty-four days because, if the number one is doubled seven times, the total is sixty-four (the number of days from Septuagesima Sunday through Easter Sunday); moreover, if one looks to the seven groupings of this larger number, the reason for the term Septuagesima is clear. The second portion of the Catalan text (ll. 6-33), entitled *Alia ratio Septuagesimae*, is basically like that of the Altamura version, but it has been abbreviated slightly by the omission of the difficult passage before the historical explanation of the origins of the pre-Lenten weeks. Prefaced also by *Alia ratio*, the third section in the Catalan text (ll. 34-37) explains that there are nine weeks of seven days from Septuagesima to Easter ($9 \times 7 = 63$ days), and it is because each week of that period consists of seven days that Septuagesima is so called.

(f. 106r)   QUARE DICTA SIT SEPTUAGESIMA

Septuagesima namque non pro septem ebdomadibus vel pro septuaginta diebus dicitur sed pro septem terminis numerorum, id est, i, ii, iiii, viii, xvi, xxxii, lxiiii, et sic colliguntur ut ebdomadae non in summulis sed summule dispertiantur in ebdomadibus per arbitrium
5 dierum qui lxiiii sunt usque in Pascha.

ALIA RATIO SEPTUAGESIMAE

Solet quaeri a nonnullis cur Septuagesima, Sexagesima, Quinquagesima, seu Quadragesima in sacris codicibus certis nominibus pretitulentur. De quibus certa ratio haec est. Cunctis namque legentibus liquet universum orbem quattuor aecclesiarum ordinibus esse
10 distributum, videlicet Romanorum, Alexandrinorum, Iherosolimorum, et Antiocenorum; quae generaliter uno vocabulo sancta aecclesia catholica nuncupantur. Hae namque singulae aecclesiae cum unam teneant catholicam fidem diversis utuntur officiorum ieiuniorumque moribus. Unde fit ut Iherosolimorum aecclesia inchoet ieiunium a Septuagesima usque in Pascha, sublatis tribus diebus de unaquaque ebdomada, id est, primo die dominico

---

[12] *Ep.* 144 (MGH *Epp.* 4.228-30, from this codex).
[13] Altamura, Archivio Capitolare, Copertina del registro di amministrazione S. N. for 1563-64.

15 et quinta feria et sabbato. (f. 106v) Alexandrinorum vero aecclesia inchoat ieiunium a
    Sexagesima usque in Pascha auferentes (sic) de singulis ebdomadibus diem dominicum et
    quintam feriam. Antiocena quoque aecclesia inchoat ieiunium a Quinquagesima consum-
    matque in Pascha, subtrahens de unaquaque ebdomada diem dominicum sicuti facit et
    Romana aecclesia quae a Quadragesima inchoare ieiunium consuevit. Quanquam hoc
20 tempore variis utentes doctrinis singulae provinciae et regiones diversos sibi mores
    usurpent prout quemque voluntas duxerit. Una enim est aecclesia sed diversae consuetudi-
    nes. Dierum vero quos auferunt de ieiunio ista est ratio. Diem dominicum pro eo quod ipso
    die conditus est mundus et ipso die resurrectio Domini nostri Iesu Christi celebratur, et
    ipso die est annunciatus Salvator noster ab angelo virgini Mariae. Quintam feriam
25 propterea quia in ipso die lavit Dominus noster pedes discipulorum suorum et tradidit
    corpus et sanguinem suum discipulis, et in ipso die conficitur chrisma, et in ipso die
    Salvator noster ascendit ad caelos. Sabbatum propter venerationem aeternae quietis quae
    promissa est sanctis in caelesti Iherusalem. Cum vero unum sit ieiunii tempus, quatuor
    illud vocabulis distinguendis providit antiquitas iuxta mores quattuor aecclesiarum me-
30 moratarum, id est, Septuagesima, Sexagesima, Quinquagesima, Quadragesima. Pro Ihero-
    solimorum aecclesia accepit vocabulum Septuagesima, similiter pro Alexandrinorum
    aecclesia Sexagesima, necnon et pro Antiocena aecclesia Quinquagesima, et pro Romana
    aecclesia vocavit antiquitas Quadragesima.

ALIA RATIO

35 Septuagesima dicta novem per septem quia a Septuagesima usque in Pascha novem
    ebdomadae sunt, et per unamquamque ebdomadam sunt septem dies; pro hoc est dicta
    Septuagesima.

II

The second text in MS. HC 380/819, a long and fanciful commentary on the
Mass whose origins go back to the early Carolingian period, was developed and
widely diffused in southern Italian manuscripts from the tenth to the twelfth
century. It begins with a pseudonymous correspondence between Pope Damasus
and Jerome dealing with the time Mass should be celebrated, into which a
pseudo-canon from the first Council of Nicea has been incorporated. This
pseudonymous correspondence can be found as early as the ninth century in canon
law and liturgical manuscripts. By the tenth century the correspondence had been
augmented in southern Italy with explanations of practices in the celebration of the
Mass, and by at least the tenth and eleventh centuries the augmented tract had
found its way into the south Italian canonical Collection in Nine Books[14] and
Collection in Five Books;[15] the eleventh-century copies of both works are written

---

[14] Vatican City, Biblioteca Apostolica Vaticana Vat. lat. 1349, fols. 81r-82v. On this codex see
Roger E. Reynolds, 'A South Italian Ordination Allocution', Mediaeval Studies 47 (1985) 441.
[15] On this collection and some of its sources and derivatives, see Roger E. Reynolds, 'Law,
Canon: to Gratian' in Dictionary of the Middle Ages 7 (New York, 1986), pp. 406-409.

in Beneventan script or have Beneventan-script symptoms.[16] The *Collection in Five Books*, as it became the canonical vademecum for clerics and monks in southern and central Italy in the eleventh century,[17] was the vehicle for the wide diffusion of our tract on the Mass. There are at least ten distinct versions of the text, and it can be found in at least thirty-three manuscripts, fifteen of which are either written in Beneventan script or have Beneventan-script symptoms.[18]

At first the appearance of this south Italian tract in a Catalan manuscript might seem curious, but it should be noted that two other versions of the text can be found in Catalan manuscripts of the twelfth century. A short form with the pseudonymous correspondence between Damasus and Jerome expanded only slightly is entered in the so-called *Pontifical of San Ramón* (Tarragona, Biblioteca Provincial 26, fol. 224r), a manuscript containing the canonical *Liber Tarraconensis* and a south Italian pontifical text.[19] A long version, but one quite unlike that in the Hispanic Society manuscript, appears in Tortosa, Biblioteca Capitular 122, fols. 42v-43v. This latter codex is important not only for the Mass commentary but also for the fact that its texts in Carolingian script are written over texts in Beneventan that have been erased.[20] In other words, the Tortosa manuscript is evidence of the transfer to Catalonia of texts written in the Beneventan script of southern Italy.[21]

---

[16] See Roger E. Reynolds, 'Odilo and the *Treuga Dei* in Southern Italy: A Beneventan Manuscript Fragment', *Mediaeval Studies* 46 (1984) 454 n. 27. A single leaf perhaps from a manuscript of the *Collection in Five Books*, containing the glossed text of 1.212-219, 220-224, is fol. 50 in the miscellany Rome, Biblioteca Vallicelliana R 32. This folio, measuring 269 × 190 mm., was written in eleventh-century Farfese script, but is likely derived from a Beneventan-script ancestor.

[17] Carlo Guido Mor, 'La reazione al *Decretum Burchardi* in Italia avanti la riforma gregoriana', *Studi gregoriani* 1 (1947) 201.

[18] See Roger E. Reynolds, 'An Early Medieval Mass Fantasy: The Correspondence of Pope Damasus and St. Jerome on a Nicene Canon' in *Proceedings of the Seventh International Congress of Medieval Canon Law: St. John's College, Cambridge, 23-27 July 1984*, ed. Peter Linehan (Monumenta iuris canonici, Ser. C, Subsidia; Vatican City, in press).

[19] On the manuscript see Roger E. Reynolds, 'The *De officiis vii graduum*: Its Origins and Early Medieval Development', *Mediaeval Studies* 34 (1972) 148 n. 130. This form is also appended to a manuscript of the *Collection in Four Books* (Paris, Bibliothèque Nationale lat. 3187, fols. 131v-132v), a text kindly brought to my attention by Professor Robert Somerville.

[20] On this manuscript see Virginia Brown, 'A Second New List of Beneventan Manuscripts (I)', *Mediaeval Studies* 40 (1978) 272, and Loew-Brown, *The Beneventan Script* 2.139. To fol. 48r this is a Beneventan-script palimpsest of the tenth or eleventh century. Traces of Beneventan script appear on fols. 7r, 21r, 22r-v, 25r, 27r, 28v, 30v, 35r, 37r, 39r, 41r, 42r-v, 43r, 44r. Fols. 41r-47v are an inserted quire of large folded folios originally written in Beneventan script in double columns of 90 mm. running sideways to the present overlying text.

[21] South Italian iconographic motifs in Catalonia have often been pointed out by art historians, who compare one version of the depiction of *Mater Ecclesia* in the Beneventan-script Exultet rolls with the fresco from San Quirze de Pedret; on which see *Exultet-Rolle: Vollständige Faksimile-Ausgabe in Originalgrösse des Codex Vaticanus Latinus 9820 der Biblioteca Apostolica Vaticana: Kommentarband*, ed. Herbert Douteil and Felix Vongrey (Codices e vaticanis selecti 35; Graz, 1975), p. 82 n. 114 and pl. 28.

The details of the version of the pseudonymous correspondence between Damasus and Jerome and the expanded commentary on the Mass in the Catalan manuscript have been treated elsewhere,[22] but it should be noted that the version here is close to one in the *Collection in Five Books*, where it is used as an introduction to canons on the Eucharist.[23] Our compiler, however, has abbreviated the text, not unlike the earlier tract on Septuagesima. For example, in the section dealing with the trinitarian significance of the priest, he repeats the explanation for the term *sacerdos* ('Pater *sa-*, et Filius *-cer-*, et Spiritus sanctus *-dos*') but omits the explanation for presbyter found in most versions ('Pater *pres-*, Filius *-bi-*, Spiritus sanctus *-ter*'). Whether the compiler was following a model which omitted the curious second comparison or was simply reflecting his own understanding is uncertain, but the same type of omission occurs in an early eleventh-century codex with Beneventan interrogation signs, Vatican City, Biblioteca Apostolica Vaticana Arch. S. Pietro H 58, where the scribe presented on fol. 46v the explanation of *sa-cer-dos*, but after writing 'Pater' left a large blank space.[24]

Although in MS. HC 380/819 the text is presented as a single paragraph, it has been divided here so as to emphasize the structure of the sometimes obscure commentary, consisting of: the pseudonymous correspondence between Damasus and Jerome (ll. 1-20); explanations as to why the Mass should not be said after the third hour, why the priest is to celebrate with two other persons, why he should wear seven vestments (ll. 21-42); the seven 'sententiae' of the Trinity or the trinities in (1) the lights at Mass with their wax, wick, and flame, (2) the incense with its odor and fire, (3) the bread, wine, and water, (4) the tersanctus, (5) the term *sa-cer-dos*, (6) the chalice, oblation, and covering on the altar, (7) the threefold Agnus Dei (ll. 43-67); and the concluding paragraph (ll. 68-71).

(f. 106v)   INCIPIT EPISTULA DAMASI PAPAE DIRECTA IHERONIMO PRESBITERO, QUALITER VEL QUIBUSMODIS SACERDOS SACRIFICARE DEBEAT

Dum quadam die resideret sanctissimus papa Damasus in sede beati Petri apostoli intentio orta est in tota aecclesia Romana de sacrifitio qua hora liceat sacerdoti sacrifitium

---

[22] See Reynolds, 'Early Medieval Mass Fantasy', and 'A South Italian Liturgico-Canonical Mass Commentary', *Mediaeval Studies* 50 (1988) (forthcoming).

[23] M. Fornasari, ed., *Collectio canonum in V libris (Lib. I-III)* 3.212 (pp. 413-15) (CCM 6; Turnhout, 1970). On the use of this text to begin the section of canons on the Mass, see Reynolds, 'Early Medieval Mass Fantasy', n. 22.

[24] Beneventan interrogation signs can be found on fol. 46r of the Mass commentary. On this manuscript see Roger E. Reynolds, 'Excerpta from the Collectio Hibernensis in Three Vatican Manuscripts', *Bulletin of Medieval Canon Law* N.S. 5 (1975) 4-9; and the literature since this date (n. 25 below). The Mass commentary in the Vatican codex (fol. 45v), although closer to the one in the *Collection in Five Books*, bears a rubric that is nearer the Catalan text: 'Incipit epistula sancti Damasi papae Hieronimo presbitero Hierusolimis transmissa: Quomodo sacerdos debet sacrificaret'.

5 offerre, et non inveniebat. Tunc misit epistulas suas ad beatissimum Iheronimum (f. 107r)
presbiterum Iherosolimis ita:

Damasus papa Iheronimo presbitero in Domino aeternam salutem. Dirigimus vestrae
fraternitati quia intentio orta est in tota aecclesia Romana de sacrifitio qua hora liceat
sacrificari et non invenimus exinde finem. Dirigat nobis sanctitas vestra quae omnia
10 scrutatur quomodo exinde agamus.

Iheronimae (*sic*). Pater sanctissime, veritas enim in vobis nulla est absconsa. Recordamini concilii Niceni ubi trecenti fuerunt decem et octo patres sancti quomodo fixum et
constitutum est ab eis: siquis die dominico resurrectionis post horam terciam ausus fuerit
canere missam, anathematizetur; aliis diebus a tercia usque ad horam nonam si presumpse-
15 rit, similiter anathematizetur; aliis vero horis licitum est sacrificare.

Cumque relecta fuisset epistula, invenerunt in concilio scriptum a trecentis decem et
octo patribus sanctis qui inflamati fuerunt de Spiritu sancto, quomodo in Nicena sancti
coram Constantino magnifico et catholico ac sanctissimo imperatore scripserunt et
constituerunt ut siquis die dominico sacrificare post horam terciam ausus fuerit aut canere
20 missam, in dampnatione anathematizetur.

Pro eo quod Spiritus sanctus hora tercia descendit ad apostolos, ideo non licet post
horam terciam die dominico nec sacrificare nec ieiunare nec ullam abstinentiam habere.
De aliis vero diebus a media hora tercia usque ad aliam mediam horam terciam in media
hora octava similiter anathematizetur. Pro eo quod ista hora Christus in passione in
25 patibulo crucis stetit pro nostra salute, ideoque si ista hora praesumpserit sacrificare, angeli
non recipiunt sacrificium ad offerendum maiestati. Ergo quid prodest sacrifitium illud?

Et quando sacrificaverit sacerdos, non praesumat solus sacrificare quia Christus quando
in sacrifitium pro tocius mundi salute imolari se permisit, duo latrones in cruce fuerunt cum
eo. Ergo si solus sacrificaverit sacerdos, cui dicit Dominus vobiscum? Certe melius est
30 dicere (f. 107v) Dominus mecum, et ipse respondeat Et cum spiritu meo. Ecce satis
blasphemat si duos vel tres non habet ministros. Et si habet, sana fide potest dicere
Dominus vobiscum, et nos optamus ut sit Dominus cum spiritu tuo. Quia si solus sacrificat
videtur Pater esse solus, Filium nec Spiritum sanctum in Trinitate non esse. Si vero cum
uno ministro sacrificaverit ergo cui dicit Dominus vobiscum? Melius est ei dicere Dominus
35 tecum vel nobiscum. Absit. Si cum duobus ministris sacrificat videtur esse perfecta Trinitas.
Ergo qui sacrificat habeat secum duos ministros. Sicut Dominus dicit in evangelio, Ubi duo
vel tres steterint in nomine meo in medio eorum sum (Mt 18:20). Et in omni loco tria
testimonia apud Deum firmata sunt. Et si plus sunt, ecce quam melius sunt apud Deum
et hominem.

40 Et habeat sacerdos secum quando sacrificat lineam et cingulum et amictum et orarium
et planetam et in manu teneat mapulam et sudarium trilice in honore sanctae Trinitatis
propter sacrifitium ponendum super altare.

Ecce una sententia sanctae Trinitatis. Et in nullo permittimus sine lumine accenso
sacrificare quia qui sine lumine accenso sacrificaverit videtur esse sacrifitium cecum. Absit
45 hoc, et non permittat Deus ut fiat sacrifitium caecum apud Christianos quia si lumen
accensum habet, perfecta Trinitas ibi videtur habere virtutem quia oleum et cerae aut papiri
flamma Trinitatem significant.

Ecce alia sententia sanctae Trinitatis. Et inde lumen pro vice Christi ponitur. Omnis sacerdos lumen habeat quando sacrificat quia ipse Dominus dixit Ego sum lux mundi (Jo
50 8:12). Et habeat incensum quia quando angeli Sathanae ceciderunt de caelo in terram in foetore ceciderunt. Cum vero odorem incensi facit sacerdos ad altarem, praesentialiter fugit diabolus et ille odor per angelos ante Deum ascendit et incensum et odor et ignis Trinitatem (f. 108r) significant.

Et quando offert sacerdos Domino in altari, non solum offert panem quia si solus panis
55 ponatur videtur Pater non habere Filium. Si panis et vinum ponatur, videtur Pater esse cum Filio et non habere Spiritum sanctum. Si panem et vinum et aquam adunatum ponitur (*sic*) videtur esse Patrem et Filium et Spiritum sanctum.

Unde dicimus Sanctus, Sanctus, Sanctus tribus vicibus in honore sanctae Trinitatis. Et si solum ignem habet ad sacrificandum videtur Patrem non habere Filium quia lumen
60 accensum Trinitatem significat.

Qui sacrificat, non in sordibus adulterii sed mundus ab omni inquinatione adulterii sacrificet quia sacerdos Trinitas interpretatur: Pater *sa-*, et Filius *-cer-*, et Spiritus sanctus *-dos*. Ecce sacerdos et presbiter Trinitas intelligi potest.

Ergo trilice posita in altari et desuper calicem cum oblatione aetiam et operimento super
65 calicem similiter sancta Trinitas figuratur.

Et dicimus ter Agnus Dei propter sanctam Trinitatem.

Ecce septem sententiae sanctae Trinitatis in honore septiformis Spiritus sancti gratiae.

Ergo non presumat sacerdos aliud facere quando sacrificat nisi quomodo supradiximus ut illuminet se et animas Christianorum. Et si aliter facere praesumpserit nec sibi lumen
70 nec aliis Christianis praestat. Sed ille caecus est et alios in cecitatem post se trahit. Audi Christum dicentem Si caecus caecum duxerit ambo in foveam cadunt (Mt 15:14, Lc 6:39).

III

In the south Italian canonical *Collection in Five Books* and some of its sources and derivatives the long Mass commentary is followed by a series of canons, many of which reflect concerns in that tract. So it is in our Catalan manuscript that three of the same canons follow the commentary, but without a break or rubrics. Surprisingly, this grouping finds a close parallel in the already-mentioned early eleventh-century codex, Vatican City, Biblioteca Apostolica Vaticana Arch. S. Pietro H 58, written in Farfese script perhaps in Rome itself, but containing south Italian texts and Beneventan-script interrogation signs.[25] In MS. Arch. S. Pietro H

---

[25] This manuscript has been dated to the early eleventh century by Professor Bernhard Bischoff; on which see Roger E. Reynolds, 'Unity and Diversity in Carolingian Canon Law Collections: The Case of the *Collectio Hibernensis* and Its Derivatives' in *Carolingian Essays: Andrew W. Mellon Lectures in Early Christian Studies*, ed. Uta-Renate Blumenthal (Washington, D. C., 1983), p. 135 n. 220, and Bernhard Bischoff, 'Eine karolingische "Vita pastoralis": "Sedulius, Carmen alpha"', *Deutsches Archiv* 37 (1981) 559. Since the *Collection in Five Books*, as it presently exists in its three more or less complete manuscripts, is to be dated after 1014 (because of the canons of Henry II), the texts in the San Pietro manuscript paralleling those in the *Collection in Five Books* may have come

58 (fol. 47r) the three canons follow the Mass commentary, but the second and third have rubrics. The first canon, corresponding to the *Collection in Five Books* 3.213,[26] deals with a topic in the longer tract: the reason for the mixture of water and wine in the Eucharist (ll. 1-4). The explanation (that the wine is the blood of Christ and the water his faithful people [cf. Apoc 17:15]) goes back at least to the time of Cyprian and was repeated in medieval liturgical commentaries, conciliar enactments, and canonical collections.[27] The second canon, corresponding to the *Collection in Five Books* 3.214,[28] deals with the purity required of the host, wine, and water (ll. 5-7). This canon, also found in the *Collection in Nine Books*,[29] justifies purity of the oblations with a reference to terms in the Mass Canon. The third text, corresponding to the *Collection in Five Books* 3.226[30] and drawn ultimately from the Council of Rome under Pope Zachary (*c.* 743),[31] prohibits bishops, priests, and deacons from bearing a staff or wearing a head covering at Mass (ll. 8-11).

from an older source and not the *Collection* itself; see Reynolds, 'Excerpta', 5 n. 28, 6 n. 34. On the Farfese script in the San Pietro codex see Bischoff, p. 559. That codices in Farfese script often bear traces of their Beneventan archetypes is illustrated, for example, in one of the manuscripts of the *Collection in Five Books* itself, namely, Vatican City, Biblioteca Apostolica Vaticana Vat. lat. 1339, on which see Loew-Brown, *The Beneventan Script* 1.179 f. On the Roman origins of the San Pietro codex see Pierre Salmon, 'Un "Libellus officialis" du xie siècle', *Revue bénédictine* 87 (1977) 257-88 and 'Un témoin de la vie chrétienne dans une église de Rome au xie siècle: le Liber officialis de la Basilique des Saints-Apôtres', *Rivista di storia della chiesa in Italia* 33 (1979) 65-73, and Raymund Kottje, *Die Bußbücher Halitgars von Cambrai und des Hrabanus Maurus* (Beiträge zur Geschichte und Quellenkunde des Mittelalters 8; Berlin-New York, 1980), pp. 65-69.

[26] Fornasari, *Collectio*, pp. 415 f.

[27] See Roger E. Reynolds, 'Mass, Liturgy of the' in *Dictionary of the Middle Ages* 8 (New York, 1987), p. 190; and W. Hartel, ed., *Cyprianus Caecilio fratri s.* [Ep. 63], c. 13 (CSEL 3.1; Vienna, 1868), pp. 71 f. For an example of a liturgical commentary with the Cyprianic passage, see Amalarius, *Liber officialis* 3.19.27-29 (*Amalarii episcopi Opera liturgica omnia* 2, ed. Jean Michel Hanssens [Studi e testi 139; Vatican City, 1948], pp. 319 f.); and for conciliar enactments and canonical collections reflecting the Cyprianic passage see Wilfried Hartmann, *Das Konzil von Worms 868: Überlieferung und Bedeutung* (Abhandlungen der Akademie der Wissenschaften in Göttingen, philol.-hist. Klasse, 3. Folge, 105; Göttingen, 1977), pp. 47, 127 f. (to which add the *Paenitentiale Vallicellanum II*, c. 50.1 [Rome, Biblioteca Vallicelliana E 62, fol. 284r]).

[28] Fornasari, *Collectio*, p. 416.

[29] Fornasari, ibid., cites the source as *Paenit. iudic.* 32, ed. Schmitz (2.249), but the text in question is drawn from the penitential book of the *Collection in Nine Books* 9.122 (Vatican City, Biblioteca Apostolica Vaticana Vat. lat. 1349, fol. 215r; also found in the *Paenitentiale Vallicellanum II*, c. 50.2 [Rome, Biblioteca Vallicelliana E 62, fol. 284r]). On the penitentials in this collection see Franz Bernd Asbach, *Das Poenitentiale Remense und der sogen. Excarpsus Cummeani* (Regensburg, 1975), p. 181, and Franz Kerff, 'Das Paenitentiale Pseudo-Gregorii III. Ein Zeugnis karolingischer Reformbestrebungen', *Zeitschrift der Savigny-Stiftung für Rechtsgeschichte*, Kan. Abt. 69 (1983) 53-56. On the reception of the *Capitula iudiciorum* in this codex see Letha Mahadevan, 'Überlieferung und Verbreitung des Bußbuchs "Capitula Iudiciorum"', *Zeitschrift der Savigny-Stiftung für Rechtsgeschichte*, kan. Abt. 72 (1986) 45, 71-73.

[30] Fornasari, ibid., pp. 425 f.

[31] *Concilium romanum (a. 743)* 13, ed. Albert Werminghoff (MGH *Leges conc.* 1; Hanover-Leipzig, 1946), p. 18.

(f. 108r) In calice Domini non debet offerri vinum solum. Si solum vinum offertur, sanguis Christi incipit esse sine nobis. Si aqua pura offeratur, sola plebs incipit esse sine Christo. Quando in vino miscetur et invicem copulantur, sacramentum spirituale perficiunt.

5 Hostiam puram et perfectam offerri liceat absque sordidatione; clarissimum vinum cum aqua mixtum prout debeat sine turbido aut aceto vel quassato aut fece, sed, quomodo legitur, hostiam puram et immaculatam et illibatam.

Ut nullus episcopus, presbiter aut diaconus ad caelebrandum missarum sollempnia (f. 108v) praesumat cum bacculo introire aut velato capite ad altare Dei assistere, quoniam 10 et Paulus apostolus prohibet viros velato capite orare in aecclesia. Et si temere presumpserint, comunione priventur.

IIII

Immediately after the canons corresponding to the *Collection in Five Books* 3.212-214, 226, the Hispanic Society manuscript contains a series of texts which are not as specifically related to south Italy as the preceding material. The first is a version of the preface to the *Regula canonicorum* of Chrodegang of Metz.[32] It is certainly not surprising to discover such a text in a manuscript from a house of canons regular, but strangely our version is closer to one used in England in the eleventh century and translated into Old English than to the more common versions.[33] How this version of the text reached Catalonia is not clear, but it is not beyond the realm of possibility that, like many English and Norman texts, it was once found in Beneventan territories[34] and was carried to Catalonia with other texts. In fact, there was at one time a manuscript in a Roman library with only the preface of the *Regula*, which Werminghoff compared to that in the English copies.[35] In any event, the text with its reference to the 318 fathers of the first

---

[32] On the versions and editions of the *Regula* see Gaston Hocquard, 'La règle de Saint Chrodegang, état de quelques questions' in *Saint Chrodegang: communications présentées au colloque tenu à Metz à l'occasion du douzième centenaire de sa mort* (Metz, 1967), pp. 58-61.

[33] Cambridge, Corpus Christi College 191, pp. 1 f., on which see: N. R. Ker, *Catalogue of Manuscripts Containing Anglo-Saxon* (Oxford, 1957), pp. 74 f.; Arthur S. Napier, *The Old English Version of the Enlarged Rule of Chrodegang together with the Latin Original* (EETS 150; London, 1916), p. 1; and Brigitte Langefeld, 'A Third Old English Translation of Part of Gregory's *Dialogues*, This Time Embedded in the Rule of Chrodegang', *Anglo-Saxon England* 15 (1986) 197, especially the literature cited in n. 2.

[34] See Roger E. Reynolds, 'The "Isidorian" *Epistula ad Leudefredum*: An Early Medieval Epitome of the Clerical Duties', *Mediaeval Studies* 41 (1979) 288 f., Richard F. Gyug, *An Edition of Leningrad MS. BAN f. 200: The Lectionary and Pontifical of Kotor* (Diss. Toronto, 1983), passim, and Virginia Brown, 'A New Commentary on Matthew', above, pp. 443-65. On the use of Insular material in Catalan liturgical books of the eleventh century, see Reynolds, 'Ordination Rite', 141.

[35] Albert Werminghoff, 'Die Beschlüsse des Aachener Councils im Jahre 816', *Neues Archiv* 27 (1902) 647. For examples of Roman manuscripts with sections of the *Regula* of Chrodegang see Roger E. Reynolds, 'Isidore's Texts on the Clerical Grades in an Early Medieval Roman Manuscript', *Classical Folia* 29 (1975) 97, and the bibliography in n. 38 below.

Council of Nicea does find a resonance in the long Mass commentary with its pseudo-canon attributed to the same 318 fathers.

Italics are used in the transcription below when the reading differs from the text printed in EETS 150 (cited in n. 33 above).

(f. 108v) Si trecentorum decem et octo reliquorumque sanctorum patrum canonum auctoritas inviolata semper et *episcopos* atque *clericos* secundum rectitudinis normam viverent, superfluum videretur a nobis exiguis super hanc rem tam *ordinatam dispositum* aliquod novi retractare aut dicere. Quid aliud agendum nobis est qui in tam gravi *crimine*
5 venimus nisi in quantum possumus si non quantum debemus ad rectitudinis lineam, Deo inspirante, clerum nostrum reducamus? Igitur divino fulti auxilio egrediamus parvum decretulum facere per quod clerus se ab illicitis choerceat et ociosa deponat, mala diu longeque usurpata derelinquat. Sic emendemus in melius illius videlicet amore qui suo sancto et precioso sanguine nos redemit. *Vigilanti* ergo studio institutionis formam
10 colligere studeamus in qua plane contineatur qualiter prelati vivere et subiectos regere et in Dei servitio constringere et bene operantes hoc ad meliora provocare, protervos et neglegentes debeant corrigere vel corripere, quantinus formula hac vivendi inspecta et Deo sibi adiutorium prebente humiliter suscepta et efficaciter impleta, cum bonorum operum lampadibus *veniente* sponso apparere atque ad eius thalamum ingredi mereantur quia nec
15 infelix potest iudicari cui continget qualemcumque partem in *paradiso* habere. Sed illis ibidem sors datur qui in quantum possunt per vitae meritum in hoc huius temporis curriculo dum licet currere *festinant.*

V

Following the preface to the *Regula* of Chrodegang with no break is an *Ordo officii* on fol. 108v divided into two sections by the rubric *Ordo Romanus.*[36] In the first section, there is an instruction regarding prayer upon rising from bed, and the reference to the Trinity echoes the trinitarian concerns of the long Mass tract. Then, beside the rubric, there is a series of instructions for the office of a group of clergy living under a prior.[37] Like the long Mass commentary and appended canons with their connection to the Vatican codex Arch. S. Pietro H 58 with its Beneventan symptoms, these instructions for the office, both before and after the rubric *Ordo Romanus,* have their connection with Roman and Beneventan codices. At least four of the sections of the text in the Catalan manuscript are reflected in

---

[36] On manuscripts in Vic with *Ordines Romani* see Roger E. Reynolds, 'The Ordination of Clerics in Toledo and Castile after the Reconquista according to the "Romano-Catalan Rite"' in *II. Congreso Internacional de Estudios Mozarabes: IX. centenario de la Reconquista de Toledo, 1085-1985,* ed. Ramon Gonzálvez Ruiz (Toledo, forthcoming), nn. 40, 44.

[37] On priors at Santa Maria del Estany, see Villanueva, *Viage literario,* pp. 234-36, and Francisco Miquel Rosell, *Liber feudorum maior. Cartulario real que se conserva en el Archivo de la Corona de Aragón* 1 (Barcelona, 1945), p. 477.

two eleventh-century liturgico-canonical codices, Vatican City, Biblioteca Apostolica Vaticana Vat. lat. 1351 (a manuscript written for a community of Roman canons regular) and Vat. lat. 4885 (a manuscript which may have been written for a Roman community of canons regular at San Lorenzo in Damaso and is related to MS. Vatican City, Biblioteca Apostolica Vaticana Barb. lat. 646, with its Beneventan notations).[38] The four sections in the Catalan manuscript also reflected in the Vatican codices are: ll. 1-6 'Cum autem de lecto ... valeamus. Per'; l. 13 'Et nulli liceat cooperto capite'; ll. 19-26 'In secunda feria ... sub una Gloria'; and ll. 29-32 'In quadragesimis namque diebus ... tribus diebus in ebdomada'.[39] Of special interest is the third section, ll. 19-26, where Pss 21-25 have been assigned in these eleventh-century Catalan and Roman texts not to Sunday Prime[40] but to the second through sixth ferias, something that according to the traditional understanding of the history of the office happened during the sixteenth century in the reform of Pius v.[41] In any event, themes found in the tracts on Septuagesima and the Mass appear in our *Ordo officii*: the Trinity, Sundays and the fifth feria, Quadragesima (although here both the Lent of St. Martin from Martinmas to Christmas and the major Lent before Easter are noted), the deacon and subdeacon as associates with the celebrant of the Mass, and the Mass itself.

(f. 108v)   Cum autem de lecto surgit, tunc dicit In nomine Patris et Filii et Spiritus sancti tribus vicibus. Postea Ego dormivi (Ps 3:6) et somnum caepi, et psalmum totum Voce mea ad Dominum clamavi voce mea (Ps 3:5), totum cum Gloria. Postea hec oratio: Gratias tibi agimus Domine Deus omnipotens qui nos de transacto noctis spacio ad matutinas
5 horas perducere dignatus es. Quesumus indones nobis hunc diem sine peccato transire quantinus ad vesperum tibi omnipotenti Deo placere valeamus. Per.

---

[38] On these manuscripts see: Werminghoff, 'Beschlüsse', 640-44; Ch. Dereine, 'Le problème de la vie commune chez les canonistes d'Anselm de Lucques à Gratien', *Studi gregoriani* 3 (1948) 293 f. and 'La prétendue règle de Grégoire VII pour chanoines réguliers', *Revue bénédictine* 71 (1961) 110 n. 1, 118; and Cosimo Damiano Fonseca, *Medioevo canonicale* (Pubblicazioni dell'Università Cattolica del Sacro Cuore, 3rd Ser., Scienze storiche 12; Milan, 1970), pp. 78-101, and especially pp. 81 (on Egger's suggestion that Vat. lat. 4885 was written for a canonical community at San Lorenzo in Damaso), 88 (items 66 f. and 71 on fols. 145v, 148r and 150r of Vat. lat. 4885), and 97 f. (items 65 f. and 70 on fols. 74v and 78v of Vat. lat. 1351). On the connection between Vat. lat. 4885 and Vat. Barb. lat. 646 see Pierre Salmon, *Les manuscrits liturgiques latins de la Bibliothèque Vaticane* 4 (Studi e testi 267; Vatican City, 1971), p. 115, item 354, and Loew-Brown, *The Beneventan Script* 2.162. Both Vat. lat. 1351 and 4885 have Beneventan interrogation signs.
[39] Mansi 14.302, 305, 307.
[40] See Roger E. Reynolds, 'Divine Office' in *Dictionary of the Middle Ages* 4 (New York, 1984), p. 227.
[41] Mario Righetti, *Manuale di storia liturgica*, vol. 2: *L'anno liturgico. Il breviario*, 2nd edition (Milan-Genoa, 1955), p. 652, noting that on these ferias Pss 23, 24, 25, 22, and 21 respectively were used. I am grateful to Mr. Jonathan Black for this reference.

Ordo Romanus

In dominicis et in illis diebus festis quando novem lectiones fatiunt novem responsa cantent. Finito responso in dominicis et in omnibus diebus festis cantent Te Deum
10 laudamus. Finito autem dicat prior versus ad ipsum diem pertinens (f. 109r) et Deus in adiutorium (Ps 69:2) et cantent matutinales laudes sicut supradictum est. Postea dicatur Prima, Deus in nomine tuo (Ps 53:3), Beati inmaculati (Ps 118:1), Retribue (Ps 118:17), Quicumque vult. Et nulli liceat cooperto capite Fides catholica canere ob honorem sanctae Trinitatis et numquam praetermittatur confessio. Expleta vero Prima, tunc dicant matutina-
15 les laudes in honore sanctae Trinitatis.

In dominicis et in omnibus festivitatibus non dicantur (sic) matutinas defunctorum neque missam neque vesperam. Sed in omni hora sive noctis sive diei unum pro eorum animabus absolutione psalmum canitet cum Requiem aeternam absque oracione et post psalmum dicit Requiescant in pace. R. In nomine Christi. Amen. In secunda feria ad
20 Primam post hymnum Deus Deus noster respice in me (Ps 21:2), et Deus in nomine tuo (Ps 53:3) sub una Gloria. In tercia feria Dominus reget me (Ps 22:1) et Deus in nomine tuo (Ps 53:3) sub una Gloria. In quarta feria Domini est terra (Ps 23:1) et Deus in nomine (Ps 53:3) sub una Gloria. In quinta feria Ad te Domine levavi (Ps 24:1) et Deus in nomine (Ps 53:3) sub una Gloria. In sexta feria Iudica me Domine (Ps 25:1) et Deus in nomine
25 tuo (Ps 53:3) sub una Gloria. In sabbato Confitemini Domino (Ps 117:1) et Deus in nomine tuo (Ps 53:3) sub una Gloria. Et omnibus diebus Beati inmaculati (Ps 118:1) et In quo corrigit (Ps 118:9) sub una Gloria. Et Retribue (Ps 118:17) cum Adhesit pavimento (Ps 118:25) sub una Gloria et semper Quicumque vult.

In quadragesimis namque diebus quod est a festivitate sancti Martini usque in natale
30 Domini omni die letaniam cantet ad Primam et post confessionem dicant septem psalmos speciales et postea surgat ebdomodarius et dicat orationem. Similiter a capite ieiunii usque in Pascha. In aliis cotidianis diebus tribus diebus in ebdomada similiter letaniam faciant et post orationem benedicatur populus et recedant. Tunc incipiantur matutinales laudes in honore omnium sanctorum. Finito de omnibus sanctis mox incipiantur (sic) Pro defunctis
35 in qua parte aecclesiae volueris. Finito Pro defunctis incipiatur missa pro defunctis ita ut diaconus et subdiaconus ministrant et omnes fratres conveniant ad missam qui infra ecclesiam sunt praeter infirmos et qui inobedientia sunt directi. Prior vero ad missam officium ita dicendo Requiem eternam.[42]

VI

On the verso side of what may have been the last folio of the original codex, there is entered under the rubric *De septem gradibus aecclesiae* an Ordinal of Christ, a text appropriate to a house of canons regular with its variety of clerics.[42]

---

[42] See, e.g., *Bernhardi cardinalis et lateranensis ecclesiae prioris Ordo officiorum ecclesiae late-ranensis*, ed. Ludwig Fischer (Munich-Freising, 1916), p. 36. In the *Libellus de diversis ordinibus et professionibus qui sunt in aecclesia*, ed. and trans. G. Constable and B. Smith (Oxford, 1972), pp. 10-13, 60, which defends the canons regular, there is an Ordinal of Christ, and it is argued that canons might be ordained to the lower as well as the higher grades. For additional uses of the

In the south Italian *Collection in Nine Books* and *Collection in Five Books*, their sources and derivatives, a form of the same Ordinal of Christ appears and, because of its characteristics, it has been called the Italo-Hibernian Chronological Ordinal of Christ.[43] The form in the Catalan text, however, is of the common Hibernian Chronological variety, widely spread throughout Europe from the seventh and eighth centuries onwards.[44] A form of this version is entered in Barcelona, Biblioteca Universitaria 228, fol. 136v (s. x, origin southern France/northern Italy? or Catalonia?),[45] but again there are differences which make it unlikely that the Barcelona text was the model for the text under consideration. In fact, the readings closest to ours appear in a group of related florilegial manuscripts, several of which were written in southern France.[46] Unlike the text in those manuscripts, however, the rubric and introduction here are slightly different, the individual grades lack specific numbers, and the verse for the *sacerdos* is slightly longer. Perhaps the most unusual thing about our text is that Christ is said to have been the exorcist when he cast out six, not seven, demons from Mary Magdalene, an error due perhaps to a misreading of a Roman numeral in the scribe's exemplar.

(f. 109v)   DE SEPTEM GRADIBUS AECCLESIAE

Quomodo implevit Christus septem gradus.
Lector fuit quando apperuit librum Esayae propheta et dixit Spiritus Domini super me.
Exorcista fuit quando eiecit sex demones de Maria Magdalena.
5   Subdiaconus fuit quando fecit de aqua vinum in Cana Galileae.
Diaconus fuit quando lavit pedes discipulorum suorum.

Ordinals of Christ in the context of rules for canons regular, see Roger E. Reynolds, *The Ordinals of Christ from Their Origins to the Twelfth Century* (Beiträge zur Geschichte und Quellenkunde des Mittelalters 7; Berlin-New York, 1978), pp. 134 f. It is interesting that from the ninth century onwards there were canons in the cathedral at Vic who lived under the *Regula* of the Council of Aachen (816) or the *Institutio canonicorum* (for manuscripts in Vic see Reynolds, '*Epistula ad Leudefredum*', 254 n. 3) and that in the *Regula* there are descriptions of the lower orders, including exorcists of whom several may have been signatories to the cartularies of Vic edited by Eduard Junyent i Subirà, *Diplomatari de la Catedral de Vic, segles IX-X* 1 (Vic, 1980), p. 21. For the influence of Vic on Estany see Freedman, *Diocese of Vic*, p. 41.
  [43] Reynolds, *Ordinals*, pp. 91-93, to which add the text edited in Reynolds, 'South Italian Ordination Allocution', 443.
  [44] Reynolds, *Ordinals*, pp. 58-75.
  [45] On this manuscript see Reynolds, 'Ordination Rite', 150 f. n. 34, and literature therein, and Susan A. Keefe, 'Carolingian Baptismal Expositions: A Handlist of Tracts and Manuscripts' in *Carolingian Essays*, p. 219. I am grateful to Professor Keefe and Dr. Gyug for obtaining a copy of this text for me in Barcelona.
  [46] For these manuscripts, on which I am preparing an extensive study, see Reynolds, *Ordinals*, p. 70 n. 9 (1)-(6). Professor Bernhard Bischoff has kindly informed me that Paris, Bibliothèque Nationale lat. 614A was written in southern France in the tenth century, and that New York, Columbia University, Butler Library Plimpton 58 was written in the second third of the ninth century in southern France and contains Spanish symptoms.

Sacerdos fuit quando accepit panem, benedixit ac fregit deditque discipulis suis.
Istos quinque gradus ante passionem suam implevit.
Hostiarius fuit quando dixit Tollite portas, principes vestras.
10   Episcopus fuit quando levavit manu (*sic*) super discipulos suos et benedixit eos.

VII

Directly beneath the Ordinal of Christ, a hand slightly later than the one designated as A by Faulhaber has copied on fol. 109v a letter of Pope Victor II (1055-57) to Bishop Guislabertus of Barcelona (1035-*c*.1062). In the text, which unfortunately breaks off in mid-sentence, the pope refers to an 'ovis' or simple lamb of Guislabertus' flock who has, according to reports, spent a year in exile and is the bearer of the letter. Since the person is not named, his identity is uncertain, but he is probably someone connected with the excommunication hurled by Victor II against Count Ramón Berenguer, Almodis, and Archbishop Guifredus of Narbonne, an excommunication reiterated at the Council of Toulouse in 1056 and mentioned by the Countess Ermessenda in her *Sacramentale* of 1057.[47]

In our text the pope places this person under the care of Guislabertus and assigns a severe penance, whose provisions again echo themes found in the liturgico-canonical texts in the three preceding folios. First, for seven years the penitent is to observe two Quadragesimas outside the major Easter Lent, one preceding the feast of John the Baptist and the other Advent, in which he is to have only bread and water three days a week. On other days he is to dine once on Lenten-type foods. Outside these Lents, he is to have bread and water for two days a week, and twice a week he is to abstain from fats and meats, although he is allowed them on Sundays, the fifth feria or Thursday, days of remission, and if sick. Beyond the seven years the penitent is to have only bread and water on Fridays and must abstain from meat on Wednesdays and Saturdays. Moreover, for three years he is not to enter church except during the Paschal season or to take communion, unless in danger of death.

(f. 109v)   Victor episcopus servus servorum Dei G. Barchinonensi episcopo salutem et apostolicam benedictionem.

Hanc tuae (*sic*) ovem post annale exilium, ut asserit, tuae dilectione (*sic*) curandam remittimus quatinus in patria degens penitentiam subscriptam testimonio tuo et compatrio-
5 tarum suorum peragat, scilicet septem annis ita ut duas quadragesimas excepta maiori singulis annis fatiat, unam ante nativitatem sancti Iohannis, alteram ante nativitatem Christi, tribus diebus in septimana pane et aqua tantum. Ceteris vero diebus semel

---

[47] On these excommunications see Rosell, *Liber feudorum*, pp. 225 f., and S. Sobrequés i Vival, *Els grans comtes de Barcelona: biografies catalanes* (Sèrie històrica 2; Barcelona, 1961), p. 64.

refficiens quadragesimalibus cibis utatur. Reliquo autem tempore duas ferias in ebdomada habeat in pane et aqua. Ceteris autem bis refitiat sine sagina et carne, quae tamen sibi
10 concessimus die dominica et quinta feria et diebus remissionis aut forte suae aegrotationis. Expletis quoque septem annis diebus vitae suae sextam feriam in pane et aqua habeat, quarta et sabbato a carne abstineat. Ecclesiam tuae dioceseos excepto pascali tempore non intret triennio, communione (*sic*) peracta penitentia percipiat nisi forte periculum mortis imineat. Porro tua cura viderit qualitatem hominis et facultatem et secundum mensuras eius
15 peni ...

XVI

The south-Italian Collection in Five Books and its derivatives: The collection of Vallicelliana Tome XXI

Among the indigenous collections of canon law circulating in southern and central Italy in the eleventh and early twelfth centuries was one styled by Carlo Guido Mor as the vademecum of canonists before and well into the period of the so-called Gregorian Reform, the *Collection in Five Books* (hereafter 5L). Although the collection itself is found in only three manuscripts and perhaps in one fragment — all of substantial size and hardly of vademecum portability — its derivatives seem indeed to have been in their size and content the handbook of many an eleventh- and twelfth-century Italian canonist.[1]

Among these derivative collections there are several types. First, there are those whose compilers simply abbreviated material from the 5L, sometimes according to the sequence of canons found in the 5L and sometimes not.[2] A second type of derivative collection is of a farraginous nature in which canons from the 5L are thrown together helter-skelter or are combined with canons from other collections in no discernible order.[3] In a third type of derivative collection canons from the 5L are combined with material from Burchard's *Decretum*.[4] And in a fourth type canons from the 5L are combined with material from the *Collection in Seventy-Four Titles*.[5] Further, it is noteworthy that several of the derivative collections, like the 5L itself, mix liturgical texts with more strictly canonistic material.[6]

---

[1] See Roger E. Reynolds, 'The South-Italian canon law *Collection in Five Books* and its derivatives: New evidence on its origins, diffusion, and use,' *Mediaeval Studies* 52 (1990) 278-95.

[2] E.g. Naples, Biblioteca Nazionale Vittorio Emanuele III, XII A28; Florence, Biblioteca Riccardiana 300; Rieti, Archivio Capitolare 5; and Rome, Biblioteca Angelica 1447.

[3] E.g. Rome, Biblioteca Vallicelliana B 32, B 63, and T. XXI.

[4] E.g. Florence, Biblioteca Medicea Laurenziana Plut. 4, sin. 4; Florence, Biblioteca Riccardiana 300; Monte Cassino, Archivio della Badia 216; Rome, Biblioteca Vallicelliana F 2, F 8, F 92; Toledo Biblioteca Capitular 22-32; Vatican, BAV Vat. lat. 3830, 4977, 8487.

[5] E.g. El Escorial, Real Biblioteca de San Lorenzo Z.III.19; Monte Cassino, Archivio della Badia 522; Rome, Biblioteca Angelica 1447; Rome, Biblioteca Casanatense 2010; and Rome, Biblioteca Vallicelliana F 54.

[6] E.g. Florence, Biblioteca Riccardiana 300; Rome, Biblioteca Vallicelliana E 62, F 2; and Vatican, BAV Vat. lat. 4317 and 7818.

Beyond the selection and arrangement of canons and the mixture of canons from the 5L with other collections and texts, the derivatives are distinctive for other reasons. First, they are all in single manuscripts. Second, many of the manuscripts were written in the Beneventan script of southern Italy or bear symptoms of that script.[7] Third, many of the derivatives can be considered monastic in character and even issued from monastic scriptoria, like manuscripts of the 5L itself.[8] Especially significant are those with connections to the central Italian abbeys of Sant'Eutizio near Nursia and Farfa, both of which produced manuscripts of the 5L itself.[9] Finally, a number of the derivative collections are penitential in nature, as the 5L itself was, as is clear from its preface and the canons in books 4 and 5.

The Biblioteca Vallicelliana in Rome, rich in manuscripts from southern and central Italy, many of which are written in Beneventan script and issued from monastic houses of the eleventh and twelfth centuries, is a depository where many of the derivative collections of the 5L are now housed.[10] The text of one of these derivatives, found in Tome XXI, was even printed in the modern catalogue of the Tomi of the Vallicelliana.[11] Regrettably, the cataloguers failed to recognize the source of the texts and thus reproduced largely those that were rubricated or capitalized, passing over in silence many that are found in the 5L as separate canons.

The codex in which the derivative of the 5L is found contains a vast miscellany of texts described in the modern catalogue. The quires containing the derivative are long and thin (160 x 300 mm.), and according to the catalogue extend from fols. 270 bis to 302. In fact, fol. 270 bis is simply pasted on to the bifolium 271-78, is in a different hand, and is differently ruled, so our quires actually run from fols. 271 to 302. As it is presently constructed, the first quire of the section consists of two bifolia (fols. 271 and 278, and 272 and 277), two halves of bifolia (fols. 273 and 276), and a final full bifolium (fols. 274-75). This is then followed by three full quires of four bifolia each (fols. 279-86, 287-94, and 295-302). The

---

[7] E.g. in Beneventan script: El Escorial, Real Biblioteca de San Lorenzo Z.III.19; Madrid, Biblioteca Nacional 373; Monte Cassino, Archivio della Badia 216, 522; Rieti, Archivio Capitolare 5; Rome, Biblioteca Vallicelliana B 32, F 2, F 8, F 54; and Vatican, BAV Vat. lat. 7818: and with Beneventan symptoms: Naples, Biblioteca Nazionale Vittorio Emanuele III, XII A28;Toledo Biblioteca Capitular 22-32; and Vatican, BAV Vat. lat. 4317.

[8] On the manuscripts written in monasteries and with monastic-oriented canons, see Reynolds, 'South-Italian canon law *Collection in Five Books*' (n. 1 supra) 294.

[9] See Reynolds, 'South-Italian canon law *Collection in Five Books*' 281-85, 292.

[10] Rome, Biblioteca Vallicelliana B 32, B 63, E 62, F 2, F 8, F 54, F 92, and T. XXI.

[11] *Catalogo dei manoscritti della Biblioteca Vallicelliana*, 1, eds. Anna Maria Giorgetti Vichi and Sergio Mottironi (*Indici e cataloghi*, N. S. 7; Rome 1961) 293-95.

ink is a brownish-black; and there are redish-orange rubrics brushed through with yellow and a few interlace initials in green, yellow, and violet.

The modern catalogue describes the hand as a central Italian minuscule of the late eleventh or early twelfth century; and in her recent study of 'romanesca' script, Paola Supino Martini also dates it to the last decade of the eleventh century.[12] Although she designates the section of Tome XXI with our derivative among 'MSS non localizzati,' our quires have features that draw them, like one of the codices of the 5L itself, Vallicelliana B 11, sharply into the number of manuscripts connected with Sant'Eutizio. Not only is there the suprascript ' used for the final 's' in words (in Beneventan and central Italian style[13]), but also a suprascript 's' is used for the final 's'. More important, however, is the use of 'dripping' letters. Here they are not of the type used in Vallicelliana B 11 and its close associates, but more like those of Vallicelliana B 4 and C 10, pt. 2, fol. 139r-279v, both manuscripts from Sant'Eutizio and dating to the end of the eleventh century.[14] In these manuscripts the dripping letters end not with the sickle-shaped curve, but with a graceful sinuous flourish, which at times loops over itself. Beyond the palaeographical features, there is also internal evidence in the texts of the quires containing our derivative that links them to Sant'Eutizio or perhaps one of her dependencies. The quires contain both the canonical derivative, beginning in the middle of the second quire (fol. 284r) and running to the end of the fourth quire (fol. 302v), and what the modern catalogue calls 'litanies,' running from fol. 271r to 283v. Actually these 'litanies' are an abbreviated martyrology, and it is in their contents that the connections of the quires with Sant' Eutizio are clear. In this martyrology the scribe has capitalized a number of his entries or has underlined them in yellow. Among these are Eutizio (with yellow underlining; added later in a small hand; fol. 276r) and a number of feasts of Spoleto (capitalized; fol. 283v), in whose diocese Sant'Eutizio lay. Also, on fol. 283r, a scribe has added in large black letters the name of 'Thomas Abbot' (of Farfa, ca. 680-720), who was venerated at Sant'Eutizio. E.B. Garrison has pointed out that such entries as these can be found in a number of central Italian liturgical books not originating at Sant'Eutizio.[15] But the case for an origin at Sant'Eutizio is strengthened if our martyrology in Tome XXI is compared with a longer one in Vallicelliana E 59, whose contents Pietro Pirri has described among his

---

[12] Paola Supino Martini, *Roma e l'area grafica romanesca (secoli x-xii)* (Biblioteca di *Scrittura e civiltà* 1; Alessandria 1987) 305f.

[13] See E.A. Loew, *The Beneventan script. A history of the south Italian minuscule*, 2nd enlarged edition prepared by Virginia Brown, 2 vols. (Sussidi eruditi 33-34; Rome 1980) 1.213-17.

[14] Martini, *Roma e l'area grafica romanesca* 206, 208.

[15] E.B. Garrison, *Studies in the history of mediaeval Italian painting*, 4 vols. (Florence 1953) 2.124, and 4.165f., 218, 237, and 251.

manuscripts from Sant'Eutizio[16] and where the dedication of the basilica of Sant' Eutizio is noted in large rubricated letters on fol. 59v. In Vallicelliana E 59, the hand is not far removed from those at Sant'Eutizio at the end of the eleventh century, and as in our quires of Tome XXI, there is the suprascript '*s*' for the final '*s*' and dripping letters occasionally with a 'flaming letter' rising into the upper margin.[17] If the long martyrology of Vallicelliana E 59 is compared with the shorter one in our Tome XXI, there are a few differences, but the correspondences are even more striking. Among these are the names of Eutizio, which is both capitalized and rubricated, and Thomas Abbot, whose *depositio* is placed on 10 December. Also there are the Spoleto entries in both martyrologies.

Since the modern Vallicelliana catalogue of incipits of the derivative of the 5L is flawed, and since the derivative is fairly short, incipits and explicits of the canons will be printed below, together with an identification of their sources in the 5L. Here the composition of the derivative as a farraginous collection can be seen clearly, but several general comments should be made regarding the method of the excerptor and his sources. First, it is clear that the excerptor has skipped freely about the 5L for his canons: a few from bk 1, some from bk 3, back to bk 1, then bk 4, and so forth. In most cases the number of canons drawn from the 5L does not extend beyond three or four in a sequence. Nor does it seem that there is much attempt at systematization. Rather, the excerptor seems to have been content to choose randomly the canons that struck his fancy. It is clear, however, that the excerptor drew more heavily from bk 4 of the 5L than from any other, and hence, like many other derivatives of the 5L, the one in our codex is heavily penitential in character.

As to the sources, the excerptor may have had a model in a farraginous collection that had drawn random canons from the 5L. It is known, in fact, that there are fragments of manuscripts from Sant'Eutizio in which such random excerpts are found.[18] On the other hand, the excerptor may have been working directly from a manuscript of the 5L. As to what form of the 5L this model codex contained, the connections of our derivative in Tome XXI to Sant'Eutizio would point to Vallicelliana B 11. But it was certainly not B 11 itself because 1) there are glosses in our manuscript not in B 11;[19] 2) in some instances the inscriptions of canons differ,[20] and 3) some of the canons, such as 63 and 64, are

---

[16] P. Pirri, *L'abbazia di Sant'Eutizio in Val Castoriana presso Norcia e le chiese dipendenti* (2nd edn; Studi Anselmiana 45; Rome 1960) 359f.

[17] Garrison, *Studies* 2.122.

[18] See above, n. 9.

[19] E.g. nrr. 98, 100, 101.

[20] E.g. nrr. 45-47.

found in the codices of the 5L, Vatican, Vat. Lat. 1339,[21] and Monte Cassino, Archivio della Badia 125,[22] but not in Vallicelliana B 11.[23] On the other hand, these very canons appear in the *Penitentiale Vallicellianum II*,[24] whose manuscript comes from Sant'Eutizio.[25] This suggests that our excerptor might have been using sources beyond the 5L itself, and this is probably indeed the case because there is a handful of canons that do not seem to appear in any reported manuscripts of the 5L.[26]

In presenting the incipits and explicits of our derivative, the following conventions have been used. Numbers in brackets have been assigned each canon for easier identification.[27] Titles and ascriptions that are rubricized in the codex are here capitalized; those merely capitalized in the codex are italicized here. As for the sources in the 5L, Mario Fornasari's edition (=F)[28] is cited for canons drawn from bks 1-3; and for those from bks 4-5, Vallicelliana B 11 (=B) has been cited. In a few instances where B 11 lacks an analogue, Vat. Lat. 1339 (=V) and Monte Cassino 125 (=C) have been cited.[29]

The *Collection of Vallicelliana Tome XXI*

<1>   <fol. 284r> DE HIS QVI IN EGRITVDINE BAPTISMA CONSECVNTVR.   EX CONCILIO CESARIENSE.
Si quis in egritudine fuerit baptizatus ... talis possit admitti.
(1.83, F 66f.)

---

[21] fol. 192r.

[22] pp. 219f., c. 63 is lacking in the text, but is added in the margin.

[23] It is interesting that in Vallicelliana B 11, fol. 192r, where these canons should lie, a blank space is left in the manuscript.

[24] H.J. Schmitz, *Die Bussbücher und die Bussdisciplin der Kirche nach handschriftlichen Quellen dargestellt*, I (Mainz 1883) 376f.

[25] Rome, Biblioteca Vallicelliana C 6, on which see Martini, *Roma e l'area grafica romanesca* (n. 12 supra) 219.

[26] See nrr. 24, 108, and 110.

[27] The principle used here is that a number is assigned a canon if 1) it is rubricated (not necessarily capitalized) in the derivative; or 2) it is a separate *capitulum* with rubric (not necessarily numbered) in the Vallicelliana codex of the 5L.

[28] *Collectio canonum in v libris (lib. i-iii)*, ed. M. Fornasari (CCCM 6; Turnhout 1970). The numbers for the canons in all of the books vary widely in the manuscripts. Regrettably, Fornasari ignored these variants in the manuscripts he used for his edition of bks 1-3.

[29] J.D. Adamson, whose edition of the derivative *Collectio Toletana* will be published soon, has undertaken a complete new edition of the 5L, in which the texts and sources of canons in bks 4 and 5 will be presented. On Fornasari's edition, see G. Fransen, 'Principes d'édition des collections canoniques,' RHE 66 (1971) 125-36; and H. Mordek, 'Anzeigen,' ZRG, Kan. Abt. 60 (1974) 477f.

82

<2> DE ORDINATIONE PRESBITERORVM ET DIACONORVM. EX DECRETA PAPE
GELASII.
Ordinationes clericorum etiam presbiterorum, diaconorum ... qui ante
ordinati sunt.
(1.103, F 77f.)

<3> VT SACERDOTES ET LEVITES CANES ADVEN(AN)DVM AVT ACCIPITRES NON
HABEANT. EX CONCILIO AGATENSE.
Episcopis, presbiteris, diaconibus canes aduenandum ... officio uel communione cessabitur.
(3.250.1, F 436f.)

<4> CONCILIVM CANONICVM.
Si quis uenationes quascumque exercuerit ... diaconus ii., presbiter iii.
(3.252.2, F 437f.)

<5> CANON GREGORII.
Presbiteri non amplius quam unam ecclesiam ... unam uxorem. <fol.
284v>
(1.181, F 116)

<6> AVGVSTINVS.
Non enim omnibus clericis maxime indoctis ... penitentem ad sanctam
communionem.
(4.47, B 172v)

<7> DE ODIO.
Odium pax pellit quicumque fratrem suum ... benefacite his qui uos ode-
runt.
(4.290, B 210r)

<8> DE GVLA. IVDICIVM COMEANI.
Qui anticipat horam canonicam ... dictum est uel etas tamen ita peniteat.
(4.411, B 222v)

<9> DE TACITVRNITATE IN ECCLESIA. CANON.
Omni tempore in ecclesia tam a populo ... <285r> ... subiaciatur ut certi
timeant.
(3.240, F 431f.)

<10> DE MVLIERE QVE IN ECCLESIA LOQVITVR. IVDICIVM CANONICVM.
Scriptum est: Turpe est enim mulieri ... non correxerit excommunicetur.
(3.239, F 431)

<11> NEC LAICI NEC FEMINE INGREDIA(N)TVR AD ALTARE.
Sinodus Bracarense. Laici sue femine non ingrediantur ... ecclesiastice
correptionis subiaceat.
(3.275, F 450)

<12>   CONCILIVM AGATENSE.
        Seculares qui in natali domini ... nec inter catholicos habeantur.
        (3.267.1, F 446)

<13>   QVOD PRESBITER(I) SEMPER EVCHARISTIA(M) PARATAM HABEANT.
        Vt presbiter semper eucharistiam ... ne sine communione moriatur.
        (3.269, F 447)

<14>   VT NVLLVS SACRIFICIVM ALTARIS IN PANNO TINCTO CELEBRETVR.
        Constitutio sancti Silvestri pape. Vt sacrificium altaris non in sirico ...
        linea munda sepultus est.
        (3.216, F 416f.)

<15>   DE MOTV ALTARE. EX CANONE PAPE VIRGILII.
        Si motum fuerit altare ... <285v> ... exorcizetur salibus tantum.
        (1.180, F 116)

<16>   CONCILIVM BRACARENSE.
        Placuit ut pro consecratione basilice ... non in merito precipitatur.
        (1.177, F 115)

<17>   VT SACERDOS NON QVERAT PRETIVM MINISTERII SVI.
        Hieronimus. Sacerdos non querat pretium ... accepit gratis det.
        (1.174, F 114)

<18>   Si quis per pecuniam episcopus (sic) aut presbiterum ... et ordinatus
        deiciatur.
        (1.72, F 63)

<19>   Si quis episcopus aut presbiter aut diaconus ... sicut Simon Magus a
        Petro.
        (1.52, F 45)

<20>   SIRICIVS PAPA.
        Monachus si uxorem accipit ... si maritus accipit.
        (2.170, F 281)

<21>   IVSTINIANVS REX.
        Nemo presbiter consecretur ... minor viiii. annorum sit.
        (1.89, F 69)

<22>   HENRICI REX.
        Si quis ante xxx. annos presbiter consecrauerit ... xii. annos nullatenus
        fiat.
        (1.90, F 69f.)

<23>   CANONIS REGVLA.
        Episcopus aut presbiter, diaconus nequaquam seculares <286r> ... sin
        aliter deiciatur.
        (3.247, F 435)

84

<24> AVRASICO.
Si quis seruum alienum diaconum aut presbiterum fecerit dupla satisfac-
tione restituat seruus.
(Source unknown)

<25> DE IVRAMENTO IN LOCVTIO(NE).
Cauendum igitur esse iurationem ... est est, non non.
(4.258, B 206r)

<26> SINODVS ARELATENSE.
Si quis iustificauerit super alium iurauit ... uindictam ego retribuam.
(4.265b, B 206v)

<27> *Hieronimus.*
Post sacramentum detrans (sic) uapulauit ... arbitrio dimittendum iurans.
(4.265c, B 206v-207r)

<28> DE EO QVOD PEIVS EST NOCENS PROVOCAT AD IVRAMENTVM QVAM ILLE
QVI IVRAT.
Si quis aut prouocauerit adiurationem ... quomodo ille qui te prouocauit.
(4.269, B 207r)

<29> AVGVSTINVS.
Quicumque hominem prouocat adiurationem ... morte satiare uoluisti.
(4.270a, B 207r)

<30> THEODORVS. <286v>
Si quis per insidiam aut insipientiam ... eo quod dubium ei erat.
(4.278, B 208r)

<31> DE SACRAMENTO VOLVNTARIE. CANON.
Si quis uoluntarie iurauerit ... secundum gradum suum et ita peniteat.
(4.283, B 208v)

<32> GREGORIVS.
Si quis in altare ubi reliquie habentur ... <287r> ... si tantum per consensum iii.
(4.272, B 207v)

<33> Si quis coactus pro qualibet neccesitate causa ... iii. annos peniteat.
(4.273, B 207v)

<34> DE DIVERSIS PERIVRIIS. IVDICIVM THEODORI.
Si quis episcopus periurium incurrerit ... periurauerit iii. annos peniteat.
(4.275a,b, B 208r)

<35> SI PER CVPIDITATE(M). THEODORVS.
Si quis laicis per cupiditatem se periurauerit ... iudicio sacerdotis communicet.
(4.276a, B 208r)

<36> SINODVS ROMANA.
Si quis inscius se periurauerit et postea ... <287v> ... diaboli strangulati sunt.
(4.279a, B 208r)

<37> SINODVS ROMANA.
Si quis per industriam quod est grauius ... uite sue cum luctu peniteat.
(4.279b, B 208r-v)

<38> Si quis iurauerit in manu hominis ... v. annos peniteat si non consecrata.
(4.276b, B 208r)

<39> *Isidorus.*
Plerumque sine sacramento dici disponimus ... loquentes iurare compellunt alium.
(4.260, B 206v)

<40> Non est conseruandum sacramentum ... permanere in stupri flagitium.
(4.280, B 208v)

<41> CONCILIVM ILERDENSE. <288r>
Qui sacramento se obligauerit ... celeriter uenire festinet.
(4.281, B 208v)

<42> *Isidorus.*
Quacumque arte uerborum quisque iuret ... proximum suum dolo capit.
(4.263, B 206v)

<43> *Hieronimus.*
Tria iuramenta soluenda sunt ... <288v> ... in comparatione peiorum.
(4.256a, B 205v)

<44> Si quis per quamcumque machinationem ... <289r> ... suum quem diligere debuit.
(4.279b, B 208v)

<45> EX CONCILIO LAVDOCENSES (sic).
Qui periurium fecerit in ecclesia x. annos peniteat iuxta gradum suum.
(4.277, B 208r)

<46> IVSTINIANVS REX.
Vt non dampnetur episcopus in sancta sinodus ... nisi xxxvi. testimonia.
(3.279, F 451)

<47> DE HIS QVI SINE CAVSA PROBATA EXCOMMVNICANTVR.
Nemo episcopus neque presbiter excommunicari ... id quod iniuste fecit iuste patiatur.
(3.285, F 453)

<48>   DE SACRILEGIO.
Sacrilegium id est sacrarum rerum furtum ... <289v> ... ne gehenne ne
ignibus tradatur.
(4.233, B 203r)

<49>   DE MINISTERIO ECCLESIE. THEODORVS.
Si quis aliquid de ministerio ... popularia uero duppliciter.
(4.235, B 203r)

<50>   DE CAPITALE FVRTVM. GREGORIVS.
Si quis furtum capitale commiserit ... fecerit vii. dies peniteat.
(4.236, B 203r)

<51>   *Paterius.*
Qui in religioso loco furatur ... sub alio priore peniteat.
(4.241, B 203v)

<52>   *Sinodus Romana.*
Decreuit sancta sinodus. Si quis uult confiteri peccata sua ... <290r> ...
conueniens tempore integra peniteat.
(4.24<4>, B 204r)

<53>   DE COMMENDATIS PER FVRTVM RAPTIS AB ECCLESIA CATHOLICA NON
REDDENDIS. SINODVS HIBERNENSIS.
Si quis clericorum depositum accepit ... pecuniam suam furatus sit.
(4.225, B 202r)

<54>   LEO EPISCOPVS.
Si quis de ministerio ecclesie sancte qualicumque opus ... <290v> ...
reddetur et vii. annos peniteat.
(4.230b, B 202v)

<55>   THEODORVS.
Si quis furatus fuerit equos aut bos ... uel dampnum sic iudicetur.
(4.237, B 203v)

<56>   In conflictu canonum.
Ita habetur quicumque furtum fecerit ... adibenda est medicinam.
(4.238, B 203v)

<57>   GREGORIVS.
Quicumque furtum commederit ... si uero maior addatur.
(4.239, B 203v)

<58>   IN CONFLICTV CANONVM.
Si quis domum uel aream ... canone iudicii subiaceat.
(4.247, B 204v)

<59> DICTA HIERONIMI, GREGORII, BONIFACII. <291r>
      Comperimus namque in penitentiale ... <292r> ... neque hic neque futu-
      ro.
      (4.89, B 181r-182r)

<60> CONCILIVM AGATENSE.
      Si quis seruum proprium ... reatum sanguinis emundabit.
      (4.136, B 191r)

<61> CONCILIVM ELIBERTANO.
      Si qua femina furore zeli ... infirmata accipia (sic) communionem.
      (4.137, B 191r)

<62> IVDICIVM COMEANI.
      Si quis falsum testimonium dixerit ... <292v> ... studens inquirit iii.
      annos peniteat.
      (4.177, B 194v)

<63> DE TRADITORIBVS HOMINVM. SINODVS ROMANA.
      Si quis alium hominem in manus inimici ... ab inimicis euaserit.
      (4.123a, V 192r; 4.82, C 220 *in marg.*)

<64> Si quis castellum uel ciuitatem aut alicuius munitionem ... nichilum ualet
      ultra.
      (4.123b(1), V 192r; 4.82, C 220)

<65> SINODVS HIBERNENSIS.
      Si quis hominem gratis expoliauerit ... fratri suo cui predauerit.
      (4.251, B 205r)

<66> Si quis seruum quale cumque hominem ... <293r> ... ut impium iudice-
      tur.
      (4.252, B 205r)

<67> LIBER EXODVS.
      Quicumque furatus fuerit ... uincitur morte moriatur.
      (4.228v, B 202v)

<68> IVDICIVM CANONICVM.
      De pecunia que in alia prouincia ... et raptor xl. dies peniteat.
      (4.246a, B 204r)

<69> DESTITVTA (sic) PATRVM.
      Si quis de preda duxerit ... ab his qui operantur iniquitatem.
      (4.246b, B 204v)

<70> DE HOMICIDIIS SCELESTIBVS. GREGORIVS.
      Qui patrem uel matrem aut fratrem ... mortem cum luctu peniteat.
      (4.125, B 188v)

88

<71> DECRETA PONTIFICIS.
Si quis proprium quod absit seniorem ... <293v> ... in monasterio cum luctu peniteat.
(4.126, B 188v)

<72> DE SEPTEM GENERIBVS NOLENTIA HOMICIDIORVM. EX CONCILIO.
Sex genera sunt nolentia homicidiorum ... <294v> ... si neglegentia hoc iniuenitur (sic).
(4.129, B 189r-v)

<73> DE DIVERSIS HOMICIDIIS SI VOLUNTARIE SIVE NOLENS.
Sancta sinodus cl. patribus sub Theodosius seniore Constantinopolim congregata. Epilogus breuiter digestus propter plerosque simplices ... <295r> ... episcopus xv. et cetera similia.
(4.135, B 190v-191r)

<74> DE OPPRESSIS INFANTIBVS.
Si qua mulier fidelis oppresserit per neglegentiam infantem ... neglectum suum iudicium sacerdotis peniteat.
(4.147a, B 192r)

<75> Iudicium Comeani.
Si qua infantem suum oppresserit ... <295v> ... a luxuria tempus peniteat.
(4.147b, B 192r)

<76> Vnde supra. Comeani.
Si qua mulier inuenerit iuxta se infantem ... si baptizatus ii. quadragesime.
(4.148, B 192r-v)

<77> DE MVLIERE QVE PEPERIT ET NON NVTRIT FILIVM SVVM. IVDICIVM COMEANI.
Si mulier fidelis peperit infantem ... animam suam iudicium sacerdotis peniteat.
(4.149, B 192v)

<78> DE MVLIERIBVS CONCEPTV SVO NECANTIBVS ET DE CONSENTIENTIBVS EIVS.
Que mulier hanc detestationem fecerit ... <296r> ... tantorum homicidorum ream esse cognouerit.
(4.151, B 192v)

<79> DE MVLIER(E) QVE OCCIDIT FILIVM SVVM IN VTERO. CONCILIVM VNDE SVPRA.
Mulier que concepit et occidit filium ... iudicium pendeat sacerdotis.
(4.155, cap. in B, 157r, can. in V 193v)

<80> QVI CONCEPTV(M) MVLIERIS DECIPIVNT.
      Si quis conceptum mulieris ... xl. dies ut homicida peniteat.
      (4.156, cap. in B, 157r, can. in V 193v)

<81> SINODVS ROMANA.
      Quicumque clericus in bello aut in noxa (sic) mortalium ... <296v> ...
      sepulture tamen non priuetur.
      (3.249.3, F 436)

<82> QVI SVPER PATREM ET MATREM.
      Orthodoxis senibus in concilio Terraconenses (sic). Quicumque super
      genitorem ... placabitur iudicium pendeat sacerdoti.
      (4.210, B 199v)

<83> Si quis patri aut matri sue iniuriam fecerit ... in pietate extiterit.
      (4.211, B 199v)

<84> Si quis super patrem suum uel matrem in iracundiam ... <297v> ... ad
      patrem uel matrem in Christo.
      (4.212, B 200r)

<85> DE VSVRA. IN CANONE APOSTOLORVM.
      Episcopus aut presbiter aut diaconus usuram ... aut certe dampnetur.
      (4.345, B 216v)

<86> Iudicium Comeani.
      Si quis usuram undecumque exigerit ... donet pauperibus sin autem ex-
      communicetur.
      (4.346a, B 216v)

<87> DE EVCHARISTIA NEGLECTA.
      Si quis eucharistiam causa neglegentie ... <297v> ... et aqua ablutionis
      in igne proiciatur.
      (4.358, B 218r-v)

<88> Iudicium.
      Si quis neglexerit sacrificium aut perdiderit ... <298r> ... posito aquam
      ablutionis sumat.
      (4.359, B 218v)

<89> Iudicium canonicum.
      Si quis sacrificium uomuerit ... si post matutinum i. superponatur.
      (4.360, B 218v)

<90> Si quis sacerdos missas celebrauerit et non communicauerit i. annum
      peniteat.
      (4.361b, B 219r)

90

<91> CONCILIVM AVRASICO.
Si quis sacerdos inormiter post solitum cibum ... atque helemosinis peniteat.
(4.362a, B 219r)

<92> Iudicium canonicum.
Qui accipit sacrificium post cibum xl. dies peniteat.
(4.361b, B 219r)

<93> DE EBRIETATE. GREGORIVS.
Placuit secundum antiquam diffinitionem. Si quis episcopus aut presbiter aut diaconus in consuetudine habuerit ... <298v> ... aut aliqua nequitia iudicio sacerdotis peniteat.
(4.313, B 212v)

<94> SINODVS ROMANA.
Omnis qui fraudat debitum fratris ... proximi tui non reddidisti.
(4.316v, B 213r)

<95> Placuit accusator mendax ... dampnetur donec peniteat.
(4.189a, B 196r)

<96> *Sinodus Romana.*
Qui falso accusat fratrem usque ad exitum non communicet.
(4.189b, B 196r)

<97> SINODVS.
Penitentes qui legem penitentie ... <299r> ... uel helemosina confirmatur.
(4.29, B 167r)

<98> DE FORNICATIONE.
Si quis pontifex faciens facilem fornicationem ... reconcilietur ad communionem.
(2.64, F 217f. Words glossed as in V and C)

<99> COMEANVS.
Si quis cum Deo sacrata ... gradum numquam accedant.
(2.65, F 218)

<100> IVDICIVM COMEANI.
Si obsculatus est episcopus per desiderium mulierem ... <299v> ... obsculum (sic) sacerdotis muliebricum.
(2.66.1-7, F 218f. Words glossed as in V and C)

<101> IVDICIVM THEODORI.
Si quis diu cum muliere aut puella ... <300r> ... susceptus ab ea xl. dies peniteat.
(2.67.2, F 220, First line glossed as in V and C)

<102> DE HIS QVI INFRA ECCLESIA(M) FORNICANTVR. IVDICIVM SINODI.
In presentiarum nihil pericolosius ... <300v> ... ut decet mulieribus.
(2.78.1, F 225f.)

<103> CONCILIVM AGATENSE.
Si quis in ecclesia fornicauerit ... ii. clerici et laici dimidium.
(2.78.2, F 227)

<104> DE INCESTIS VEL DIVERSIS COMMIXTIONIBVS. EPILOGVS BREVITER DEGE-
STVS (sic).
Sinodus Calcidonensis sex centorum xxx. sacerdotum sub Martino principe ... <302r> ... et his similiaque secuntur.
(4.227, cap in B, 237v; 5.113 cap. and can. in C 330)

<105> CONCILIVM CESARIENSE.
Presbiter aut diaconus si post leuiticam benedictionem uxorem ... inter
laicos redigi oportet.
(2.70, F 221)

<106> GREGORIVS.
Si quis filius cum matre fornicauerit tam funestum atque nefarium ... et
arma relinquat nec communicet usque ad mortem.
(Cf. 5.113, C 329; 5.231, V 310v)

<107> Si qua mulier duobus fratres nupserit ... in morte promiam (sic) ei detur.
<302v>
(=?5.225, cap. in B 238v; cf. 5.112, C 329; 5.230, V 310v)

<108> Si quis cum sorore sua disponsata alterius dormierit ... non communicet
usque ad mortem.
(Source unknown)

<109> GREGORIVS. THEODORVS.
Si quis cum matre uel sorore fornicauerit xv. annos ... nec communicet
usque ad mortem nisi inminentem diem mortis periculo.
(Cf. 5.113, C 329f.; 5.231, V 360v)

<110> SINODVS ROMANA.
Clericus qui semel fornicans prouidentia sacerdotis ... et si forsitan nescit
eum v. annos peniteat.
(Source unknown)

<111> SINODVS ROMANA.
Qui cum commatre siue matre aut filia in Christo fornicauerit ... clerici
et laici x. secundum paternam ....
(B 239r, addit. between list of capitulationes and 5.1; 5.119a, C 334)

XVII

THE TURIN COLLECTION IN SEVEN BOOKS:[*] A POITEVIN CANONICAL COLLECTION

In a recent article honoring René Crozet, Professor Le Bras has drawn together several late eleventh-century canonical collections and described them as Poitevin collections.[1] Among those he mentions are the *Collection in Seventeen Books*,[2] the *Liber Tarraconensis*,[3] the Bordeaux *Collection in Seven Books*,[4] and the Berlin *Collection in Thirteen Books*.[5] The purpose of this note is to suggest that one more late eleventh-century collection be added to this array of Poitevin or Poitevin-influenced collections, the Turin *Collection in Seven Books* (Turin MS Univ. D. IV. 33)[6] (hereafter *Coll VIIL*).

In their *Histoire des collections canoniques* Fournier and Le Bras classified the Turin *Coll VIIL* as one of the Italian collections written between Gregory VII and Gratian which were influenced by the Gregorian reform. They alluded to two French texts in the Turin Collection, the canons of the Council of Poitiers of A.D. 1078[7] and a letter of Hincmar of Reims,[8] but correctly they pointed out that these texts are occasionally found in Italian canonical collections.[9] Presumably because the *Coll VIIL* is found in a manuscript now in the Biblioteca Nazionale in Turin, it was classified as Italian and no explicit connection was made with French collections of the same period.[10] A close

---

[1] G. Le Bras, 'L'activité canonique à Poitiers pendant la réforme grégorienne (1049-1099),' *Mélanges René Crozet* 1 (Poitiers 1966) 237-9.

[2] Cf. Fournier-Le Bras, *Histoire* 2.230-5. For this note both MS Lat. 675 (olim G 528) of the Bibliothèque municipale in Reims and MS lat. Phill. 1778 of the Deutsche Staatsbibliothek in Berlin have been consulted. Hereford Cathedral Library MS 0.2.VII has not been consulted. Cf. Z. N. Brooke, *The English Church and the Papacy from the Conquest to the Reign of John* (Cambridge 1931) 238f.; and P. Fournier, 'Note sur les anciennes collections canoniques conservées en Angleterre,' RHD[4] 12 (1933) 129f.

[3] Cf. Fournier-Le Bras, *Histoire* 2.240-7. Vat. lat. 6093 has been consulted.

[4] Cf. Fournier-Le Bras, *Histoire* 2.247-50. Bordeaux Bibl. mun. MS Lat. 11.

[5] Cf. Fournier-Le Bras, *Histoire* 2.251-9. MS lat. Savigny 3 of the Staatsbibliothek der Stiftung Preussischer Kulturbesitz in Berlin has been consulted.

[6] Cat. Pasini 239 (Mazzatinti 507). This MS has been consulted in Turin. The author wishes to thank the IMCL for lending him its microfilm of this MS. This collection has been extensively treated in Fournier-Le Bras, *Histoire* 2.163-7, and P. Fournier, 'De quelques collections canoniques issues du *Décret* de Burchard,' *Mélanges Paul Fabre* (Paris 1902) 208-13.

[7] Mansi 20.498.

[8] PL 126.132. Turin MS D. IV. 33, fol. 87[r] f.

[9] The letter of Hincmar is found, e.g., in the *Collection of MS M 11*, fol. 51[r], of the Archivio Capitolare of the Basilica di S. Ambrogio in Milan. On this collection, cf. Fournier-Le Bras, *Histoire* 2.222-4; and V. Foffano, 'Descrizione paleografica del Cod. M 11 dell'Archivio della Basilica di S. Ambrogio di Milano: "Decretales de Sacerdotio",' *La vita comune del clero nei secoli XI e XII* 2 (Milan 1962) 48-65.

[10] Fournier - Le Bras, *Histoire* 2.167. In his article in the *Mélanges Paul Fabre*, 207 n. 3, P. Fournier states that the Turin Collection 'ne semble nullement poitevine.' The

[*] See Addenda and Corrigenda

scrutiny of the components seems to suggest, however, that the Turin Collection should be connected with late eleventh-century French collections, specifically the Poitevin collections. A comparison of the general sources and many specific texts within the Turin Collection and Poitevin collections shows that if not written in Poitou, the *Coll VIIL* was at least heavily influenced by the Poitevin collections.

Among the general sources for the Turin Collection are the *Collection in 74 Titles*, Burchard's *Decretum*, the *Collectio canonum* of Cardinal Deusdedit, the *Pseudo-Isidorian Decretals*, and the *Collectio canonum* of Anselm of Lucca.[11] Of these the *Collection in 74 Titles* and Burchard's *Decretum* supplied the majority of texts. These are the very sources which Professor Le Bras stresses as being the major *fontes* for the Poitevin collections. While a few late eleventh-century Italian collections depended heavily on both of these sources,[12] it is primarily the Poitevin collections which Professor Le Bras lists which show a heavy reliance on them. In these collections the spirit of the Gregorian reform remains, but its exclusivism has been blunted by the inclusion of texts from Burchard's *Decretum*, texts which the high Gregorian reformers had rejected.[13] This spirit of the Poitevin collections also pervades the Turin *Coll VIIL*.

More specific ties between the Poitevin collections and the Turin Collection are suggested by the inclusion and rather unusual recensions of several individual canonical texts within the Turin Collection.

---

reason for his opinion seems to be that several texts from the *Collectio canonum* of Deusdedit and Italian councils of the late eleventh century are found in the Collection. Although it is true that the *Collectio canonum* of Deusdedit primarily influenced Italian collections, traces are certainly found in the *Collectio Caesaraugustana* (ca. 1110-1120) and perhaps in the *Collection of Ste.-Geneviève* (Paris Bibl. Ste.-Geneviève MS lat. 166) and the *Collection of St.-Germain-des-Prés* (Wolfenbüttel Gud. lat. 212). Cf. Ch. Lefebvre, 'Deusdedit,' DDC 4 (Paris 1949) 1189. Moreover, canons from the councils of Melfi and Piacenza are occasionally found in French collections. Cf. F. J. Gossman, *Pope Urban II and Canon Law* (The Catholic University of America Canon Law Studies 403; Washington 1960) 104-6. It seems especially significant that c. 1 of the Council of Benevento (1091) (Mansi 20.738), which is listed on fol. 135ᵛ of the *Coll VIIL* as a canon of the Council of Melfi, is confined almost exclusively to French canonical collections from 1091 until the appearance of Gratian's *Decretum*. Cf. Gossman, *loc. cit.* 106. The only purely Italian collection with the canon which Bishop Gossman lists is the Italian *Collection in Nine Books* of Vat. Bibl. S. Petri C 118, fol. 14ᵛ. On examining the occurrence of the Beneventan decree in this MS, it appears that it was added by a later hand and did not belong to the original collection. To be added to Bishop Gossman's list are: Ivo's *Tripartita*, Paris BN 3858B, fol. 151ʳ; Haimo's *Abridgment of the Collection in Ten Parts*, Clm 2594, fol. 13ʳ; the *Sententiae Magistri A*, Vat. lat. 4361, fol. 123ᵛ; and the *Sententiae Sidonenses*, Vat. lat. 1345, fol. 141ʳ (written perhaps after Gratian's *Decretum*).

[11] Fournier - Le Bras, *Histoire* 2.164-6.

[12] The eleventh-century Italian collections listed by Fournier-Le Bras which use substantial amounts of both Burchard's *Decretum* and the *Collection in 74 Titles* are the *Collectio canonum* of Anselm of Lucca and the so-called *Collection in Two Books* (Vat. lat. 3832) (and its early twelfth-century dependent, the *Collection of Assisi BC 227*).

[13] Le Bras, *loc. cit.* 239; and S. Kuttner, *Harmony from Dissonance: An Interpretation of Medieval Canon Law* (Wimmer Lecture 10; Latrobe 1960) 23.

First, there are two professions, uncommon in pre-Gratianic canonical collections, which link together the Turin Collection and the *Liber Tarraconensis*, a canonical collection which Professor Le Bras lists as Poitevin.[14] The professions of Berengar are almost never found in canonical collections outside France.[15] Among the French collections containing the professions is the *Liber Tarraconensis*.[16] Outside France they are contained in only two canonical collections, our Turin *Coll VIIL*[17] and the recently discovered Italian *Collectio Barberiniana*.[18] The other profession, an episcopal oath drawn from the *Ordines Romani* or the *Pontificale Romanum*, 'Beatissimo pape N apostolice sedis dignitate . . . ,' is common again to the Turin *Coll VIIL* and the *Liber Tarraconensis*.[19]

An especially close tie between the Turin Collection and Poitiers is the inclusion in the Turin Collection of ten canons of the reforming Council of Poitiers of A.D. 1078.[20] These Poitevin canons are also found in the *Liber Tarraconensis*,[21] the Berlin *Collection in Thirteen Books* (hereafter *Coll XIIIL*),[22] the provenance of which was Poitiers,[23] and the Bordeaux *Collection in Seven Books*,[24] which Tardif long ago located in Poitou.[25]

---

[14] Professor Fransen has reported, in the proceedings of the *Congrès de Droit Canonique Médiéval* (Louvain 1959) 102, another MS of the *Liber Tarraconensis* unknown to P. Fournier when he wrote his article, 'Le *Liber Tarraconensis*: Étude sur une collection canonique du xiᵉ siècle,' *Mélanges Julien Havet* (Paris 1895) 261f. The new MS, Tarragona Bibl. Prov. 26, is a short version of the *Liber Tarraconensis* much like Milan Amb. D 59 Sup. (As long ago as 1929, Valls Taberner reported the Tarragona MS as containing the *Collection in 74T*. Cf. G. Le Bras, 'Notes pour servir à l'histoire des collections canoniques,' RHD⁴ 10 [1931] 131 n. 1.) Since the long and short recensions of the *Liber Tarraconensis* come from different types of texts, the collection as a whole will bear further study. Until that time it cannot be stated with certainty that the *Liber Tarraconensis* is a Poitevin collection.

[15] Fournier - Le Bras, *Histoire* 2.239.

[16] 5.58; Vat. Lat. 6093, fol. 91ʳ⁻ᵛ. Also cf. Bordeaux MS 11, fol. 74ʳ.

[17] Fol. 77ʳ⁻ᵛ. Cf. Mansi 20.524.

[18] M. Fornasari, 'Collectio Canonum Barberiniana,' *Apollinaris* 36 (1963) 289f.

[19] *Liber Tarraconensis* 5.82; Vat. Lat. 6093, fol. 94ʳ. *Coll VIIL* 6.96; Turin MS D. IV. 33, fol. 122ᵛ. And cf. P. Fournier, 'Le *Liber Tarraconensis*' 266 and 271. This episcopal oath is found in the *Ordo Romanus* XXXV B, where the incipit is 'Beatissimo papae A. . . .' M. Andrieu, *Les Ordines Romani du haut moyen âge* 4 (Louvain 1956) 100. The oath with this incipit appears only in *Ordo XXXV B*, found in Rome Bibl. Aless. MS 173, and can be dated ca. 975-1000. The 'A' probably refers to either Pope Anastasius III (911-913) or Pope Agapetus II (946-955). The form of the oath which appears in the Turin and Tarragona Collections is also found in the *Pontificale Romanum s. XII*, 10.3. M. Andrieu, *Le Pontifical romain du moyen âge* 1 (Studi e Testi 86; Vatican City 1938) 139.

[20] 6.192-200; Turin MS D. IV. 33, fol. 134ᵛ-135ʳ.

[21] 6.83; Vat. lat. 6093, fol. 106ᵛ-107ʳ.

[22] 11.1; Berlin Savigny 3, fol. 134ʳ⁻ᵛ. In the list of capitula on fol. 132ᵛ the rubrics for the canons of Poitiers are listed simply as 'Diversa capitula.' The rubric on fol. 134ʳ reads 'Decrevit sancta synodus' with no reference to Poitiers.

[23] Fournier - Le Bras, *Histoire* 2.251.

[24] Bordeaux MS 11, fol. 156ᵛ-157ʳ. The canons appear immediately before L. II.

[25] Cf. E. J. Tardif, 'Une collection canonique poitevine,' *Nouv. rev. hist. dr. fr. étr.* 21 (1897) 149-216.

Four texts on the ecclesiastical orders further connect the Turin Collection with Poitiers. The extended 'Leonine' sermon, 'Fratres, presbyteri et sacerdotes . . . ,'[26] early appeared in canonical collections in the late ninth-century northern Italian collection, the *Collection of Milan Amb. MS Lat. A 46 Inf.*[27] Thereafter it was confined chiefly to French collections, including the Bordeaux *Collection in Seven Books* (ca. 1080-1090),[28] and later the Thérouanne *Collection in Ten Parts,*[29] and to our Turin *Coll VIIL.*[30]

Since the compiler of the Turin *Coll VIIL* was heavily dependent on Burchard's *Decretum,* it is not surprising that in his recension of the 'Isidorian' *Epistula ad Leudefredum* he followed the Burchardian recension by listing the ecclesiastical orders in the sequence: psalmist, doorkeeper, lector, exorcist, acolyte, subdeacon, deacon, presbyter, bishop, and archdeacon.[31] This same sequence is found in a few Italian collections of the second half of the eleventh century, but it is rare.[32] It was much more common in French collections. In the four collections which Professor Le Bras calls Poitevin, the Burchardian recension appears three times, once in the *Collection in Seventeen Books,*[33]

---

[26] Cf. Fournier-Le Bras, *Histoire* 2.164; P. Fournier, 'Un groupe de recueils canoniques inédits du xᵉ siècle,' *Annales de l'Université de Grenoble* 11 (1899) 394; G. Morin, 'L'auteur de l'*Admonition synodale* sur les devoirs du clergé,' *Revue bénéd.* 9 (1892) 99-108; and now R. Amiet, 'Une "Admonitio synodalis" de l'époque carolingienne : Étude critique et édition,' *Mediaeval Studies* 26 (1964) 12-82, who argues that the sermon is from a provincial or regional synod of the early ninth century.

[27] Fol. 158ᵛ-159ᵛ.

[28] Bordeaux MS 11, fol. 179ʳ.

[29] 4.31.2; Paris BN MS lat. 10743, pp. 232-5. Cf. Berlin MS Phill. 1746, fol. 74ʳ sq.

[30] 1.1; Turin MS D. IV. 33, fol. 19ʳ. The sermon is also found in the early twelfth-century Italian collection in Vat. lat. 1350, a collection based primarily on Burchard's *Decretum.* Cf. P. Fournier, *Mélanges Paul Fabre* (n. 6 *supra*) 197. R. Amiet *loc. cit.* lists two pre-twelfth-century canonical MSS in which the sermon appears: Munich lat. 6241, fol. 97ʳ-100ʳ (a canonical MS of the late tenth century); and Lucca Bibl. cap. 124, fol. 193ᵛ-194ᵛ (an eleventh-century MS containing the *Decretum* of Burchard). Among the pre-Gratianic twelfth-century canonical MSS which Amiet lists are: Vat. Barb. lat. 535, fol. 7ʳ-8ᵛ (a MS with the *Collectio canonum* of Anselm of Lucca); Wolfenbüttel Gud. lat. 212, fol. 47ʳ-ᵛ (the *Collection of Saint-Germain-des-Prés*); Vat. lat. 1355, fol. 310ʳ-311ᵛ (a Burchard MS of unknown provenance); and Bordeaux Bibl. mun. 11, fol. 76ᵛ-77ʳ, 179ʳ-ᵛ.

[31] 4.209; Turin MS D. IV. 33, fol. 64ᵛ. Cf. Burchard's *Decretum,* 3.50; PL 140.681f. In a forthcoming study this author will examine the origins and early medieval recensions of the *Epistula ad Leudefredum.*

[32] The only Italian canonical collections with the 'Burchardian' sequence known to this author are Bonizo's *Liber de vita christiana* 5.71 (ed. E. Perels [Berlin 1930] 201f.); the *Collectio Barberiniana* c. 75 (without bishop) (ed. Fornasari, *loc. cit.* [n. 18 *supra*] 277f.); and the *Collection in Five Books* of Vat. lat. 1348, fol. xlviiʳ-xlviiiⁱ (without psalmist and archdeacon).

[33] 3.40; Reims MS 675, fol. 36ʳ. Presumably because this collection contains canons from seventeen or eighteen books of Burchard's *Decretum* (LL. VI and XX are missing and LL. XV and XVI are combined), Fournier-Le Bras, *Histoire* 2.231, call this collection the *Collection in Seventeen Books.* (In his description in *Mélanges Paul Fabre* 205, P. Fournier calls this collection the *Collection of Saint Hilary of Poitiers* and notes that the Berlin MS contains only sixteen books.) The tables of contents in more 'modern'

512

and twice in the Bordeaux *Collection in Seven Books* and accompanying canonical fragments.[34] Further, there are traces of the Turin canon in the Berlin *Coll XIIIL* where the Turin incipit for the *Epistula ad Leudefredum* has
been attached as the desinit to the text of the *De distantia graduum* or *De
officiis vii graduum.*[35] It appears that the compiler of the *Coll XIIIL* did not
wish to include duplicative texts listing the functions of the ecclesiastical officers and hence omitted a canon which the compiler of the Turin Collection
had chosen to include.

Unique recensions of two ancient texts on the ecclesiastical orders in the
Turin Collection bind it very closely to the Berlin *Coll XIIIL* and thus to the
Poitevin tradition. In both the Turin Collection and the *Coll XIIIL* the fol-
lowing canon appears:[36]

> De vii gradibus ęcclesię
>
> Hii sunt vii gradus ecclesie in quibus christus affuit: idest lector fuit quando aperuit
> librum *evangelii*; exorcista quando eiecit vii demonia de maria magdalena[a]; subdia-
> conus quando fecit vinum de aqua; diaconus quando pedes discipulorum lavit; pres-
> byter quando benedixit panem; ostiarius quando portas inferni aperuit; episcopus
> quando elevavit manus super apostolos ut benediceret eis[b]. Episcopus[c] oportet eum
> iudicare, interpretari et *congregrare*, ordinare[d], consumare[e], offerre, [f]baptizare; sa-
> cerdos idest[f] presbyter oportet eum offerre et praeesse et praedicare et baptizare;
> levita idest minister oportet eum ministrare ad altare et baptizare et communicare;
> subdiaconus[g] oportet eum praeparare aquam[h] administrationem altaris et ministrare
> diacono et de[i] honestare altare; exorcista[j] oportet eum abiecere demones et dicere
> his qui non comunicant[k] ut recedant et aquam ministerii effundere; *ostiarius*[l] eum
> oportet percutere cimbalum et aperire ecclesiam et sacrarium et librum qui praedi-
> cat; *lector* oportet eum legere ei qui praedicat et lectiones canere et benedicere panem
> et omnes fructus[m].

---

hands in both the Reims and Berlin MSS suggest that there were formally only three books
with other sections added. A close examination of the structure and rubrics of the Collection further suggests that the eleventh-century compiler actually did not view his Collection as one in seventeen books. In the Reims MS, e.g., the first three books are clearly
labelled as books. Thereafter the 'books' are usually signalled by the words 'incipit'
or 'incipiunt.' Of the books which Fournier-Le Bras list, LL. V, VII, VIII, XII, and
XVI are books only in the vaguest sense. In the Reims MS 'L. V' has no 'incipit' and
is found on fol. 48r-v. 'L. VII' (fol. 49v-55r [?]) has no 'incipit' and is a farrago of diverse canons. 'L. VIII' has no 'incipit,' is contained on fol. 55r-56r, and is hardly distin-
guishable from 'L. VII.' 'L. XII' has no 'incipit' and is found on fol. 61r-v. (The 'modern'
table of contents, however, lists it as a distinct book.) 'L. XV,' although not having an
'incipit,' does appear to be a formal book (fol. 63r-69r). 'L. XVI' on penance does not
begin with a rubric and appears only on fol. 69r-70v. On the peculiarities of the Hereford
MS of this collection, cf. P. Fournier, 'Note sur les anciennes collections' 130; and Brooke
loc. cit. (n. 2 *supra*).

[34] 3.25; Bordeaux MS 11, fol. 163r. As a canonical fragment the *Epistula* in a Burchardian recension appears on fol. 75r.

[35] Berlin Savigny 3, fol. 127r: 'Hii sunt vii gradus et opera eorum digna in sancta ecclesia
catholica.' In the Turin *Coll VIIL* 4.209, fol. 64v, the rubric for the *Epistula ad Leudefredum* reads 'Ysidorus de eadem re.'

[36] *Coll VIIL* 4.208; fol. 64v: *Coll XIIIL* 10.220; fol. 126v-127r.

Variants in Berlin Savigny 3: [a] magdalene [b] eos [c] episcopum [d] consummare [e] ordinare [f-f] et [g] subdiaconem [h] aqua [i] om. [j] exorcistam [k] communicant [l] ostiarium [m] add. Hii sunt vii gradus et opera eorum digna in sancta ecclesia catholica.

This canon has two components, an Ordinal of Christ and the 'Isidorian' *De distantia graduum* or *De officiis vii graduum.* Neither of these two texts was especially uncommon in pre-Gratianic canonical collections,[37] but the recensions in the Turin and Berlin manuscripts are highly unusual.

In almost all recensions of the Ordinals of Christ, whether they appeared in canonical collections, ordinational rites, or florilegial tracts, Christ was said to have fulfilled the grade of lector when he read from Isaiah.[38] In the unique Turin-Berlin recension Christ is the lector when he reads from the Gospels.

There are two peculiarities in the second text of the canon, the *De distantia graduum* or *De officiis vii graduum.* In most recensions of this text the bishop's functions were 'iudicare, interpretari et consecrare, consummare, ordinare, offerre, et baptizare.'[39] In the Turin-Berlin text 'consecrare' has been omitted and 'congregare' put in its place. Far more unusual is the sequence of the lower ecclesiastical orders. In the Turin-Berlin text they are listed in the descending hierarchical order: subdeacon, exorcist, doorkeeper, and lector. The common sequence — sometimes descending, sometimes ascending — in this text in almost all canonical collections, ordinational formulae, and florilegia was: subdeacon, (acolyte), exorcist, lector, and doorkeeper. The basic difference between the common sequence and that of the Turin-Berlin text is that in the latter text the lector is placed hierarchically lower than the doorkeeper. This placement of the lector and doorkeeper is virtually unique to the *De distantia graduum* or *De officiis vii graduum* of the Turin-Berlin text.[40]

To claim unreservedly that the Turin Collection comes from Poitiers would clearly be going beyond the limits of the available evidence. In fact, not all of the collections mentioned by Professor Le Bras have been definitely established as Poitevin.[41] Nevertheless, the general sources and specific texts which have here been noted in connection with the *Coll VIII* point to a locality far west and north of Turin as the place of its origin. The professions of faith and obedience, the canons of the Council of Poitiers of 1078, and the unique recensions of texts and unusual canons on the ecclesiastical grades,

---

[37] In forthcoming studies this author will examine the origins and early medieval recensions of the *De distantia graduum* or *De officiis vii graduum* and what he has called the Ordinals of Christ.

[38] E.g. *Collectio Hibernensis* 8.1; ed. H. Wasserschleben, *Die irische Kanonensammlung,* 2nd ed. (Leipzig 1885) 26: and the Pseudo-Isidorian *De vetere et novo testamento quaestiones* c. 41; ed. R. E. McNally, 'The Pseudo-Isidorian "De vetere et novo testamento quaestiones",' *Traditio* 19 (1963) 48.

[39] *Pontificale Romano-germanicum saeculi decimi* 14.1-4; ed. C. Vogel and R. Elze, *Le Pontifical romano-germanique du Xe siècle* 1 (Studi e Testi 226; Vatican City 1963) 12-13. Cf. *Collectio Hibernensis* 8.2; ed. Wasserschleben, *loc. cit.* 26.

[40] In the early twelfth-century Ordinal of Christ in the *Liber de diversis ordinibus* possibly belonging to Raimbaud of Liège (PL 213.811f.), the sequence of the lower grades is that found in the *De distantia graduum* of the Turin and Berlin MSS.

[41] Cf. *supra,* n. 14.

514

all texts connected with canonical collections probably emanating from Poitou, suggest that the Turin *Coll VIIL* should be counted as another product of the eleventh-century canonical activity centered around Poitiers.

XVIII

LITURGICAL SCHOLARSHIP AT THE TIME OF THE INVESTITURE CONTROVERSY: PAST RESEARCH AND FUTURE OPPORTUNITIES*

To state that the period dominated by events at Canossa was a watershed in the history of ecclesio-political relationships is almost trite. But it is not so commonplace to state that this same period was also a high plateau in- the history of liturgical scholarship. For modern students the picture of investiture by ring and staff represents the struggle between Church and State in the late eleventh and early twelfth centuries,[1] but it should not be overlooked that the tradition of these tangible instruments was a liturgical act also signaling an intensity of concern for the liturgy and its proper performance and interpretation unequaled since the Carolingian age. Thus it comes as a surprise to many students of ecclesio-political theory to find that a majority of the publicists of the age of the Investiture Controversy whose works fill the three fat volumes of the *Libelli de lite* of the *Monumenta Germaniae historica* were avid observers of the liturgy. Peter Damian, Humbert of Silva Candida, Bonizo of Sutri, Bernold of Constance, Ranger of Lucca, the Norman Anonymous, Ivo of Chartres, Sigebert of Gembloux, Hildebert of Le Mans, and Honorius "of Autun" all wrote tracts in which aspects of liturgy were described and explained.[2] And while the political ideas of these publicistic worthies have lost their

*This paper was presented at the meeting of the Rocky Mountain Medieval and Renaissance Association in Ft. Collins, Colorado, 16 May 1977, whose theme was "Castello di Canossa—Ft. Collins, 1077–1977: Two Conferences in Rocky Mountains." Materials used in this paper were collected under grants from the Canada Council, the American Philosophical Society, and the American Council of Learned Societies.

[1]E.g., see the study of Robert L. Benson, *The Bishop-Elect: A Study in Medieval Ecclesiastical Office* (Princeton, 1968) *passim*.

[2]The following authors whose works appear in *MGH, LDL* (3 vols.; Hanover, 1891–7) are attributed with liturgical works: *LDL* 1: Humbert, *Adversus simoniacos, LDL* 1. 95; *Adversus Graecorum calumnias*, PL 143. 929; Peter Damian, *De dominus vobiscum*, PL 145. 231; Bonizo of Sutri, *Libellus de sacramentis*, ed. Walter Berschin, *Bonizo von Sutri: Leben und Werk* (Beiträge zur Geschichte und Quellenkunde des Mittelalters 2; ed. H. Fuhrmann; Berlin–New York, 1972).

LDL 2: Bernold of Constance, *Libelli* (especially *De presbyteris*), *LDL* 2. 1; *Micrologus*, PL 151. 977; Sigebert of Gembloux, *Apologia contra eos qui calumniantur missas*

cogency in modern times, their liturgical scholarship still graces the footnotes of many a modern popular exposition of the liturgy.[3]

Prior to the era of the Investiture struggles, liturgical scholarship had been at a low ebb for nearly two hundred years. The early ninth century had witnessed a spectacular output of liturgical *expositiones*. It had begun with several short, sometimes anonymous explanations of the eucharistic and baptismal rites occasioned by the liturgical reforms of Pepin and Charlemagne.[4] These were followed then by the luxuriant and allegorical *Liber officialis* of Amalarius of Metz, the more literal *De exordiis* of Walafrid Strabo, and the *De clericorum institutione* and *De sacris ordinibus* of Rabanus Maurus.[5] These tracts, copied extensively in manuscripts of the ninth century and beyond, were joined by a host of

---

coniugatorum sacerdotum, *LDL* 2. 436; *De differentia iv temporum*, PL 160. 813; Ranger of Lucca, *Liber de anulo et baculo*, *LDL* 2. 505; Ivo of Chartres, *Epistolae ad litem investiturarum spectantes*, *LDL* 2. 640; *Sermones de ecclesiasticis sacramentis*, PL 162. 505; Hildebert, *Epistolae de Paschali papa*, *LDL* 2. 667; *Versus de mysterio missae*, PL 171. 1177.

LDL 3: Honorius Augustodunensis, *De offendiculo, De apostatis, Summa gloria*, *LDL* 3. 38,57,63; *Gemma animae*, PL 172. 541; *Sacramentarium seu de causis et significatu mystico rituum divini in ecclesia officii liber*, PL 172. 737; *Speculum ecclesiae*, PL 172. 813 [on the manuscripts of Honorius see V. I. J. Flint, "The Place and Purpose of the Works of Honorius Augustodunensis," *RBén* 87 (1977) 119-27]. Norman Anonymous, *Tractates*, ed. Karl Pellens, *Die Texte des Normannischen Anonymus unter Konsultation der Teilausgaben von H. Böhmer, H. Scherrinsky und G. H. Williams neu aus der Handschrift 415 des Corpus Christi College Cambridge* (Veröff. des Instituts für Europäische Geschichte 42; Wiesbaden, 1966).

[3]See, e.g., Mgr. Lamothe-Tenet, *Les saints ordres: 2, Les ordres mineurs* (2d ed.; Toulouse, 1891) 41f., or P. Gontier, *Explication du pontifical, Texte et commentaire* 2 (2d ed.; Angers, 1899) 148f.

[4]For studies and lists of these shorter texts see Raphael Schulte, *Die Messe als Opfer der Kirche* (Liturgiewissenschaftliche Quellen und Forschungen 35; Münster / W., 1959) 121-38, dealing with the tracts *Dominus vobiscum, Prima in ordine*, and *Quotiens contra se*; and Cyrille Vogel, *Introduction aux sources de l'histoire du culte chrétien au moyen âge* (reedited with preface by B. Botte; Spoleto, 1975) 11f., listing the works of Charlemagne, *Ad Odilbertum episcopum Mediolanensis* and responses, Alcuin, *Ad Oduinum sacerdotem*; Leidrad, *Liber de sacramento baptismatis ad Carolum Magnum*; Magnus of Sens, *Libellus de mysterio baptismatis iussu Caroli Magni editus*; Theodulf of Orléans, *De ordine baptismi*; Maxentius of Aquileia, *De significatu rituum baptismatis*; various anonymous tracts on baptism, Jesse of Amiens, *Epistola de baptismo*.

[5]On the works of Amalarius, Walafrid Strabo, and Rabanus see Vogel, *Introduction*, 12; and on Rabanus especially see Raymund Kottje, "Hrabanus Maurus—'Praeceptor Germaniae'?" *Wissenschaft zwischen Forschung und Ausbildung* (Schriften der Philosophische Fachbereiche der Universität Augsburg 1; ed. J. Becker and R. Bergmann; Augsburg, 1975) 89 (repr. with manuscript citations in *Deutsches Archiv* 31 [1975] 540f.).

lesser known commentaries representing the liturgical thought of nearly all the intellectual luminaries of the Carolingian renaissance.[6]

Shortly after the middle of the ninth century reflective liturgical scholarship abruptly ceased.[7] Liturgists seem to have been content to repeat, copy, and excerpt from the liturgical geniuses of the first half of the ninth century. The only bright spots in liturgical scholarship for the next two centuries were a short *Explicatio missae* attributed to Remigius of Auxerre (d. 908), and a longer tract to which the *Explicatio* was often attached, the *Liber de divinis officiis*, attributed to Alcuin but actually written during the early tenth century.[8]

The dearth of liturgical commentaries from the mid-ninth through the mid-eleventh centuries by no means signaled a stagnation of liturgy. Rather than musing on the meaning of the liturgy, men of the two hundred years following Amalarius were busy practicing and creating liturgical forms and compiling books of the rites themselves.[9] The origins of liturgical drama are always connected with this period; many of the *Ordines romani* were written in the post-Carolingian age; and it was in the middle of the tenth century that the *Pontificale romano-germanicum* was composed and taken to Rome, there to become the basis for the Roman Pontifical used into the twentieth century. But despite the creation and use of new liturgical forms from the middle of the ninth to the middle of the eleventh century, reflective scholarship on the meaning of the liturgy did not keep pace. There was, to be sure, a host of didactic tracts, sometimes in dialogue form between master and student, in which select liturgical words and actions were explained, but these tracts, few of which have been edited, were more at the level of catechesis than liturgiology.[10]

[6]See the works noted in n. 4 above, as well as those listed by Vogel, *Introduction*, 11f., including Agobard of Lyons, *Liber de correctione antiphonarii, Contra libros iv Amalarii*; Florus of Lyons, *Liber de divina psalmodia, De actione missae*; and Hincmar of Rheims, *Epistola ad presbyteros Remensis ecclesiae*.

[7]See Adolph Franz, *Die Messe im deutschen Mittelalter: Beiträge zur Geschichte der Liturgie und des religiösen Volkslebens* (repr. Darmstadt, 1963) 407.

[8]On the *Liber* see my "Marginalia on a Tenth-Century Text on the Ecclesiastical Officers," *Law, Church and Society: Essays in Honor of Stephan Kuttner*, (ed. K. Pennington and R. Somerville; Philadelphia, 1977) 115–29.

[9]Beryl Smalley, *The Study of the Bible in the Middle Ages* (2d ed.; Oxford, 1952) 44f., notes a similar phenomenon in the production of commentaries on the Bible as opposed to the *lectio divina* in choir.

[10]See, e.g., *Albi Bibl. mun. 43 (15)*, fol. 16v; *Clm 14532*, fol. 92v; and *Clm 17043*, fol. 151v.

112

With the second half of the eleventh century complaints began to surface that abuses had crept into the liturgy,[11] but there were few objections that liturgical practice itself was neglected. In fact, it was in the second half of the eleventh century that an overpowering concern developed to Romanize a liturgy which had been dominated previously by practices imposed by the Ottonian and Salian emperors. The early popes of the so-called Gregorian Reform were fairly content to maintain the liturgical status quo of their imperial patrons,[12] but by the pontificates of Alexander II and Gregory VII there was a concerted effort not only to make the rite used in Rome more Roman and less Germanic, but also to impose that rite elsewhere. As a result a new Roman pontifical was compiled,[13] new liturgical regulations were enacted for Rome,[14] and attempts were made to suppress indigenous rites in Armenia, Milan, and Spain and supplant them with the Roman rite.[15]

---

[11]See Gregory VII, *Regula canonica* [*Vat. Lat. 629*], ed. Germain Morin, *Etudes, textes, découvertes: Contributions à la littérature et à l'histoire des douze premiers siècles* (2d ser., Anecdota Maredsolana 1; Maredsous, 1913) 459f. Gregory complains about those who daily use in the Office three psalms and three lessons due to negligence of ancient customs and fastidiousness. Vogel, *Introduction*, 363, now notes that according to Mabillon these complaints would have been voiced by Hildebrand at the Lateran Council of 1059 under Nicholas II.

[12]In fact, Stephen IX, a Lotharingian and former abbot in the long line of German abbots at Monte Cassino attempted in 1058 to suppress Ambrosian chant at Monte Cassino, so Klaus Gamber speculates, to assure conformity to the Romano-Germanic rite imposed by the emperors. See Klaus Gamber, *Codices liturgici latini antiquiores* (Spicilegii Friburgensis, Subsidia 1. 1; Freiburg/Sch., 1968) 250; and Myrtilla Avery, "The Beneventan Lections for the Vigil of Easter and the Ambrosian Chant Banned by Pope Stephen IX at Monte Cassino," *Studi gregoriani* 1 (1947) 433–58.

It must be emphasized that the Gregorian champions, Anselm of Lucca and Deusdedit, later even used large sections from the *Pontificale romano-germanicum* in their canonical collections, referring to the texts as Roman.

[13]The *Roman Pontifical of the Twelfth Century* (*PR XII*) is the result. Our earliest manuscripts of this pontifical are from the late eleventh century, *Troyes Bibl. de la Ville 2272*, and *Vat. Barb. Lat. 631*, on which see Michel Andrieu, *Le Pontifical romain au moyen-âge: 1, Le Pontifical romain du XIIᵉ siècle* (Studi e Testi 86; Vatican, 1938) 61, 81. Also elements of the *PR XII* were already appearing in manuscripts of the *Pontificale romano-germanicum*, on which see my "The *De officiis vii graduum*: Its Origins and Early Medieval Development," *Mediaeval Studies* 34 (1972) 145–48. In the *PR XII* the *Pontificale romano-germanicum* was reworked to fit the Roman situation: archaic rites and texts were omitted (e.g., *iudicia dei*, rites of exorcism, excommunication, etc.), and there was a general simplification of rites (e.g., multiple prayers were dropped) so characteristic of the Roman liturgy.

[14]E.g., there was inserted into the sanctorale the feasts of popes unknown in Frankish lands, and these were to be solemnly celebrated everywhere "cum pleno officio." See Vogel, *Introduction*, 204.

[15]On these suppressions see Karl F. Morrison, *Tradition and Authority in the Western Church, 300–1140* (Princeton, 1969) 273. For more extensive discussions of the

Accompanying these reforms in the practice of liturgy there blossomed a new interest in the explanation and interpretation of the liturgy. The fruits of this renewed concern are now counted among the works of the liturgists and publicists whose names were mentioned at the beginning of this paper as well as many others whose works have been published outside the *Libelli de lite*.[16] The importance of these works to liturgical scholarship both in quantity and quality can be illustrated dramatically by looking at one of the more complete compendia of medieval liturgical commentaries made since the Council of Trent, the *De divinis catholicae ecclesiae officiis et mysteriis* of Melchior Hittorp.[17] Of the nearly 1,500 columns in this folio-sized collection, a full third is taken up with tracts written by scholars working during the Investiture Controversy.

Given the quality and frequency of liturgical commentaries written in this well-studied period of medieval history, one might conclude that historians of medieval liturgy would long ago have collected, edited, and reedited where necessary the works of this fertile period, and then on the basis of these editions investigated every nuance of liturgical growth. But surprisingly, many of the liturgical commentaries of the period of the Investiture Controversy lie unedited in the manuscripts, and of the commentaries which have been printed, all but two, the *Libellus de sacramentis* of Bonizo of Sutri and the *De divinis officiis* of Rupert of Deutz, are still begging for modern critical editions and studies. Hence in treating the opportunities for future research in liturgical scholarship during the Investiture Controversy, this paper will first deal with several commentaries which should be the object of modern investigation and

---

suppression of rites under Alexander and Gregory see Archdale A. King, *Liturgies of the Primatial Sees* (London, 1957) 305,503ff.; Richard G. Donovan, *The Liturgical Drama in Medieval Spain* (Studies and Texts 4; Toronto, 1958) 21–23; J. N. Hillgarth in *Speculum* 52 (1977) 725; and Gregory's letter to Archbishop Gregory of Sivas in Armenia, *MGH, Epist. Sel.* 1. 510–14.

[16]To be added to the list of authors whose works appear in the *LDL* are the following, whose works have been edited elsewhere: Berno of Reichenau, *Libellus de quibusdam rebus ad missae officium pertinentibus*, PL 142. 1055; *Dialogus qualiter quatuor temporum ieiunia per sua sabbata sint observanda*, PL 142. 1087; Rupert of Deutz, *Liber de divinis officiis*, (ed., H. Haake; Corpus christianorum, Cont. med. 7; Turnhout, 1967); John of Avranches, *De officiis ecclesiasticis*, ed. R. Delamare, *Le "De officiis ecclesiasticis" de Jean d'Avranches, archevêque de Rouen, (1067–79)* (Bibliothèque liturgique du Chanoine U. Chevalier 22; Paris, 1923); Odo of Cambrai, *Expositio in canonem missae*, PL 160. 1053; Bruno of Segni, *De sacramentis ecclesiae, mysteriis atque ecclesiasticis ritibus*, PL 165. 1089; Alger of Liège (?), *De sacrificio missae*, PL 180. 853; Drogo of Laon, *Liber de divinis officiis*, PL 166. 1557.

[17]Melchior Hittorp, *De divinis catholicae ecclesiae officiis et mysteriis, varii vetustorum aliquot ecclesiae patrum ac scriptorum ecclesiasticorum libri, quorum catalogum pagina decimasexta complectitur* . . . (Paris, 1610, repr. Westmead, 1970).

editions; second, it will demonstrate some of the vistas open in manuscript research by bringing to light a few little known and hitherto unexamined liturgical commentaries, several of which are attributed to major publicists; and third, it will give an example of how an investigation of manuscripts containing the liturgical rites themselves can shed new light on the liturgical scholarship of one of the major publicists of the late eleventh century, the Norman Anonymous.

Before the history of liturgical scholarship during the period of the Investiture Controversy can be written, the commentaries must be uncovered and edited.[18] The major ones were printed long ago by Hittorp and others, but in many instances these editions are faulty. One thinks, for example, on the *Micrologus*, a tract often attributed to Ivo of Chartres but which has been shown to be the work of Bernold, canon of the cathedral of Constance. Bernold, a canon law expert and gifted liturgist,[19] was an ardent champion of Gregorian reform, and his *Micrologus* is the first significant commentary on the liturgy since the ninth-century *Liber officialis* of Amalarius. In this commentary, which is written to publicize and defend Roman practice, Bernold explains the Mass, Divine Office, fasts, and the liturgical calendar. He uses some of the allegorical explanations so dear to Amalarius, but his commentary is generally more descriptive and practical than that of his famous ninth-century forebear, and hence Bernold has at times been called the "rubricist" of the eleventh century. Two aspects in particular of the *Micrologus* have drawn the attention of liturgiologists. There is, first, Bernold's frequent reference to the memory of Gregory VII in order to justify the Roman customs he advocates.[20] Second, in one of its chapters, chap. 23, the *Micrologus* contains a brief outline of the Roman Mass and some of its formularies which played the role of fixing the Roman rite for large sections of medieval Europe.[21] So widespread was the diffusion of Bernold's text and so clear its exposition that in at least

[18]It is interesting to note that a study like Schulte's (see above, n. 4) dealing with the Mass in the commentaries stops with the beginning of the eleventh century. Perhaps this is indicative of the realization of how many more tracts there are which must be uncovered, edited, and studied.

[19]On Bernold's work see Johanne Autenrieth, *Die Domschule von Konstanz und zweier Kleriker dargestellt auf Grund von Handschriftenstudien* (Forschungen zur Kirchen- und Geistesgeschichte, N.F. 3; Stuttgart, 1956).

[20]In the *Micrologus*, chap. 14, *De signis super oblationem*, Bernold mentions the varieties of numbers of crosses made over the oblation and appeals to the memory of Gregory VII to support his contention that the number of signs must be uneven. In chap. 17, Bernold also cites Gregory VII, saying that the pope would have approved of five signs of the cross at the touching of the chalice.

[21]See Joseph A. Jungmann, *The Mass of the Roman Rite: Its Origins and Development (Missarum Sollemnia)* (trans. F. Brunner; New York, 1951) 1. 103.

one area, Hungary, the bishops in synod established the *Micrologus* as the norm for the performance of the Roman rite.[22]

Some twenty years ago Fr. Vincent Kennedy demonstrated that the edition we now have of the *Micrologus* is incomplete and defective.[23] With a view to editing the *Micrologus* anew Fr. Kennedy began to collect photographs and microfilm of manuscripts of the text (over forty-five thus far) and to collate them. Unfortunately, Fr. Kennedy's dream of a new edition of the *Micrologus* was unfulfilled at his death several years ago,[24] and a new edition and study of this tract so critical in liturgical history remains a chief desideratum of scholars of the medieval cult.

Almost as important as Bernold's *Micrologus* in the history of liturgical commentaries are the sermons ascribed to Ivo of Chartres, the canonist-liturgist-theologian whose moderate ecclesio-political "thesis" provided a partial basis for the final settlement of the Investiture Controversy. In many of his sermons Ivo dealt with baptism, ordination, liturgical vestments, the dedication of churches, the Mass, and the liturgical calendar[25] in ways so attractive that large sections were repeated verbatim by the sentence collectors and later medieval liturgical commentators.[26]

The edition of Ivo's sermons we now find printed in the *Patrologia Latina* is somewhat more satisfactory than the *Micrologus* of Bernold. But unlike the case of Bernold, little systematic search seems to have been undertaken for manuscripts containing Ivo's sermons.[27] A preliminary study reveals that dozens of European manuscripts (fifty-four at last rough count with *Sermo II* alone) contain the sermons in

---

[22]Jungmann, *The Mass of the Roman Rite*, 1. 103. The reference here is to a synod of Hungarian bishops who met ca. 1100 and published a group of decrees with the rubric *Ordo divinorum officiorum et ieiuniorum secundum libellum quem conlaudabimus ab omnibus teneatur.* In the manuscript, *Budapest Nat. Mus. Nyelvemlékek N. 1,* where the canons are found there is also the *Micrologus.* It must be noted, however, that chap. 23 is missing in the text.

[23]V. L. Kennedy, "For a New Edition of the *Micrologus* of Bernold of Constance," *Mélanges en l'honneur de Monseigneur Michel Andrieu, Rev. des. sc. relig.,* vol. hors sér. (Strasbourg, 1956) 229–41.

[24]For a list of Fr. Kennedy's works see "Vincent Lorne Kennedy: 1899–1974," *Mediaeval Studies* 37 (1975) 4f.

[25]PL 162. 505.

[26]See my "Ivonian Opuscula on the Ecclesiastical Officers," *Studia Gratiana, Mélanges G. Fransen II* 20 (1976) 312.

[27]Many of the manuscripts noted in the Institut de Recherche et d'Histoire des Textes appear to have been the result of the Abbé Guizard's researches on the works of Ivo in general.

various forms.[28] Hence, a new critical edition and study of these texts would prove invaluable not only to the historian of the liturgy but also to the historian of dogma.

Even with new critical editions of the *Micrologus* of Bernold and the sermons of Ivo we would have only a limited picture—albeit a very important one—of liturgical scholarship during the Investiture Controversy. There are additional critical editions and studies of other liturgical commentaries already mentioned which should be undertaken. But beyond all these, editions of commentaries which are still known primarily in manuscript form should be made. Here only a few can be mentioned to illustrate the wealth of liturgical commentaries still to be investigated.

There is one group of late eleventh-century commentaries which are conservative or traditional and reflect little of the "new" or "modern" liturgical scholarship represented in the works of Bernold or Ivo. These conservative commentaries follow for the most part the *expositiones* of the Carolingian age.

One of the most widely distributed of these tracts is the so-called *Liber Quare*, which first appears in a late eleventh-century manuscript in Turin.[29] Its dialogue format, explaining the Mass, Divine Office, and diverse liturgical practices, resembles the old catechetical tracts, but the responses bear the sophistication of Amalarius and his ninth-century confreres. An edition of this tract is in typescript at the Gregorian University in Rome,[30] and scholars eagerly await the published version to which Dr. Götz has devoted many years.

Another of the conservative commentaries of the late eleventh century has been known for many years from a Bamberg manuscript

---

[28]For lists of the manuscripts of Ivo's sermons see my "Marginalia," 14. To be added to the list are *Liverpool Public Libraries f091.RAB*, fols. 150–63 (a reference kindly brought to my attention by Mr. Neil Ker, who says this is a former Helmingham manuscript of the mid-twelfth century written in England with a Peterborough abbey provenance); *Library of the Bishop of Portsmouth s.n.*, noted in P. Blanchard, "Un traité *De benedictionibus patriarcharum* de Paschase Radbert?" *RBén* 28 (1911) 425f. These manuscripts all contain at least *Sermo II*, and there are many more manuscripts that contain the other sermons of Ivo, but not *Sermo II*. See e.g., J. B. Schneyer, *Wegweiser zu lateinischen Predigtreihen des Mittelalters* (Munich, 1965) 296,437; *Repertorium der lateinischen Sermones des Mittelalters* 2 (Beiträge zur Geschichte der Philosophie und Theologie des Mittelalters 48.2: Münster/W, 1970) 156; and Flint, "Place and Purpose of the Works of Honorius," 112 n. 3.

[29]*Turin Bibl. Naz. Univ. D.IV.42 (Pasini 1136)*.

[30]Georg P. Götz, *Der "Liber Quare": ein Katechismus der Liturgie, Untersuchungen und Text* (Dissertation; Rome, 1971). Also see *Iohannis Beleth Summa de ecclesiasticis officiis*, (ed. H. Douteil; Corpus christianorum, Cont. med. 41; Turnhout, 1976) 24*.

and has occasionally been attributed to Frutolf of Michelsberg.[31] It is no longer possible to attribute the tract to Frutolf, as Fr. Kennedy showed some forty years back,[32] but the commentary of the Bamberg manuscript, which is now known in at least one other manuscript, still awaits an edition and study.[33]

Many manuscripts, including three from Paris[34] and one from Milan,[35] contain conservative texts, several attributed to Amalarius, which seem in reality to be extensive excerpta from a variety of ninth-century liturgical commentators. These tracts offer little that is original, but like the collections of theological sentences of the early twelfth century, these collections of liturgical sentences also deserve to be studied and perhaps edited.

A second group of unedited liturgical commentaries from the late eleventh and early twelfth centuries is potentially more interesting than the conservative variety just mentioned. The members of this group bear all the marks of the "modern" commentaries by Bernold and Ivo, and a thorough examination of them could shed new light on the chronology and sources of the works of these two major liturgist-publicists.

Several of these tracts go under the name of Ivo. One, which is found ∗ in variant forms in Stuttgart and Munich manuscripts, is entitled *Sententia Ivonis Carnotensis episcopi de divinis officiis* and deals with the Mass and Divine Office.[36] Some of the text resembles Ivo, but other sections are more like the *De officiis ecclesiasticis* of John of Avranches. Another commentary attributed to Ivo is in manuscripts in London, Oxford, and Cambridge. The tract, entitled *Incipit liber Ivonis Carnotensis episcopi de officiis ecclesiasticis*, is a combination of the *De divinis officiis* of Drogo of Laon and the *Micrologus* of Bernold.[37]

---

[31] *Bamberg Staatsbibliothek Lit. 134 (Ed.V.13)*.

[32] Vincent L. Kennedy, "The 'De officiis divinis' of MS. Bamberg Lit. 134," *Ephemerides liturgicae* 52 (1938) 312–26.

[33] *Vienna ÖNB 273* (11th-12th centuries).

[34] *Paris BN Lat. 12942*, on which see my *The Ordinals of Christ from their Origins to the Twelfth Century* (Beiträge zur Geschichte und Quellenkunde des Mittelalters 7; ed. H. Fuhrmann; Berlin-New York, 1975) 115f.; *Paris BN Lat. 14848*, fol. 127v; and *Paris BN Lat. 11493*, fol. 94r (both containing anonymous extracts from Rabanus Maurus' *De clericorum institutione*).

[35] *Milan Ambrosiana T 62 Sup.*, on which see my *Ordinals of Christ*, 119–21.

[36] *Stuttgart Landesbibliothek Cod. Theol. 8°51* , fol. 001r; *Clm* 22273, fol. 89v; and *Clm 13105*, fol. 73r.

[37] *Oxford All Souls College 28*, fol. 137r; *London Lambeth Palace 363*, fol. 60r; *Lambeth Palace 380*, fol. 195r; and *Cambridge Corpus Christi College 68*, fol. 120v. Professor Kuttner, who kindly pointed out to me the Oxford manuscript, has noted the combination of the works of Drogo and Bernold.

Finally, manuscripts now in London, Oxford, Reims, and elsewhere contain sermons on facets of the liturgy, which are occasionally ascribed to Ivo. Some of these sermons belong to Geoffrey Babion (d. 1110) and have been edited, but others seem not to have been, and there is a possibility that they might have been written by the publicistic bishop of Chartres.[38]

To reedit all the liturgical commentaries written in the period of the Investiture Controversy which are found today printed in the *Patrologia Latina* and to edit *de novo* those commentaries still in the manuscripts would contribute immeasurably to our understanding of the medieval cult. But to appreciate fully the commentaries there must be editions and studies of the liturgical books themselves, i.e., the sacramentaries, missals, pontificals, and so forth. There has been a host of fine editions of the earliest liturgical books, the Veronese, Gelasian, and Gregorian sacramentaries and the *Ordines romani* and Roman pontificals, but despite the valiant efforts of such series as those of the Henry Bradshaw Society, we are still light-years away from editions of the vast majority of high and late medieval liturgical books. In fact, the liturgical manuscripts in some areas of Europe have never been catalogued properly, let alone studied or edited.

To conclude this paper, one example will be given of how a study of manuscripts of some of the rites themselves can illuminate a liturgical tract of one of the best-known "imperialist" publicists of the Investiture Controversy, the Norman Anonymous.

For decades scholars have been drawn repeatedly to the tractates of the anonymous champion of regal prerogatives over the Church found in the unique manuscript, *Cambridge Corpus Christi College 415*.[39] Not only have they been fascinated by the ecclesio-political ideas of the

---

[38]In *Oxford Bodl. 548* (12th century), fol. 26v, a slightly later hand has written "Sermo venerabilis Yvonis Carnotensis episcopi" beside a homily now attributed to Geoffrey, *Sermo in dedicatione ecclesiae* (PL 171. 731) (incipit: *Facta sunt encenia ierosolimis*): on fol. 145r, a much later hand has written the same words beside the *Sermo in dedicatione ecclesiae* (PL 171. 736) (incipit: *Inquit apostolus Paulus Christus dilexit ecclesiam*). In this same manuscript, fol. 91r, there are anonymous sermons directed to the clerical grades of cleric, doorkeeper, lector, exorcist, acolyte, subdeacon, deacon, and presbyter on their ordinations. There are the same sermons in *London Brit. Lib. Royal 8.F.III*, fol. 131v, and *Reims Bibl. mun. 579*, fol. 83r. On Geoffrey Babion and some of these sermons see André Wilmart, "Les sermons d'Hildebert," *RBén* 47 (1935) 12–51, esp. 20f. n. 4; Willibrordus Lampen, "De Sermonibus Gaufredi Babionis Scholastici Andegavensis," *Anton* 19 (1944) 145–68, esp. 160f.; Jean-Paul Bonnes, "Un des plus grands prédicateurs du XIIᵉ siècle Geoffroy du Loroux dit Geoffroy Babion," *RBén* 56 (1945–46) 174–215; and Schneyer, *Repertorium* 2. 150–59.

[39]For the most recent studies on the Anonymous see Kennerly M. Woody, "Marginalia on the Norman Anonymous," *HTR* 66 (1973) 273–88; Karl Pellens, *Das Kirchendenken*

Anonymous, but his identity and sources have provided them with countless hours of sleuthing, including liturgical sleuthing. The tractate *De consecratione pontificum et regum* has been studied most intensely for its liturgical sources and parallels,[40] but another short tract on the ecclesiastical hierarchy has also puzzled scholars for years. In this tract, J-19, the Anonymous attempts to justify each of the grades of the ecclesiastical hierarchy by citing an event or saying in Christ's life.[41]

[Tractate J-19]

Thus he [Christ] discharged first the office of diaconate—as we are taught by the testimony of sacred scripture—then [the office] of lector and thereafter the exorcist and acolyte, then doorkeeper and finally the subdeacon together with the priest.

[1] Thus he discharged the office of deacon at the time when he began to preach and say, "Do penance, for the kingdom of heaven is at hand."

[2] And indeed he did this before the book of the prophet Isaiah was given to him when he had gone into the synagogue, whence he first established the office of lector.

[3] But after that he cast out demons from the bodies of those possessed, and [4] he illumined the blind, whence he discharged the office of exorcist and acolyte.

[5a] And thus before entering the temple he cast out the sellers and buyers from the temple, whence he first discharged the office of doorkeeper.

[6] Finally at length he began to fulfill the office of subdiaconate when at supper he washed the feet of his disciples.

[7] Also on that day he discharged the office of priest when he took bread and offering thanks he blessed, broke, and gave it to his disciples saying, "Take and eat all etc."

[5b] But according to some he discharged the office of doorkeeper when he opened the gate of hell and leading capitivity captive he opened the doors of paradise, which afterward he did. . . .

Such texts, called the Ordinals of Christ, were frequently repeated in medieval liturgical books, canonical collections, and elsewhere. Hence, scholars have attempted to find precedents for the Anonymous in the

---

des Normannischen Anonymus (Veröff. des Instituts für Europäische Geschichte Mainz 69; Wiesbaden, 1973); and Wilfrid Hartmann, "Beziehungen des Normannischen Anonymus zu frühscholastischen Bildungszentren," *Deutsches Archiv* 31 (1975) 108–43.
[40]See, e.g., George H. Williams, *The Norman Anonymous of 1100 A.D.: Toward the Identification and Evaluation of the so-called Anonymous of York* (Harvard Theological Studies 18; Cambridge, Mass., 1951) 36–46, 74–82; Norman Cantor, *Church, Kingship, and Lay Investiture in England, 1089—1135* (Princeton, 1958) 185–89; and Ruth Nineham, "The so-called Anonymous of York," *JEH* 14 (1963) 31–45.
[41]*C.C.C. 415*, p. 119. Cf. Pellens, *Die Texte des Normannischen Anonymus*, 108.

120

major sources he was using in constructing his Ordinal of Christ. Since in another tract, J-11,[42] the Anonymous had varied one of these texts also found in the sermons of Ivo of Chartres,[43] it has been thought that the Anonymous in J-19 was modifying Ivo even further.[44] But if the text of J-19 and the complete text of Ivo are compared, it will be seen that there is very little agreement.

[Tractate J-11]	[Ivo]
It is read that on the night on which Christ was betrayed he ordained them subdeacons, deacons, and priests. For at that time he exercized these offices and then gave them at first the example, mandate, and power of those offices. . . .	These offices are divided into seven grades because the holy Church is adorned with the gift of septiform grace. These offices our Lord in his own person disclosed and left them for an example to his Church so that the form which went before in the head might be represented in the body.
	[1. Doorkeeper] This office our Lord initiated for us when, having made a whip from cords, he cast out the sellers and buyers from the temple and overturned the seats of the money-changers. . . . Wherefore he also showed himself a doorkeeper when he said, "I am the door; if any will enter by me, let him go in and out."
	[2. Lector] This office our Lord in his own person disclosed when in the midst of the elders he opened the book of the prophet Isaiah and read distinctly that they might understand, "The Spirit of the Lord is over me, and the remainder which follows in that chapter."
	[3. Exorcist] This office the Lord exercized when with his saliva he touched the ears of the deaf and dumb and said, "Epheta," which is "Be you open."
	[4. Acolyte] This office the Lord is shown to have had in himself when he says in the Gospel, "I am the light of the world; he who follows me shall not walk in the shadows, but shall have the light of life."

[42]See my "The Unidentified Sources of the Norman Anonymous: C.C.C.C. MS 415," *Transactions of the Cambridge Bibliographical Society* 5.2 (1970) 126f.

[43]See my "The Unidentified Sources," 127f.; and *Sermo II*, PL 162. 514–19.

[44]Williams, *Norman Anonymous*, 85.

When he washed the feet of the disciples he exercized the office of subdiaconate, and he said to the disciples, "I have thus given you an example so that whatsoever I have done to you, you may do similarly to one another." In this act he enjoined them to fulfill the office of subdiaconate.

[5. Subdeacon] This office the Lord exercized when, supper having been made with his disciples, he wrapped about himself a towel and pouring water into a bowl he washed the feet of the disciples and dried them with the towel.

But the diaconate [he enjoined] when he extended to them his body saying, "Take and divide it among you." For the division of the body of Christ is the duty of the deacons.

[6. Deacon] This office the Lord exercized when after supper he dispensed the sacraments confected with his own mouth and his own hands, and when he aroused the sleeping apostles to prayer saying, "Watch and pray lest you enter into temptation."

But he bestowed on them the priesthood when he began saying, "Do this in my memory."

[7. Presbyter] This office the Lord Jesus Christ exercized when after supper he changed the bread and wine into his body and blood and commanded his disciples that they should do the same in memory of his passion. Even more clearly and perfectly did he fulfill this office when he himself as priest and host offered himself on the altar of the cross for the sins of mankind and by his own blood, entering into glory, pacified heaven and earth.

Thus Christ made and established the apostles, giving them a mandamus and example. In everything we ought to imitate them.

Other sources with similar texts available to the Anonymous which scholars have compared with Tractate J-19 are in the canonical *Collectio hibernensis*[45] and a variety of English pontificals[46] widely used in both England and Normandy. But again the texts in these two sources do not agree with the Anonymous.

---

[45]L. VIII, chap. 1. The translation below is based on *Orléans Bibl. mun. 221 (193)*, pp. 38f.

[46]*Egbert Pontifical*, ed. W. Greenwell, *The Pontifical of Egbert, Archbishop of York, A. 732–766* (Durham, 1853) 10f.; *Dunstan Pontifical*, ed. E. Martène, *De antiquis ecclesiae ritibus libri tres . . .*, Lib. I, cap. viii, art. xi, Ordo III, t. 2 (Venice, 1793) 37; *Lanalet Pontifical*, ed. G. H. Doble, *Pontificale Lanaletense (Bibliothèque de la Ville de Rouen A. 27, Cat. 368): A Pontifical formerly in use at St. Germans, Cornwall* (Henry Bradshaw Society 74; London, 1937) 49; *Anderson Pontifical, London Brit. Lib. Addit. 57337*, fols. 36v–37v; *Pontifical of Canterbury, C.C.C.C. 44 (olim I.1)*, pp. 200–204. The translation below is based on the *Egbert Pontifical*.

122

[Collectio hibernensis]	[English Pontificals]
Regarding the grades in which Christ was present	Regarding the seven grades of the Church which Christ fulfilled
[1] He was the doorkeeper because he opened the gates of hell.	[1] He was the doorkeeper when he closed and opened the ark of Noah and when he opened the portals of hell.
[2] He was the exorcist because he cast out seven demons from Maria Magdalena.	[2] He was the lector when he opened in the synagogue of the Jews the book of Isaiah the prophet and read, "The Spirit of the Lord is over me, etc."
[3 He was the lector when he opened the book of Isaiah.	[3] He was the exorcist when he cast out seven demons from Maria Magdalena.
[4] He was the subdeacon because he made wine from water in Cana of Galilee.	[4] He was the subdeacon when he blessed water in Cana of Galilee and converted it to wine.
[5] He was the deacon when he washed the feet of his disciples.	[5] He was the deacon when he broke five loaves among five thousand men and seven loaves among four thousand, or when he washed the feet of his disciples.
[6] He was the priest because he took bread and broke and blessed it.	[6] He was the presbyter when he took bread in his holy hands, likewise the chalice, and looking unto heaven and giving thanks to God his Father, he blessed them.
[7] He was the bishop when he lifted his hands to heaven and blessed the apostles.	[7] He was the bishop when with raised hands he blessed his disciples and apostles in Bethania and, leading them out, was raised to heaven.

Since most modern research tends to locate the Anonymous in Normandy, perhaps in Rouen, it is strange that the Norman and especially Rouen pontificals have not been thoroughly examined as the source for, or at least for parallels to Tractate J–19. But if one searches carefully through the pontifical manuscripts used in Norman territories, especially Rouen, from the twelfth century, one can find a distinct parallel to the Norman Anonymous.[47] While the sequence of grades in the Ordinal of Christ in the Norman pontificals is arranged according to the order in which the grades were conferred by a bishop and the sequence in the Anonymous is due perhaps to his hagiographical

---

[47] *Paris BN NAL 306*, fols. 111r–29r; *Paris Bibl. Maz. 539*, fols. 95v–110r; and *Vat. Lat. 3748*, fols. 106v–22v.

preference for the proto-deacon Stephen,[48] the events and sayings from Christ's life are remarkably similar. Since the Rouen pontifical manuscripts date from thirty to three hundred years after the manuscript of the Anonymous' tractates,[49] there is no ironclad proof of a direct dependence, but it is interesting that virtually the same text, with a major variant in only the verse for the doorkeeper, can be found in a pontifical manuscript for the province of Canterbury written at virtually the same time as *C.C.C. 415.*[50]

[Norman Pontificals]

[Rouen Pontificals]

[1. Doorkeeper] This office our Lord Jesus Christ exercized when having entered the temple he cast out with a whip made of cords the sellers and buyers of sheep and cattle.

[Canterbury Pontifical]

[1] Christ was worthy to become doorkeeper when he closed and opened the ark of Noah or when he opened the portals of hell and then led out his elect but left the reprobate.

[2. Lector] But this office our Lord discharged when having entered the synagogue there was given to him the book of the prophet Isaiah.

[3. Exorcist] This office the Lord also discharged when demons were cast out by him from the bodies of those possessed.

[4. Acolyte] This office Christ discharged when he restored sight to the blind and those darkened by the blackness of sins, and when as the sun of righteousness he shone forth.

[5. Subdeacon] But this office the Lord discharged when he washed with water the feet of the apostles and dried them with a towel.

[6. Deacon] But Christ discharged the office of deacon while he preached to us. . . . This office the Lord administered when with a clear voice he proclaimed, "Do penance, for the kingdom of heaven is at hand."

[48]Williams, *Norman Anonymous*, 86, 107.
[49]For Professor Bischoff's dating of the manuscript see Hartmann, "Beziehungen," 110 n. 8.
[50]*Cambridge Univ. Lib. Ee 2. 3*, fols. 93v–105r. The Latin texts of the Norman pontificals printed below may be found in my *Ordinals of Christ*, pp. 136f.

> [7. Priest] For the Lord was a priest
> when hanging on the cross he offered
> himself a living host to the Father on
> high for the salvation of his people; for
> concerning him the prophet said, "You
> are a priest unto eternity according to
> the order of Melchisedek."

If the texts from the Rouen and Canterbury pontifical manuscripts are compared with Tractate J–19, it appears that the Anonymous simply abbreviated the texts of the pontificals for all the grades except the *sacerdos* and rearranged the grades so the deacon was in the lowest, not his customary antepenultimate position in the hierarchy and the doorkeeper was raised to a level immediately below the subdeacon. For the doorkeeper the Anonymous gave alternative sanctions represented in the Rouen and Canterbury texts, and for the *sacerdos* he used a common Christic sanction found in the *Collectio hibernensis* and English pontificals, both sources used elsewhere in the Tractates.[51]

Recently Dr. Hartmann has shown how an examination of the canonical and theological sources of the Anonymous casts this enigmatic author in a new light in the milieu of early scholasticism.[52] In a way, his study was not unlike those of Mgr. Ryan and Dr. Hoesch, who have substantially altered our understanding of such other publicists as Peter Damian and Humbert of Silva Candida with studies of their canonical sources.[53] The parallels drawn in this paper between the tracts of the Norman Anonymous and contemporary pontificals illustrate the importance of investigating the manuscripts of the rites themselves in conjunction with liturgical scholarship of the publicists. Only when the texts of the liturgical formulae themselves have been edited can the new and reedited texts of the liturgical scholarship of the late eleventh and early twelfth centuries be placed in their proper historical perspective.

---

[51] Williams, *Norman Anonymous*, 48f.

[52] Hartmann, "Beziehungen."

[53] J. Joseph Ryan, *Saint Peter Damiani and His Canonical Sources: A Preliminary Study in the Antecedents of the Gregorian Reform* (Pontifical Institute of Mediaeval Studies: Studies and Texts 2; Toronto, 1956); and Henning Hoesch, *Die kanonischen Quellen im Werk Humberts von Moyenmoutier: ein Beitrag zur Geschichte der vorgregorianischen Reform* (Forschungen zur kirchlichen Rechtsgeschichte und zum Kirchenrecht 10; Vienna, 1970).

ADDENDA AND CORRIGENDA

II. Basil and the Early Medieval Latin Canonical Collections

p. 518: The late Professor Maurice Sheehy has kindly pointed out that a knowledge of the work of Basil was in Ireland before the compilation of the *Collectio canonum hibernensis*. The *Amra Coluim Cille* (ed. W. Stokes, *Revue Celtique*, vols. 20 and 21), dating to ca. 590–600, refers to Columcille's keeping of the Rule of Basil.

p. 527, n. 63, 4.69: This canon is found without attribution in the *Poenitentiale Casinense* (Montecassino, Archivio della Badia MS 372), on which see Herm. Jos. Schmitz, *Die Bussbücher und die Bussdisciplin der Kirche*, 1 (Mainz, 1883) 428.

IV. Unity and Diversity in Carolingian Canon Law Collections: the Case of the *Collectio Hibernensis* and its Derivatives

On the *Collectio Hibernensis* and its derivatives, see now my 'The *Collectio canonum hibernensis* and its Influence in the Early Middle Ages,' *Studies in Medieval and Early Modern Canon Law*, eds. W. Hartmann and K. Pennington (Washington, D.C., in press).

V. Excerpta from the *Collectio hibernensis* in three Vatican manuscripts

p. 5: On the construction of the manuscript, Vatican, Archivio di San Pietro H 58, see Raymund Kottje, *Die Bussbücher Halitgars von Cambrai und des Hrabanus Maurus: ihre Überlieferung und ihre Quellen* (Beiträge zur Geschichte und Quellenkunde des Mittelalters 8, ed. H. Fuhrmann: Berlin–New York, 1980) 65–69; and the precisions in my 'The *Collectio canonum hibernensis* and its Influence in the Early Middle Ages,' *Studies in Medieval and Early Modern Canon Law*, eds. W. Hartmann and K. Pennington (Washington, D.C., in press). On the important penitential in the manuscript, possibly the earliest 'Roman' tariff penitential, see Ludger Körntgen, 'Ein italienisches Bussbuch und seine fränkischen Quellen. Das anonyme Paenitentiale der Handschrift Vatikan, Arch. S. Pietro H 58,' in *Aus Archiven und Bibliotheken: Studien zum Recht und zur Kirchengeschichte des Mittelalters: Festschrift für Raymund Kottje zum 65. Geburtstag*, ed. H. Mordek (*Freiburger Beiträge zur mittelalterlichen Geschichte* 3: Bern, Frankfurt/M, Las Vegas, 1991) 189–205.

XV. South Italian *Liturgica* and *Canonistica* in Catalonia (New York, Hispanic Society of America MS. HC 380/819)

p. 482: For a somewhat different version of the text on Septuagesima, see the codex, Madrid, Biblioteca Nacional, 19, fol. 28v.

XVII.   The Turin *Collection in Seven Books:* A Poitevin Canonical
Collection

On the Turin collection see Linda Fowler-Magerl, 'Vier französische und spanische
vorgratianische Kanonessammlungen,' in *Aspekte europäischer Rechtsgeschichte:
Festgabe für Helmut Coing zum 70. Geburtstag* (Ius Commune, Sonderheft 17:
Frankfurt a. Main, 1982) 124–41.

XVIII.   Liturgical Scholarship at the Time of the Investiture
Controversy: Past Research and Future Opportunities

p. 117: On the *Sententia Ivonis* see now Ronald John Zawilla, 'The *Sententia
Ivonis Carnotensis episcopi De divinis officiis*, the "Norman School," and
Liturgical Scholarship: Study and Edition,' *Mediaeval Studies* 49 (1987)
124–51.

INDEX OF MANUSCRIPTS

T - #0029 - 270225 - C0 - 224/150/18 [20] - CB - 9780860784050 - Gloss Lamination